Literature-Based Teaching in the Content Areas

40 Strategies for
K–8 Classrooms

Literature-Based Teaching in the Content Areas

Carole Cox

California State University, Long Beach

Los Angeles | London | New Delhi
Singapore | Washington DC

For information:

 SAGE Publications, Inc.
2455 Teller Road
Thousand Oaks, California 91320
E-mail: order@sagepub.com

SAGE Publications Ltd.
1 Oliver's Yard
55 City Road
London EC1Y 1SP
United Kingdom

SAGE Publications India Pvt. Ltd.
B 1/I 1 Mohan Cooperative Industrial Area
Mathura Road, New Delhi 110 044
India

SAGE Publications Asia-Pacific Pte. Ltd.
33 Pekin Street #02–01
Far East Square
Singapore 048763

Printed in the United States of America

Library of Congress Cataloging-in-Publication Data

Cox, Carole, 1943-
Literature-based teaching in the content areas : 40 strategies for K–8 classrooms / Carole Cox.
    p. cm.
Includes bibliographical references and index.
ISBN 978-1-4129-7493-6 (pbk. : alk. paper)
    1. Literature—Study and teaching (Elementary) 2. Literature—Study and teaching (Middle school) I. Title.

LB1575.C799 2012
372.64—dc22   2010034406

This book is printed on acid-free paper.

12   13   14   15   16   10   9   8   7   6   5   4   3   2   1

Acquisitions Editor:	Diane McDaniel
Editorial Assistant:	Terri Accomazzo
Production Editor:	Belinda Thresher
Copy Editor:	Jenifer Dill
Typesetter:	C&M Digitals (P) Ltd.
Permissions Editor:	Adele Hutchinson
Proofreader:	Victoria Reed-Castro
Indexer:	Michael Ferreira
Cover Designer:	Janet Kiesel
Marketing Manager:	Erica DeLuca

Contents

Preface

As the students in my 3rd- and 4th-grade combination class packed up at the end of the day, I watched in dismay as two of them struggled over possession of a paperback book, each one wanting to take it home. Each one held onto it, yanking it back and forth until they finally ripped it in half. I was stunned. The class was stunned. The two students, each holding half of the book, were stunned. And embarrassed. And feeling guilty. They started to cry. I took them out into the hall so they could explain to me in private what had happened. One said "I love that book." The other one said "No, I love it."

The ripped book was *Search for a Living Fossil: The Story of the Coelacanth* (Clymer, 1966). In 1938, a strange, 5-foot long, 250 pound fish was discovered off the coast of South Africa. It was previously known only in the fossil record of the Cretaceous period and was thought to have been extinct for 70 million years. This book told the story for children. I had checked it out of the school library during our class's science study of the behavior of mealworms. While observing, recording information, and reading books about mealworms, I had encouraged my students to read about other living organisms. The two students who ripped the book loved reading and re-reading it and talking about it. They began to read other books about marine life and asked if we could have an aquarium in our classroom to observe fish as well as mealworms.

As we talked in the hall after the incident, the students made up and agreed to buy a new copy of the book with their own money to replace the ripped one. We talked about what they had learned about cooperating with other students and respecting school property. I learned something too. This experience brought new meaning to the saying I had heard about how important it is to "Put the right book in the hands of a student"—even if they rip it in half.

PURPOSE OF THE BOOK

The same might be said for putting the right book in the hands of a teacher, a book that can engage both the students and the teacher, lead to meaningful discussions related to students' prior experiences and current interests, and become a jumping off place for teaching and learning in the content areas. And indeed, after I left the elementary classroom and earned a PhD in Education, I found this to be true. I taught undergraduate and graduate courses in children's literature and in language arts and reading methods. I learned how powerful it is for a preservice teacher in a methods class with field experiences, or an inservice teacher in her or his own classroom, to find books they not only loved but thought their students would love and that they could align with standards and strategies in the content areas.

The purpose of *Literature-Based Teaching in the Content Areas* is to describe literature-based strategies for teaching K through 8 content areas: language arts and reading, social studies, mathematics, science, and the arts. Each strategy includes extensive lists of literature for the classroom, both fiction and nonfiction trade books as distinguished from textbooks. Grounded in current theory and research on best practices, the emphasis of *Literature-Based Teaching in the Content Areas* is on practical activities that teachers can use in the classroom.

AUDIENCE

The primary courses for *Literature-Based Teaching in the Content Areas* are general methods for multiple subjects in a preservice teacher preparation program, courses on integrated teaching across the curriculum, methods courses that blend subjects (e.g., language arts/social studies or the arts, or mathematics/science, or a short course in one or more of the content areas). Students in these courses could be either undergraduate students at a college or university that offers a BA in Education with certification, or graduate students in a fifth-year certification program.

Literature-Based Teaching in the Content Areas builds a bridge between the principles and content of the college course and K through 8 classroom practice, with examples of literature-based strategies college students can put to use immediately in any content area in their applied field experiences in schools. There is a trend in some teacher certification programs to move toward more general methods courses, or to blend two or more content area courses, but there are few textbooks available that take this approach. Literature is used in every subject in the K through 8 curricula, and the strategies in this book will allow preservice teachers to gain practical experience across the content areas in their early field experiences as well as in their student teaching. *Literature-Based Teaching in the Content Areas* can serve as a supplement to a core text or as one of several books in a course that does not use a core text. The book could also be used by practicing teachers and school districts for professional development.

ORGANIZATION OF THE BOOK

The book is organized into five sections, one for each of five content areas in the K–8 curriculum: language arts and reading, mathematics, social studies, science, and the arts. Each section includes the following: information on what research has to say about literature-based teaching in this specific content area, guidelines for selecting books, and the national standards for the specific content area addressed.

Eight teaching strategies are included in each section. Each strategy is organized as follows:

- *Rationale:* A summary of the strategy with key, evidenced-based research and best teaching practices introduces the strategy.

- *Strategy:* The idea behind the strategy and how it can be carried out in the classroom is described in a few paragraphs.

- *Grade-Level Modifications:* The teaching example for each strategy is differentiated for Grades K through 2, 3 through 5, and 6 through 8. Within each grade level, books are suggested for use with the strategy. Ideas for technology integration are included as appropriate.

- *English Learners:* English language development strategies that can be used for the example are explained, such as demonstrating meaning and illustrating vocabulary at a nonverbal level by using visuals, real objects, models, meaningful actions and gestures, tapping the five senses, Total Physical Response (TPR), dramatization, singing illustrated songs, tapping into and relating to student's background knowledge and prior experience, and primary language support through the use of cognates and bilingual books.

- *Struggling Students:* Ideas for adapting each strategy for struggling students are provided.

- *Assessment:* Ideas for authentic teacher assessment and assessment tools will be shown as well.

- *Resources:* Books with more information on a strategy for teachers or students are included.

- *References:* Evidence-based research and best practices are provided.

In addition, individual strategies may include mini-lessons, student work samples, graphic organizers, writing frames, and other teaching tools. These strategies are a beginning point for literature-based teaching in the content areas. I encourage you to try them out but also to adapt them according to your own ideas and the unique characteristics, abilities, strengths, and needs of the students you teach.

SPECIAL FEATURES

While *Literature-Based Teaching in the Content Areas* is practical, it is guided by Louise Rosenblatt's (1995) transactional theory of the reading process, which views the reading of any book as personal, experienced meaning. It is also based on my own longitudinal studies of children's patterns of response to literature and the implications of this research for teaching, such as the questions and prompts teachers can use for leading discussions and for student writing (Cox, 2008). This approach is a natural gateway to differentiate instruction because students can respond based on personal experiences, ideas, and interests in the content area.

The text provides the following pedagogical aids:

- Research-based reader response questions and prompts for discussion and writing differentiated for each grade level in a strategy.

- Detailed teaching ideas for one or more key books for each of the grade levels, K through 2, 3 through 5, and 6 through 8, in each strategy.

- Extensive book lists of both classic and contemporary children's literature tailored for different grade levels and English learners in each strategy.
- Whole class and small group discussions and activities, and ideas for student independent learning.
- Graphic organizers, charts, frames, templates, sentence starters, and planning and data sheets for teachers and students.
- Mini-lessons on skills and writing conventions that are important in a strategy.
- Technology integrated throughout the book with teaching ideas for using websites, software programs, Internet research, online discussion boards, interactive games, YouTube, digital photography, Smart Boards, WebQuests, and virtual field trips on the World Wide Web.
- Assessment tools such as rubrics, checklists, self- and peer-editing and assessment forms, student journals and logs, conference sheets and record keeping forms.
- Student work samples and classroom vignettes to bring the content to life.
- Resources for teachers for reading more about a strategy.

USING THIS BOOK IN THE K–8 CLASSROOM

To use *Literature-Based Teaching in the Content Areas,* the teacher only needs to dip in and choose one of the strategies from any of the content areas. Everything she or he needs to get started is in each strategy: a classroom example that models the strategy; a research-based rationale; target content standards; specific books; reader response questions and prompts; teaching ideas for Grades K through 2, 3 through 5, and 6 through 8 as well as for English learners and struggling students; assessment ideas; and teacher resources for further reading. I encourage each teacher to adapt each strategy to her or his own experience, ideas, interests, and learning styles as well as to those of the students in the class.

REFERENCES

Clymer, E. (1966). *Search for a living fossil: The story of the Coelacanth.* New York: Scholastic.

Cox, C. (2008). *Teaching language arts: A student-centered classroom* (6th ed.). New York: Pearson.

Rosenblatt, L. M. (1938/1995). *Literature as exploration.* New York: Modern Language Association.

Acknowledgments

I would like first to acknowledge the two students who ripped the book *Search for a Living Fossil: The Story of the Coelacanth* in half, as well as the many other students I had as a classroom teacher, who always reminded me of the power of putting the right book in a student's hands. I have seen that same power at work with the many teacher education students I have taught at the university level when I modeled an instructional strategy with a children's book and they tried it on their own with students. When it was a book they were enthusiastic about and their students enjoyed, I knew that the book, more than my modeling, was what made for a successful experience. The most common response I have heard over the years when this happened was "Dr. Cox, it worked!" They actually did the work, with the right book, and I thank them for sharing their experiences with me. They have contributed immeasurably to *Literature-Based Teaching in the Content Areas*.

I have also observed so many wonderful teachers using literature-based strategies in the classrooms where I placed my own preservice teacher education students, and I am grateful to them for not only mentoring my students but for inspiring many of the ideas in this book. In particular, I would like to thank Dr. Paul Boyd-Batstone, who I first encountered when he was a 3rd-grade Spanish/English bilingual teacher, and who subsequently earned his doctorate and joined the faculty where I teach at California State University, Long Beach. We share a common interest in teaching with literature from a reader response perspective and have co-authored a book on it, titled *Engaging English Learners: Exploring Literature, Developing Literacy, and Differentiating Instruction* (Pearson, 2009). I observed Paul effectively use many of the strategies in the book when he was a classroom teacher, and he offered many excellent suggestions for others, reviewed sections of the book, and provided invaluable feedback.

I also wish to acknowledge my excellent editor, Diane McDaniel. Diane actually proposed the idea for this book to me, and I thought it was wonderful. It filled a gap in the literature as I knew of no other books of literature-based strategies across all the content areas. It related to my own research of longitudinal studies of children's responses to literature from a reader response perspective, specifically Louise Rosenblatt's (1938/1995) transactional theory. And it allowed me to look at all the wonderful new books of children's literature being published today, as well as look at the many classics of children's literature with new eyes.

Diane also provided excellent reviewers for the book, and I wish to acknowledge them as well for their insightful critiques and suggestions:

Deborah Bowditch, University of Wisconsin-Whitewater

Ingrid S. Graves, Tarleton State University

Robert Reising, University of the Cumberlands

Susan Soroka, Arizona State University

Louise B. Swinarski, Salem State University

Finally, I know that my passion for books and reading is due to my parents. I had a mother who read to me—Alice J. Shirreffs. I also had a father who kept the house filled with books and wrote about 90 books himself—Gordon D. Shirreffs, a writer of paperback Western fiction for adults and children. My own three children, Wyatt, Gordon, and Elizabeth, are grown, but as children they reminded me over and over again as I read to them, as my mother had read to me, of the power of literature to entertain and delight us and to take us all over the world to learn so many things and, even more important, to learn about ourselves.

Introduction

This book describes literature-based strategies to teach K through 8 content areas: language arts and reading, mathematics, social studies, science, and the arts. Grounded in current theory and research on best practices, the emphasis is on practical activities that teachers can make their own in the classroom. The goal is to provide teachers with a detailed description of teaching strategies and activities that begin with a book and lead to learning standards-based knowledge, skills, understandings, concepts, and processes in each of the content areas using an inquiry-based model of integrated teaching.

The book takes a transactional, reader response approach to teaching with literature (Rosenblatt, 1938/1995). Through the use of a series of open questions based on my own research (Cox, 2008) on student stance to literature from a reader response perspective, students will connect a book to their own experience and prior knowledge and, further, will question, challenge, or hypothesize about concepts in the book through whole class or small group discussion and writing. Engaging students through a personal exploration of literature will serve as a basis for connecting their own experiences and prior knowledge with learning in the content areas. This approach also provides a framework for teachers to differentiate instruction for students across grade levels, including English learners at different stages of English proficiency and struggling students.

LITERATURE AND THE CONTENT AREAS

Literature used in classrooms is both fiction and nonfiction trade books, as distinguished from textbooks. Integrating such literature into content areas is a recommended best practice and can be accomplished through teacher read alouds and questions and prompts for class discussions, book clubs and other small group activities, graphic organizers and teacher modeling, journals and other types of writing, cooperative learning, choice of books and student independent reading and research on a topic, projects, and technology (Alvermann, Phelps, & Gillis, 2010).

Recent research examining the classrooms of outstanding teachers revealed several findings about literature-based teaching in the content areas (Allington & Johnston, 2002; Pressley, Allington, Wharton-McDonald, Block, & Morrow, 2001; Taylor, Pearson, Clark, & Walpole, 2000; Wharton-McDonald, Pressley, & Hampston, 1998). Reading and writing were integrated in these classrooms—and integrated with the content areas as well. Many cross-curricular connections were made. The rooms were full of books, and reading and writing took place throughout the day. Teachers used reading, science, social studies, and other textbooks but rarely followed the lesson plans provided in teacher's guides for these materials. Instead, students read nonfiction informational books and biographies and historical fiction, and they also made use of magazines and the Internet to find information in the content areas. In these classrooms, students did a great deal of reading and writing across a range of topics and content areas and were highly engaged in reading and writing activities.

Another important feature of teaching with literature that was revealed in these studies was that teachers provided many opportunities for students to discuss the books they read. The teachers modeled higher-level thinking strategies through the questions and prompts they used, and they used an inquiry-based approach by asking students what they thought and how they could find out about a topic rather than looking for right or wrong answers to a question. They asked open questions that had more than one possible answer. Teachers also used a variety of grouping formats, from whole class to small groups to individual activities. Students had opportunities to discuss literature with each other.

English learners were the focus of a recent review of research, titled *Developing Literacy in Second-Language Learners: Report of the National Literacy Panel on Language-Minority Children and Youth* (August & Shanahan, 2006), and key recommendations for English learners were that teachers develop more thorough discussions of reading material and literature and that English language materials be read by students beyond the instructional day, in order to build vocabulary and comprehension. Given the growing numbers of English learners in classrooms across the country, these recommendations have important implications for how teachers approach not only teaching with literature in the content areas, but teaching English learners in general. Strategies that are especially designed for English learners can facilitate such discussions.

A READER RESPONSE PERSPECTIVE TOWARD TEACHING WITH LITERATURE

Reader response theories can inform teachers of how to make the experience of reading and discussing literature meaningful for all students. The transactional model of reading developed by Louise Rosenblatt (1938/1995) focuses on the active role of the reader in creating meaning from the text. Rosenblatt and other reader response theorists maintained that the reader and the text/author construct meaning together. Each reading event is unique, involving a particular reader, text, and context and occurring at a particular moment in time. Rosenblatt described this process as a two-way transaction, a live-circuit between the reader and the text.

Stance Toward Literature

According to Rosenblatt (1938/1995), although all reading occurs as experienced meaning, readers assume a stance—or focus their selective attention in different ways when reading. Stance represents a reader's readiness to organize thinking about what is read according to a more efferent or more aesthetic framework. The reader's adoption of a stance, either conscious or unconscious, guides their experiencing of the text. Any text can be read efferently or aesthetically, and readers move back and forth on a continuum from more efferent to more aesthetic, eventually settling on one predominant stance.

During a more efferent reading, the reader's focus is on the information to be taken away from the text, or the more public, lexical, analytical, abstracting aspects (e.g., reading the label on a bottle of prescription medicine to find the correct dosage). During a more aesthetic reading, the reader's focus is on the lived-through experience of the reading event, or the more private, experiential, affective, associational aspects (e.g., reading a novel and picturing yourself as one of the characters).

A more efferent reading focuses on what is in the text. A more aesthetic reading focuses on the associations, feelings, attitudes, and ideas that the text arouses in the reader. Most readings are a mix of both stances, and any text can be read more efferently or more aesthetically (e.g., reading the sports page to find out who won a baseball game and what the score was, or reading the same page and imagining yourself as a player in the game). Rosenblatt (1938/1995) maintained that, for most experiences with literature, teachers should encourage students to take an aesthetic stance.

Research on Stance

Studies of children's and adolescent's stance toward literature from Rosenblatt's transactional, reader response perspective have shown that students take a primarily aesthetic stance to literature when asked an open question such as "What did you think of the story?" (Cox, 1997, 2002, 2008; Cox & Many, 1992a, 1992b, 1992c), that students who take a primarily aesthetic stance reach higher levels of understanding of a story (Many, 1991, 2004), and that more aesthetic teaching approaches improve writing (Many & Wiseman, 1992).

A key to guiding discussions of literature, and encouraging students to take an aesthetic stance toward literature, is in the questions and prompts that teachers use.

Reader Response Questions and Prompts for Teachers

The following types of questions and prompts for talking about a book are based on my longitudinal study of categories of children's stance in response to literature on a continuum from a more aesthetic stance, focused on a personal experiencing of the book, to a more efferent stance, focused on the content of the book. Because I found that the same cohort of children took a predominantly aesthetic (71.6%) rather than efferent (28.4%) stance in their responses over a 6-year period, from kindergarten through 5th grade, I recommend that teachers begin discussions of literature with more open, aesthetic questions and prompts.

These questions and prompts represent each of the more aesthetic categories of stance children took toward a literary work. This means that teachers would first direct their students to reflect on their personal experiencing of the book (Cox & Boyd-Batstone, 2009). Directing children to reflect on their uniquely personal experiencing of the book allows teachers to better understand questions they have about the book, parts of the book that struck them or attracted their attention, their associations with life experience and background knowledge, and any hypothesis they might have formed about the book. These aspects of a more aesthetic stance allow a teacher a glimpse into each child's unique understanding of the book by engaging them with further explorations of literature and a basis for connecting literature to learning in the content areas. While children may also have a shared understanding of many aspects of the book, it is the personal understanding of each one that can lead to higher levels of understanding and learning.

Teachers can think of a book as a springboard to a discussion of their students' responses and the unique stance of each one to the book. That is the real beginning of meaningful learning. First, use more open and aesthetic questions and prompts, and allow them to tell you and other students what they were thinking and feeling as they heard or read a book. Then build on their questions, their ideas about the parts of the book that struck them, their associations, and their hypotheses as you extend the book as a basis for learning in one or more of the content areas.

1. *Questioning*—Children are puzzled by something in the book; wonder about it; want to know something

- What did you think of the story?

- Tell anything you want about the story.

2. *Focusing on a part*—Children are struck by a part of the book; something attracted their attention

- What was your favorite part of the story?

- Tell about it.

3. *Associating*—Children relate a personal experience or background knowledge or make an intertextual link (other books, movies, TV, etc.)

- Has anything like this ever happened to you? Tell about it.

- Have you ever had feelings like a character in the story? Tell about them.

- Does this story remind you of any other stories? Tell about them.

4. *Hypothesizing*—Children wonder about something in the book; make predictions; extend the story in a unique way

- Was there anything in the story you wondered about? Tell about it.

- Did something puzzle you? Tell about it.

- What else do you think might happen?

- Is there anything you would change in the story? What? How?

5. *Performing*—Younger children act out a part of the book verbally or nonverbally; role play a character using their actions or voice; make sound effects; pantomime an event in the book

- If you were a character in the story, what would you say?

- Show how you would act if you were a character in the story.

- If you could talk to a character in the story, what would you say?

- What sounds would you hear in the story?

In each of the literature-based strategies in the book, I suggest specific questions that branch off of the main stems of aesthetic questions but are then tailored to a particular book. These questions can be used for a whole class discussion, a small group discussion, or a prompt for writing in a literature journal.

REFERENCES

Allington, R. L., & Johnston, P. H. (2002). *Reading to learn: Lessons from exemplary fourth grade classrooms*. New York: Guilford.

Alvermann, D. E., Phelps, S. F., & Gillis, V. R. (2010). *Content area reading and literacy: Succeeding in today's diverse classroom*. Boston: Pearson/Allyn & Bacon.

August, D., & Shanahan, T. (Eds.). (2006). *Developing literacy in second-language learners: Report of the National Literacy Panel on language-minority children and youth*. Mahwah, NJ: Erlbaum.

Cox, C. (1997). Literature-based teaching: A student response-centered classroom. In N. Karolides (Ed.), *Reader response in elementary classrooms: Quest and discovery* (pp. 29–49). Mahwah, NJ: Erlbaum.

Cox, C. (2002). Resistance to reading in school. In M. Hunsberger & G. Labercane (Eds.), *Making meaning in the response-based classroom* (pp. 141–153). Boston: Allyn & Bacon.

Cox, C. (2008). *Teaching language arts: A student-centered classroom* (6th ed.). Boston: Pearson/Allyn & Bacon.

Cox, C., & Boyd-Batstone, P. S. (2009). *Engaging English learners: Exploring literature, developing literacy, and differentiating instruction*. Boston: Pearson/Allyn & Bacon.

Cox, C., & Many, J. E. (1992a). Beyond choosing: Emergent categories of efferent and aesthetic stances. In J. Many & C. Cox (Eds.), *Reader stance and literary understanding: Exploring the theories, research and practice* (pp. 103–126). Norwood, NJ: Ablex.

Cox, C., & Many, J. E. (1992b). Stance towards a literary work: Applying the transactional theory to children's responses. *Reading Psychology: An International Quarterly, 13,* 37–72.

Cox, C., & Many, J. E. (1992c). Toward an understanding of the aesthetic response to literature. *Language Arts, 69,* 28–33.

Many, J. E. (1991). The effect of reader stance and age level on children's literary response. *Journal of Reading Behavior, 21,* 61–85.

Many, J. E. (2004). The effect of reader stance on students' personal understanding of literature. In R. B. Ruddell & N. J. Unrau (Eds.), *Theoretical models and processes of reading* (pp. 914–928). Newark, DE: International Reading Association.

Many, J. E., & Wiseman, D. (1992). The effect of teaching approach on third grade students' responses to literature. *Journal of Reading Behavior, 24,* 265–287.

Pressley, M., Allington, R. L., Wharton-McDonald, R., Block, C. C., & Morrow, L. (2001). *Learning to read: Lessons from exemplary first-grade classrooms*. New York: Guilford.

Rosenblatt, L. M. (1938/1995). *Literature as exploration*. New York: Modern Language Association.

Taylor, B. M., Pearson, P. D., Clark, K., & Walpole, S. (2000). Effective schools and accomplished teachers: Lessons about primary grade reading instruction in low-income schools. *Elementary School Journal, 101*(2), 121–166.

Wharton-McDonald, R., Pressley, M., & Hampston, J. M. (1998). Literacy instruction in nine first-grade classrooms: Teacher characteristics and student achievement. *The Elementary School Journal, 99,* 101–128.

PART I

Language Arts and Reading

WHAT RESEARCH HAS TO SAY ABOUT LITERATURE-BASED TEACHING AND LANGUAGE ARTS AND READING

Over the last 40 years, there have been several major research studies of literacy, which have informed language arts and reading instruction. This research has either been conducted on a national scale or funded by U.S. federal agencies, institutes, or associations. Overall, this research supports the use of a balanced approach to literacy instruction that considers all the language arts that support learning to read as well as the importance of students learning the alphabetic principle, word study, and phonics to decode new words.

More specifically, here is what this research has to say about literature-based teaching and language arts in reading:

• *The First-Grade Studies* (Bond & Dykstra, 1967/1997) analyzed 27 studies that were commissioned to compare methods of beginning reading instruction in the United States. The results showed that an integrated program that included learning phonics, reading meaningful text, and reading and writing for meaning was most effective.

• *Learning to Read: The Great Debate* (Chall, 1967) was a synthesis of reading research from 1900 to 1965 that showed the importance of learning the code as well as reading aloud to young children and reading extensively to develop fluency and comprehension.

• *Becoming a Nation of Readers: The Report of the Commission on Reading* (Anderson, Hiebert, Scott, & Wilkinson, 1985) supported the findings of Bond and Dykstra and Chall but showed a need for a greater emphasis on reading comprehension as part of a balanced, integrated approach to teaching reading and language arts; for more time allotted for children to read quality children's literature; for reading aloud by teachers; and for writing integrated into the reading period.

- *Beginning to Read: Thinking and Learning About Print* (Adams, 1990) showed that the most important instructional activity was reading literature aloud to children and providing time for children to read many types of texts to develop fluency.

- *Preventing Reading Difficulties in Young Children* (Snow, Burns, & Griffin, 1998) summarized research on reading, pre-K through 3rd grade. Essential elements of best practices included fluency development through practice with engaging literature at students' independent level.

- The *Report of the National Reading Panel* (National Institute of Child Health and Human Development [NICHD], 2000), commissioned by the U.S. Congress, established five pillars of reading instruction: phonemic awareness, phonics (alphabetics), fluency, vocabulary, and comprehension. The report found that vocabulary can be learned incidentally in the context of storybook reading or from listening to the reading of others and that active participation during storybook readings has an impact on learning. The report recommended an integrated, balanced reading program.

In *Classrooms That Work: They Can all Read and Write* (Cunningham & Allington, 2007), there are several recommended best practices that were derived from studies based on observations of unusually effective teachers. These best practices include several that can be implemented with literature-based teaching of language arts and reading:

- Offering many opportunities to read

- Providing opportunities to discuss what is read

- Integrating the teaching of reading and writing

- Having books everywhere and using them in many ways

- Reading aloud frequently

- Having children read and write throughout the day and at home

Characteristics of these teachers' instructional approaches included several features that are a part of literature-based teaching:

- Managed choice, meaning students were presented with options to choose from

- Multiple class instructional formats, such as whole class, small group, student pairs, and student-teacher conferences

- Collaborative learning

- Student self-evaluation

The studies described in this book revealed an important characteristic of the best practices of these unusually effective teachers that supports the idea of literature-based teaching. They all used the widest variety of reading materials available to them. None used a single reading program or set of materials. Practices that were regularly used by these teachers were reading aloud to students every day, scheduling time every day for self-selected reading, talking to students about their reading, making time for sharing and responding to reading, and providing a wide array of reading materials for students to choose from. One of the best ways to put these best practices into place in your own classroom is through literature-based strategies for teaching literacy.

GUIDELINES FOR SELECTING BOOKS FOR TEACHING LANGUAGE ARTS AND READING

Every year, a committee appointed by the Children's Literature Assembly of the National Council of Teachers of English (NCTE) selects 30 titles for the Notable Children's Books in the Language Arts. The charge of the seven-member national committee is to select books each year that best exemplify the criteria established for the award. Books considered for this annual list are works of fiction, nonfiction, and poetry written for children in Grades K through 8. The books must meet one or more of the following criteria:

1. Deal explicitly with language, such as plays on words, word origins, or the history of language

2. Demonstrate uniqueness in the use of language or style

3. Invite child response or participation

   In addition, books are to

4. Have an appealing format;

5. Be of enduring quality; and

6. Meet generally accepted criteria of quality for the genre in which they are written.

For more information about the Notable Children's Books in the Language Arts, see the Children's Literature Assembly's website at http://www.childrensliteratureassembly.org/.

Other excellent book selection guides are Children's Choices, Young Adult Choices, and Teacher's Choices which are joint projects of The International Reading Association (IRA) and the Children's Book Council (CBC). Children's Choices is an annual list of favorite new books chosen by 12,500 school children. An annotated version of the list appears in the October issue of the IRA publication The Reading Teacher. An annotated list of Young Adult Choices appears each year in the November issue of the Journal of Adolescent & Adult Literacy, also an IRA publication, and an annotated list of Teacher's Choices appears in the November issue of The Reading Teacher. For more information go to the IRA website at www.reading.org and click on Booklists.

NATIONAL STANDARDS FOR THE ENGLISH LANGUAGE ARTS

The national standards for the English language arts were written jointly by two professional teaching organizations of educators focused on language and literacy: The IRA and the NCTE. These standards represent what students should know and be able to do in the English language arts.

The vision guiding these standards is that all students must have the opportunities and resources to develop the language skills they need to pursue life's goals and to participate fully as informed, productive members of society. These standards assume that literacy growth begins before children enter school as they experience and experiment with literacy activities—reading, writing, and associating spoken words with their graphic representations. Recognizing this fact, these standards encourage the development of curriculum and instruction that make productive use of the emerging literacy abilities that children bring to school. Furthermore, the standards provide ample room for the innovation and creativity essential to teaching and learning. They are not prescriptions for particular curriculum or instruction.

Standards for the English Language Arts (International Reading Association [IRA]/National Council of Teachers of English [NCTE], 1996) names and defines six language arts:

Reading. The complex, recursive process through which we make meaning from texts, using semantics; syntax; visual, aural, and tactile cues; context; and prior knowledge.

Writing. The use of a writing system or orthography by people in the conduct of their daily lives to communicate over time and space.

Listening. Attending to communication by any means; includes listening to vocal speech, watching signing, or using communication aids.

Speaking. The act of communicating through such means as vocalization, signing, or using communication aids such as voice synthesizers.

Viewing. Attending to communication conveyed by visually representing.

Visually Representing. Conveying information or expressing oneself using nonverbal visual means, such as drawing, computer graphics (maps, charts, artwork), photography, or physical performance.

IRA/NCTE Standards for the English Language Arts

1. Students read a wide range of print and nonprint texts to build an understanding of texts, of themselves, and of the cultures of the United States and the world; to acquire new information; to respond to the needs and demands of society and the workplace; and for personal fulfillment. Among these texts are fiction and nonfiction, classic and contemporary works.

2. Students read a wide range of literature from many periods in many genres to build an understanding of the many dimensions (e.g., philosophical, ethical, aesthetic) of human experience.

3. Students apply a wide range of strategies to comprehend, interpret, evaluate, and appreciate texts. They draw on their prior experience, their interactions with other readers and writers, their knowledge of word meaning and of other texts, their word identification strategies, and their understanding of textual features (e.g., sound-letter correspondence, sentence structure, context, graphics).

4. Students adjust their use of spoken, written, and visual language (e.g., conventions, style, vocabulary) to communicate effectively with a variety of audiences and for different purposes.

5. Students employ a wide range of strategies as they write and use different writing process elements appropriately to communicate with different audiences for a variety of purposes.

6. Students apply knowledge of language structure, language conventions (e.g., spelling and punctuation), media techniques, figurative language, and genre to create, critique, and discuss print and nonprint texts.

7. Students conduct research on issues and interests by generating ideas and questions and by posing problems. They gather, evaluate, and synthesize data from a variety of sources (e.g., print and nonprint texts, artifacts, people) to communicate their discoveries in ways that suit their purpose and audience.

8. Students use a variety of technological and information resources (e.g., libraries, databases, computer networks, video) to gather and synthesize information and to create and communicate knowledge.

9. Students develop an understanding of and respect for diversity in language use, patterns, and dialects across cultures, ethnic groups, geographic regions, and social roles.

10. Students whose first language is not English make use of their first language to develop competency in the English language arts and to develop understanding of content across the curriculum.

11. Students participate as knowledgeable, reflective, creative, and critical members of a variety of literacy communities.

12. Students use spoken, written, and visual language to accomplish their own purposes (e.g., for learning, enjoyment, persuasion, and the exchange of information).

REFERENCES

Adams, M. J. (1990). *Beginning to read: Thinking and learning about print.* Cambridge, MA: MIT Press.

Anderson, R. C., Hiebert, E. H., Scott, J. A., & Wilkinson, I. A. G. (1985). *Becoming a nation of readers: The report of the commission on reading.* Washington, DC: National Institute of Education.

Bond, G., & Dykstra, R. (1967/1997). The cooperative research program in first-grade reading instruction. *Reading Research Quarterly, 32,* 345–427.

Chall, J. (1967). *Learning to read: The great debate.* New York: McGraw-Hill.

Cunningham, P. M., & Allington, R. (2007). *Classrooms that work: They can all read and write* (4th ed.). Boston: Pearson/Allyn & Bacon.

International Reading Association (IRA) & National Council of Teachers of English (NCTE). (1996). *Standards for the English language arts.* Newark, DE: IRA, Urbana, IL: NCTE.

National Institute of Child Health and Human Development (NICHD). (2000). *Report of the National Reading Panel: Teaching children to read: An evidence-based assessment of the scientific research literature on reading and its implications for reading instruction* (NIH Publication No. 00–4769). Washington, DC: U.S. Government Printing Office.

Snow, C. E., Burns, M. S., & Griffin, P. (Eds.). (1998). *Preventing reading difficulties in young children.* Washington, DC: National Academy Press.

Strategy
1

All About Book

A kindergarten student drew a picture of himself and wrote a caption by copying words from the graphic organizer his teacher used to record students' responses to the following question: "What is incredible about you?" which was asked after reading the book *Incredible Me!* The student's creation (Figure 1.1) will be a page in the class's *All About the Incredible Students in Our Class* book.

Figure 1.1 Kindergarten student drawing and writing in response to *Incredible Me!*

RATIONALE

This literature-based strategy can be used across grade levels with any book or any topic. Students listen to a read aloud of a book and discuss the book, responding first to open and aesthetic reader response questions and prompts. The teacher uses the book as a model for students to share ideas of their own on a topic, recording them on a graphic organizer. Students begin with these ideas and write an All About Book on the topic.

Research supports the idea that when students are given an adult model to follow, such as a teacher reading a story aloud and recording students' responses on a graphic organizer, and materials and opportunities to write, they begin to experiment with and build a repertoire of knowledge about written language (Sulzby, 1992). Donald Graves (1983) described the writing process, or what students do as they continue to develop as writers, as having the following steps: (1) pre-write, (2) draft, (3) revise, (4) edit, and (5) publish. Each of these aspects can involve students in a number of different ongoing activities, from the pre-writing and discussing of a book to the publication of their own All About Book.

Source: From Standards for the English language arts, by the International Reading Association (IRA) and the National Council of Teachers of English (NCTE), 1996. Newark, DE: NCTE, Urbana, IL: IRA.

English Language Arts Standard

13. Students use spoken, written, and visual language to accomplish their own purposes (e.g., for learning, enjoyment, persuasion, and the exchange of information).

STRATEGY

Read aloud a book that provides a model for students to tap into their own prior experience as a source of ideas to write an All About Book. For example, a book with characters that are around the age of the students in the class, that have good self-images, and that are able to describe themselves positively might provide such a model.

Lead the discussion using aesthetic, reader response questions and prompts that move from a focus on the book to a focus on the students, asking them to describe their strengths and what they like about themselves or how they imagine themselves in a positive way. Record students' responses on a cluster graphic organizer, or older students can do this on their own, to model the writing process.

Student writing can be published in an All About Book with a page for each child, or older students can write and publish an All About Book independently.

GRADE-LEVEL MODIFICATIONS

K–2ND GRADE

Introduce the book *Incredible Me!* (Appelt, 2003), a rhyming book in which a child joyfully explains "I'm the one, the only, most marvelous me!" (This book would also be appropriate for pre–K.) Ask students what they think the word *incredible* means and then write down their ideas in the corner of a piece of chart paper; add to their ideas with synonyms for incredible (e.g., *great, amazing, awesome, fabulous, marvelous, extraordinary,* and *remarkable*). Then, read the book aloud and lead a discussion using aesthetic reader response questions and prompts: What do you think was the most incredible thing about the character in the story? What is something incredible about you?

Record students' responses to the last question on a graphic organizer on a piece of chart paper like in Figure 1.2. Draw a circle in the center and write "Incredible Me." Extend lines around the circle to connect to student responses in a spider-shaped cluster. (Use chart paper so that you can save the graphic organizer and add to it with subsequent re-readings of the book.) Model by writing about yourself (e.g., "I am incredible because I have incredible students in my class.") Write the name of each child next to their response.

| Figure 1.2 | Graphic organizer "Incredible Me!" |

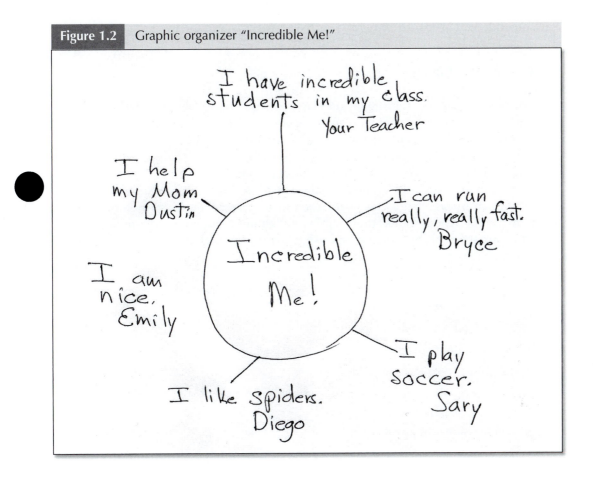

Students use their own ideas from the graphic organizer if they responded during the class discussion, or they can use other ideas they have. They can draw a picture and write a caption by either copying the response that was written on the graphic organizer, writing a new one, writing on their own, or dictating their response to you. Students can share their drawing and writing with the class.

Publish student writings by putting them together in a class book with a title: for example, *All About the Incredible Students in our Class.* Student writing can also be published by mounting it on a bulletin board with the same title.

Plus Technology

Students can use KidPix (Riverdeep), a multimedia graphics software program that they can use to draw and write, and then print out, or they can add sounds and produce multimedia slide shows.

Books

Appelt, K. (2003). *Incredible me!* New York: HarperCollins.

Beaumont, K. (2004). *I like myself.* New York: Harcourt.

Carlson, N. (1988). *I like me.* New York: Viking.

Carlson, N. (1997). *ABC, I like me.* New York: Viking.

Curtis, J. L. (2002). *I'm gonna like me.* New York: HarperCollins.

Richmond, M. (2003). *Hooray for you!* New York: Marianne Richmond Studios.

3RD GRADE–5TH GRADE

Read *Amazing Grace* (Hoffman, 1991), a picture book about a young African American girl with lots of talent who achieves her goal of starring in the class play with the support of her understanding mother and grandmother. Lead a discussion using aesthetic reader response questions and prompts: What do you think was the most amazing thing about Grace? What's something amazing about you?

Students can do a personal graphic organizer with several ideas about what is amazing about them by creating a cluster for each idea. Each of these can become a paragraph in an All About Book they will write about themselves. Do a mini-lesson on writing a paragraph by creating and using a poster with students that contains the following key ideas:

Writing a Paragraph

1. Paragraphs are sentences on a main idea

2. Start with a topic sentence

3. Add facts and details in supporting sentences

4. Number your topic sentence and supporting sentences on your cluster
   - Put a 1 next to the topic sentence
   - Number supporting sentences in order, 2, 3, and so on

5. Write a paragraph with a lead sentence and details in supporting sentences

---

Students could also write a short All About Book about themselves. Guide students to brainstorm a list of possible topics they could use for chapter titles (e.g., My life, Family, School, Interests, Goals, etc.). The purpose of this activity would be to create multiple-paragraph compositions for each chapter of the book around a topic that engages the reader and to develop the topic with supporting details and vivid imagery. When revised and edited, the chapters could be word processed and published as a book.

Books

Hoffman, M. (1991). *Amazing Grace*. New York: Dial.

Hoffman, M. (2001). *Starring Grace*. New York: Puffin.

Hoffman, M. (2003). *Encore, Grace*. New York: Dial.

Hoffman, M. (2008). *Princess Grace*. New York: Dial.

Hoffman, M. (2011). *Bravo, Grace*. New York: Puffin.

6TH GRADE–8TH GRADE

Read aloud *Boys of Steel: The Creators of Superman* (Nobleman, 2008), a picture book about the two high school boys who created the character of Superman. Lead a discussion using aesthetic reader response questions and prompts: If you were a superhero like Superman, what powers would you have? What special abilities do you already have?

Students can identify what special abilities they already have and the super powers they would have if they were a superhero, and students can record them on a personal graphic organizer. Using their alter ego superhero character, they can write and illustrate an All About comic strip or a story about the character in the form of a graphic novel, which tells a story through a combination of text and illustrations.

Books

Colfer, E., & Donkin, A. (2007). *Artemis Fowl: The graphic novel*. New York: Hyperion.

Horowitz, A., & Johnston, A. (2007). *Point blank: The graphic novel*. New York: Philomel.

Kinney, J. (2007). *Diary of a wimpy kid: A novel in cartoons*. New York: Amulet Books.

Nobleman, M. T. (2008). *Boys of steel: The creators of Superman*. New York: Knopf.

ENGLISH LEARNERS

For English Learners (ELs) at the beginning level, use visuals and draw pictures next to student responses on the graphic organizer. Also use gestures to demonstrate student responses through Total Physical Response (TPR). Students can draw and utilize dictation for their writing.

For intermediate and advanced ELs, show the word *incredible* on a white board, chart, or on a sentence strip. Tap into students' prior knowledge by asking if anyone knows what it means or can give an example. If ELs are Spanish speakers, show the cognate *incredible*. Ask for synonyms and write those down on a chart as you talk about them.

STRUGGLING STUDENTS

Take dictation by writing labels, captions, or phrases on a student drawing. Use a sentence starter ("I am incredible...") by modeling and writing it on the bottom of the graphic organizer with the students' ideas. Provide students with a frame for an individual graphic organizer. They may use this in a conference with you, working with a buddy who is a more capable peer, or on their own.

ASSESSMENT

The following checklist with comments for drawing and writing, K through 2nd, can be used and adjusted by grade level according to state, district, or school standards.

Checklist With Comments for Pre-writing and Writing, K–2

*Name*_____ *Date* _____

Title

Check those that apply	**Comments**
Draws in lieu of writing	
Draws as pre-writing	
Draws to illustrate writing	
Writing	
Gave dictation	
Wrote name	
Letters to represent words	
Words: label or caption	
Phrases	
Sentences	
Strengths	
Needs	

RESOURCES

Corgill, A. M. (2008). *Of primary importance: What's essential to teaching young writers*. Portland, ME: Stenhouse.

Horn, M., & Giacobbe, M. E. (2007). *Talking, drawing, writing: Lessons for our youngest writers*. Portland, ME: Stenhouse.

REFERENCES

Graves, D. H. (1983). *Writing: Teachers and children at work*. Portsmouth, NH: Heinemann.

Sulzby, E. (1992). Research directions: Transitions from emergent to conventional writing. *Language Arts, 69*, 290–297.

Strategy
2

Biopoems

Elizabeth wrote this biopoem in free verse in an 8th-grade Honors English class.

"I am

MANATEES, FRIENDS, ARROWBEAR

I like reading and spending time with friends

Acceptance, kindness, and love are important to me in people

I fight for what I believe in—and believe in it

I am stubborn and won't change my mind

But I change other peoples' and help them see

I love all of my friends

I despise shallow people who just don't understand

I strongly believe all killing is wrong

This is who I am!"

RATIONALE

This literature-based strategy guides students to tap into their own life experience, something they know a lot about, to find ideas for writing. It also provides structure through the use of the biopoem frame. Model biopoem writing by reading, and having students read, autobiographical poetry.

Research on writing has shown that literacy develops when reasons for writing exist, when the writing is social and helps mediate relationships with other people, and when students are given opportunities to reflect on their own lives (Farr, 1994; Heath, 1983). Reading, discussing, writing, publishing, and sharing autobiographical poetry in the form of biopoems gives students such reasons and opportunities.

Source: From Standards for the English language arts, by the International Reading Association (IRA) and the National Council of Teachers of English (NCTE), 1996. Newark, DE: NCTE; Urbana, IL: IRA.

English Language Arts Standard
2. Students read a wide range of literature from many periods and many genres to build an understanding of the many dimensions (e.g., philosophical, ethical, aesthetic) of human experience.

STRATEGY

Model writing biopoems by reading autobiographical poetry aloud and providing examples in a collection of books in the classroom. Students can also read selections and read aloud for the class or in small groups. Lead discussions using aesthetic reader response questions and prompts that direct students to tap into their own life experiences as a source of ideas to write about.

With support, the students can brainstorm ideas to write their own autobiographical poetry in the form of a biopoem, and they can be provided with biopoem frames appropriate for each grade level on chart paper or on an overhead transparency or each student can be given a copy. Students can write independently, in pairs, or in groups, and students can also adapt the frames and create their own biopoem frame or choose to write autobiographical poetry in another poetic form.

GRADE-LEVEL MODIFICATIONS

K–2ND GRADE

Read autobiographical poetry aloud for young children from Jack Prelutsky's (2007) *Me I Am!* Then lead a discussion using aesthetic reader response questions and prompts: These poets describe themselves with words in their poems. What are some words you would use to describe yourself, your family, or things you like?

Record students' words on a graphic organizer with five columns to correspond to the final biopoem frame, labeled as follows: First name, Me, My family, Things I like, Last name. Put this biopoem frame on chart paper and model writing a biopoem using the words from the graphic organizer describing one student; then give each student a blank writing frame to write their own biopoem.

First name
3 words about me
3 words about my family
3 words about things I like
Last name

Students can complete the frame or ask someone to take dictation for them. Students can illustrate their biopoem with a self-portrait.

Trace an outline of each student's body on butcher paper and have the student cut it out. The student can draw on it, glue or staple their biopoem to it, and write other words, phrases, and sentences that describe his or her self on it. A student effigy can be created by backing the outline collage with a second cutout and stapling the front and back together, leaving a space, and stuffing it with crumpled newspaper to create a three-dimensional effect.

Books

Greenfield, E. (1988). *Nathaniel talking*. New York: Black Butterfly Children's Books.

Prelutsky, J. (2007). *Me I am!* New York: Farrar, Straus & Giroux.

3RD GRADE–5TH GRADE

Read autobiographical poetry and writing such as Ashley Bryan's (2009) *Words to My Life Song*, a beautifully illustrated picture book autobiography of the writer and illustrator that is a seamless blend of words and art. Lead a discussion using aesthetic reader response questions and prompts: What did you picture in your mind when you heard the words in the poems and song? What words would you use to create a picture of yourself in a poem or song?

The students can use a cluster graphic organizer to write down words and phrases to describe themselves, and they can write and illustrate an autobiographical poem or song. (The teacher and students can adapt a biopoem frame for K–2 or 6–8, or see Strategy 33: Songwriting.) The students and teacher can also plan a poetry slam, where students do a performance reading of their biopoem accompanied by gestures, props, music, or dance. Students could work in pairs or small groups, one assisting the other as each reads their poem.

Plus Technology

Software programs for poetry writing include Poetry Express, Poetry Palette, and interactive poetry writing sites such as KidzPage (http://gardenofsong.com/kidzpage), Poetry Express (www.poetryexpress.org), or Scholastic's Poetry Writing with Karla Kuskin, Jack Prelutsky, and Jan Marzallo (http://teacher.scholastic.com/writewit/poetry/).

Books

Bryan, A. (2009). *Words to my life song*. New York: Atheneum.

Grimes, N. (1986). *Something on my mind*. New York: Puffin.

Mak, K. (2001). *My Chinatown: One year in poems*. New York: HarperCollins.

Rylant, C. (1984). *Waiting to waltz: A childhood*. Seattle, WA: Bradbury Press.

6TH GRADE–8TH GRADE

Read aloud from the collections of autobiographical poetry by Gary Soto, who wrote about growing up Mexican American in the Central Valley of California: *Canto Familiar* (1995); *Fearless Fernie: Hanging out With Fernie and Me* (2002); *Worlds Apart: Fernie and Me* (2005); *A Fire in My Hands,* a revised and expanded edition

(2006); and *Neighborhood Odes* (1992). Provide a copy of the poem for each student, or display it on a chart or overhead projector transparency. Then lead a discussion using aesthetic reader response questions and use the following prompts: The poet described himself through events in his life and his feelings. If you were a poet, how would you describe yourself?

Ask students to write down one way the poet described something about himself and one way they would describe something about themselves. Then, suggest that they describe themselves on the outside (what they look like) or on the inside (how they feel or what they think). Create a T-chart graphic organizer on chart paper or on a whiteboard. Title the graphic organizer "Poets Describing," and create two columns under the title: (1) Gary Soto and (2) Our Class.

Using a pair-share cooperative learning activity, ask students to share with a buddy what they wrote about how Gary Soto described himself and how they described themselves. They can add to their notes during their conversation. The students can share what they wrote about Gary Soto and themselves with the whole class and record their ideas on the T-chart graphic organizer. In the left-hand column, record students' ideas about how the poet described himself. In the right-hand column, let students record their ideas about how they would describe themselves. After this discussion, ask students to add to their list of ways they would describe themselves, which they will then use to write a biopoem or an autobiographical poem.

Provide a blank of one of the biopoem frames shown in this chapter or display one on chart paper or overhead transparency for students to create their own biopoems. Here is a biopoem frame commonly used in upper elementary and middle school.

BIOPOEM
First name
Four words that tell about you
Child of
Lover of (3 things)
Who feels (3 things)
Who needs (3 things)
Who would like to see (3 things)
Resident of
Last name

Student biopoems can be published in a variety of ways: They can be mounted on a bulletin board display, collected in a class poetry anthology that can be reproduced, or shared on an overhead projector transparency and read aloud.

Plus Technology

Direct students to Gary Soto's website (www.garysoto.com). Students can word process poems and print out and publish a class anthology of biopoems. They can also use PowerPoint to present their poetry, adding decorative borders, clip art images or photographs, sound effects, and fade ins and outs.

Books

Angelou, M. (1993). *Life doesn't frighten me*. New York: Stewart, Tabori, and Chang.

Grimes, N. (1998). *A dime a dozen*. New York: Dial.

Nelson, M. (2001). *Carver. A life in poems.* New York: Front Street.

Soto, G. (1992). *Neighborhood odes.* New York: Harcourt.

Soto, G. (1995). *Canto familiar.* New York: Harcourt.

Soto, G. (2002). *Fearless Fernie: Hanging out with Fernie and me.* New York: Putnam.

Soto, G. (2005). *Worlds apart: Fernie and me.* New York: Putnam.

Soto, G. (2006). *A fire in my hands.* New York: Harcourt.

ENGLISH LEARNERS

Beginning English learners can use visuals by drawing a picture of themselves or attaching a photograph to a piece of paper and labeling it with describing words, phrases, or sentences. Create a word bank of describing words they can copy onto their poem. In a group, intermediate and advanced English learners can brainstorm describing words, phrases, or sentences. Record these on chart paper as a phrase or sentence bank. Students can choose from these and write the phrases or sentences on strips of paper, arranging them in a pattern and using a glue stick to attach them to a piece of paper. There is also culturally sensitive literature that provides primary language support with English-Spanish poetry collections.

Books

Alarcon, F. S. (1998). *From the belly button of the moon and other summer poems.* San Francisco: Children's Book Press.

Argueta, J. (2001). *A movie in my pillow/Una pelicula en mi almohada.* San Francisco: Children's Book Press.

Carlson, L. M. (Ed.). (1994). *Cool salsa: Bilingual poems on growing up Latino in the United States.* New York: Holt.

Medina, J. (1999). *My name is Jorge: On both sides of the river.* Honesdale, PA: Boyds Mills Press.

Mora, P. (1996). *Confetti.* New York: Lee & Low.

STRUGGLING STUDENTS

Create a blank frame with the categories from the previously shown biopoem on chart paper, whiteboard, or overhead transparency. The frame can also be adapted by using fewer categories or changing the categories to meet the needs of students. Model writing the biopoem on the frame with students and record their responses on chart paper. Provide a blank copy of the frame for each student to write their biopoem.

You could also take dictation, provide a word bank for each student to use, and adjust the frame as needed for individual students. Copies of the student biopoems can be reproduced for reading aloud.

Assessment

Use a Peer-Editor Form so students who are reading and writing can respond to, review, and edit the poetry of another student. Students can find or be assigned a buddy, and then they can read and review each other's writing, including suggesting changes before the poetry is published in a class book, displayed on a bulletin board, or shared in a PowerPoint presentation.

Peer-Editor Form

The piece I read was _____

by _____

The best thing about this piece is _____

_____

_____

If the writer wanted to change something, I would suggest _____

_____

_____

Peer editor _____   Date_____

Resources

Tiedt, I. M. (2002). *Tiger lilies, toadstools, and thunderbolts: Engaging K–8 students with poetry.* New York: Scholastic.

Wood, J. (2006). *Living voices: Multicultural poetry in the middle school classroom.* Urbana, IL: National Council of Teachers of English.

References

Farr, M. (1994). En los dos idiomas: Literacy practices among Chicano Mexicanos. In B. J. Moss (Ed.), *Literacy across communities* (pp. 9–48). Cresskill, NJ: Hampton Press.

Heath, S. B. (1983). *Ways with words: Language, life, and work in communities and classrooms.* Cambridge, England: Cambridge University Press.

Book Clubs

In a 5th-grade class, the teacher had read aloud Betsy Byars' (2000) book *The Summer of the Swans*, about a 14-year-old girl who realizes how much she cares about her developmentally disabled brother when he runs away. The students have written in their literature journal and now meet in book clubs to discuss the book:

Doug: You know in the story, I was wondering. . . . Why did he run away?

Jada: He wanted to see the swans.

Samrith: Yeah, but why did he want to see the swans so desperately?

Huong: I know why. I know you all probably like to talk to yourself, and if he can't talk to himself he probably wanted to go see the swans. To have something interesting to do. To keep himself company. We all want to do that.

RATIONALE

Book clubs are a way to organize teaching language arts and reading with literature. Students choose books they will read in groups. Different groups read different books, and the teacher meets with each group on a rotating basis to facilitate book discussions, guide writing in response to the book, and possibly suggest other special projects. The teacher may provide a focus for book clubs, such as a genre, author, theme, or a combination of these. Book clubs typically last two to three weeks.

This is a very flexible strategy that can provide for differentiated instruction in a variety of ways that engage students with reading literature and the language arts. Research shows that book clubs can lead to rich discussions of literature (Eeds & Wells, 1989). They can be varied and used across grade levels and across the curriculum to complement learning in the content areas at different grade levels, K through 8, and for diverse students. Martinez-Roldan and Lopez-Robertson (2000) reported on the use of book clubs in a 1st-grade bilingual classroom and found that "young bilingual children, no matter their linguistic background, are able to have rich discussions if they have regular opportunities to engage with books from a transactional perspective" (p. 2770).

Source: From Standards for the English language arts, by the International Reading Association (IRA) and the National Council of Teachers of English (NCTE), 1996. Newark, DE: NCTE, Urbana, IL: IRA.

> ## English Language Arts Standard
>
> 11. Students participate as knowledgeable, reflective, creative, and critical members of a variety of literacy communities.

STRATEGY

Students form small groups and read the same self-selected book. Collect multiple copies of a book from the school and public libraries. Do brief *book talks* to introduce these books to students by showing the book, giving a brief summary, and reading an excerpt. Instead of using multiple copies of a book, students can also rotate a copy of the book to read during sustained silent reading, at other times during the school day, and at home.

Students begin reading and writing about whatever attracted their attention or whatever they thought about the book in a journal. While students are reading and writing in journals, schedule a rotation of conferences with each group (e.g., one group a day for five days). During the conference with a group, discuss the chapters students have been reading using aesthetic reader response questions and prompts and have students share what they have written in their journals while reading the book. These questions and prompts can be posted on a chart in the room.

Reader Response Questions and Prompts

- Tell me about the book you are reading.
- What did you think about as you were reading it?
- What questions did you have about the book?
- Ask your own questions and respond to other students' questions.
- What part of the book attracted your attention? Why?
- Has anything like what happened in the book ever happened to you?
- Does the book remind you of other stories, books, movies, television shows, or games you have experienced?
- What else do you think might happen in this book?
- What would you change about the book?

Record student ideas on one side of a piece of chart paper to keep an ongoing record of Book Club discussions during teacher conferences. After at least one of these discussions, guide students to suggest other ideas for writing and further reading or for developing special projects that would be presented to the class using a Book Club plan (e.g., writing stories, poems, songs, or scripts for dramatizing a scene from the book;

reader's theatre; and art projects). On the other side of the paper, record, or have students record, the group discussions. The components of this plan can vary depending on the interests, ideas, and abilities of the students.

Students can continue reading the book and can begin writing ideas they developed for the Book Club plan. The teacher continues to conference with groups, adjusting the conferences according to their interests and needs. Students share writing and special projects with other book clubs at the end of the book club cycle.

GRADE-LEVEL MODIFICATIONS

K–2ND GRADE

Introduce One-Day Book Clubs using humorous poetry in the primary grades. Begin by reading several selections of humorous poetry aloud, from a poetry collection such as Jack Prelutsky's (1991) *For Laughing out Loud: Poems to Tickle Your Funny-Bone;* then lead a discussion using reader response questions and prompts: What was your favorite poem? What did you like about it?

Students can vote on their favorite poems. The next day, they can form One-Day Book Clubs. Give individual copies of one or more of the favorite poems to each book club for discussion. Rotate among the groups to conference with students and record their ideas on a chart titled "Our Ideas About the Poem _____."

One-Week Book Clubs could also be formed with students in the primary grades around books that are one title in a popular series of humorous stories about the same characters for children in the primary grades.

Books

Florian, D. (1999). *Laugh-eteria*. New York: Harcourt.

Lewis, P. (1996). *Riddle-Icious*. New York: Knopf.

McNaughton, C. (1998). *Who's been sleeping in my porridge? A book of wacky poems and pictures.* Cambridge, MA: Candlewick Press.

Parish, P. (1963). *Amelia Bedelia*. New York: Harper & Row.

Park, B. (2002). *Junie B., first grader: Toothless wonder.* New York: Random House.

Prelutsky, J. (1991). *For laughing out loud: Poems to tickle your funny-bone.* New York: Knopf.

3RD GRADE–5TH GRADE

Read aloud a chapter a day from *Holes* by Louis Sachar (1998), a Newbery Award winning book, or other humorous book for middle grades. Lead a discussion after reading each day, using reader response questions and prompts: What did you think of the part of the story I read today?

Then do book talks on other humorous books, have students vote on their favorite books, and collect multiple copies of favorite titles. School or public librarians can help.

Or students can rotate reading of the book for each book club during independent reading or reading at home.

The students can read and discuss books using aesthetic reader response questions and prompts posted in the room. Rotate among groups to conference and develop a Book Club Plan for each group and to record and discuss ideas on the plan as well as ideas for writing or other special projects.

Plus Technology

For virtual book clubs, see Book Raps (http:rite.ed.qut.edu.au/old_oz-teachernet/projects/book-rap/) and Spaghetti Book Club (www.spaghettibookclub.com).

Books

Blume, J. (1972). *Tales of a fourth grade nothing.* New York: Dutton.

Criswell, P. K. (2007). *The book club kit.* New York: American Girl.

Levy, E. (1997). *My life as a fifth grade comedian.* New York: Harper Collins.

Robinson, B. (1972). *The best Christmas pageant ever.* New York: Harper & Row.

Rockwell, T. (1973). *How to eat fried worms.* New York: Watts.

Sachar, L. (1998). *Holes.* New York: Farrar, Straus, & Giroux.

The following books are from various popular series of humorous stories for students in the middle grades. Students in book clubs could read different titles in a series.

Byars, B. (1991). *Wanted . . . Mud Blossom.* New York: Delacorte.

Cleary, B. (1999). *Ramona's world.* New York: Morrow.

Danziger, P. (1995). *Amber Brown goes fourth.* New York: Putnam.

Delton, J. (1999). *Angel spreads her wings.* New York: Houghton Mifflin.

Gantos, J. (1999). *Jack on the tracks: Four seasons of fifth grade.* New York: Farrar, Straus & Giroux.

Hurwitz, J. (1979). *Aldo Applesauce.* New York: Morrow.

Lowry, L. (1979). *Anastasia Krupnik.* New York: Houghton Mifflin.

McDonald, M. (2003). *Judy Moody predicts the future!* Cambridge, MA: Candlewick Press.

McKay, H. (1992). *The exiles.* New York: McElderry.

Sachar, L. (1993). *Marvin Redpost: Why pick on me?* New York: Farrar, Straus & Giroux.

Sachar, L. (1995). *Wayside School gets a little stranger.* New York: Morrow.

Smith, J. L. (1993). *Serious science: An Adam Joshua story.* New York: HarperCollins.

6th Grade–8th Grade

Book clubs can be formed in 6th grade self-contained classrooms, or in English classes in middle school, related to the English curriculum or student interests. See Strategy 4: Online Discussion Boards for how to have students discuss the same book online in a virtual book club. Avid and capable readers could self-select groups and books to read, based on interests and abilities. Students could suggest individual projects that interest them during book club discussions.

The following titles are one in a popular series of humorous books appropriate for adolescent students.

Books

Byars, B. (1990). *Bingo Brown, gypsy lover.* New York: Viking.

Cooper, I. (1992). *Queen of the sixth grade.* New York: Morrow.

Park, B. (1982). *Skinnybones.* New York: Knopf.

Paulsen, G. (1993). *Harris and me.* New York: Harcourt Brace.

English Learners

Introduce the key vocabulary in a book, story, or poem using English Language Development (ELD) strategies, depending on the level of English proficiency of the students in each Book Club. ELD strategies, such as context-embedded instruction with peer support and tapping into prior knowledge, are all part of the structure of book clubs. Read aloud to students. Introduce academic vocabulary from the books, using visuals, drawing, or showing a pictorial representation of the word. Use gestures that provide clues to the word meanings and have students respond by using TPR. Also use props or realia, cognates, and graphic organizers.

Differentiation for beginning, intermediate, and advanced ELs can also be provided for the types of writing or special projects each child does. For example, a beginning level English learner might draw a picture and label it, an intermediate level EL could write sentences and illustrate them, and an advanced EL could write and illustrate a short book.

Use primary language support with bilingual books or books published in languages other than English: for example, books by Gary Soto published in English and Spanish.

Books

Soto, G. (1990). *Baseball in April and other stories.* San Diego, CA: Harcourt

Soto, G. (1993). *Beisbol en abril y otras historias.* Mexico: Fondo de Cultural Economica.

Struggling Students

For struggling readers, read aloud to a book club group, have students read in pairs with a buddy, or have them read along with a taped version of the book. Students could have a copy of the book, story, or poem so they can follow along. Students could also take turns and join in the reading or do a choral reading. Students could have book buddies who team up and support each other during reading and writing.

For struggling writers, highlight phrases on a graphic organizer for the discussion of the book for students to use to begin writing. Also take dictation at the beginning of the writing or allow students to be assisted by a buddy writer. Create writing frames based on the ideas of the students in a book club to scaffold students' writing.

ASSESSMENT

Use a Book Club Log to conference with students and monitor and assess student progress in a book club.

Book Club Log

Name: _____   Date: _____

Book Title: _____   Author: _____

Date	Pages Read	Journal Entry (check)	Conference Notes

RESOURCES

Cox, C., & Boyd-Batstone, P. (2009). *Engaging English learners: Exploring literature, developing literacy, differentiating instruction.* Boston: Pearson/Allyn & Bacon.

Daniels, H. (2002). *Literature circles, voice and choice in book clubs and reading groups.* Honesdale, PA: Stenhouse.

Day, J. P., Spiegel, D. L., McLellan, J., Brown, V. B., & Allington, R. L. (2002). *Moving forward with literature circles.* New York: Scholastic.

Samway, K. D., & Whang, G. (1996). *Literature circles in a multicultural classroom.* York, ME: Stenhouse.

REFERENCES

Byars, B. (2000). *The summer of the swans.* New York: Scholastic.

Eeds, M., & Wells, D. (1989). Grand conversations: An exploration of meaning construction in literature study groups. *Research in the Teaching of English, 23,* 4–29.

Martinez-Roldan, C., & Lopez-Robertson, J. (2000). Initiating literature circles in a first grade bilingual classroom. *The Reading Teacher, 52,* 270–281.

Online Discussion Boards

The 6th-grade student excitedly told her friend as she ran to catch her bus: "I'll read the next chapter of the book on the bus and write on the discussion board when I get home! Look for it. I'll look for yours too."

RATIONALE

With this strategy, teachers use technology as a tool for their students to respond to literature in online discussions. Students write their responses to a book on an online discussion board, and then they respond to teach other in a continuing online discussion about the book. Since students can go online at any time, and other students can respond at any time, a specific time does not have to be scheduled for this asynchronous activity. Students can participate during class, or from the library, or from home with access to a computer and the Internet. The teacher can also participate in the online discussion at any time. This strategy provides an effective merger of literature discussion and technology in literacy instruction (McKenna, Labbo, & Reinking, 2004).

In the examples here, the technology strategy is teamed with a graphic novel—two relatively recent communication and literary forms used in the classroom for reading, writing, and thinking. The teacher can use this strategy for a book that is assigned to the whole class for reading (e.g., required literature in middle school English classes) or for a book that all students read in an English/Social Studies block schedule (e.g., a work of historical or regional fiction in English set in the period of history or region studied in social studies). It can also be used with book clubs (see Strategy 3 Book Clubs), or students can form buddy groups where at least two students read the same book and respond to the book and each other in the online discussion.

English Language Arts Standard

8. Students use a variety of technological and information resources (e.g., libraries, databases, computer networks, video) to gather and synthesize information and to create and communicate knowledge.

Source: From Standards for the English language arts, by the International Reading Association (IRA) and the National Council of Teachers of English (NCTE), 1996. Newark, DE: NCTE, Urbana, IL: IRA.

STRATEGY

Collect a text set of graphic novels for the classroom. Have students find a reading buddy or form small groups to read the same graphic novel during independent reading, in the library, or at home.

Set up an online discussion board on a learning management system with a discussion board capability, such as a public domain Wiki. Many public schools utilize a Web-based system that includes e-mail and discussion board features. Create guidelines and a schedule for writing a response to the book in an online discussion board.

Online Discussion Board Log

Directions: Write an online response to the assigned pages by the scheduled date. Write a response to at least two other students by the scheduled date.

Suggested Reader Response Questions and Prompts:

What did you think of the story?

What did you think about the graphic novel format?

Has anything like this ever happened to you?

Did the story remind you of anything?

What else do you think could have happened in the story?

What did you wonder about?

Schedule

Read and write an online response   Write to two other students

Chapter/Pages   Date   Date

Plan whole class or small group discussions with students during the online discussion board cycle. Direct students to not only reflect on their personal experiencing of the book, but to also reflect on the experiences of other students as evidenced by their online responses. During the online discussion board cycle for the graphic novels students are reading with a buddy or in a small group, they may post comments about other graphic novels they are reading as well.

Team up with another teacher who is reading the same book or assigning the same books to be read by students and establish online discussion boards either with other classes in your school or with other schools in your district or elsewhere. With online discussion boards, students can read and discuss the book with students in other classrooms in the school, as well as with students in their own class. The same would be true for district required reading. Or simply team up with a teacher anywhere by choosing the same book for students to read. It might be interesting to team with a teacher in another country whose students are learning English and would have access to the same book, either in print or online.

GRADE-LEVEL MODIFICATIONS

K–2ND GRADE

Share and make available graphic novels for younger students, for example *Benny and Penny in Just Pretend* (Hayes, 2008), *Billions of Bats: A Buzz Beaker Brainstorm*

(Nickel, 2007), or *Otto's Orange Day* (Cammuso & Lynch, 2008), or use this strategy with any illustrated picture book.

Team up with another teacher reading the same book through a guided threaded discussion feature on a discussion board. Take dictation from younger students by using a Smart Board and project the threaded discussion on a Smart Board screen between two or more classrooms anywhere. Employ guided writing or interactive writing strategies (see Strategy 5, Interactive Writing) while sharing the students authentic responses to a book in real-time across multiple classrooms.

Books

Cammuso, F., & Lynch, J. (2008). *Otto's orange day.* New York: TOON Books.

Hayes, G. (2008). *Benny and Penny in just pretend.* New York: RAW Junior.

Nickel, S. (2007). *Billions of bats: A Buzz Beaker brainstorm.* Mankato, MN: Stone Arch Books.

3RD GRADE–5TH GRADE

Read aloud graphic novels for middle grade students (e.g., the books listed in the section that follows) and either set up an online discussion board, as described previously, or take dictation and project their responses on a Smart Board screen using the guided threaded discussion feature on a discussion board as described for students in K through 2nd grade.

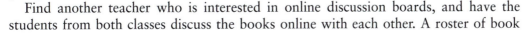

Books

Gaiman, N. (2008). *Coraline.* New York: HarperCollins.

Holm, J. L. (2007). *Babymouse: Heartbreaker.* New York: Random House.

Morse, S. (2008). *Magic pickle.* New York: GRAPHIX.

Piley, D. (1997). *The adventures of Captain Underpants: An epic novel.* New York: Blue Sky Press.

Steinberg, D. J. (2008). *Sound off! The adventures of Daniel Boom aka Loud Boy.* New York: Grosset & Dunlap.

Stine, R. L. (2007). *Terror trips: Goosebumps.* New York: Graphix.

Trondheim, L. (2009). *Tiny tyrant.* New York: First Second.

Wood, D. A. (2008). *Into the volcano.* New York: Blue Sky Press.

Yeh, P. (2007). *Dinosaurs across America.* New York: Nantier Beall Minoustchine.

6TH GRADE–8TH GRADE

Collect multiple titles and copies of graphic novels such as *The Invention of Hugo Cabret* by Brian Selznick (2007), a book which combines characteristics of the picture book, graphic novel, and film genre and which was the winner of the 2008 Caldecott Medal for the most distinguished American picture book from those published in the United States during the previous year. Students can team with a buddy or form small groups to read the same title and participate in an online discussion board.

Find another teacher who is interested in online discussion boards, and have the students from both classes discuss the books online with each other. A roster of book titles and students reading those titles could be planned and used to guide students to a discussion group for the same book they are reading.

Students could also research and implement other forms of technology communication. Using digital photography and a photo editing program, students can create their own graphic novels. They may photograph their own drawings in order to publish them online in a Wiki or blog.

Books

Colfer, E., & Donkin, A. (2007). *Artemis Fowl: The graphic novel.* New York: Hyperion.

Hale, S., Hale, D., & Hale, N. (2008). *Rapunzel's revenge.* London: Bloomsbury.

Jacques, B. (2007). *Redwall: The graphic novel.* New York: Philomel.

Kinney, J. (2007). *Diary of a wimpy kid: A novel in cartoons.* New York: Amulet Books.

MacHale, D. J., & McNeil, C. S. (2008). *The merchant of death: Pendragon graphic novel.* New York: Aladdin.

Petrucha, S. (2007). *Nancy Drew graphic novels, girl detective #9: Ghost in the machinery.* New York: Papercutz.

Siegel, S. C. (2007). *To dance: A ballerina's graphic novel.* New York: Atheneum.

Storrie, P. D. (2007). *Beowulf: Monster slayer.* New York: Graphic Universe.

English Learners

Using graphic novels provides visual clues to the story for ELs. Use primary language support by pairing an EL with another EL whose home language is the same when both students are literate in that language. ELs can also be paired with a buddy to write in English, they can dictate to their buddy, or you can take dictation for them in English using the guided threaded discussion feature on a discussion board. Learning is communicative-based and context-embedded as students can participate in the discussion with the support of the teacher and more English-proficient students.

Struggling Students

Create a word document template with blank textboxes for students to write an online response. Students can be paired with a buddy to write a response, where students work together and discuss their responses with each other and support each other in writing an online response. You or an aide can also take dictation and project their responses on a Smart Board screen using the threaded discussion feature of an online discussion board.

ASSESSMENT

Use the Online Discussion Board Log as a record of a student's participation, and use the following rubric, Table 4.1, for assessment.

Table 4.1	Online Discussion Rubric		
Criteria	**3**	**2**	**1**
Rumination	Posed a new idea or developed an opinion in depth	Opinion stated clearly	Opinion not stated clearly
Storytelling	Provided vivid personal examples or story	Provided personal examples or story	No use of personal examples
Evocative	Justified reasoning or use of metaphorical thinking	Interesting idea or metaphor posed with some justification	Argument without justified reason
Reference	Appropriately cited relevant ideas beyond the reading	Appropriately cited ideas beyond the reading	No references cited, or inaccurate

Source: Adapted from "Rubric to Determine a Quality Online Discussion Posting," by L. L. Larson, Boyd-Batstone, P., & C. Cox, 2009. In J. Salmons & L. Wilson (Eds.), *Handbook of Research on Electronic Collaboration and Organizational Synergy, Vol. I.* (pp. 387–398). Hershey, PA: Information Science Reference/IGI Global.

RESOURCES

Richardson, W. (2008). *Blogs, wikis, podcasts and other powerful web tools for classrooms.* Thousand Oaks, CA: Corwin.

REFERENCES

Larson, L. L., Boyd-Batstone, P., & Cox, C. (2009). Rubric to determine a quality online discussion posting. In J. Salmons & L. Wilson (Eds.), *Handbook of research on electronic collaboration and organizational synergy, Vol. I* (pp. 387–398). Hershey, PA: Information Science Reference/IGI Global.

McKenna, M. C., Labbo, L. D., & Reinking, D. (2004). Effective use of technology in literacy instruction. In R. D. Robinson, M. C. McKenna, & J. M. Wedman (Eds.), *Issues and trends in literacy instruction* (pp. 259–281). Boston: Pearson/Allyn & Bacon.

Strategy 5

Interactive Writing

The kindergarten teacher begins interactive writing in her class by writing "Today is . . ." on a piece of chart paper. She asks for a volunteer to take the pen and write the day, which she has written on a sentence strip and clipped to the top of the chart. Michael raises his hand and the teacher offers him the pen. He comes forward proudly to take it and carefully starts to write M for Monday.

RATIONALE

The teacher shares the writing experience with young students on chart paper or a whiteboard that is large enough for the whole class to see. Students participate by giving the teacher ideas and also by "taking the pen" and writing words, phrases, or sentences with the teacher's guidance. Older students can participate in shared and collaborative writing as well (Button, Johnson, & Fergerson, 1996; McCarrier, Pinnell, & Fountas, 2000).

Reading literature is an excellent way to initiate interactive writing in the class, and the teacher can continue using literature as the class does interactive writing with any new book that is read throughout the year. The teacher can begin with what is happening that day in class, or a holiday, or a special event in the school. Topics could also be any idea of interest to the students or any interesting event that has occurred: a new class pet, a special activity, a guest speaker that visited the class, a field trip the class went on, a change in the weather (e.g., it rained, snowed, or it was sunny for a change), or something special happened to a child (e.g., they took a trip, have a family visitor, or participated in an after school activity).

This strategy could be modeled on the first day of school, and it could continue to be used throughout the school year daily or several times a day, with other books read aloud during the week or other topics of interest to the students. Mini-lessons can be used to teach writing conventions in the authentic writing context of interactive writing.

Source: From *Standards for the English language arts,* by the International Reading Association (IRA) and the National Council of Teachers of English (NCTE), 1996. Newark, DE: NCTE, Urbana, IL: IRA.

> ### English Language Arts Standard
>
> 6. Students apply knowledge of language structure, language conventions (e.g., spelling and punctuation), media techniques, figurative language, and genre to create, critique, and discuss print and nonprint texts.

STRATEGY

Read literature that introduces a topic for discussion and interactive writing and do mini-lessons on the conventions of writing as the need for them occurs during interactive writing. For example, for kindergarten, model how to (1) capitalize the first letter or the first word in a sentence and (2) indent the first sentence of a paragraph using the title as the first sentence.

The First Day of School

The first day of school is . . . .

Ask students for ideas to complete the sentence. Remind them of the ideas they shared in response to the reader response questions and prompts. When the class agrees on how to complete the sentence, ask for a volunteer to come to the chart and take the pen to complete the sentence. If a child volunteers and is not yet writing, take dictation for them and write the words as they speak them. If a child is not yet writing but knows the alphabet, spell the words letter-by-letter as they write or write the words in pencil and have the child trace over them with a marking pen. Continue writing the story this way. Ask the students for ideas and for volunteers to take the pen.

Other mini-lessons on the conventions of writing can be modeled during interactive writing as they occur in context.

Older students can practice interactive writing by sharing the pen and collaborating with each other on letters, memos, invitations, or any kind of narrative story, as well as on reports in the content areas.

GRADE-LEVEL MODIFICATIONS

K–2ND GRADE

Read aloud a book about school. *Off to Kindergarten* by Tony Johnson (Cartwheel/Scholastic, 2007) can be used for a kindergarten class. In this rhyming text, a little boy names all of the things he wants to bring to school on the first day of kindergarten, from a sandbox to a chair for his stuffed bear, until his mother assures him that his teacher will have everything he needs. For 1st- or 2nd-grade students, use *Hamsters, Shells, and Spelling Bees: School Poems* in a collection edited by Lee Bennett Hopkins (2008) in his *I Can Read* poetry anthology series. Lead a discussion using aesthetic reader response questions and prompts: How do you feel about the first day of school? How do you feel about school? What do you wish will happen in school this year?

Tell students they will all share their ideas about school through interactive writing. Students can sit on the rug and form a semicircle facing an easel with a piece of paper on it. Ask students for title suggestions for the piece of interactive writing (e.g., "Today at School," "School," "The First Day of School," or another title that emerges from the discussion of the book). Discuss the title choice with the students and either write the title at the top of the chart paper or whiteboard or ask for a child to volunteer to take the pen (marking pen) and write the title. Provide scaffolding to support the student writer with spelling, capitalization, punctuation, or other writing conventions.

For days other than the first day of school, here are some topics and sentence starters: "Today is Monday" (or any other day of the week), "Today is President's Day" (or any other holiday), "It's a Rainy Day" (or any other weather), or "We're Going to the Zoo" (or any other field trip).

Mini-Lessons on Conventions of Writing During Interactive Writing, K–2

- Alphabet and forming letters
- Upper- and lowercase letters
- Capitalize words in a title, the first word in a sentence, and names, days, months, place names, and a person's title
- Indent the first sentence
- Punctuation
  o At the end of a sentence, use a period, question mark, or exclamation mark
  o Commas in dates, a series, and addresses
  o Apostrophes in contractions and possessives
  o Periods in abbreviations
  o Commas in compound and complex sentences
  o Quotation marks in dialogue
- Spelling
  o Ask for ideas about how to spell the word; model the conventional spelling of the word
- Writing the date

Plus Technology

Through the use of a Smart Board, take dictation and project students' interactive writing on a screen. Revisions can be made to the writing as students watch the changes made on the screen, and mini-lessons may be modeled as well. The interactive writing can also be in the form of an e-mail message that can be sent anywhere—to another teacher's classroom, other school personnel (e.g., the principal or the librarian), or to family members with e-mail access.

Books

Cleary, B. (1968). *Ramona the pest.* New York: HarperCollins.

Collicott, S. (2008). *Mildred and Sam go to school.* New York: HarperCollins.

Danneberg, J. (2000). *First day jitters.* Watertown, MA: Charlesbridge Publishing.

Harris, R. H. (2003). *I am not going to school today!* New York: McElderry.

Hopkins, L. B. (2008). *Hamsters, shells, and spelling bees: School poems.* New York: HarperCollins.

Johnson, T. (2007). *Off to kindergarten.* New York: Scholastic.

Klise, M. S. (2007). *Imagine Harry.* New York: Harcourt.

Lillegard, D. (2001). *Hello school! A classroom full of poems.* New York: Knopf.

Wells, R. (2004). *My kindergarten.* New York: Hyperion.

Wolff, N. (2007). *It's time for school with Tallulah.* New York: Holt.

3RD GRADE–5TH GRADE

Students can write interactively in response to a read aloud book such as *Tales of a Fourth Grade Nothing* (Blume, 1972). Letters can be written interactively by the whole class to someone who visited the class as a guest speaker, to the author of a book they enjoyed, to another class to join them for an activity, to the principal or other school staff in appreciation for something, to a student who is at home for medical reasons, or to the editor of a newspaper on an issue of concern to students. Students can also form groups and write stories, narratives, or short reports in the content areas interactively.

Students can form more than one group but agree to write on the same topic. For example, in response to a chapter book like *Ramona the Pest* (Cleary, 1968), more advanced primary students could plan to write their own memoir of school patterned after the book. They could identify a main character together but write separate chapters on different topics such as friends, recess, favorite school subjects, least favorite school subjects, or most embarrassing moments. The groups could meet periodically as a whole and discuss the continuity among the chapters and revise accordingly.

Writing conventions appropriate for Grades 3 through 5, or as needed, can be taught in mini-lessons during interactive writing.

- Indenting paragraphs
- Punctuation: Hyphens, colons, parentheses, or commas in a series of adjectives
- Strong verbs, specific nouns, and colorful adjectives and adverbs
- Complete and incomplete sentences
- Contractions
- Pluralization rules
- Plural possessives
- Quotation marks and underlining in published titles
- Homonyms
- Onomatopoeia

Books

Blume, J. (1972). *Tales of a fourth grade nothing.* New York: Dutton.

Cleary, B. (1968). *Ramona the pest.* New York: W. Morrow.

6TH GRADE–8TH GRADE

Students can do shared or collaborative writing in response to a favorite book many have read—for example, one of the Harry Potter books. They can form groups and work together to write a mission statement for Hogwarts' school, a memo to the Headmaster on an issue, or a letter from Gryffindor House to one of the other houses, challenging them to a competition.

In addition to writing in response to literature, students in Grades 6 through 8 can write a class mission statement or manifesto on something of interest (e.g., classroom expectations, guidelines, behavior, or goals for the semester), which can be done through interactive writing by the whole class. Letters can be written interactively to the editor of a newspaper at school or a local paper, or letters can be written for purposes of advocacy (e.g., to question or protest the actions of local, state, or federal government officials or businesses), or to request information or guidance from an organization. Students can also write interactively in groups in the content areas, writing reports collaboratively.

The interactive writing strategy can be used by older students working in groups independently, without the teacher. Students can discuss an idea for writing, take turns taking the pen, and peer-edit each other's writing. Conference with such a group periodically, providing instruction in writing conventions as needed by the group. This same process could be used for writing a script for reader's theatre or for a play or a movie, with each group writing a different scene. The reader's theatre script or the play could be performed, or the movie filmed.

Writing conventions appropriate for Grades 6 through 8, or as needed for a class or group, can be taught during interactive writing:

- Capital letters: nationality, ethnicity, language, events, associations, institutions, trade names, commercial products, company names
- Colons and semicolons
- Dashes and parentheses
- Commas after introductory words or phrases
- Word choice
- Figurative language and metaphors

Books

Rowling, J. K. (1998). *Harry Potter and the sorcerer's stone*. New York: Scholastic.

ENGLISH LEARNERS

Interactive writing makes the writing process visual to the whole class, and English learners who are not yet writing can contribute by illustrating the interactive writing. Interactive writing is context-embedded instruction that taps the prior knowledge of students. It also involves social interaction and cooperation among students. If an English learner is not yet writing, they could "hold the space" between words as another student or the teacher writes the words.

English learners see writing modeled and can copy sentences into their own writing in journals or stories. Use the interactive writing strategy with small groups of English learners, using primary language support as well.

Needs-based groups can be formed and can write interactively in a variety of ways (e.g., responding to a book read aloud or any previously read text, or writing conventions specifically needed by the group).

STRUGGLING STUDENTS

Students participate by verbally sharing ideas for interactive writing. Take dictation for students, either by writing their ideas for them or by writing them in pencil first and having the student write over them with a marking pen.

Do interactive writing in a small group of three to five struggling readers and writers while other students write in journals or write stories. The same procedure would be used, but each child would have more opportunity to participate and there would be more time to assess and differentiate instruction for each one.

ASSESSMENT

1. Initialing Interactive Writing: Show each child how to initial their writing on the chart. This provides a record of their progress in writing and a means to identify strengths and needs of each child over time. In small groups or writing conferences, provide mini-lessons for each child's assessed needs.

2. Interactive Writing Record: Use a loose-leaf notebook to keep a record of each child's writing during interactive writing. Word process and print out a facsimile of the form that follows, 3-hole punch it, and include it in the notebook. Use alphabet tabs for last names, and put each child's record under the letter of their last name. Periodically, go through the interactive writing pieces and note the following for each child on their sheet of paper:

Interactive Writing Record

Name:

Date:

Strengths	Needs/Mini-lesson	Date Completed	Results

RESOURCES

McCarrier, A., Pinnell, G. S., & Fountas, I. C. (2000). *Interactive writing: How language and literacy come together, K–2.* Portsmouth, NH: Heinemann.

REFERENCES

Button, K., Johnson, M. J., & Fergerson, P. (1996). Interactive writing in a primary classroom. *The Reading Teacher, 49*, 446–454.

Journal Writing

Figure 6.1 is a journal entry of a kindergarten student in a class of all Khmer speaking Cambodian Americans who were learning English. He copied the date from a small whiteboard in the Journal Center, drew a picture, and dictated an entry to his teacher who wrote the words for him in the lined spaces at the bottom.

Figure 6.1   A kindergarten journal entry

October 18

October

We threw bean bags into the jack-o-lantern.
Jada

RATIONALE

Writing in journals can be a powerful strategy for students to respond to literature, gain writing fluency, dialogue in writing with another student or the teacher, or write in the content areas. While journaling is a form of writing in its own right, students can also freely generate ideas for other types of writing as they journal.

Teachers can use literature that takes the form of a journal by reading excerpts and discussing them with students. There are also books that focus on the idea of using diaries, journals, and logs to write about life experiences. Responding to students' journals and using dialogue journals between the teacher and student can be an effective means of communication and assessment as well (Atwell, 1998).

Source: From *Standards for the English language arts*, by the International Reading Association (IRA) and the National Council of Teachers of English (NCTE), 1996. Newark, DE: NCTE, Urbana, IL: IRA.

English Language Arts Standard

5. Students employ a wide range of strategies as they write and use different writing process elements appropriately to communicate with different audiences for a variety of purposes.

STRATEGY

Introduce journal writing through reading aloud an illustrated picture book for younger students, or a chapter book for older students, that uses the journal or diary format. Discuss the book using aesthetic reader response questions and prompts, and model journal writing features: noting the date, using an interesting sentence starter for a journal entry, and mini-lessons on writing conventions.

Journal writing can be done at a set time during a class period or day, or students can write in journals sometime during the day. Monitor the latter through a checklist, noting whether or not students are writing in them.

Journals can also be part of writing conferences with individuals or small groups. They can also be used to address writing conventions and questions and needs students may have about spelling, punctuation, word usage, or grammar. Students can choose to share what they have written, or they can share an idea from the journal that they would like to explore further with another type of writing (e.g., poetry, story, or letter). Journals can be used in conferences to discuss these other writing forms.

For example, students could write from the perspective of a personified character, such as an animal or other nonhuman, to personify, research, and learn more about the personified character, and they could write a fictionalized version of a diary. The same could be done with a historical figure or a fantasy creature. Students could put themselves in the place of the character they have learned about, personified, or imagined and write from their point of view.

Students could form pairs and personify, pick, or create characters that would have very different points of view. For example, two 5th-grade students learning about the Civil War could work as a team and read about the lives of soldiers from the North and the South. They could discuss similarities and differences and each write a journal from the perspective of one of the soldiers, either a Yankee or a Rebel.

Students could do the same in groups, each writing a journal from the perspective of one person in a mutual context. For example, a 3rd-grade class learning about world communities could write a journal about a single issue (e.g., the environment, from the point of view of a leader from one of several countries—the United States, China, India, a member of the European Union, Egypt, etc.). Students in a 6th-grade class learning about the ancient world could do the same from the perspective of an ancient Greek or Roman citizen.

Do a mini-lesson on point of view in writing and make a poster that students can refer to when writing.

Point of View

- Point of view lets the reader know who is doing the writing

- First-person: One character is writing, using *I*

- Omniscient: The writing is from an all knowing perspective, where the author can see and report everything about all of the characters

- Limited omniscient: The writer knows and reports all about one or more characters, but not about all of the characters

- Objective: Just the facts are told

- Most journal writing uses the first-person point of view, but other perspectives could also be used.

GRADE-LEVEL MODIFICATIONS

K–2ND GRADE

Introduce kindergarten or 1st-grade students to journaling by reading aloud a picture book, such as *An Island Scrapbook: Dawn to Dusk on a Barrier Island* (Wright-Frierson, 1998), or an illustrated book in a journal format for 2nd-grade students, such as *Amelia's Notebook* (Moss, 1995), and lead a discussion using aesthetic reader response questions and prompts: What was your favorite part of the journal? What would you write in a journal?

Record students' responses on chart paper to model the journaling process. The chart could be titled "Our Class Journal" and the date added. Continue modeling with the class journal and have students take the pen and add to the entries using interactive writing (see Strategy 5 Interactive Writing) until students are ready to begin their own journals.

Students who are just beginning to write can also go to a Journal Center, which would include multiple copies of a blank frame for drawing and writing a journal entry that could be kept in a file box. The day's date could be written on a sentence strip or a small whiteboard in the center. Beginning writers can go to the center, copy the date, draw a picture, write, or have someone else take dictation and write for them—perhaps an aide, a classroom volunteer, a more capable peer, or an older student in another grade who spends time assisting in the class. Each student who uses the Journal Center can keep his or her journal entry in a manila file folder labeled with their name. They can also choose to share journal entries during time for sharing with the class.

Books

Moss, M. (1995). *Amelia's notebook*. Berkeley, CA: Tricycle Press.

Wright-Frierson, V. (1998). *An island scrapbook: Dawn to dusk on a barrier island*. New York: Simon & Schuster.

Wright-Frierson, V. (1999). *A North American rainforest scrapbook*. New York: Walker.

3RD GRADE–5TH GRADE

Read *Diary of a Worm* (Cronin, 2003) aloud. *Diary of a Worm* is a fictional daily journal of a personified worm, revealing some of the good news and bad news about being a worm. The good news is he never has to take a bath. The bad news is he can never do the hokey pokey. The book models journal writing with humor. Lead a discussion using aesthetic reader response questions and prompts: What do you think of the things the worm wrote about in his diary? What would you write about in your diary?

Record students' ideas on a cluster chart titled "Our Journal Ideas." Next, conduct a mini-lesson on sentence starters to write an interesting journal. Ask students if they were struck by any sentence starters in *Diary of a Worm* that made the journal exciting and fun to read. Make a list on chart paper or a whiteboard. Re-read sections of the book to find more and add to the list. Take suggestions from students for other interesting sentence starters for a journal. Make a poster titled "Journal Sentence Starters" that students may refer to with the list of sentence starters from *Diary of a Worm* and their own suggestions.

Provide students with their own journals: a bound notebook, lined paper in a three-hole binder, or lined paper stapled together. Students can make and decorate a journal cover. Students can write in journals at a designated time during the day, or anytime during the day, but should write daily. Collect a text set of books that use the diary or journal format and do a book talk to introduce each one—provide a brief summary and read an excerpt aloud. Students may read these independently, or they may choose one for a book club group (see Strategy 3 Book Clubs).

Books

Blos, J. (1979). *A gathering of days: A New England girl's journal, 1830–1832*. New York: Scribner's.

Byars, B., Duffey, B., & Myers, L. (2007). *Dog diaries: Secret writings of the WOOF society*. New York: Henry Holt.

Cronin, D. (2003). *Diary of a worm*. New York: HarperCollins.

George, J. (1988/1959). *My side of the mountain*. New York: Dutton.

Hest, A. (1995). *The private notebook of Katie Roberts, age 11*. Cambridge, MA: Candlewick Press.

Little, J. (1989). *Hey world, here I am*. New York: Harper & Row.

Monroe, M. A. (2007). *Turtle summer: A journal for my daughter*. New York: Sylvan Dell.

O'Brien, R. C. (1975/1987). *Z for Zachariah*. New York: Macmillan.

Reig, J. (1978). *Diary of the boy King Tut Ankh Amen*. New York: Scribners.

Sparks, D. C. (1995). *The bittersweet time*. New York: Eerdman's.

Williams, V. B. (1981). *Three days on a river in a red canoe*. New York: Greenwillow.

6TH GRADE–8TH GRADE

Read a chapter book that uses the diary or journal format to discuss and model journal writing. After each reading, lead a discussion using aesthetic reader response questions and prompts: What was your favorite part today? What ideas did you have about writing in your own journal?

Create a list of sentence starters for journals. As the book is read aloud over time, students may also add ideas for sentence starters to the list.

Plus Technology

Students may word process their journal entries. If a computer or laptop is not available for each student, they may each have a folder on the central unit and keep their journal entries in that folder.

Books

Byars, B. (1988). *The burning questions of Bingo Brown.* New York: Viking Penguin.

Cleary, B. (1983). *Dear Mr. Henshaw.* New York: Morrow.

Cleary, B. (1991). *Strider.* New York: Morrow.

Cushman, K. (1994). *Catherine called Birdy.* New York: Clarion.

Frank, A. (1952). *Anne Frank: The diary of a young girl.* New York: Doubleday.

Grimes, N. (1998). *Jazmine's notebook.* New York: Dial.

Holm, J. L. (2007). *Middle school is worse than meatloaf: A year told through stuff.* New York: Atheneum.

Klise, K. (2001). *Trial by journal.* New York: HarperCollins.

ENGLISH LEARNERS

Journals offer many English language development strategies for ELs. Journaling taps into each student's prior experience and knowledge and is therefore context-embedded communication. Students can also write in their primary language.

Use visuals through graphic organizers by recording students' ideas for journal writing and do a mini-lesson on sentence starters using a poster to be displayed in the classroom.

Journal Sentence Starters

- Today is . . . (use date displayed in the room)

- Today I . . . will, feel, need, did, want, saw, heard, played, sang . . .

- I . . . want to, wish I had, went to, used, read, wrote, watched . . .

Dialogue journals are also useful with ELs. The students can write in either a home language or English, or both. More proficient English speakers can respond in English. Then, you or another student can write in the journal to create a written dialogue.

Dialogue journals can also be used at home with family members. Students take a journal home and have a family member write in the journal in English or the home language, or students can read what they have written in the journal, a family member can listen and respond, and the student can note in writing in the journal what the family member said. This increases home-school connections and social interaction, leading to language development for ELs.

STRUGGLING STUDENTS

Model journal writing using a graphic organizer. Students can be provided with a one-page blank frame that has a fill-in for the date: Today is . . . . Take dictation or do a class journal writing interactively (see Strategy 5 Interactive Writing) or in small groups. Students can also do an oral journal entry and have another student write what they say and read it together, checking for writing conventions.

ASSESSMENT

1. Journal: The journal itself becomes a valuable, ongoing record of a student's development in writing over a semester or school year.

2. Checklist: If journal writing is required on a regular schedule (e.g., three days a week or every day), students can record the date of each journal entry on a checklist that can be kept in the front of the journal—so the number and dates of the entries can be seen at a glance. Students could also download a blank calendar for each month and check off the days they made a journal entry.

3. Conference: Students can bring journals to teacher conferences if there are ideas they would like to share, or discuss writing options, or if they have questions about writing conventions.

RESOURCES

Trueit, T. S. (2005). *Keeping a journal*. Danbury, CT: Children's Press.

REFERENCES

Atwell, N. (1998). *In the middle* (2nd ed.). Portsmouth, NH: Heinemann.

Strategy 7

Poetry Walks

The 4th-grade student rubbed a dry leaf between his fingers. He had picked it up off the ground while on a poetry walk with his class in early winter, after the trees had shed their leaves. He stared out the window at a bare tree and wrote a haiku.

Haiku

Bare trees shiver now

Without their cloak of green leaves

Cold, in the winter

RATIONALE

In his landmark book *Writing: Teachers and Children at Work,* based on his research observing students writing in classrooms over several years, Donald Graves (1983) emphasized the importance of helping students write about things they know. He suggested conferencing with students to help students identify something they know, something that is unique to them. It can be an interest, a collection, or an experience. He further recommended that this is what they should begin to write about. He also recommended surrounding children with literature to serve as models for their writing. A teacher can do both of these by reading poetry with nature imagery aloud and providing poetry collections for students to read independently, and by taking students on poetry walks where they can experience nature firsthand as a source of ideas and images to use in writing their own poetry.

English Language Arts Standard

12. Students use spoken, written, and visual language to accomplish their own purposes (e.g., for learning, enjoyment, persuasion, and the exchange of information).

Source: From Standards for the English language arts, by the International Reading Association (IRA) and the National Council of Teachers of English (NCTE), 1996. Newark, DE: NCTE, Urbana, IL: IRA.

STRATEGY

Read and discuss poetry with nature imagery with students. Use a graphic organizer with students to classify describing words that draw on the senses, model poetry writing using words and phrases from the graphic organizer for younger students, and model forms of traditional Japanese poetry for older students.

Take students on a poetry walk around the school, neighborhood, or community to observe and collect sensory images from direct experience with nature: the sights, sounds, smells, and textures of things outdoors. Students can take a poetry journal with them to write down words as they observe, listen, smell, and touch things outside the classroom. They can also add drawings to help them remember what they are observing. They can simply list what they observe, the poetry journal can include a page with a category for each of the senses so they can classify them as they collect them, or they can use a combination of the two. They can also collect objects to take back to the classroom such as rocks or pebbles and small branches or leaves on the ground (not living things). They can continue to observe these in the classroom as they develop their vocabulary for poetic imagery.

Guide students to write poetic forms appropriate for each grade level using the nature images they collected on poetry walks.

Plus Technology

Use a digital camera or iPhone to take nature photographs students choose on the poetry walk, which can be uploaded to the computer and viewed again in the classroom by all students.

GRADE-LEVEL MODIFICATIONS

K–2ND GRADE

Read aloud the picture book *Frederick* by Leo Lionni (1967). Frederick is a mouse who collects images and words about nature in spring and summer while the other mice are gathering and storing food for the winter. When it is cold and the food is gone, Frederick cheers up the other mice with the images he collected and a poem. Lead a discussion using aesthetic reader response questions and prompts: What was your favorite thing Frederick described? What did you picture in your mind? What are some things you could describe?

Take a poetry walk with students on the school grounds or in the neighborhood. Ask students to describe things they are seeing, hearing, smelling, or touching related to the season, such as the weather or trees and plants, and then record what they say on a clipboard with paper (students who can write can record ideas in a notebook they take with them). Back in class, ask students for words to describe the things they saw on the poetry walk and record them under headings for four of the senses:

Sense Words Describing Nature

Smell	Touch	Sight	Sound

Complete a class triante with students using sense words to describe nature.

Triante Poem Using Sense Words	Poem
Line 1: One word (Title)	Trees
Line 2: Two words (Smell)	Fresh, green
Line 3: Three words (Touch)	Hard scratchy bark
Line 4: Four words (Sight)	Tall, thin, many branches
Line 5: Five words (Sound)	Soft rustling in the breeze

Continue reading nature poetry, and students can continue taking poetry walks and drawing or writing nature images in a journal to write more nature poems. Students can continue to write nature poetry throughout the school year, noting the changes in seasons in their journals and poetry.

Books

Lionni, L. (1967). *Frederick*. New York: Pantheon.

Otten, C. F. (1997). *January rides the wind: A book of months*. New York: Lothrop, Lee & Shepard. (These are short poems about each month of the year.)

Paolilli, P., & Brewer, D. (2001). *Silver seeds: A book of nature poems*. New York: Viking. (These are acrostic poems about familiar sights in nature.)

3RD GRADE–5TH GRADE

To introduce writing traditional Japanese haiku nature poetry, read aloud *Wabi Sabi* by Mark Reibsten (2008). This is a beautifully illustrated book with collages by Caldecott award winning artist Ed Young. The book ostensibly tells the story of a cat from Kyoto, Japan who goes in search of the true meaning of her name, Wabi Sabi. The spare text and haiku poetry explain that it means finding real beauty in unexpected places. Traditional Japanese haiku by famous Japanese poets Basho and Shiki are written in Japanese on each page and translated in an addendum. Tell students that *Wabi Sabi* is both a story and a collection of haiku, or a form of traditional Japanese poetry that focuses on nature and uses a pattern. Students can take turns reading the haiku poem found on each page. Lead a discussion using aesthetic reader response questions and prompts: Which of the haiku was your favorite? If you wrote a haiku, what would you write about? Students can talk to a partner and think-pair-share some words, phrases, or sentences and write down their ideas in a poetry journal.

Take a poetry walk and have students write and draw nature images they might use for writing haiku. Back in the class, model how to write haiku, a short, traditional Japanese poem, usually about the seasons or nature, which is approximated in English by writing a first line of five syllables, a second line of seven syllables, and a third line of five syllables. Make a poster or overhead projector transparency with the pattern.

> **Haiku**
>
> - Haiku is a short, traditional Japanese poem, usually about the seasons or nature.
> - In English, it uses a pattern of 17 syllables in three lines:
>   Line 1: 5 syllables
>   Line 2: 7 syllables
>   Line 3: 5 syllables

Students can write a haiku using the nature images they wrote and drew in a poetry journal on the poetry walk. Introduce students to other patterns of traditional Japanese poetry writing as well.

> **Senryu**
>
> - Senryu uses the same pattern as haiku, but can be written on topics other than the seasons or nature.
>
> **Tanka**
>
> - Tanka is a short, traditional Japanese poem, usually about the seasons or nature.
> - In English, Tanka uses a pattern of 31 syllables in five lines:
>   Line 1: 7 syllables
>   Line 2: 5 syllables
>   Line 3: 7 syllables
>   Line 4: 5 syllables
>   Line 5: 7 syllables
>
> **Haiga**
>
> - Haiga is haiku with a drawing.

Plus Technology

Digital photographs collected on a walk could be uploaded to a computer, leaving space for writing. A student could write and edit a poem to go with the photograph and word process it on the same page as the photograph.

Books

Demi. (Ed.). (1992). *In the eyes of the cat: Japanese poetry for all seasons.* New York: Holt.

Gollub, M. (1998). *Cool melons—turn to frogs! The life and poems of Issa.* New York: Lee & Low.

Janeczko, P. (2000). *Stone bench in an empty park.* New York: Orchard.

Lewis, J. P. (1995). *Black swan/white crow.* New York: Atheneum.

Mannis, C. (2002). *One leaf rides the wind*. New York: Viking.

Muth, J. J. (2005). *Zen shorts*. New York: Scholastic.

Nishimoto, K. (2008). *The haiku picture book*. New York: Heian.

Prelutsky, J. (2004). *If not for the cat*. New York: Greenwillow.

Raschko, C. (2001). *Simple gifts: A Shaker hymn*. New York: Henry Holt.

Reibsten, M. (2008). *Wabi Sabi*. New York: Little Brown.

6TH GRADE–8TH GRADE

Introduce haiku by reading *Wabi Sabi* (Reibsten, 2008), take students on a poetry walk, and have students write haiku as described previously for Grades 3 through 5. The book *Wabi Sabi* also includes information on the development of haiku in Japan and 14 poems by the haiku masters Masaoka Shiki (1867–1902) and Matsuo Basho (1644–1694) in the Addendum, in Japanese characters and in English. Basho wrote perhaps the most famous Japanese haiku:

An ancient pond
A frog jumps in
The sound of water.

Students can read and learn more about Basho, write about him, or dramatize episodes from his life and travels writing haiku and reading his poems for other students.

Students who have read and written haiku or other traditional forms of Japanese poetry can work individually or in pairs to create their own original poetry form. After writing samples, they can make a poster modeling the new form, demonstrate it to other students, and add it to the repertoire of poetry in a writing center.

Plus Technology

Students can word process haiku and print out and publish a class anthology, and they can use Kid Pix to illustrate them. Model the Japanese poetry patterns with a PowerPoint presentation. Students can also use PowerPoint to present their poems to others, adding decorative borders, clip art images or photographs, sound effects, and fade ins and fade outs.

An interesting combination of pattern writing and technology can be introduced to students through a mini-lesson on Renga, which is a collaborative, cooperative linked haiku that students can write with their friends using an online discussion board. See Strategy 4: Online Discussion Board for information on how to set up and use an online discussion board. Make a chart with directions on renga.

Renga Online Discussion Board

- Renga is a form of traditional Japanese poetry writing.
- It is created with linked haiku or other patterns you can write with friends.
- Traditional renga begins with the haiku pattern of 5–7–5 syllables in three lines, and another person responds with a pattern of 7–7 syllables in two lines.
- Write renga on an online discussion board with other students.

Books

Myers, T. (2000). *Basho and the fox*. New York: Marshall Cavendish Children's Books.

Myers, T. (2004). *Basho and the river stones*. New York: Marshall Cavendish Children's Books.

Spivak, D. (1997). *Grass sandals: The travels of Basho*. New York: Atheneum.

ENGLISH LEARNERS

Important English language development strategies for ELs are using realia—or real objects—and the senses in teaching vocabulary, reading, and writing. Bring nature items into the class; take students on poetry walks so that ELs can observe, smell, and touch them; and introduce describing words that can be recorded on the chart. To write a triante, provide each child with a blank copy of the graphic organizer to classify words describing nature by one of the senses and a frame for the triante. Do the same for haiku or for any of the other forms of traditional Japanese poetry about nature.

Books

See collections of nature poetry written in both English and Spanish:

Alarcon, F. X. (2005). *Iguanas in the snow/Iguanas en la nieve*. San Francisco: Children's Book Press.

Nye, N. S. (1995). *This tree is older than you are: A bilingual gathering of poems and stories from Mexico*. New York: Simon & Schuster.

The well-known poet and translator Alicia Zavala Galvan collaborated with author Michael Moore in this collection of haiku poems in both English and Spanish, which can be shared with students whose first language is Spanish:

Moore, M., & Galvan, A. Z. (Trans.). (1996). *Contemporary view of haiku/Vista contemporanea de haiku*. New York: Mustard Seed Press.

STRUGGLING STUDENTS

Use nature photos and objects from poetry walks in the classroom. By uploading images to the computer and printing them out, struggling students can label the pictures with words from the graphic organizer in a blend of free verse and concrete poetry.

Conference with small groups of students and use the graphic organizer to develop describing words and model writing a triante or haiku with these words. Each child can record words on their own blank copy of the chart and write a triante or a haiku on a blank frame of this poetry pattern.

Using a haiku syllable word bank—a graphic organizer with columns for words of one, two, three, or more syllables—students can place words in the correct column to use when writing haiku. One member of the group, you, or an aide can write down words and images for the whole group, and these can be recorded on a poster that can be copied by each student on their own copy of the word bank and used to write a haiku on the haiku pattern frame. The use of frames and templates introduced through mini-lessons and displayed on a poster, along with an individual student handout, can provide scaffolding for students to write the pattern, drawing words from the word bank they have created in small groups.

Words can also be written on sticky notes that can be first placed on a poster and then added to an individual students' word bank to use as a model for writing the word in the haiku pattern frame.

ASSESSMENT

Students can use a form of traditional Japanese poetry writing called haibun, which combines haiku or other poetry patterns with a story. For each poem written, students write a short prose passage to set up each poem. This form was often used to record a journey. Students could write haibun throughout the journey of the school year and discuss them with the teacher periodically in writing conferences. Introduce haibun with a mini-lesson.

Haibun

- Haibun is a type of traditional Japanese poetry that combines a poem and a story.

  1. Write a poem (haiku, senryu, tanka, or haiga) with a drawing.

  2. Write a paragraph to set up your poem.

- Continue to do this and to tell a story with your poetry.

RESOURCES

Donegan, P. (2003). *Haiku*. Boston: Turtle Publishing.

Ehmann, S., & Gayer, K. (2009). *I can write like that! A guide to mentor texts and craft studies for writer's* workshop, K–6. Newark, DE: International Reading Association.

REFERENCES

Graves, D. H. (1983). *Writing: Teachers and children at work*. Portsmouth, NH: Heinemann.

Performance Reading

Strategy 8

The 7th-grade students were in groups, helping each other plan for a performance reading of passages from Shakespeare for a program they were going to present to the rest of the school called "Meet Shakespeare's Men and Women." Anne was going to be A Fairy and read Act 2, Scene 1 from A Midsummer Night's Dream. She said "I'm not going to wear shoes." Another student said "You can't go on the stage barefoot!" But Anne had clearly stepped into the role of A Fairy and replied "No. Fairies don't wear shoes."

RATIONALE

Performance reading, or fluent oral reading, can be practiced when young students join in a repeated reading of a book with memorable phrases or sound effects and added gestures, or when older students plan how to read passages of a book with expression for an audience. Fluent oral reading has three aspects: accuracy, or reading the words in a text without error in pronunciation; automaticity, or reading the words in a text correctly and effortlessly; and prosody, or reading with appropriate expression and phrasing to reflect the meaning of a passage. Research has shown that fluent oral reading learned through performance reading leads not only to engagement in and enjoyment of reading for students, but to reading comprehension (Rasinski & Hoffman, 2003), and it is one of the goals established in the research report of the National Reading Panel (NICHD, 2000).

English Language Arts Standard

3. Students apply a wide range of strategies to comprehend, interpret, evaluate, and appreciate texts. They draw on their prior experience, their interactions with other readers and writers, their knowledge of word meaning and of other texts, their word identification strategies, and their understanding of textual features (e.g., sound-letter correspondence, sentence structure, context, graphics).

Source: From Standards for the English language arts, by the International Reading Association (IRA) and the National Council of Teachers of English (NCTE), 1996. Newark, DE: NCTE, Urbana, IL: IRA.

Strategy

Engage young readers by choosing a book with memorable repeated language or refrains that they can act out with gestures, sound effects, props, and voices. Have students listen to the read aloud, and then model the use of gestures, sound effects, props, and voices. Students participate during the reading and repeated readings of the book and can act it out as they discuss it. Mini-lessons on phonemic awareness, phonics, and word study can be embedded in performance reading.

After acting it out, students can draw in response to the book and write. Kindergarten students could draw and have someone take dictation for them if they are not yet writing. Students in 1st and 2nd grade can label the drawing, write a caption, or do more—depending on their writing ability.

Older students can plan performance readings of texts that feature monologues, dialogues, speeches, songs, or any text that can be voiced by students. They can discuss the text and make decisions about how to use their voices, facial expressions, gestures, movements, props, and costume pieces. Students can do this independently or in pairs or groups. Performance readings can be shared with others in the class, school, or with parents.

Grade-Level Modifications

K–2nd Grade

Read aloud *We're Going on a Bear Hunt*, retold by Michael Rosen (1989), a traditional rhyming tale that tells of a family who take a walk and encounter a bear. Model gestures (rubbing hands together), sound effects, and voices (chanting "swishy swashy") when the family is going through grass. Read dramatically, and slowly. Students can join in the reading with gestures, sound effects, and voices as they were modeled, and they can act out the story narrative. To use a prop, provide a small blanket or square of cloth to represent the blanket at the end of the story. This prop could be rotated among students as the story is acted out.

After reading and engaging students in acting out the story, lead a discussion with students using aesthetic reader response questions and prompts: Show us your favorite part. Act it out! Has anything like this ever happened to you? Is there anything you would change in the story? Act it out!

Re-read the story and pause for students to add gestures, sound effects, and voices. The phrases that students use to join in performing the story can be written on chart paper or sentence strips. Point to the phrases as the students perform them, linking the speaking and performing to the words. During further readings, gradually release responsibility for the phrases that students repeat to increase fluency and comprehension of the story.

Students can draw and write about the story and their experience of acting it out. Kindergarten students can draw a picture. On their own or with help, they can add labels or a caption to the picture. They can also use dictation. More proficient kindergarten writers and 1st- and 2nd-grade students can add a caption and more to their drawings.

Mini-lessons on word study can be added to repeated readings of the book. For the book *We're Going on a Bear Hunt* (Rosen, 1989), do a mini-lesson on chart paper or whiteboard using an onset (*sw-*) and rime (*-ash*) from the story. (Every syllable in

English has a rime, or the vowel and any consonant after it, and may have an onset, or the consonant before the vowel in the syllable.)

Onsets and Rimes

- The words *Swishy swashy* begin with what two letters?

- What other words begin with *sw-*?
    Swim, swam, swum, swell, swollen. . .

- The word *swashy* has *-ash* in it. What other words have *-ash* in them?
    Bash, cash, dash, gash, gnash, hash, lash, mash, rash, splash . . .

- If you think of more words that begin with *sw-* or have *-ash* in them, we will add them to our list.

Collect a text set of other books good for performance reading to read and act out with the class, or for students to read and act out independently in small groups and share with the rest of the class.

Books

Burleigh, R. (2009). *Clang! Clang! Beep! Beep! Listen to the city.* New York: Simon & Schuster.

Butler, J. (2007). *Can you growl like a bear?* Atlanta, GA: Peachtree Publishers.

Carle, E. (2002). *"Slowly, slowly, slowly," said the sloth.* New York: Philomel.

Fleming, D. (1991). *In the tall tall grass.* New York: Holt.

Gray, L. M. (1994). *Small green snake.* New York: Scholastic

Joose, B. (2009). *ROAWR!* New York: Philomel/Penguin.

Moss, L. (1995). *Zin! Zin! Zin! A violin.* New York: Scholastic.

Rosen, M. (1989). *We're going on a bear hunt.* New York: Margaret K. McElderry Books.

Tafuri, N. (1984). *Have you seen my duckling?* New York: Greenwillow.

3RD GRADE–5TH GRADE

Good Masters! Sweet Ladies! Voices From a Medieval Village (Schlitz, 2007), the 2008 Newbery Award-winning book, is a collection of 19 monologues and two dialogues from characters living in an English village in 1255. The book can be read independently or aloud, but it is clearly intended as a text for performance reading by students. Introduce it with either a book talk, paging through it as a preview for students, or by passing it from student to student to read a monologue of one of the colorful characters (e.g., Otho, the miller's son; Barbary, the mud slinger; Will, the plowboy; Alice, the singing shepherdess, etc.) Lead a discussion after several monologues, using aesthetic reader response questions and prompts: Which character was your favorite? What did you wonder about that character? How would you use your voice, face, and gestures to communicate the emotions, attitudes, and motives of that character? The students can continue reading and discussing the characters.

To do a performance reading of the book, take volunteers for characters. Model a plan for each student to decide how to use voice, facial expressions, gestures, movements, props, and costume pieces for the lines their character speaks to bring the character to life. Students can work in pairs to develop their plan.

Planning Sheet for My Character From *Good Masters! Sweet Ladies!*

Lines _____

Voice

Facial expression

Gestures

Movement

Props

Costume

Students can read to each other in pairs, putting their plan into action, and do a performance reading of the book a few characters at a time, leading up to a continuous performance reading of the whole book. This can be performed for other classes at school, or for parents and community members.

To continue performance readings, collect a text set of good books for performance reading that students can read independently and act out in pairs or small groups and present to the class. Students can also choose books on their own that they would like to use for performance reading.

Books

Bagert, B. (1992). *Let me be the boss.* Honesdale, PA: Wordsong.

Esbensen, B. J. (1986). *Words with wrinkled knees.* New York: HarperCollins.

Gunning, M. (1993). *Not a copper penny in me house: Poems from the Caribbean.* Honesdale, PA: Wordsong.

Odanaka, B. (2009). *A crazy day at the Critter Café.* New York: McElderry Books/Simon & Schuster.

Olaleye, I. (1995). *The distant talking drum.* Honesdale, PA: Wordsong.

Palatini, B. (2009). *Lousy rotten stinkin' grapes.* New York: Simon & Schuster.

Schlitz, L. A. (2007). *Good masters! Sweet ladies! Voices from a medieval village.* Cambridge, MA: Candlewick Press.

Spilka, A. (1994). *Monkeys write terrible letters.* Honesdale, PA: Wordsong.

Springer, N. (1994). *Music of their hooves.* Honesdale, PA: Wordsong.

Thayer, E. L. (2000). *Casey at the bat: A ballad of the republic sung in 1888.* New York: Handprint.

6TH GRADE–8TH GRADE

Read books that tell the story of one of Shakespeare's plays, and lead a discussion of the stories using aesthetic reader response questions and prompts: What did you wonder about? Who was your favorite character?

Plan a performance reading of scenes from Shakespeare's plays: "Meet Shakespeare's Men and Women." Students can choose a scene to read and can interpret the character using voice, facial expressions, gestures, movements, props, and costume pieces. Scenes can be edited for length, appropriate to each student. Good scenes and characters from Shakespeare for performance reading include the following:

Play	Scene	Characters
As You Like It	Act 2, Scene 7	Jacques
Hamlet	Act 5, Scene 1	Hamlet
Macbeth	Act 1, Scene 7	Macbeth
Romeo and Juliet	Act 2, Scene 2	Romeo and Juliet
Much Ado About Nothing	Act 2, Scene 1	Beatrice
Much Ado About Nothing	Act 2, Scene 3	Benedick
A Midsummer Night's Dream	Act 2, Scene 1	A Fairy
The Taming of the Shrew	Act 2, Scene 1	Petruchio

Each student can write a brief summary of the story of the play, the scene they are reading, and something about the character as an introduction.

Meet Shakespeare's Character _____

The Play

The Scene

My Character

Students can continue performance reading of Shakespeare, first reading the story of the play and finding a character and a scene from the original play. Students may choose to read the plays as well.

Books

Chute, M. (1993). *Stories from Shakespeare.* New York: Meridian.

Claybourne, A. (2005). *Usborne stories from Shakespeare.* Tulsa, OK: EDC Publishing.

Lamb, C., & Lamb, M. (2007). *Tales from Shakespeare*. New York: Random House.

Nexbit, E. (2009). *Green Tiger's illustrated stories from Shakespeare*. Seattle, WA: Green Tiger Press.

Packer, T. (2004). *Tales from Shakespeare*. New York: Scholastic.

English Learners

Choose books that contain the content and vocabulary of the cultural and language group of the English learners in the class. For example, for Spanish speaking ELs, see these picture books, in which the text is primarily in English but is interspersed with words in Spanish and where the story lends itself to acting out and performance reading:

Deedy, C. A. (2007). *Martina the beautiful cockroach: A Cuban folktale*. Atlanta, GA: Peachtree Publishers. (There is also a Spanish version of this book with a CD of the story in Spanish, published in 2008.)

Mora, P. (2006). *!Marimba! Animales from A to Z*. New York: Clarion.

The teacher can focus on using nonlinguistic strategies to make the story comprehensible (i.e., props and realia and gestures).

Students can be paired with a buddy—a student who is a more proficient English speaking EL or an English speaker. The EL uses props, gestures, and sound effects, while the buddy speaks the words and phrases. When using an English text that also has words in Spanish, such as the picture books listed previously, the less English proficient student can say the words in Spanish and gradually add words in English as they become more comfortable with speaking them, while the more proficient English speaker can say the words in English.

Struggling Students

Scaffold performance reading by making, or helping the students make, cue cards with words and phrases in large print. The cue cards can be used initially for the student to repeat the words after the teacher models them, and then students can use them as they practice.

Students can be paired for performance reading of a picture book, poem, song, or book excerpt. The teacher can pair students by how well they work together, and a more able reader can be paired with one who struggles. Students can read and practice performing a text together and share it with other pairs or the class.

Cocreate a rubric for performance reading with students that can both guide and assess a student's ability to use repeated phrases and language, characters' voices, gestures, sound effects, or props, as appropriate for each story or poem used. Younger students can discuss their performance readings with others, first noting their strengths and then making suggestions for things on which they can improve. Older students can do a peer-assessment with another student, again first noting strengths and then areas needing improvement. Here is an example of a teacher created rubric for kindergarten through 2nd grade.

Rubric for Performance Reading, K–2

Aspect of Performance Reading	NA for this story	3	2	1
Language: Repeated words or refrains		Always correctly joins refrain; speaks/reads enthusiastically	Usually joins refrain; some omissions or errors	Occasionally joins or does not join refrain; frequent errors or omissions
Story Characters' Voices		Correctly uses voices; changes expression and volume to reflect voices of different characters	Usually uses voices; some difference in expression and volume	Limited, inappropriate, or no use of voices of characters
Gestures, Sound Effects, Props		Consistently and appropriately uses throughout the story; even adds appropriate variations	Usually uses appropriately	Does not use or use is limited and may be incorrect or inappropriate

Cox, C. (2009). *Shakespeare kids: Speaking his words, performing his plays*. Denver, CO: Libraries Unlimited.

Rasinski, T. (2003). *The fluent reader: Oral reading strategies for building word recognition, fluency, and comprehension*. New York: Scholastic.

References

National Institute of Child Health and Human Development. (2000). *Report of the National Reading Panel. Teaching children to read: An evidence-based assessment of the scientific research literature on reading and its implications for reading instruction: Reports of the subgroups* (NIH Publication No. 00–4754). Washington, DC: Government Printing Office.

Rasinski, T. V., & Hoffman, J. V. (2003). Theory and research into practice: Oral reading in the school literacy curriculum. *Reading Research Quarterly, 38*(4), 510–522.

PART II

Social Studies

WHAT RESEARCH HAS TO SAY ABOUT LITERATURE-BASED TEACHING AND SOCIAL STUDIES

While different curricular models for social studies have been proposed over the years, many experts in the field of social studies education today have advocated an inquiry and problem solving approach that reflects a constructivist theory of learning and is grounded in an experiential and developmentally appropriate use of strategies and materials (Levstik & Tyson, 2008).

However, the most commonly used tool of social studies instruction over the years has been the textbook, which has also tended to define the curriculum, or what is taught (Armento, 1993; Kon, 1995; Thornton, 2008; Wade, 1993). Critics have advocated replacing the textbook or changing it by shifting from broad coverage to a more in-depth focus on powerful ideas, including activities that require higher level thinking, adding more global and multicultural content, and moving away from just reading textbooks and answering questions on worksheets. For example, students could be engaged with more discussion or debate, role play, cooperative learning, use of primary sources, and an inquiry approach to learning (Brophy & Alleman, 2007).

Research has identified several problems associated with the use of textbooks in teaching social studies. Social studies textbooks in the primary grades contain limited content that is often trite, familiar to students, and lacking a focus on meaningful big ideas (Brophy, 1992; Haas, 1991; Larkins, Hawkins, & Gilmore, 1987). Students have tended to not learn much of lasting value from this curriculum and to not like it very much either (Zhao & Hoge, 2005). An unrealistic level of background knowledge is required for comprehension of these texts (Beck & McKeown, 1991; Beck, McKeown, & Gromoll, 1989), and the reading level of textbooks is frequently two grade levels above that of students using them (Chall & Conrad, 1991). In studies of 5th-grade American history texts, Beck and McKeown (1991) and Beck, McKeown, Sinatra, and Loxterman (1991) found that explanations were so simplified and the text structure so often interrupted that students struggled to understand historical events and lost the narrative flow. Goodlad (1984) called for a change from classrooms where students listen to lectures to the whole class, work individually on written assignments, and read textbooks that are often too difficult to understand. But if not the textbook, then what?

Literature for children and young adults can serve as an alternative to the social studies textbook (Rycik & Rosler, 2009). A teacher can read an informational or biographical picture book aloud to students K through 8 or a factually accurate chapter book of historical or cultural fiction, a nonfiction book, or a biography for upper elementary through middle school students and present social studies content in a narrative form. Students should experience a variety of sources of information in learning social studies, including primary sources, Internet websites, and learning from listening to or reading biographical and historical fiction as well as traditional textbooks (Fertig, 2005; Moss, 2005; Villano, 2005). Rationales for incorporating literature into the teaching of social studies have been persuasive (McGowan, Erickson, & Neufeld, 1996).

There is a wealth of well-written, beautifully illustrated, and engaging literature that can be used with many different instructional strategies to teach social studies content (Brophy & Alleman, 2007; Seefeldt, 1993): for example, books with multicultural perspectives (Field, 2003; Sullivan, 1996) and books on economics (Suiter & Meszaros, 2005; VanFossen, 2003). Levstik (1995) found that historical fiction is the most commonly used type of literature in social studies instruction; because it tends to elicit a moral response, due to the reader identifying with the main character's perspective, recognizing and understanding various perspectives in the text requires teacher mediation.

Furthermore, research on the use of informational books in social studies in elementary schools has shown that while these books are read less frequently than fiction, with teacher mediation students respond favorably to nonfiction and use it to carry out inquiries in social studies (Levstik, 1995; Pappas, 1991). An added bonus of more frequent reading of nonfiction is that it leads to better progress in literacy than a literacy curriculum focused primarily on fiction (Duke, 2000; Pappas, 1991). Smith and Niemi (2001) also found that the use of materials other than, or in addition to, textbooks was associated with higher scores on achievement tests in American history. Finally, on the National Assessment of Educational Progress (NAEP) (2007) U.S. history assessment, students who reported reading historical literature (biographies, historical stories) at least a few times a year outperformed those who did not.

Informational books for social studies can be written in the first person, lending a strong voice to the narrative of a historical figure's life. Studies have shown that the presence of this text voice can improve students' understanding of the content (Beck, McKeown, & Worthy, 1995). An informational book can also use multiple voices to show different perspectives on a historical event or on a problem of social living today. Since children often conceptualize and organize knowledge in narrative structures that closely resemble stories they have heard or read in books, it may be that these are more useful for teachers than the more conceptual structures used by adults in the social sciences (Bruner, 1990). Young children are capable of learning history, especially when content is conveyed through the narrative structures in literature and focuses on the broad concepts rather than through a straight chronological presentation centered around dates, names, places, and events (Barton, 1996; Seefeldt, 1993; VanSledright & Brophy, 1992).

Teachers can read literature, present new information, and lead discussions using a more informal, narrative style that includes modeling by sharing the teacher's own experiences and asking students to share experiences from their own lives. Building on this base of narrative structure using literature and the story of students' lives, the concepts can be extended to society, the past, and other cultures. Social studies content and concepts are presented, discussed, applied, and understood in a meaningful way using narrative or story structure, which continues as students read more or write in the social studies. Continuing with this approach, students and teachers co-construct resources such as graphic organizers for displaying content, timelines, maps, data charts, posters, technology projects such as wikis, curriculum drama, and the accompanying vocabulary to collect, organize, analyze, synthesize, and interpret content and to extend ideas into subsequent learning experiences (Alleman, Brophy, & Knighton, 2003).

GUIDELINES FOR SELECTING BOOKS FOR TEACHING SOCIAL STUDIES

The National Council for the Social Studies (NCSS), in collaboration with the Children's Book Council, publishes a list titled "Notable Social Studies Tradebooks for Young People" each year as an insert to the May/June issue of the NCSS official journal, *Social Education*. Lists for all previous years are on the NCSS website at www.socialstudies.org/notable. Books selected for these annotated bibliographies are written primarily for students in Grades K through 8.

The selection committee uses the following criteria for inclusion on their list of books:

- Emphasize human relations

- Represent a diversity of groups and are sensitive to a broad range of cultural experiences

- Present an original theme or a fresh slant on a traditional topic

- Are easily readable and of high literary quality

- Have a pleasing format and, when appropriate, illustrations that enrich the text

Titles are arranged by broad subject categories and subthemes. Annotators have also indicated the thematic strand of *Expectations of Excellence: Curriculum Standards for Social Studies,* to which the book relates.

NATIONAL STANDARDS FOR SOCIAL STUDIES

The NCSS developed content and process standards with 10 themes that can guide teachers as they develop social studies instruction using engaging learning strategies and children's and young adult literature instead of instruction focused solely on the use of textbooks. The 10 themes that form the framework of the social studies standards as outlined in *Expectations of Excellence: Curriculum Standards for Social Studies* (1994) are as follows:

1. Culture: Students will learn the common characteristics and significant differences among the world's cultural groups. The content related to this theme comes primarily from the social science field of anthropology.

2. Time, Continuity, and Change: Students will learn how to reconstruct the past and develop a historical perspective to interpret the present. The content related to this theme comes primarily from the social science field of history.

3. People, Places, and Environments: Students will learn to understand the significance of place and develop a geographic perspective to interpret current social conditions. The content related to this theme comes primarily from the social science field of psychology.

4. Individual Development and Identity: Students will learn how culture, social groups, and institutions shape personal identity. The content related to this theme comes primarily from the social science field of psychology.

5. Individuals, Groups, and Institutions: Students will learn how institutions such as schools, churches, families, and government influence people's lives. The content related to this theme comes primarily from the field of sociology.

6. Power, Authority, and Governance: Students will learn how forms of government distribute power and authority. The content related to this theme comes primarily from the social science field of political science.

7. Production, Distribution, and Consumption: Students will learn that resources are limited and that people must make decisions on what things will be produced, how those things will be distributed, and the rate at which they will be consumed. The content related to this theme comes primarily from the social science field of economics.

8. Science, Technology, and Society: Students will learn that new technology changes the way people live. The content related to this theme comes from several social science fields.

9. Global Connections: Students will learn about the global connections among the world's societies. The content related to this theme comes from social science fields.

10. Civic Ideals and Practices: Students will learn the importance of civic participation in a democratic society. The content related to this theme comes primarily from political science.

REFERENCES

Alleman, J., Brophy, J., & Knighton, B. (2003). Co-constructing classroom resources. *Social Studies and the Young Learner, 16,* 5–8.

Armento, B. (1993). Reform revisited: The story of elementary social studies at the crest of the 21st century. In V. Wilson, J. Litel, & G. Wilson (Eds.), *Teaching social studies: Handbook of trends, issues, and implications for the future* (pp. 25–44). Westport, CT: Greenwood.

Barton, K. C. (1996). Narrative simplifications in elementary children's historical understanding. In J. Brophy (Ed.), *Advances in research on teaching: Vol. 6. Teaching and learning history* (pp. 51–83). Greenwich, CT: JAI Press.

Beck, I. L., & McKeown, M. G. (1991). Research directions: Social studies texts are hard to understand: Mediating some of the difficulties. *Language Arts, 68,* 482–489.

Beck, I., McKeown, M., & Gromoll, E. (1989). Learning from social studies texts. *Cognition and Instruction, 6*(2), 99–158.

Beck, I. L., McKeown, M. G., Sinatra, G. M., & Loxterman, J. A. (1991, Summer). Revising social studies from a text processing perspective: Evidence of improved comprehensibility. *Reading Research Quarterly, 26*(3), 251–276.

Beck, I. L., McKeown, M. G., & Worthy, J. (1995). Giving a text voice can improve students understanding. *Reading Research Quarterly, 30,* 220–239.

Brophy, J. (1992). The de facto national curriculum in U.S. elementary social studies: Critique of a representative example. *Journal of Curriculum Studies, 24,* 401–447.

Brophy, J., & Alleman, J. (2007). *Powerful social studies for elementary students* (2nd ed.). Belmont, CA: Thomson Wadsworth.

Bruner, J. (1990). *Acts of meaning.* Cambridge, MA: Harvard University Press.

Chall, J. S., & Conrad, S. S. (1991). *Should textbooks challenge students?* New York: Teachers College Press.

Duke, N. (2000). 3.6 minutes per day: The scarcity of informational texts in 1st grade. *Reading Research Quarterly, 35,* 202–225.

Fertig, G. (2005). Teaching elementary students how to interpret the past. *Social Studies, 96,* 2–8.

Field, S. (2003). Using children's literature and the universals of culture to teach about Mexico. *The Social Studies, 96,* 123–127.

Haas, M. (1991). An analysis of the social science and history concepts in elementary social studies textbooks Grades 1–4. *Theory and Research in Social Education, 19,* 211–220.

Goodlad, J. (1984). *A place called school: Prospects for the future.* New York: McGraw-Hill.

Kon, J. H. (1995). Teachers' curricular decision making in response to a new social studies textbook. *Theory and Research in Social Education, 23*(2), 121–146.

Larkins, A., Hawkins, M., & Gilmore, A. (1987). Trivial and noninformative content of elementary social studies: A review of primary texts in four series. *Theory and Research in Social Education, 15,* 299–311.

Levstik, L. S. (1995). Narrative constructions: Cultural frames for history. *The Social Studies, 86*(3), 113–116.

Levstik, L. S., & Tyson, C. A. (Eds.). (2008). Handbook of research in social studies education. New York: Routledge.

McGowan, M., Erickson, L., & Neufeld, J. (1996). With reason and rhetoric: Building the case for the literature-social studies connection. *Social Education, 60,* 203–207.

Moss, B. (2005). Making a case and a place for effective content area literacy instruction in the elementary grades. *The Reading Teacher, 59*(1), 46–55.

National Assessment of Educational Progress. (2007). 2006 U.S. History. Retrieved January 10, 2010, from http://nces.ed.gov/nationsreportcard/ushistory/

National Council for the Social Studies. (1994). *Expectations of excellence: Curriculum standards for social studies.* Washington, DC: National Council for the Social Studies.

Pappas, C. (1991). Fostering full access to literacy by including information books. *Language Arts, 68,* 449–462.

Rycik, M. T., & Rosler, B. (2009). The return of historical fiction. *The Reading Teacher, 63*(2), 163–166.

Seefeldt, C. (1993). History for young children. *Theory and Research in Social Education, 21,* 143–155.

Smith, J., & Niemi, R. G. (2001). Learning history in schools: The impact of course work and instructional practices on achievement. *Theory and Research in Social Education, 29,* 18–42.

Suiter, M., & Meszaros, B. (2005). Teaching about saving and investing in the elementary and middle school grades. *Social Education, 69,* 92–95.

Sullivan, J. (1996). Real people, common themes: Using tradebooks to counter stereotypes. *Social Education, 60,* 399–401.

Thornton, S. J. (2008). Continuity and change in social studies curriculum. In L. S. Levstik & C. A. Tyson (Eds.), *Handbook of Research in Social Studies Education* (pp. 15–32). New York: Routledge.

VanFossen, P. (2003). Best practice economic education for young children? It's elementary! *Social Education, 67,* 90–94.

VanSledright, B. A., & Brophy, J. (1992). Storytelling, imagination, and fanciful elaboration in children's historical reconstructions. *American Educational Research Journal, 29,* 837–859.

Villano, T. L. (2005). Should social studies textbooks become history? A look at alternative methods to activate scheme in the intermediate classroom. *The Reading Teacher, 59*(2), 122–130.

Wade, R. C. (1993). Content analysis of social studies textbooks: A review of ten years of research. *Theory and Research in Social Education, 21*(3), 232–256.

Zhao, Y., & Hoge, J. (2005). What elementary students and teachers say about social studies. *Social Studies, 96,* 216–221.

Strategy 9

Curriculum Drama

A 6th-grade class was studying the Renaissance. One group of students had shown a keen interest in the life of Henry VIII and the events leading to the Protestant Reformation in England, especially as it related to Henry's six wives. Based on biographies and other informational books they read about this period, they planned and presented a mock interview with Henry and all six of his wives at the same time, as if it were a contemporary television show with an interviewer and guests who present different and even opposing points of view. The interview was lively to say the least as Henry faced all six wives (he beheaded two, divorced two, one died in childbirth, and one survived him). Henry and the feather in his beret seemed to wilt as he responded to all the wives. His response to the interviewer's last question, "Do you have any final words, Henry?" revealed something of the student's reflecting on Henry's life as it might pertain to his own when he answered "I'm never getting married. . ." (what the student seemed to be thinking) ". . . again" (as Henry might have said).

RATIONALE

The word *drama* comes from a Greek word meaning "to do or live through." Curriculum drama is a strategy teachers can use to engage students with social studies content by stepping into a role and doing things other people would do, living through the lives of other people, past and present; representing different roles people in power or authority take; and communicating curriculum content in the social studies to others.

Learning theory supports the use of drama in the classroom. From his extensive research on child development, Piaget (1962) found that language development goes through three stages: (1) actual experience with an action or object, (2) dramatic reliving of this experience, and (3) words that represent this whole schema verbally. From Vygotsky's (1986) sociohistorical theory of learning, *activity* is the major explanatory concept in the development of human thought and language. The use of drama in the classroom reflects a social constructivist perspective of learning that is active, social, and centered in students' experience and that provides an effective way to teach language, literacy, and content (Wagner, 2003).

Curriculum drama combined with children's and adolescent literature can be a powerful means to teach social studies, to actively engage students, and to enliven, expand, and enrich learning (Kornfield & Leyden, 2005; Rosler, 2008). Research has also shown that using curriculum drama in social studies helps students of varying ability achieve higher levels of understanding of history content, the ability to evaluate evidence and develop concepts, and to visualize future implications of historical information to a greater extent than more conventional teaching strategies (Goaien & Hendy, 1993). Curriculum drama can take a variety of forms: role play, improvisation, monologues, dialogues, reenactments, scriptwriting, mock debates and interviews, "you are there" moments in history, and plays. Students can read and do research on a topic, use improvisational techniques or write scripts incorporating social studies content, and present it dramatically. Potentially dramatic moments in social studies are many, and under a teacher's guidance, students in K through 8 can act out contemporary social problems and current events, and they can relive events in history, step into the lives of people of other cultures, or read a biography of a historically important person and bring that person to life.

Source: From *Expectation of excellence: Curriculum standards for the social studies*, by the National Council for the Social Studies, 1994. Washington, DC: Author.

Social Studies Standards

Strand 2: Time, Continuity, and Change
Strand 6: Power, Authority, and Governance
Strand 10: Civic Ideals and Practices

STRATEGY

Introduce the various forms of curriculum drama to students in connection with reading a picture or illustrated book aloud. Through questioning, discussion, modeling, collaboration, and student-centered group work, plan how to use curriculum drama to bring the social studies content of the book to life.

Choose literature that lends itself to potentially dramatic moments related to the social studies content, theme, or standard to be taught. Reader response questions and prompts can be used to direct students to reflect on their experience of the book, and students can record their ideas on chart paper using a graphic organizer. Discuss the book, the students' personal experiencing of the book, and the key events and central concepts.

Guide students to think about how the concepts and events might be dramatized. Prepare a poster with a list of types of drama strategies that can be used to teach social studies curriculum content:

- Role playing
- Improvisation
- Monologues
- Dialogues
- Interviews
- Debates
- Reenactments

Choose one of the students' ideas recorded on the graphic organizer and ask them to choose a type of curriculum drama that might be used to further explore and learn about it and to present and communicate what has been learned to others. Use collaborative learning strategies such as Think-Pair-Share, where students think on their own, pair with a partner to talk over their ideas, and share with the rest of the class. They may also work in small groups, with each group choosing an idea or event in the book and a way to dramatize it. Record their different ideas for dramatizing next to the different concepts and events on the graphic organizer.

Plan how to carry out dramatizing the curriculum. For example, if a book describes a series of events in the life of a person or a historical period, a timeline could be created and student groups assigned to reenact part of the timeline in chronological order. Each group would collaborate on how to do this, do further reading and research, and practice. Students could write an introduction to the whole sequence, and an announcer could begin with the introduction and then announce each group's contribution in sequence. Another approach would be to take the same concept or event and let different groups choose one of the drama strategies to present their view on it to the other groups. In this way, different ways of communicating create multiple perspectives on the content. More improvisational techniques can be used after students discuss, read more on a topic, prepare notes, take different roles, and participate in an interview or a debate.

Plus Technology

Film and video clips of important events in recent history can easily be found on the Internet. Go to Google, click on Video, and search for specific people or events. Do the same with YouTube. Students can search these on their own, or the teacher can select the film and video clips to share with the whole class on a Smart Board, if one is available, or on a computer monitor.

Also, check with school, local, or university libraries for the online collection *American History in Video,* by the electronic publisher Alexander Street (www.alexanderstreet.com). This is a themed resource with 5,000 complete newsreels and documentaries equaling 2,000 hours with synchronized, scrolling text. Film and video clips can be found dating back to the first half of the 20th century through the current period, showing everything from the lives of everyday people to the famous World War II speeches by Franklin D. Roosevelt after Pearl Harbor, Winston Churchill during the Battle of Britain, as well as Hitler, to the often quoted Presidential Inaugural addresses such as John F. Kennedy's and Barack Obama's.

Grade-Level Modifications

K–2nd Grade

Choose, read, and discuss a picture book with social studies content appropriate for young children. Good books for primary students include biographies of important figures in American and world history. A common teaching theme in primary social studies is "People who make a difference." For example, read aloud *Big George: How a Shy Boy Became President Washington* (Rockwell, 2009).

Discuss the book using reader response questions and prompts that can lead into appropriate forms of curriculum drama for young children: "What event in George Washington's life do you remember most? If you were George Washington, how would you feel and act during those events? What are some things you would say?"

Record students' responses on a tree chart graphic organizer.

George Washington's Life			
Event	*Feelings*	*Actions*	*Words*

Re-read and discuss the book, adding student ideas to the graphic organizer. Discuss what students might do if they were George at any given point in his life. As a whole class, students can improvise gestures, actions, and spoken responses, and these can be added to the chart as well. Ask students questions such as the following:

- How would he stand?
- What gestures might he use?
- How would he move?
- What facial expressions would he make?
- What would his voice sound like?
- What would he say?
- Who might he be talking to?
- What would they do or say?

Take volunteers to choose one of the events in his life and role play and use improvisation to bring it to life. Students could plan and do this individually or in groups. There are many excellent picture books and illustrated biographies for young children to use with curriculum drama that can be collected in a text set in the classroom and used for more curriculum drama or for student independent reading.

Books

Grimes, N. (2008). *Barack Obama: Son of promise, child of hope.* New York: Simon & Schuster.

Krull, K. (2003). *Harvesting hope: The story of Cesar Chavez.* New York: Harcourt.

Pinkney, A. D. (2009). *Boycott blues: How Rosa Parks inspired a nation.* New York: HarperCollins, Greenwillow, Amistad.

Rockwell, A. (2008). *Big George: How a shy boy became President Washington.* New York: Harcourt.

Van Steenwyk, E. (2009). *First dog Fala.* Atlanta, GA: Peachtree. (Franklin D. Roosevelt)

3RD GRADE–5TH GRADE

Curriculum drama can be especially effective in fostering understanding of different points of view when learning about conflicting positions on an issue, whether among people in one group or nation or between two groups or nations: for example, during the Revolutionary War, the Civil War, World War II and the Holocaust, the Vietnam War, the Cold War era, or during movements such as antislavery, women's suffrage, or Civil Rights.

Assemble a text set of books that provide information from multiple perspectives on the conflict. As students read and discuss what they are reading, record ideas on a graphic organizer—a T-chart with two columns, each one representing a position in the conflict. An expanded T-chart graphic organizer could be used if there are clearly more than two main positions.

The Conflict	
One Side	*The Other Side*

The class could be divided and each half could focus on learning about one of the positions. Using curriculum drama such as role playing and dialogues between leaders of each position, team debates on the position, or mock interviews with representatives of each position, students learn about and advocate for a position that may not necessarily be their own, but by stepping into a role, their engagement in and learning about the conflict is enhanced.

Picture books can be paired with a chapter book. The picture book can be read aloud to introduce the students to the conflict, and the paired chapter book can be read aloud or read by students. Other books on the conflict can form a text set to be used in the classroom by students as they plan how to dramatize the differences among people in different periods in history. For example, introduce the conflict of the Revolutionary War with *George vs. George: The Revolutionary War as Seen by Both Sides* (Schnazer, 2004), and continue by reading aloud the chapter book *My Brother Sam Is Dead* (Collier & Collier, 1974).

Books

Collier, J. L., & Collier, C. (1974). *My brother Sam is dead.* New York: Four Winds.

Schnazer, R. (2004). *George vs. George: The Revolutionary War as Seen by Both Sides.* Washington, DC: National Geographic Books.

6TH GRADE–8TH GRADE

In middle school, students learning about a period in ancient or modern world history can stage reenactments of important events with students playing different roles. They can write narrations or scripts with speaking parts, add settings with backdrops drawn and painted on butcher paper, or make simple costume pieces like a toga or a classical drape out of a length of fabric for ancient Greek or Roman history; simple headbands, headdresses, or collars for ancient Egypt; or berets, other hats, and lengths of fabric for capes for Renaissance and European history.

Picture books or illustrated books can provide images as well as information for reenactments, showing what the people and their world looked like at a given time and place in history, as well as information about the period. After introducing curriculum drama, groups could be formed and assigned a period to reenact on a rotating basis—one group a week, for example. Students could plan and rehearse during group work time when students not doing a reenactment are working on other assignments.

Books that show as well as tell about these periods could be read aloud and be the source of ideas for simple settings, costumes, and props for each group. For example, Diane Stanley wrote or illustrated many beautiful biographies. They are rich in information about the historical period, but because of their wonderful images, they are especially helpful in getting students to envision the period they are learning about. These and other illustrated books, combined with chapter books that could be read aloud or read silently by students, would provide a source of information and imagery to explore, reimagine, and present to others using curriculum drama.

Books

Ancient world:

Stanley, D., & Vennema, P. (1988). *Shaka, king of the Zulus*. New York: HarperCollins.

Stanley, D., & Vennema, P. (1994). *Cleopatra*. New York: William Morrow.

Middle East:

Stanley, D. (2002). *Saladin, noble prince of Islam*. New York: HarperCollins.

Europe:

Stanley, D. (1999). *Peter the Great*. New York: HarperCollins.

Stanley, D. (2002). *Joan of Arc*. New York: HarperCollins.

Stanley, D., & Vennema, P. (2001). *Good Queen Bess: The Story of Elizabeth I of England*. New York: HarperCollins.

ENGLISH LEARNERS

All students must tap into prior experience, knowledge, and cultural experiences during drama, which is an especially important strategy to use for English learners. English learners can also benefit from the many elements of curriculum drama that are excellent ELD strategies: visual cues through the use of illustrated books and scene backgrounds; realia such as costumes and props; nonverbal means of communication, such as gestures, actions, sound effects, and Total Physical Response (TPR); and graphic organizers for planning drama that use visual and organizational structures that scaffold learning for ELs.

There are books about individuals who may themselves have been English learners or that are representative of the many countries and cultures English learners represent, which can be used by a teacher to make a connection with students' background and heritage. Some of these books are in two languages and can introduce students' primary language into the classroom.

Books

Bernier-Grand, C. T. (2004). *Cesar: ¡Si, se puede! Yes we can!* New York: Marshall Cavendish.

Cohn, D. (2002). *¡Si, se puede!/Yes, we can! Janitor Strike in L.A.* El Paso, TX: Cinco Puntos Press.

Krull, K. (2003). *Cosechando esperanza: La historia de Cesar Chavez.* San Anselmo, CA: Sandpiper.

STRUGGLING STUDENTS

Social studies textbooks, which are often two or more grade levels above the average reading level of a grade, leave many struggling readers also struggling with social studies content. Curriculum drama based on engaging literature at varying levels of readability offers a way of learning that is an alternative to more conventional teaching strategies such as answering written questions or writing a report after reading a textbook.

Cooperative learning strategies used with curriculum drama support inclusion of all students in a classroom community and are a wonderful strategy for differentiating instruction. Differences among students—such as cognitive and learning styles, social class, race and ethnicity, language, and disabilities—are viewed as resources. Inclusion is rooted in frequent student-to-student interaction, in which students learn about each other as individuals and learn to respect each other and to see each other as contributing members of the group.

Struggling readers and writers and students with disabilities may experience success in several ways with curriculum drama: by playing a role suited to their strengths, by listening to literature read aloud for information, by becoming engaged with and learning content through drama activities, and by gaining independence through their contributions to a curriculum drama project

ASSESSMENT

Authentic assessment of curriculum drama can take a variety of forms. As students plan and rehearse, they can evaluate throughout the process. Prompt them to think, respond to, and discuss the curriculum drama project as well as the social studies content they are learning. Students can take notes to use during discussions.

Students can also write to demonstrate what they have learned using different types of writing: a script for a scene they will perform, a poem, or short essays that answer specific questions. Writing may be combined with illustration in the form of posters and political or social commentary cartoons. Younger students can draw and write, and in the case of emergent writers or beginning English learners, someone can take dictation and write captions on their drawings for them.

When different groups in a class are researching different aspects of a period in history, for example, and using a form of curriculum drama to learn and communicate what they have learned, they may also develop questions that students in other groups can answer. These questions would reflect what the group hoped to communicate, and the responses of other students would demonstrate whether or not they succeeded.

Rubrics may be cocreated with students so that the goals and outcomes of curriculum drama are clear and relative to both the use of drama and the social studies content to be learned. A self-assessment by students can be especially sensitive to a wide range of possible learning about drama, literature, social studies, and themselves.

Self-Assessment for Curriculum Drama in Social Studies

Tell About the Drama

1. Tell about the drama we did for social studies.

2. What is the most important thing you learned?

3. Which role did you play?

4. Tell about your character.

5. What is the most important thing about your character?

6. Tell how you felt about doing drama and social studies.

RESOURCES

Fennessey, S. M. (2000). *History in the spotlight: Creative drama and theatre practices for the social studies classroom.* Portsmouth, NH: Heinemann.

Schneider, J. J., Crumpler, T. P., & Rogers, T. (2006). *Process drama and multiple literacies: Addressing social, cultural, and ethical issues.* Portsmouth, NH: Heinemann.

Swartz, L. (1995). *Dramathemes.* Portsmouth, NH: Heinemann.

Taylor, P. (1999). *Red coats and patriots: Reflective practice in drama and social studies.* Portsmouth, NH: Heinemann.

REFERENCES

Goaien, P., & Hendy, L. (1993). "It's not just fun, it works!" Developing children's historical thinking through drama. *Curriculum Journal, 4*(3), 363–384.

Kornfeld, J., & Leyden, G. (2005). Acting out: Literature, drama, and connecting with history. *The Reading Teacher, 59*(3), 230–238.

Piaget, J. (1962). *Play, dreams, and imitation in childhood.* New York: Norton.

Rosler, B. (2008, November/December). Process drama in one fifth-grade social studies class. *The Social Studies,* pp. 265–272.

Vygotsky, L. S. (1986). *Thought and language.* Cambridge, MA: MIT Press.

Wagner, B. J. (2003). Imaginative expression. In J. Flood, D. Lapp, M. R. Squire, & J. M. Jensen (Eds.), *Handbook of research on teaching the English language arts* (3rd ed.). Sponsored by the International Reading Association/National Council of Teachers of English. Mahwah, NJ: Erlbaum.

Strategy 10

Map Making

Gordon was learning about maps in his kindergarten class. His teacher read a beginning book about maps to the class, *As the Crow Flies: A First Book of Maps* (Hartman, 1993), and asked students to paint a map of anything they wanted. Figure 10.1 is Gordon's map of the world.

Figure 10.1 Gordon's world map

(Continued)

| Figure 10.1 | (Continued) |

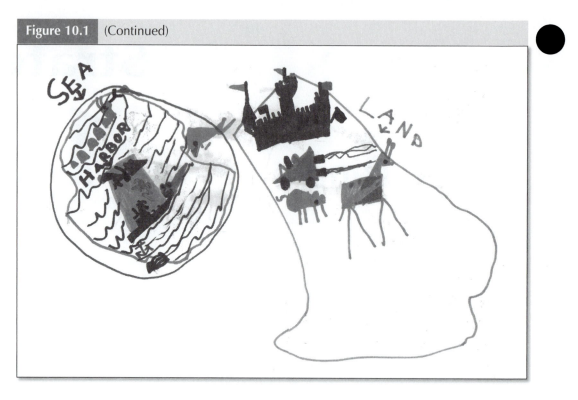

RATIONALE

Children's ability to read maps was one of the many things investigated by Jean Piaget as he built his theories about child development (Piaget & Inhelder, 1969). As he frequently did, Piaget described the stages children go through as they learn to see things from different perspectives, a necessary skill in learning to read and understand maps. The three stages are as follows:

1. Topographical—children are able to use directional labels such as north, south, east, and west

2. Projective—children are able to use their own position to determine a location, such as knowing what is in front, back, left, or right of them

3. Euclidian—children can accurately perceive spatial relationships such as those that are used on a map

Piaget's stage theory can provide a teacher with a general framework in thinking about developmentally appropriate practices for different ages and grades, and students probably move through these stages in the same order, if not all at the same age.

Research on learning and teaching geography has further explored this relationship between the development of thinking and map reading skills (Forsythe, 1995; Gregg & Leinhardt, 1994; Stoltman, 1991). Findings show that children are able to understand map symbols and that they represent places and things on a map, but it is more difficult for them to read and interpret more abstract symbols and to understand the relationships between the symbols. Scale, measurement, and the frame of reference for maps can also be difficult for children. Instruction in map skills should therefore be clear, structured, and developmentally appropriate. It's important to note in addition that Trifonoff's (1997) research revealed that even young children demonstrate the ability to use advanced mapping skills with appropriate instruction.

To address the difficulty that research shows students may have with more abstract map symbols and the relationship among these symbols on a map, introduce map skills with literature that contextualizes mapping in a narrative, can be related to where in the world each student lives, and engages students by "doing geography." Recommended best practices today reflect this constructivist approach to teaching geography, particularly the value of hands-on, active learning and inquiry approaches, such as activities and projects (Bednarz, 2003). For example, relating new concepts to locations in the students' world and using visualizations, demonstrations, and student-created models, charts, and graphs enhanced student learning (Hickey & Bein, 1996); map-makers learned more than map-readers (Gregg, 1999), and students making maps in groups had a better understanding of map concepts than those who worked individually (Leinhardt, Stainton, & Merriman Bausmith, 1998).

Social Studies Standards

Strand 1: Culture
Strand 3: People, Places, and Environments
Strand 9: Global Connections

Source: From Expectation of excellence: Curriculum standards for the social studies, by the National Council for the Social Studies, 1994. Washington, DC: Author.

STRATEGY

Choose and read a book appropriate for the grade level that introduces key concepts and terms in either a narrative book of fiction or an engaging informational book. After reading and discussing the book, and encouraging students to relate the terms and concepts to their own experience through reader response questions and prompts, students can learn to both read and make maps that show the spatial relationships among people, places, and environments. They can use primary data to make their own maps and secondary data in the form of maps they read.

Primary data: Students can collect the primary data necessary to create their own maps in the classroom and school, or in the community on a field trip. They can count and measure spaces in their own environment, such as the school, or take photographs with digital cameras on a field trip, such as one to city hall. They can also keep records of observations in both types of places. These data can be used to construct their own maps.

Secondary data: Students can use maps as a secondary source of information. A good way to begin is to link their experiences to the map. Other secondary sources are online databases and books, such as an atlas. In these sources, they can read maps, charts, tables, and graphs with geographic information.

To provide developmentally appropriate instruction in map skills, begin with the locations most familiar to students in Grades K through 2—such as their own rooms or houses or the classroom, school, or community. Instruction in Grades 3 through 5 can be expanded to cities, states, the United States, and the world; in Grades 6 through 8, a historical view can be added through the use of maps of the ancient world and other historical periods.

Plus Technology

Even the youngest students can go online to http://www.mapquest.com and request a map for any location, such as their home, school, or community. Digital cameras can be used to photograph sites in the school and community to help students create maps and use symbols to represent the sites on maps. The U.S. Geological Survey (USGS) website (www.education.usgs.gov) includes numerous map collections that students can search. Maps.com at www.maps.com and www.maps101.com offers access to thousands of maps, mapping software, and ideas for teaching activities and lesson plans.

Geographic Information System (GIS) merge various layers of information in a computer environment that allows for retrieval, storage, manipulation, analysis, and visualization of geographic information (www.ccdmd.qc.ca/en/gis/before.html). Research on GIS use in elementary schools has shown that it can help students practice geographic skills, that it is extremely motivating, and that it enhances student learning (Keiper, 1999).

The popular PBS television game show for children *Where in the World Is Carmen Sandiego?* built knowledge of geography, taking children around the world as they searched for the elusive Carmen. Carmen Sandiego began as a detective in a computer software game by Broderbund Software, and animated adventures on DVD and other products are available worldwide (www.riverdeep.net, www.broderbund.com). The game can be projected from the computer onto a screen or large monitor. Students observe and take notes, and they acquire knowledge of geography and maps as Carmen travels worldwide.

GRADE-LEVEL MODIFICATIONS

K–2ND GRADE

Read aloud *Mapping Penny's World* by Laureen Leedy (1998). In the book, a young girl makes a map of her room for a school assignment. She then becomes inspired to map all the places that her dog Penny loves. While the book is in a narrative form, it also provides good explanations of map vocabulary, such as *compass rose, scale, key,* and *symbols*. It provides examples of the kinds of maps that young children can read, understand, and make themselves. Ask students reader response questions and prompts: What part was the most interesting to you? What map would you like to make?

Do a mini-lesson on map vocabulary by preparing a chart with key vocabulary, asking students what they already know about the terms, using the book to model the meaning of the terms, and planning how they can use each of the concepts the terms represent when they make maps on their own:

Key Map Vocabulary

- Compass rose
- Scale
- Key
- Symbols

Students can first make a map of their own room, drafting it from memory and then revising it at home. Then make a map of the classroom with students by first measuring it and then creating an appropriate scale to make a map. For example, one foot in the classroom could equal one inch on the map. For the youngest students, model making a map to scale with the measurements on a piece of chart paper or butcher paper. A more advanced project would be for each student to use graph paper or simply measure one inch to one foot for the scale of the map. Students can add a compass rose, scale, key, and symbols to their maps.

Books

Chesanow, N. (1995). *Where do I live?* Hauppauge, NY: Barrons.

Fanelli, S. (1995). *My mapbook.* New York: Harper Festival.

Hartman, G. (1993). *As the crow flies: A first book of maps.* St. Louis, MO: Turtleback Books.

Leedy, L. (1998). *Mapping Penny's world.* New York: Henry Holt.

Sweeney, J. (1996). *Me on the map.* New York: Knopf.

3RD GRADE–5TH GRADE

The book *People,* by Peter Spier (1980), while not a book specifically about maps, takes a global view of the world and all the people in it. It is a wonderful read aloud that tells how people all over the world are alike and different, but that each one of us is unique in our own way. After using reader response questions and prompts to talk about the book, such as "What is unique about you?" and writing about their unique qualities, students can build on this experience to learn map skills. Students can collect data that identify their own birthplace or the birthplaces of their parents, grandparents, and other family members. Use the following tree map template to help them collect this data.

Where in the World Are We From?

Where I was born: _____

Where members of my family were born:

Mother _____   Father _____

Grandmother _____   Grandfather _____

Grandmother _____   Grandfather _____

Where I live now: _____

On a large map of the world in the classroom, students can use sticky notes or stick pins of one color with labels attached to show where they were born. The birthplaces of parents can be shown with another color, and grandparents, if known, using another color. In most classrooms in the United States, the plotting of these birthplaces would cover many parts of the world. Each student could also connect their birthplace and that of their parents and grandparents to show the relationship among the locations for each one of them.

Each student can identify the cities, stages, countries, continents, and hemispheres of their birthplace and that of their parents or grandparents on the large world map, and they can then share these with the rest of the class. On their own copy of a world map, they can then identify the following:

- Hemispheres: Northern and Southern

- Continents: Africa, Antarctica, Asia, Australia, Europe, North America, South America

- Oceans: Antarctic, Atlantic, Arctic, Indian, Pacific

Books

Knowlton, J. (1999). *Maps and globes*. St. Louis, MO: Turtleback Books.

Ritchie, S. (2009). *Follow that map! A first book of mapping skills*. Toronto, Ontario, Canada: Kids Can Press.

Spier, P. (1980). *People*. New York: Doubleday.

Treays, R. (1998). *My town*. Tulsa, OK: Educational Development Corporation.

6TH GRADE–8TH GRADE

Students can travel back in time and look at historical maps of the world. The class could divide into groups based on their own heritage. If most students share a similar heritage (e.g., European American or African American), they could choose a continent to research at different periods in history: Ancient World, Middle Ages, Renaissance, and so on. They can make maps to accompany reports or presentations on their family history or on another period of time they are learning about.

Students who read fantasy novels such as J. K. Rowling's *Harry Potter* series, Brian Jacques' *Redwall* series, or J. Tolkien's *The Hobbit* or *Lord of the Rings* trilogy can create a map of it based on the information about the locations in the story narrative. Fantasy novel writers often do this to help the reader picture the world they have imagined. Like the fantasy writers of these books, challenge students to create their own fantasy world, write about it, and map it.

Books

Adams, S. (2007). *The Kingfisher atlas of the ancient world*. Boston: Kingfisher.

Adams, S. (2007). *The Kingfisher atlas of the medieval world*. Boston: Kingfisher.

Johnson, S. (1999). *Mapping the world*. New York: Atheneum.

Mattern, J. (2009). *The big book of the Civil War: Fascinating facts about the Civil War including maps, historic photographs, and timelines*. Philadelphia: Running Kids Press.

National Geographic. (2007). *National Geographic world atlas for young explorers* (3rd ed.). Washington, DC: National Geographic Children's Books.

Wagner, M., & Bryant, D. (2009). *The big book of World War II: Fascinating facts about World War II including maps, historic photographs, and timelines*. Philadelphia: Running Kids Press.

ENGLISH LEARNERS

Tapping into the background and prior knowledge of English learners is a first step in meaningful instruction for students whose home language is other than English. This is accomplished when students do research and create maps of their own homes, schools, communities, and places of family origin. Other important strategies for ELs include using visuals such as maps and models such as a globe, which are also used in learning about maps.

Primary language support can be used with books in the home languages of ELs. For example, the book *People* (Spier, 1987) is available in Spanish.

Books

Spier, P. (1987). *Gente/People* (Spanish edition). Lyndhurst, NJ: Lectorum Publications.

STRUGGLING STUDENTS

Map frames with labels can be used for students creating their own maps. For the classroom, provide a black line outline for the room measurements to scale. Add labels for Compass Rose, Key, and Scale, with space for the student to fill them in after the information has been modeled for each one. Together, create a list of symbols that the students can then copy and place on their maps.

ASSESSMENT

The maps students create will demonstrate their understanding of mapping skills. Checklists for different types of maps and grades can also be used not only to assess whether students have used map making tools correctly, but also to guide them in doing it. They can use these checklists as a to-do and self-editing list. They can also work in pairs and assess and edit each other's maps, revising and improving as necessary. They can also include written comments explaining how they created each item and how each one is used.

Checklist for Maps, K–2			
	Yes	No	Comments
Compass Rose			
Scale			
Key			
Symbols			

RESOURCES

Corn, J. (2003). *Making and using maps.* New York: Scholastic.

REFERENCES

Bednarz, R. S. (2003). Nine years on: Examining implementation of the national geography standards. *Journal of Geography, 56*(1), 99–109.

Forsythe, A. S. (1995). *Learning geography: An annotated bibliography of research paths.* Indiana, PA: National Council for Geographic Education.

Gregg, M. (1999). Mapping success: Reversing the Matthew effect. *Research in Geographic Education, 1*(2), 118–135.

Gregg, M., & Leinhardt, G. (1994). Mapping out geography: An example of epistemology and education. *Review of Educational Research, 64,* 311–361.

Hickey, G. M., & Bein, F. L. (1996). Students' learning difficulties in geography and teachers' interventions: Teaching cases from K–12 classrooms. *Journal of Geography, 95*(3), 118–125.

Keiper, T. A. (1999). GIS for elementary students: An inquiry into a new approach to learning geography. *Journal of Geography, 98*(2), 47–59.

Leinhardt, G., Stainton, C., & Merriman Bausmith, J. (1998). Constructing maps collaboratively. *Journal of Geography, 97*(1), 19–30.

Piaget, J., & Inhelder, B. (1969). *The psychology of the child.* (H. Weaver, Trans.). New York: Basic Books.

Stoltman, J. P. (1991). Research on geography teaching. In J. P. Shaver (Ed.), *Handbook of research on social studies teaching and learning* (pp. 437–447). New York: Macmillan.

Trifonoff, K. M. (1997). Introducing thematic maps in the primary grades. *Social Studies and the Young Learner, 11*(1), 17–22.

Strategy
11

Timelines

The first people were the pirates. The pirates went all around to all the worlds and got all the treasure. Next came the cave men. The cave men lived in the caves at Disneyland. But there weren't any castles or Popsicle stands yet. But that was all right because the cavemen didn't like fun. They liked dark and carried big things on their shoulders. Then came the Indians and the Pilgrims. They came at the same time. Then came us.

World History by Elizabeth, age 5

RATIONALE

Timelines are graphic representations of the chronology of events in time. While they are often used as a way to display information in visual form in textbooks as an alternative to written narrative, students can also become more actively engaged in learning the sequence of events in history by constructing timelines themselves.

The strategy of timelines can be used with students in Grades K through 8. Research shows that even young children have an understanding of temporal order of events in history and have the ability to think about and try to explain continuity and change over time (Barton, 1997, 2002, 2008; Barton & Levstik, 1996; Downey & Levstik, 2008; Harnett, 1993; Levstik, 1991). For example, see the explanation of world history that Elizabeth dictated to her kindergarten teacher around Thanksgiving when the class was learning about the Pilgrims. She was clearly thinking about where the Pilgrims fit in the sequence of people in world history. Most upper elementary and middle school students can identify historical developments, especially related to national history, even though they may lack a detailed understanding of those developments (Barton & Levstik, 1998; Lee, 2004; Yeager & Terzian, 2007). A study by Barton and Levstik (1996) with children from kindergarten through Grade 6 using the method of placing pictures and photographs from 1772 to 1993 in sequence showed that kindergarten and 1st-grade students are able to demonstrate understanding of differences in historical time. Dates were more useful for older students in Grades 3 and 4, and this ability increased in Grades 5 and 6 as students could match dates with specific pictures.

It's advisable to keep timelines fairly simple, to cocreate them with students, and to consider alternative chronological representations given the content taught, such as vertical or horizontal timelines, timelines at an angle, timelines that replicate a path taken by people or travelers, or circles (Alleman & Brophy, 2003; Lynn, 1993; Masterman & Rogers, 2002). Timelines as a teaching strategy can help students construct an understanding of historical events over time, even the youngest students. Literature can be used to show, model, and help students develop concepts about time, continuity, and change in social studies as a basis for creating timelines (Hoodless, 2002). Haas (2000) explained how to do this with the book *A Street Through Time* (Steele, 2004), using timelines and other powerful instructional strategies for social studies.

Source: From Expectation of excellence: Curriculum standards for the social studies, by the National Council for the Social Studies, 1994. Washington, DC: Author.

Social Studies Standards

2. Time, Continuity, and Change
4. Individual Development and Identity
5. Individuals, Groups, and Institutions

STRATEGY

Students can begin with timelines of their own lives. Literature about a child's birthday can begin a study of timelines with younger students. Many books of children's and young adult literature for older students, particularly nonfiction history, show timelines. Read and discuss a book with students, leading into the activity of constructing a timeline with events from each of their own lives using a reader response prompt such as "Think about the important events in your life over the years, and you can each make a timeline."

Each student can begin with their date of birth and then make a list of the subsequent years of their lives, with at least one important event for each year. These lists should be developmentally appropriate for each grade but can become increasingly complex through the grades. Information on what was happening in the world around them can be added as well. Teachers can co-construct the guidelines for creating a timeline with students, depending on their grade and area of study in the social studies (e.g., the family in kindergarten, the community in Grade 3, U.S. history in Grade 5, world history in Grade 6, etc.). These parallel timelines afford students a view of the world during their own lifetime, situating themselves in the context of the historical events of the time.

There are several types of timelines a teacher can choose, depending on the grade, area of study in social studies, and needs of students:

- Horizontal: from left to right

- Vertical: from bottom to top

- Illustrated: pictures added

- Table top timelines: add objects, artifacts, photographs in frames, etc. to a timeline on a table or counter in a classroom

- Circles: this could be a clock or represent a journey that ended where it began

- Computer generated: use Word, Excel, or PowerPoint, adding information to create a personal or historical timeline

- Meandering: a timeline could represent a journey or migration that did not follow a linear path

- Map: put a timeline directly on a map to show both distance, place, and time on a journey

- Parallel timelines: put a student's life on the left and world events on the right

- Living timelines: construct a large timeline that uses the walls or floor of the room using lengths of butcher paper; students can learn about and dress to represent historical events and then tell other member of the class, or an audience of other classes, about the period

Plus Technology

Go to the International Reading Association created website for teachers—www.read writethink.org—for an interactive timeline creator.

GRADE-LEVEL MODIFICATIONS

K–2ND GRADE

Read aloud *On the Day You Were Born,* by Debra Frasier (2005). Use reader response questions and prompts to discuss the book and connect the concept of birth date to each student's own life: "What do you know about what happened on the day you were born?" Use the following template for students to record dates and events. They can take it home and do it with the help of family members and also add information in class on their own.

On the Day I Was Born
I was born on (Month, day, year)
In   I was one year old and I
In   I was two years old and I

The calendar and months and dates of the year are often taught as social studies content in kindergarten. Kindergarten students could use the first line of the template provided, either writing their birth date themselves or telling it to someone for dictation. Each student could illustrate the sentence. Then, make a list of the months of the year, with each student's birth date written next to the month of their birth, in order by days. After making a wall timeline with the months of the year, each student's birth date could be added in the correct month. Students in Grades 1 and 2 could create a vertical timeline of their life, using the template provided, with the correct number of years for the grade—typically six years for Grade 1 and seven years for Grade 2.

Books

Curtis, J. L. (2000). *Tell me again about the night I was born.* New York: HarperCollins. (for adopted children)

Frasier, D. (2005). *On the day you were born.* New York: Harcourt.

Hennesy, B. G. (2005). *Because of you.* Cambridge, MA: Candlewick Press.

Tillman, N. (2006). *On the night you were born.* New York: Feiwel & Friends.

3RD GRADE–5TH GRADE

Timelines can be created to match appropriate social studies content in Grade 3 (the community), Grade 4 (the state), and Grade 5 (U.S. history). An excellent book to read aloud and have available for students to read in the classroom is *How Children Lived* (Rice & Rice, 2001). The book introduces the concepts of time and distance and describes 16 children living in different eras of the past, from ancient Egypt in 1200 B.C. up to the 1920s in the United States. It begins with a double page spread showing each child standing where they lived on a world map. Then the life of each child is described in chronological order, with a timeline of the period in which they lived. Discuss the book using reader response questions and prompts such as "What would a timeline of your life look like? How could you also describe the world you live in?" Students can construct a timeline of their own lives like the one Elizabeth made, shown in Figure 11.1.

In all three grades, the study of a period of history can begin with the students' own community: for example, 100 Years of Our Town. Contact the local historical society for resources. Students in Grade 4 can move on to constructing timelines for state history, and students in Grade 5 can construct one for U.S. history. They can also create parallel timelines by continuing to add to their own personal timeline, as well as adding current events in the world. If they use the vertical format, personal events could be on one side, world events on the other. If they use a horizontal format, the line could run through the middle of a paper, with personal events below and world events above the line.

There are other books with timelines related to American history that could be collected for a text set in the classroom.

Books

Aronson, M., & Glenn, J. W. (2007). *The world made new: Why the age of exploration happened and how it changed the world.* Washington, DC: National Geographic Children's Books.

Panchyk, R. (2002). *World War II for kids: A history with 21 activities.* Chicago: Review Press.

Rice, C., & Rice, M. (2001). *How children lived.* New York: DK Children.

Waldman, C. (1994). *Timelines of Native American history.* New York: Macmillan.

6TH GRADE–8TH GRADE

Teachers can also introduce students in Grades 6 through 8 to timelines by having them construct a personal timeline. As students in these grades move into the study of

Figure 11.1   "Timeline of My Life" by Elizabeth

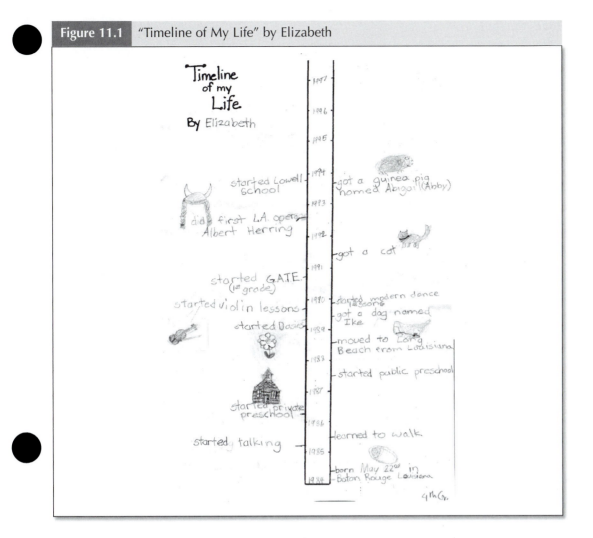

the history of the world, there are several books that focus on the concept of change over time in history to read aloud and have available in the classroom. The book *A Street Through Time* (Millard, 1998) is an illustrated timeline, tracing the development of an unnamed European riverside location through 14 different periods in time, from 10,000 B.C. when it was a Stone Age hunter's camp through modern times. The same format is used in two other books in this series: *A Port Through Time* (Millard, 2006) and *A City Through Time* (Steele, 2004). Discuss any of these books with students using reader response questions and prompts: What do you think our town or city looked like over time?

Students could work in cooperative learning groups, each taking a different era to study and creating a timeline of their own city or of a region of the world that they were studying. They could also construct different types of timelines appropriate for this age group, such as a computer generated timeline or a living history timeline with students acting, speaking, and dressing as the historical part.

After studying past historical events in any era, students could work in groups and project possible future events on a timeline with an explanation based on real events that have occurred in the past. Different students or groups with differing views of the future could debate and present a rationale for why they made the predictions they did and why they believe their predictions to be more valid than another group.

Books

Adams, S., & Plantagenet, S. F. (2004). *History of the world.* New York: DK Children.

Chisholm, J. (2003). *Timelines of world history.* Tulsa, OK: Usborne Books.

Millard, A. (1998). *A street through time.* New York: DK Children.

Millard, A. (2006). *A port through time.* New York: DK Children.

Steele, P. (2004). *A city through time.* New York: DK Children.

ENGLISH LEARNERS

The context-embedded instruction that is so important for English learners to succeed can be achieved with personal timelines. Students draw on their own life experiences and that of their families as they construct this type of timeline. The timeline itself provides visual support, which is also important in the instruction of students learning English; teachers can use illustrations to clarify timeline content and students can illustrate their own timelines. Students can work in pairs, providing support through cooperative learning as well. Another ELD strategy is to use props, realia, and artifacts, which could be included in a table top timeline.

STRUGGLING STUDENTS

Construct a timeline frame for struggling students and use templates for gathering information that will be placed on a personal timeline. Model a template on a piece of chart paper using one student as an example, and then each student could complete their own template: "In _____ I _____" completing one for each year of the timeline. The year and event could be transferred to a timeline with intervals for each year.

ASSESSMENT

Authentic assessment of timelines could include a guideline for the elements expected in each timeline, which could also serve as a self-editing checklist for students as they produce the timeline. Elements on the timeline would vary depending on the age, developmental level, varying needs and abilities of the students, and the area of social studies for which the timeline was constructed.

RESOURCES

Marsh, C. (2003). *Terrific timeline tools for teachers.* Peachtree, GA: Gallopade.

REFERENCES

Alleman, J., & Brophy, J. (2003). History is alive: Teaching young children about changes over time. *Social Studies, 94*(3), 107–111.

Barton, K. C. (1997). History—it can be elementary: An overview of elementary students' understanding of history. *Social Education, 61,* 13–16.

Barton, K. C. (2002). "Oh, that's a tricky piece!" Children, mediated action, and the tools of historical time. *Elementary School Journal, 103,* 161–185.

Barton, K. C. (2008). Research on students' ideas about history. In L. S. Levstik & C. A. Tyson (Eds.), *Handbook of research on social studies teaching and learning* (pp. 239–258). New York: Routledge.

Barton, K. C., & Levstik, L. S. (1996). "Back when God was around and everything": Elementary children's understanding of historical time. *American Educational Research Journal, 33,* 419–454.

Barton, K. C., & Levstik, L. S. (1998). "It wasn't a good part of history": Ambiguity and identity in middle grade students' judgments of historical significance. *Teachers College Record, 99,* 478–513.

Downey, M. T., & Levstik, L. S. (2008). Teaching and learning history. In L. S. Levstik & C. A. Tyson (Eds.), *Handbook of research on social studies teaching and learning* (pp. 400–410). New York: Routledge.

Haas, M. (2000). A street through time used with powerful instructional strategies. *Social Studies and the Young Learner, 13*(2), 20–23.

Harnett, P. (1993). Identifying progression in children's understanding: The use of visual materials to assess primary school children's learning in history. *Cambridge Journal of Education, 23,* 137–154.

Hoodless, P. A. (2002). An investigation into children's developing awareness of time and chronology in story. *Journal of Curriculum Studies, 34,* 173–200.

Lee, P. (2004). "Walking backwards into tomorrow": Historical consciousness and understanding of history. *International Journal of Historical Learning, Teaching and Research, 4*(1), 226–234.

Levstik, L. (1991). Teaching history: A definitional and developmental dilemma. In V. A. Atwood (Ed.), *Elementary school social studies: Research as a guide to practice* (pp. 68–84). Washington, DC: National Council for the Social Studies.

Lynn, S. (1993). Children reading pictures: History visuals at key stages 1 and 2. *Education, 3–13, 21*(3), 23–29.

Masterman, E., & Rogers, Y. (2002). A framework for designing interactive multimedia to scaffold young children's understanding of historical chronology. *Instructional Science, 30,* 221–241.

Yeager, E. A., & Terzian, S. (2007). "That's when we became a nation": Urban Latino adolescents and the designation of historical significance. *Urban Education 42,* 52–81.

Strategy 12

Oral History

The students in the 8th-grade social studies class had all done a family oral history project where they interviewed family members. The teacher asked each one to share the most interesting thing they learned about their family. Phillip shared that in 1937, when his father's grandfather was 13 years old, there was a terrible famine in Fizhou on mainland China so the boy was put on a boat with his little sister, who was 11. They were told to get off when they reached Singapore and look for relatives. When the boat docked, they got off. It was not Singapore, however; it was Taipei on the island of Taiwan. The boat left, and the children stayed and had to fend for themselves. Phillip told the class that one of his goals was to learn Chinese so that he could learn more about his heritage from his family in Taiwan.

RATIONALE

Oral history is a method to learn about past events from the spoken stories of people who lived through them. When students conduct oral history research with members of their families or community they are participating in what John Dewey (1938) called *active learning,* which could move to a "more objective intellectual scene of organization" (p. 82) rooted in the student's own experience. Students are actively engaged in collecting data when they do oral histories. Not only are they learning history, they are learning to be historians.

Engaging students in historical research should begin with students exploring their own personal, family, or local history (Leigh & Reynolds, 1997; Schwartz, 2000). Students can do this by interviewing family and community members and creating oral histories—a type of primary source material in the study of history.

Other source materials to use with oral histories could be physical artifacts such as photographs, journals, documents, and other materials that the subject of an oral history could provide (Barton, 2001; Field, Labbo, Willhem, & Garret, 1996: Hickey, 1997). There are a variety of ways to use primary sources such as oral histories, documents, photographs, and artifacts in social studies education, but teachers should be mindful of using these in constructive and meaningful ways (Barton, 2005).

Source: From Expectation of excellence: Curriculum standards for the social studies, by the National Council for the Social Studies, 1994. Washington, DC: Author.

> ### Social Studies Standards
>
> Strand 2: Time, Continuity, and Change
> Strand 4: Individual Development and Identity
> Strand 5: Individuals, Groups, and Institutions

STRATEGY

Introduce oral histories by reading literature that is on a social studies topic to be explored, such as grandparents for young children, or that models the use of oral histories as a data collection method. Discuss the books using reader response questions and prompts: "What did you find most interesting about the person's life or what they said? What would you ask this person if you were interviewing them? What else would you like to know about them? Who might you want to interview to do an oral history?"

Choose a topic for oral histories that is related to an area of study in social studies and is developmentally appropriate for the grade level of students. In some cases, the people who are telling their life story may be the same, but the topic would be different. For example, 2nd-grade students might be focusing on learning about grandparents and family heritage, and they could interview their grandparents. Students in 5th grade might be studying U.S. history and interviewing those same grandparents about their related experiences or memories of events. For students in 5th grade today, a grandparent might be interviewed about the Vietnam War or the Civil Rights Movement.

Help students plan ways to gather information through oral histories. Cocreate questionnaires and surveys. Have students plan and practice interview techniques and make decisions about whether to use an audio or video recorder, take written notes, or, in the case of young children who may not be writing themselves, ask the person interviewed to write comments on a survey. In some cases, the oral history interview could be less structured and take the form of a conversation beginning with open questions in semi-structured interviews, followed by more structured follow-up questions. Permission to use the oral histories should be given by the interviewee.

Offer students options for communicating what they have found:

- Written reports summarizing the oral history

- Q&A Reports: Turning the questions with answers into statements

- A poster about the person

- Role playing the person interviewed

- Inviting the person interviewed as a guest speaker

- PowerPoint presentation using video clips of the interview

- Scriptwriting: Write a script using the words of the interviewee and dramatize it

The final oral history project may also incorporate photographs, letters, and artifacts, or copies of these used with the interviewee's permission.

GRADE-LEVEL MODIFICATIONS

K–2ND GRADE

Young students can be introduced to the strategy of oral histories by interviewing family members. In many states, a primary grade social studies focus is on grandparents. By interviewing grandparents, or interviewing other family members about grandparents if they cannot be interviewed, young children learn about their historical and cultural heritage, their families, and themselves.

Introduce a study of grandparents by reading the Caldecott Award-winning book *Grandfather's Journey* by Allen Say (1994), a beautifully illustrated account of the author-illustrator's grandfather's journey from Japan to the United States and back again over the course of his lifetime. The story continued with the author's father as a child and then the author himself. Allen Say learned about his family and Japanese heritage from stories told by his father and grandfather. Use reader response questions and prompts to discuss the book and lead into using the strategy of oral history with the class: What do you think was the most interesting thing about Grandfather's journey? What do you know about your own grandparents? What questions would you like to ask them about their lives?

Record a list of questions suggested by students, discuss the list, suggest questions related to the social studies standards, and decide on a set of questions that all students can either ask their grandparents or ask their family about their grandparents. Use the questions on a form with space for answers and make a copy for each student.

Model asking the questions for students, and let them practice asking the questions in pairs. Write a memo to parents about the oral history project on grandparents and send home a form with the questions developed in class. Attach a permission form.

When students have interviewed a grandparent, or another family member about a grandparent, give students a writing frame that turns the question format into statements so that they can write a Q&A Report on their grandparents.

Q&A Oral History Report

Questions

When were you born?

Where were you born?

What was it like when you were a child my age?

What are the most important things that have happened to you?

Answers

I was born on _____ in _____. When I was a child your age
I _____.

The most important things that have happened to me are _____
_____
_____.

Books

Ackerman, K. (1988). *Song and dance man.* New York: Knopf.

De Paola, T. (1978). *Nana upstairs and nana downstairs.* New York: Penguin.

Miller, M. (1987). *My grandmother's cookie jar.* Los Angeles: Price Stern Sloan.

Say, A. (1994). *Grandfather's journey.* New York: Houghton Mifflin.

Schwarz, A. (1978). *When I grew up long ago: Older people talk about the days when they were young.* New York: J. B. Lippincott.

3rd Grade–5th Grade

Read excerpts from *Remember Pearl Harbor: Japanese and American Survivors Tell Their Stories* (Allen, 2003) and lead a discussion using reader response questions and prompts: Which story interested you the most? What other events would you like to learn more about?

With students, plan an oral history project related to a period of modern history they are learning about, or they can identify any number of people who might participate in an oral history project and provide a first-hand account of past key historical events. Students can reach beyond the family or community for oral histories they would like to conduct. Notify other teachers in the school about an area of interest, or students can search online for participants (e.g., members of historical societies, veterans' organizations, city officials, or advocacy organizations). With supervision, they can arrange telephone interviews with people they want to interview but cannot meet face to face. Students can use eye to eye technology, e-mail, and so on.

Put together a text set of books that model the use of oral histories as they pertain to modern American and world history.

Books

Allen, N. (2003). *Remember Pearl Harbor: Japanese and American survivors tell their stories.* Washington, DC: National Geographic Society.

Bruchac, J. (1999). *Lasting echoes: An oral history of Native American people.* New York: Harper Trophy.

Denenberg, B. (1995). *Voices from Vietnam.* New York: Scholastic.

Drez, R. J. (2004). *Remember D-Day: Both sides tell their stories.* Washington, DC: National Geographic Children's Books.

Marsh, C. (1990). *Out of the mouths of slaves: African American oral history.* Peachtree City: Gallopade International.

Nicholson, D. M. (2005). *Remember World War II: Kids who survived tell their stories.* Washington, DC: National Geographic Children's Books.

Nieuwsma, M. J. (1998). *Kinderlager: An oral history of young Holocaust survivors.* New York: Holiday House.

6th Grade–8th Grade

Students in Grades 6 through 8 often study their own family heritages, including the immigration of their family to this country, even if it took place long before they were born. Family members today can be interviewed about family members in the past. Family stories are often passed down from generation to generation.

Introduce the idea of studying family heritage and immigration by reading examples of oral histories from *I Was Dreaming to Come to America: Memories From the Ellis Island Oral History Project* (Lawlor, 1997). Discuss using reader response questions and prompts: What do you know about when your own family came to America? What would you like to know about that period and what happened to them? Brainstorm ideas for topics and questions to ask, and create a guide for students to follow when interviewing family members.

Books

Atkins, S. B. (1993). *Voices from the fields: Children of migrant farm workers tell their stories.* Boston: Little, Brown & Company.

Bode, J. (1991). *New kids in town: Oral histories of immigrant teens.* New York: Scholastic.

Bode, J. (2000). *The colors of freedom: Immigrant stories.* London: Franklin Watts.

Harlan Rowe Junior High. (2008). *Everyday heroes: Biographies and memoirs from the Athens area school district eighth grade oral history project.* Bloomington, IN: Pen & Publish.

Lawlor, V. (1997). *I was dreaming to come to America: Memories from the Ellis Island oral history project.* New York: Viking.

Weinberger, K. (2000). *Journey to a new land: An oral history.* New York: Mondo Publishing.

ENGLISH LEARNERS

Oral histories are an effective strategy for learning social studies because they can tap into students' prior knowledge and increase home–school connections often cited as lacking among ELs. English learners can also use two languages: the home language for interviewing family members and English for writing the results of an oral history to share with other members of the class.

STRUGGLING STUDENTS

Scaffold learning for struggling students with writing frames and templates, modeling, and cooperative learning. Use the Q&A Report format, turning questions they ask into statements as they write up the report of what they discovered from the interview. Model asking questions with students and then reverse roles so the students can practice asking the teacher questions. Students can work in pairs to practice the interview.

ASSESSMENT

Combine a guideline for conducting an oral history with a cover sheet checklist that has a description of the step in conducting an oral history, the date it was completed, and space for a student to comment for self-reflection and evaluation.

RESOURCES

Hazareesingh, S. (1994). *Speaking about the past: Oral history.* Staffordshire, England: Trentham Books.

REFERENCES

Barton, K. (2001). A picture's worth: Analyzing historical photographs in the elementary grades. *Social Education, 65,* 278–283.

Barton, K. (2005). Primary sources in history: Breaking through the myths. *Phi Delta Kappan, 86,* 745–753.

Dewey, J. (1938). *Experience and education.* New York: Macmillan.

Field, S., Labbo, L., Willhem, R., & Garrett, A. (1996). To touch, to feel, to see: Artifact inquiry in the social studies classroom. *Social Education, 60,* 141–143.

Hickey, M. G. (1997). Bloomers, bellbottoms, and hula hoops: Artifact collections aid children's historical interpretation. *Social Education, 61,* 293–299.

Leigh, A., & Reynolds, C. (1997). Little windows to the past. *Social Education, 61,* 45–47.

Schwartz, S. (2000). My family's story: Discovering history at home. *Social Studies and the Young Learner, 12*(3), 6–9.

Data Charts

After reading and learning about marine life in school, an 8th-grade class in California took a field trip to Sea World. They interviewed trainers there to collect data about the food budget for the animals and made a data chart, Figure 13.1.

Figure 13.1	8th-grade student's data chart: Animal food consumption and budgeting

Animal food consumption and Budgeting

Animal Food %	Average weight of Adult in kilograms	X 2.2 = average weight in pounds	X average % of body weight eaten per day	= pounds/day total food into pounds	% of each food type = pounds/day each	X cost of each food type	= cost per food type	total cost per animal per day	individual pounds/week	individual pounds/month	individual pounds/year	X number of animals equals	total lbs/day	total lbs/week	total lbs/month	total lbs/year
Killer Whale	340.2	748.4	.35	262				90.40	1834 lb	7702 lb	95368 lb	6	1572 lb	11004 lb	46212 lb	572208 lb
Mackerel 10%					26	$.30	7.80									
Smelt 30%					79	.35	27.65	$632.80	$2657.76	$32916			$5424.00	$37,980.0	$159,448	$1,974,96
Herring 50%					131	.35	45.85									
Squid 10%					26	.35	9.10									
Bottlenose Dolphin	215.5	474	.5	24.1				8.27	168 lb	706 lb	8736 lb	10	240 lb	1688 lb	7060 lb	87360 lb
Mackerel 5%					1.2	$.30	.36									
Smelt 60%					14	.35	4.40	$57.84	$243.14	$3016		$82.70	$578.90	$2431.40	$30,160.00
Herring 20%					5	.35	1.75									
Squid 15%					3.6	.35	1.26									
Sea Lions	225	495	.65	32				10.95	224 lb	941 lb	11648 lb	19	608 lb	4056 lb	17879 lb	221312 lb
Mackerel 20%					6.4	.30	1.92									
Smelt 20%					6.4	.35	2.24	$76.65	$321.93	$4004		$208	$1456.35	$6118	$76076
Herring 40%					13	.35	4.55									
Squid 20%					6.4	.35	2.24									
Sand tiger Sharks	100	220	.7	1.5				1.21	10.5 lb	44 lb	596 lb	6	9 lb	63 lb	264 lb	3276 lb
Ladyfish 50%					.75	.80	.60									
Blue Runner 50%					.75	.81	.61	$8.47	$35.57	$442		$7.26	$50.82	$213.00	$2652.00
Emperor Penguin	3.11	7.48	.55	4				1.44	28 lb	118 lb	1436 lb	8	32 lb	229 lb	944 lb	11648 lb
Herring 80%					3.2	.35	1.12									
Sardines 20%					.8	.40	.32	$10.8	$45.36	$572		$11.52	$86.40	$363	$4576.00
Sea Otter	31.5	69.3	.25	17				34.50	119 lb	500 lb	26000 lb	5	85 lb	596 lb	2500 lb	30000 lb
Shrimp 30%					5.1	3.50	17.85									
Clams 55%					9	1.50	13.50	$241.50	$1014.30	$12584		$172.50	$1208.00	$5070.00	$63,420.00
Crabs 10%					1.7	1.15	1.96									
Sea Urchins 5%					.85	1.40	1.19									
park totals
total pounds													2646 lb	17823 lb	74859 lb	1035288 lb
total cost													$1024.38	7173	$30143	$2,741,880.00

RATIONALE

Data charts, surveys, and graphs are tools students can use to practice some of the many methodological tools of a social scientist doing research: observing, recording, describing, defining, measuring, estimating, classifying, comparing and contrasting, gathering and processing data, communicating, analyzing, synthesizing, hypothesizing, predicting, generalizing, evaluating, and verifying (Christensen & James, 2001).

Teachers can use data charts along with literature as part of an investigation of a question, problem, or hypothesis or to compare and contrast differing points of view on a topic in the social studies. Data charts, surveys, and graphs can be useful when exploring economics education. Research has shown that young children's thinking about economics follows stages similar to Piaget's description of their cognitive development (Brophy & Alleman, 2002; Diez-Martinez & Ochoa, 2003) and that their understanding of economics can be improved through focused, direct instruction (Gretes, Piel, & Queen, 1991; Sosin, Dick, & Reister, 1997). Not only are data charts a way to gather and organize information, they are also an alternative to using a written report to present and communicate information to others.

Economics educators have recommended children's literature to teach economic principles and concepts (Kehler, 1998; Suiter & Meszaros, 2005; VanFossen, 2003). Beginning with an experience with literature to contextualize or model the use of data charts, teachers can use them with students to collect and display information on the production, distribution, and consumption of goods and services and to engage students in economic activities and decision making. Discussions about planning, creating, completing, and analyzing a data chart can lead to understanding of principles of economics based on students' own experiences (Laney, 2001; Laney & Schug, 1998).

Source: From Expectation of excellence: Curriculum standards for the social studies, by the National Council for the Social Studies, 1994. Washington, DC: Author.

Social Studies Standards

Strand 7: Production, Distribution, and Consumption
Strand 8: Science, Technology, and Society

STRATEGY

Literature can be used to introduce a question or hypothesis in an area of social studies, such as economics. Students can then gather and analyze data and suggest answers to the question or a solution for the hypothesis.

Record students' ideas on a graphic organizer cluster and then use those ideas to identify the key ideas and questions students will answer. In this way, data charts can be created by the teacher or cocreated with students for students to do research in books or online, or students can survey and gather data to place in the chart to address the question. The question can be combined with a survey that will chart the related experience of the students or others or the differences in students' interpretations, conclusions, or opinions.

Students can retrieve data and it can be entered on a chart for the whole class. This class chart can be the end product or serve to model data retrieval and entry on a chart for subsequent activities. Students can do data charts in groups or on their own. Individual student's data charts can be combined to get a bigger picture of data collection in answer to a question.

Data charts can be used with any subject if students need to collect, organize, classify, analyze, and interpret information. They are an excellent strategy for not only inquiry learning based on student research but for displaying and communicating what has been learned. Data charts can take different forms to collect and display information in different ways: tables with multiple columns and rows, pie charts, T-charts, and so on.

Plus Technology

Students can search online to find data to use in data charts. Students can also create charts of the production, distribution, and consumption of goods and services using Word (e.g., box charts, pie charts, graphs, and other ways of displaying comparisons). Other technology tools to use are online surveys and spread sheets on Excel.

For more on economics education, the National Council of Economics Education (NCEE) has published more than 400 Internet-based lessons at its *EconEdLink* site (http://econedlink.org/).

GRADE-LEVEL MODIFICATIONS

K–2ND GRADE

Read aloud Anne Rockwell's (2004) *Four Seasons Make a Year*, in which a young girl shares her experience of each of the seasons of the year. Lead a discussion asking reader response questions and prompts: Which was your favorite season? What do you like about that season?

Record student ideas on a cluster graphic organizer and use these ideas to begin a data chart on the four seasons. With students, cocreate a data chart from their ideas, and add categories they think are appropriate for their grade and class. After reading more books on the seasons and calendar, and after discussions about each season, students can classify ideas from the books and their own experience on the data chart.

Data Chart for the Four Seasons				
Season	*Winter*	*Spring*	*Summer*	*Fall*
Temperature				
Weather				
Holidays				
Play				
Sports				

Introduce the idea of a survey of consumer choices and costs related to the seasons. After reviewing the data chart on the four seasons, develop questions that can be answered on a survey form. For example, (1) What is one thing you would buy in each season? (2) How much would each thing cost? The survey can be completed in class by the students, but it could also be expanded to other classes, the school, home, and the community.

Survey on Consumer Goods by Season

In fall I would buy: _____

It would cost: _____

In spring I would buy: _____

It would cost: _____

In summer I would buy: _____

It would cost: _____

Add two more rows to the data chart on the four seasons: what people buy, and what these things would cost. Students could find out what time of year they would spend the most. They could also survey other students in the school, teachers, and family and community members. Data from completed surveys could be collapsed, analyzed, and displayed using another data chart or graph to see what time of the year Americans spend the most on consumer goods.

Books

Adams, B. J. (1992). *The go-around dollar.* New York: Simon & Schuster.

Gibbons, G. (1988). *The seasons of Arnold's apple tree.* San Anselmo, CA: Sandpiper.

Gibbons, G. (1996). *The reason for seasons.* New York: Holiday House.

Maestro, B. (1993). *The story of money.* New York: Clarion Books.

Rockwell, A. (2004). *Four seasons make a year.* New York: Walker Books.

Viorst, J. (2009). *Alexander, who used to be rich last Sunday.* New York: Atheneum.

Zimelman, N. (1992). *How the second grade got $8,205.50 to visit the Statue of Liberty.* Morton Grove, IL: Albert Whitman & Co.

3rd Grade–5th Grade

Use literature to introduce the concept that investing in the stock market means you can buy stock in a company and be a part owner—and make or lose money, depending on how well the company performs and the ups and downs of the stock market. Read and discuss *A Kid's Guide to Stock Market Investing* (Orr, 2008). Ask reader response questions: What would you do if you invested in the stock market?

Students can begin to play the stock market, individually or in teams. The class can decide how long they will play, but it should be a minimum of two weeks. To build a stock portfolio, students can pretend they have $100,000 to invest in the stock market. They can read the newspaper or go online to look at the listings of companies on the New York Stock Exchange (NYSE) or American Stock Exchange (AMEX OR ASE) and choose five companies whose stocks they would like to buy. The class, group, or individual students can create a Stock Purchase Chart, Figure 13.2, and write down the closing prices listed in the newspaper or online. Convert the prices to dollar amounts by using the conversion chart, Figure 13.3.

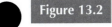

Figure 13.2   Stock purchase chart

Example:

Stock name						
Closing price						
Number of shares purchased	100					
Total value of shares						

_____ Total value of investment

Figure 13.3   Conversion chart

(Fractions into dollar amounts)

1/8 = .13	5/8 = .63
1/4 = .25	3/4 = .75
3/8 = .38	7/8 = .88
1/2 = .50	

(Example: If a stock is listed as 50 1/4, its value is $50.25)

Next, students can chart the progress of each stock using the newspaper. They can record the gains or losses for each stock and write down the closing prices for the day on a Stock Activity Chart, Figure 13.4.

Figure 13.4   Stock activity chart: Gains or losses and closing price

Stocks	Day 1	Day 2	Day 3	Day 4	Day 5	Day 6	Day 7	Day 8	Day 9	Day 10

On the final day of the project, students can sell their stock and calculate how much money they would have made or lost. They could record this on a gain/loss chart, Figure 13.5. They would complete the chart by writing down their initial investment for each stock and comparing it to the present market value. They can determine whether or not their initial investment of $100,000 grew or declined.

| Figure 13.5 | Gain/loss chart |

Stocks						
Closing price, Day 10						
Number of shares owned						
Present market value						
Initial value						
Gain/loss (+ or –)						

_____ Total gain/loss

Students can continue this project and build a class portfolio of stock individually or in groups, graph the ups and downs of the stock market each day, or research the companies whose stocks they have chosen.

Plus Technology

Students charting data on the stock market could learn to use Excel or Word and develop a spread sheet with the information they are using.

Books

Bateman, K. R. (2008). *The young investor: Projects and activities for making your money grow.* Chicago: Chicago Review Press.

Fuller, D. J. (2006). *The stock market.* Minneapolis, MN: Lerner Classroom.

Orr, T. (2008). *A kid's guide to stock market investing.* Hockessin, DE: Mitchell Lane.

Zuravicky, O. (2005). *The stock market: Understanding and applying ratios, decimals, fractions, and percentages.* New York: PowerKids Press.

6TH GRADE–8TH GRADE

Students can learn about today's economic and financial situation relative to the past and make predictions for the future. Read *Six Days in October: The Stock Market Crash of 1929* (Blumenthal, 2002) with students and discuss it using reader response questions and prompts: What do you know about your family during the Depression? How do you think you would have felt during that time? How are things that are happening during the current recession affecting you?

Students can read and research further on the Depression and compare it to the current recession. Organize classes into groups using a jigsaw cooperative learning strategy, with each group finding information on a piece of the puzzle of the Depression of the 1930s and the great recession of the 2000s.

Figure 13.6	Comparison chart

	The Great Depression 1930s	The Great Recession 2000s
U.S. and world events		
Causes		
Effects		
Recovery		
Other interesting facts		

Each group could also be responsible for discovering the different aspects associated with each of the broad topics on the chart, Figure 13.6. For example, a group researching Effects could look at the effects on the stock market and employment among different groups of Americans, such as city dwellers, farmers, the rich, middle class, poor, or members of different political parties. This information can be used to expand the range of the chart.

Students can present their information, compare and contrast these two periods of economic downturn along a continuum of different aspects, and make predictions about the future of the economy based on what they have learned about the past.

Books

Blumenthal, K. (2002). *Six days in October: The stock market crash of 1929.* New York: Atheneum.

Cooper, M. L. (2004). *Dust to eat: Drought and depression in the 1930s.* New York: Clarion.

Freedman, R. (2005). *Children of the depression.* New York: Clarion.

Gow, M. (2003). *The stock market crash of 1929: Dawn of the great depression.* Berkeley Heights, NJ: Enslow Publishers.

Hesse, K. (1999). *Out of the dust.* New York: Scholastic.

Lied, K. (2002). *Potato: A tale from the Great Depression.* Washington, DC: National Geographic Children's Books.

Moss, M. (2003). *Rose's journal: The story of a girl in the great depression.* San Anselmo, CA: Sandpiper.

Stanley, J. (1993). *Children of the dustbowl: The true story of the school at weedpatch camp.* New York: Crown Books.

ENGLISH LEARNERS

Charts provide a visual display of information that is an important English language development strategy. The student-student interaction in the group work activities associated with charts can scaffold learning for English learners. Presenting information learned on a chart is also a meaningful alternative to writing a more lengthy report to gather and present information for students still emerging into English literacy, as well as speaking. The use of universal numbers on some charts can provide more comprehensible input for students as well.

STRUGGLING STUDENTS

Model the use of charts with the class or a group, and each student can have an individual copy of the chart and copy the group information onto his or her own chart. Students can work in teams of mixed ability levels and use cooperative learning strategies such as the jigsaw strategy to fully participate in an activity.

ASSESSMENT

Students can create a work portfolio of data charts they have created individually, in groups, or with the class. With the teacher or on their own, they can self-evaluate their work with data charts using a form answering questions such as the following: (1) What question did I answer? (2) What data did I gather to answer it? (3) How did I classify and organize the data? (4) What did I learn?

Students could also be assessed as they use data charts to present the information they have gathered and discuss what they have learned.

RESOURCES

Kellett, M. (2005). *How to develop children as researchers.* Thousand Oaks, CA: Sage.

REFERENCES

Brophy, J., & Alleman, J. (2002). Primary-grade students' knowledge and thinking about the economics of meeting families' shelter needs. *American Educational Research Journal, 39*(2), 423–468.

Christensen, P., & James, A. (Eds.). (2001). *Research with children: Perspectives and practices.* London: Routledge Falmer.

Diez-Martinez, E., & Ochoa, A. (2003). Mexican children's and adolescent's development of occupational hierarchy related to consumption and saving. *Children's Social and Economic Education, 5*(3), 148–163.

Gretes, J., Piel, J., & Queen, J. A. (1991). Teaching economic concepts to fifth graders: The power of simulations. *Social Science Record, 28*(2), 71–83.

Kehler, A. (1998). Capturing the "economic imagination": A treasury of children's books to meet content standards. *Social Studies and the Young Learner, 11*(2), 26–29.

Laney, J. (2001). Enhancing economic education through improved teaching methods: Common sense made easy. In J. Brophy (Ed.), *Subject-specific instructional methods and activities* (pp. 411–435). New York: Elsevier Science.

Laney, J., & Schug, M. (1998). Teach kids economics and they will learn. *Social Studies and the Young Learner, 11*(2), 13–17.

Sosin, K., Dick, J., & Reiser, M. L. (1997). Determinants of achievement of economics concepts by elementary school students. *Journal of Economics Education, 28*(2), 100–121.

Suiter, M., & Meszaros, B. (2005). Teaching about saving and investing in the elementary and middle school grades. *Social Education, 69,* 92–95.

VanFossen, P. (2003). Best practice economic education for young children? It's elementary! *Social Education, 67,* 90–94.

Strategy 14

Multiple Perspectives Jigsaw

A 3rd-grade teacher provided books on multiple perspectives on the first people in the Americas and Columbus for students to read in groups. One group read the book *Encounter* (Yolen, 1992), written from the perspective of the Taino people who lived on the island of San Salvador when Columbus landed there in October 1492. The group shared what they learned with groups reading about Columbus from other perspectives: "It's a sad story. Columbus took the Taino people as slaves to Spain. Many died. Only one survived in the story. He was little. A child. He was sad because he had his people and his land taken away."

RATIONALE

An inquiry approach to learning encourages students to think about multiple perspectives on what really happened in history (Banks et al., 2005). There are often multiple perspectives on controversial issues or beliefs about people, events, and movements, and students can consider the differences among these as they learn to analyze, compare and contrast, interpret, and generalize from among them. However, students may often overlook the diverse experiences and perspectives of people at any given point in history, thinking that each period is characterized by a single group of people (Barton, 1996).

However, when multiple perspectives and human diversity are emphasized in teaching approaches and student activities, studies have shown that students achieve a better understanding of how human experience and perspectives differed both within and among groups of people in the past (Barton, 2001; Brophy, 1999; Grant, 2001). When multiple historical sources are used, students learn to compare and contrast and critically evaluate these sources (Britt & Aglinskas, 2002; Stahl, Britton, Hynd, McNish, & Bosquet, 1996). Using multiple sources and examining multiple perspectives in historical inquiry in more open-ended classroom contexts, students also demonstrate a high level of engagement and a greater enjoyment of the study of history (Brush & Saye, 2001).

This way of approaching social studies forms a natural fit with cooperative learning strategies such as the jigsaw strategy, where students work in groups looking at different perspectives or pieces of a puzzle (Aronson, 1997). Research on cooperative learning, which can be accomplished using a strategy like looking at multiple perspectives through literature and social studies instruction, shows the following results: higher achievement and better retention of information, growth in moral and cognitive reasoning, enhanced motivation to learn, enhanced self-esteem, and an improved attitude toward school, school subjects, teachers, and other students (Qin, Johnson, & Johnson, 1995).

STRATEGY

Literature can be used to introduce a social studies concept or issue about which there may be conflicting views. One book may present more than one perspective, or it may present a perspective that is not commonly known or accepted. A text set of several books with different information on the same topic from different perspectives can be kept in the classroom.

Choose and read aloud books on a controversial historical issue or real-life problem for students to solve and discuss the book using reader response questions and prompts: "The book shows differing points of view. What did you think of each one?"

Students can research, discuss, and compare and contrast differing accounts of historical events. They can also identify the reliability of the source of information, whether primary or secondary. Students can learn about and also present what they have learned about multiple perspectives in several interesting ways, such as data charts, debates, curriculum drama, and reader's theatre, which can showcase and highlight differences.

The jigsaw cooperative learning strategy can also be used. Students in small groups can work on a different piece of the problem, or puzzle to be solved, each taking responsibility for a different part. The same issue and chart can be used for all groups, and they can compare what they found with other groups. Or each group can take a different piece of the puzzle if the issue or problem is broad enough. Students can work together toward a common goal while each has individual responsibilities within a group to achieve the goal. Students in groups of three to five students each take responsibility for finding out about one of the multiple perspectives that can exist, each one a piece of the jigsaw puzzle. Students work independently on their piece, but work toward the goal of the whole group.

Use a poster or whiteboard to display a large data chart, and each student and group can use a smaller version to begin collecting data. As data is filled in, more questions may arise in a group, and they can be added to the data chart as well.

GRADE-LEVEL MODIFICATIONS

K–2ND GRADE

Help young students take an inquiry approach to history or issues by questioning commonly held assumptions that are often taught as unquestionable facts. For example, October 12 is Columbus Day, and there is no doubt that his voyage to the Americas was important for Europe in the 15th century. However, not only was Columbus not the first European to sail to North America, Europeans were not the first people in the Americas.

Begin an inquiry and ask: Who discovered America? Make a list of student responses. Over several periods, read aloud *The Discovery of the Americas: From Prehistory Through the Age of Columbus* (Maestro & Maestro, 1992), a picture book introduction to new world exploration that avoids the traditional Eurocentric approach. The authors combine maps, illustrations, tables, and notes along, with accessible writing, for younger students. They begin with what is known of people crossing the Bering Land Bridge over 20,000 years ago from Asia, possible visits by Phoenician and Japanese seafarers, early civilizations such as the Maya and Inca, the fairly well-documented Viking settlements, and many explorers, including Columbus. As you read each section of the book, add names of people who came to America to the list. Make a large class chart to compare and contrast each person or people on the list.

Who Discovered America?				
	When	*How*	*Facts to Support*	*What We Know About Them*
Land Bridge				
Maya and Inca				
Chinese				
Vikings				
Europeans				

Use the jigsaw cooperative learning technique. Begin by forming small groups. Give each student in the group a form to record information on the person or people they are learning about, using the headings of the class chart: When, How, Facts to Support, All About Them, What We Know About Them. Rotate and meet with each group, read aloud books on the person or people, and discuss the books; students can record information on their chart or dictate their responses to others. While you are with one group, the other groups can read, discuss, and take notes on their own.

Each group can report to the whole class what they learned about a person or people, each adding their piece to the jigsaw puzzle. Students can use other strategies to continue comparing and contrasting what they learn in answer to the question, Who discovered America?: for example, a timeline showing when each group came to America, a world map showing where they came from and how they got to the Americas, or a curriculum drama to act out scenes showing what might have happened with each group. Here are more books and a sample text set on Vikings.

Books

Freedman, R. (2007). *Who was first? Discovering the Americas.* New York: Clarion.

Hart, A. (2001). *Who really discovered America: Unraveling the mystery and solving the puzzle.* Charlotte, VT: Williamson Publishing.

Maestro, B., & Maestro, G. (1992). *The discovery of the Americas: From prehistory through the age of Columbus.* New York: Harper Collins.

Wulffson, D. (2007). *Before Columbus: Early voyages to the Americas.* Breckenridge, CO: Twenty-First Century Books.

Vikings

Chisholm, J., Roxbee, P., & Reid, S. (2002). *Who were the Vikings?* Tulsa, OK: E.D.C. Publishing.

D'Aulaire, I., & D'Aulaire, E. P. (1994). *Leif the Lucky.* San Luis Obispo, CA: Beautiful Feet Press.

Langley, A. (2000). *You wouldn't want to be a Viking explorer.* Danbury, CT: Children's Press.

Schachnen, J. (2002). *Yo, Vikings!* New York: Dutton.

Sciezka, J. (2004). *Viking it and liking it.* New York: Viking/Puffin. (Time Warp Series).

Wargin, K. (2003). *V is for Viking.* Chelsea, MI: Sleeping Bear Press.

3rd Grade–5th Grade

Guide students to not only compare and contrast different historical perspectives in books, but to examine the sources of information that support these perspectives, such as relying on either primary or secondary source information. Read *Encounter,* by Jane Yolen (1992). It is an account of Columbus landing in the Americas from the first-person perspective of a Taino person (the native people who lived on the island of San Salvador when Columbus landed there in October of 1492). *Encounter* tells how the Taino people and their culture were devastated as a result of their encounter with Columbus and his men. This offers an alternative perspective from other books about Columbus that students may read, which do not mention what happened to the Taino or report history differently.

Discuss the book using reader response questions and prompts: What did you think of the book? How would you have felt when Columbus landed in San Salvador if you were Taino? Has anything like this ever happened to you?

As you plan to read other books about Columbus, do a mini-lesson on primary and secondary sources of information.

Primary and Secondary Sources of Information

- Primary source
- Secondary source

Read other books about Columbus and the Taino from multiple perspectives, discuss and identify the sources of information that are used as primary or secondary. Create a class chart with each book listed, a description of Columbus and the Taino people, and sources of information as primary or secondary:

Compare and Contrast: Columbus and the Taino people in books

Book	Columbus	Taino people	Primary Source	Secondary Source

The jigsaw cooperative learning strategy can be used by forming small groups. Each group would read and discuss one of the books in the text set to help complete the chart. When completed, the chart can be discussed and each viewpoint analyzed on the basis of using primary or secondary source information and the validity of each viewpoint based on accurate, inaccurate, complete, or incomplete information.

Books

European perspective

D'Aulaire, I., & D'Aulaire, E. P. (1955). *Columbus*. New York: Doubleday.

Dagliesh, A. (1955). *The Columbus story*. New York: Scribner's.

Columbus's perspective

Columbus, C. (1992). *The log of Christopher Columbus, selected by S. Lowe*. New York: Philomel.

Roop, P., & Roop, C. (Eds.). (1990). *I, Columbus: My Journal: 1492–1493*. New York: Avon.

Taino Perspective

Dorris, M. (1992). *Morning Girl*. New York: Hyperion.

Yolen, J. (1992). *Encounter*. New York: Harcourt, Brace, Jovanovich.

6TH GRADE–8TH GRADE

Literature can be used with middle school students to compare and contrast war and conflict throughout American and world history. Issues such as the reasons for a war, from the perspective of each side in the conflict or from differing perspectives on one side, can be researched, analyzed, and discussed using text sets of literature written from the viewpoints of many people.

There are many beautifully illustrated picture books that deal with serious issues and could be read aloud to middle school students to initiate this strategy. Patricia Polacco has mined her own family history for serious and moving books about war, like *Pink and Say* (1994), about the friendship between a white and an African American Union soldier during the Civil War, and *The Butterfly* (2000), about a family that hides a Jewish family from the Nazis during the German occupation of France in World War II. Discuss books like these using reader response questions and prompts: How would you feel if you were the characters in the book? Does the story remind you of anything in your own life or anything that is happening in the world today?

For any period in history that is under study, identify major conflicts and wars. Put together a text set of books in the area that represents multiple perspectives. To use the jigsaw cooperative learning strategy, form the class into groups, each group choosing one perspective of the conflict. Students in each group read, research, and prepare information to add to a class study. Students can present what they have learned in a variety of ways: a class chart, debates, mock news interviews, curriculum drama, or reports written from one perspective. Conflict in the past can be compared to current events, such as the wars in Iraq and Afghanistan.

This strategy could be used for other historical events around which there is controversy or just differing perspectives: for example, the Westward movement from the perspective of the European American pioneers or the Native Americans; the dropping of the atomic bomb on Hiroshima and Nagasaki, Japan, at the end of World War II from the perspective of the Japanese people; Japanese Americans who were interned in America; Japanese American soldiers who fought in Europe; and other Americans.

Students could also seek sources of primary information on historical conflicts and issues (see Strategy 12: Oral History). For example, interview living veterans of foreign wars: the Korean War, Vietnam, the Gulf War, Iraq and Afghanistan, and possibly

World War II. Students would read and research the conflict to prepare interview questions, conduct interviews, take notes or do an audio or video recording and make written transcripts, and make a chart of the perspectives of these living sources of information. They could apply what they have learned about from first person accounts of these conflicts and wars to today's conflicts and wars around the globe, speculate on the future, and suggest actions nations can take to address these conflicts.

Below is a sample text set for multiple perspectives on World War II, organized by the war in America, Japan, and Europe. However, in each of these areas, students will encounter stories told from the multiple perspectives on a war that covered the entire world. An excellent book to introduce World War II and multiple perspectives is *Passage to Freedom: The Sugihara Story* (Mochizuki, 2003). It is the true account of Chiune Sugihara, the Japanese consul in Lithuania in 1940 who saved the lives of hundreds of Polish Jewish refugees by writing visas by hand so they could escape the Nazis, which he did at great risk to himself and his family.

Books

Civil War

Polacco, P. (1994) *Pink and Say*. New York: Scholastic.

World War II

Adams, S. (2007). *World War II*. New York: DK Children.

Ambrose, S. E. (2001). *The good fight: How World War II was won*. New York: Atheneum.

In America:

Colman, P. (1998). *Rosie the Riveter: Women working on the home front in World War II*. New York: Crown.

Cooper, M. L. (2002). *Remembering Manzanar: Life in a Japanese relocation camp*. New York: Clarion.

Fleischman, J. (2007). *Black and white airmen: Their true story*. New York: Houghton Mifflin.

Houston, J., & Houston, J. D. (1983). *Farewell to Manzanar*. New York: Bantam Books.

McKissak, P. C., & McKissak, F. L. (1996). *Red-tail angels: The story of the Tuskegee Airmen of World War II*. New York: Walker Books.

Uchida, Y. (2004). *Journey to Topaz: A story of the Japanese-American evacuation*. Berkeley, CA: Heyday Books.

In Japan:

Coerr, E. (1997). *Sadako*. New York: Putnam.

Coerr, E. (2004). *Sadako and the thousand paper cranes*. New York: Puffin.

Maruki, T. (1982). *Hiroshima no pika*. New York: HarperCollins.

Polmar, N. (2004). *The Enola Gay: The B-29 that dropped the atomic bomb on Hiroshima*. Dulles, VA: Potomac Books.

Spencer, L. (2003). The *war at home: Japan during World War II*. San Diego, CA: Lucent.

Yep, L. (1996). *Hiroshima*. New York: Scholastic.

In Europe:

Borden, L. (2003). *The little ships: The heroic rescue at Dunkirk*. New York: Margaret K. McEdlerry.

Borden, L. (2004). *The greatest skating race: A World War II story*. New York: Margaret K. McEdlerry.

Cooper, M. L. (2000). *Fighting for honor: Japanese Americans and World War II*. New York: Clarion.

Ippisch, H. (1996). *Sky: A true story of resistance during World War II*. New York: Simon & Schuster.

Lowry, L. (1998). *Number the stars*. New York: Houghton Mifflin.

Mochizuki, K. (2003). *Passage to freedom: The Sugihara story*. New York: Lee & Low.

Myers, W. D. (1999). *The journal of Scott Pendleton Collins: A World War II soldier, Normandy, France, 1944*. New York: Scholastic.

Russo, M. (2005). *Always remember me: How one family survived World War II*. New York: Atheneum.

Smith, F. D. (2005). *Elsie's war: A story of courage in Nazi Germany*. London: Frances Lincoln Books.

Smith, F. D. (2008). *My secret camera: Life in the Lodz ghetto*. London: Frances Lincoln Books.

ENGLISH LEARNERS

The jigsaw cooperative learning activity provides English learners with support through student to student interaction. Students working in small groups can assume different roles in the groups. An English learner could be actively listening and responding in non-linguistic ways, such as by drawing a response or illustrating group writing. They also benefit from the small group setting through increased teacher and student interaction because there are fewer students. Take dictation for students, use visuals and graphic organizers to contextualize information, and tap into students' prior knowledge.

For example, many English learners or their families are from areas of the world where America has been at war, or where there has been conflict: former Soviet bloc countries such as East Germany and, more recently, the Ukraine; Southeast Asian countries such as Vietnam and Cambodia; and countries in the Middle East where we are still engaged in war. By tapping into their own prior experience, or asking them to interview family members, students can make a great contribution to comparing and contrasting perspectives on what really happened in history.

STRUGGLING STUDENTS

The use of charts for the whole class, charts for each student, and prepared frames can assist struggling students. A word bank can be included with a chart for each student with words needed to complete it: for example, the names of historical figures or locations they will need (e.g., Christopher Columbus and the Taino).

The jigsaw cooperative learning activity in an inclusive classroom would ensure that struggling students or students with disabilities would interact and learn alongside their more advanced or nondisabled peers.

ASSESSMENT

Authentic assessment could take place with you as a participant or observer in the small groups, noting the level of participation of each student. Student work, such as individual charts, notes on books read, and contributions to reports, could be compiled in a portfolio for each project.

RESOURCES

Johnson, D., & Johnson, R. (2004) *Assessing students in groups: Promoting group responsibility and individual accountability.* Thousand Oaks, CA: Corwin.

Miller, W. (1997). *U. S. history through children's literature: From the Colonial period to World War II.* Denver, CO: Libraries Unlimited.

Miller, W. (1998). *U. S. history through children's literature: Post World War II.* Denver, CO: Libraries Unlimited.

REFERENCES

Aronson, E. (1997). *The jigsaw classroom.* New York: Longman.

Banks, J., Cookson, P., Gay, G., Hawley, W., Irvine, J., Nieto, S., et al. (2005). Education and diversity. *Social Education, 69,* 36–40.

Barton, K. C. (1996). Narrative simplifications in elementary children's historical understanding. In J. Brophy (Ed.), *Advances in research on teaching: Vol. 6. Teaching and learning history* (pp. 51–58). Greenwich, CT: JAI Press.

Barton, K. C. (2001). "You'd be wanting to know about the past": Social contexts of children's historical understanding in Northern Ireland and the United States. *Comparative Education, 37,* 89–106.

Britt, M. A., & Aglinskas, C. (2002). Improving students' ability to identify and use source information. *Cognition and Instruction, 20,* 485–522.

Brophy, J. (1999). Elementary students learn about Native Americans: The development of knowledge and empathy. *Social Education, 63,* 38–45.

Brush, T. A., & Saye, J. W. (2001). The use of embedded scaffolds with hypermedia-supported student-centered learning. *Journal of Educational Multimedia and Hypermedia, 10,* 333–356.

Grant, S. G. (2001). It's just the facts, or is it? The relationship between teachers' practices and students' understandings of history. *Theory and Research in Social Education, 29,* 65–108.

Qin, Z., Johnson, D. W., & Johnson, T. R. (1995). Cooperative versus competitive efforts and problem solving. *Review of Educational Research, 65,* 129–143.

Stahl, S. A., Britton, B. K., Hynd, C., McNIsh, & Bosquet, D. (1996). What happens when students read multiple source documents in history? *Reading Research Quarterly, 31,* 430–456.

Strategy

15

WebQuests

"We're going to go to Japan. Our class. We're going to get there by flying on the Internet."

A kindergarten student describing a WebQuest on
Japan her teacher announced to the class.

RATIONALE

With the recent emphasis on the use of technology in education, various technologically mediated learning experiences have been developed for classroom use that can be combined with literature-based teaching for social studies instruction (Lamb & Teclehaimonot, 2005; Swan & Hofer, 2008; Teclehaimonot & Lamb, 2004). With computer access and technological support, structures such as WebQuests that are designed for inquiry learning using the Internet can be used (Dodge, 1995; March, 2003/2004).

There are many WebQuest sites that provide self-contained modules on elementary and middle school curriculum including social studies content, many of which are literature based (Teclehaimonot & Lamb, 2004). These modules scaffold Internet-based content with an inquiry process resulting in a project for students to complete. Search for and preview already produced WebQuests, including many for young children (VanFossen, 2004): for example, one that leads 3rd-grade students through a day in the life of a Japanese child today. WebQuests can be created to align with any aspect of the social studies curriculum and the curriculum standards for social studies, as well as National Educational Technology Standards (NETS) (ISTE, 1998). WebQuests can be used with students K through 8 with scaffolding appropriate for each level. They also use many features that are important when teaching students with disabilities (Skylar, Higgins, & Boone, 2007). Students can also create their own websites (Peterson & Koeck, 2001).

Research on the use of technology in social studies education has shown that the use of technology such as WebQuests is effective in guided inquiry (Sunal & Sunal, 2003) and that it is most effective with scaffolding and support along with the structured WebQuest design (Brush & Saye, 2000; Milson, 2002; Saye & Brush, 2006).

Source: From *Expectation of excellence: Curriculum standards for the social studies,* by the National Council for the Social Studies, 1994. Washington, DC: Author.

Social Studies Standards

Strand 5: Individuals, Groups, and Institutions
Strand 8: Science, Technology, and Society
Strand 9: Global Connections

STRATEGY

WebQuests are inquiry-oriented, collaborative student activities that use web-based information for solving problems through focused analysis, synthesis, and evaluation. Students are given a task and provided with access to online resources to help them complete the task. Create a WebQuest or use a variety of online sources to find ready-to-use WebQuests created by other teachers.

A literature-based WebQuest uses a book or books as a focal point for activities and includes bibliographies of books that can be used in concert with a WebQuest. In this way, both literature and a WebQuest can be used to introduce a topic in social studies. Discuss a book with students and have them read more about the topic using text sets of books along with information online to complete WebQuest activities. WebQuests can be especially useful in introducing topics with which students may have little or no experience (e.g., homelessness), to visit another time or place in history (e.g., Medieval times), or to go global and learn about another part of the world through images, videos which can be embedded in a WebQuest (e.g., Japan).

Conducting a WebQuest

1. Introduce the topic. Identify a topic, problem, or question of interest to students, building on their prior knowledge. Explain the basic concepts related to the topic.

2. Set the task. The task requires students to use multiple sources of information, analyze and synthesize it, and summarize it in order to make a generalization, take a position, or argue a point of view.

3. Identify resources. Start students on the task by directing them to various web-based sites with links to other related sites they can begin to explore.

4. Activate the process. Students will spend the majority of time on a WebQuest following up on resources; making links with new sources; analyzing, summarizing, and synthesizing what they find; and drawing conclusions or taking positions.

5. Assess the project. Students present their resources, findings, and conclusion or position to others. They must organize all the information they processed and carefully plan the presentation to communicate what they have learned.

Depending on the age of students and their skill level, students can work alone, in groups, or in collaboration with the teacher in using WebQuests. A teacher can create a WebQuest as long as he or she can create a document with hyperlinks, which means a WebQuest can be created in Word, PowerPoint, or Excel. There are also free authoring tools, such as Filamentality, zWebQuest, PHPWebQuest, and others with a fee, such as TeacherWeb or QuestGarden, which offers a 30-day free trial. Go to http://webquest.org for more detailed information on creating a WebQuest.

To start using WebQuests and to learn about, find, or create your own WebQuests, begin with the following:

- http://webquest.org. Bernie Dodge at San Diego State University, the originator of the WebQuest, maintains this site, which includes information about WebQuests, how to get started (with YouTube demonstrations), and a matrix of the top sites that a teacher can search.

- http://www.bestwebquests.com. Tom March, at San Diego State University and a co-creator of WebQuests, provides a list of WebQuests that have been evaluated.

For the National Educational Standards (NETS), go to http://cnets.iste.org, as well to the website for the International Society for Technology in Education (ISTE), www.iste.org for teacher support.

GRADE-LEVEL MODIFICATIONS

K–2ND GRADE

Young children are given the role of student ambassadors to learn as much as they can about Japan before they travel there with the literature-based WebQuest "Student Ambassadors to Japan" (go to www.questgarden.com/49/72/0/070416194049/ or go to questgarden.com and search the Curriculum X Grade Level Matrix for Social Studies K–2). The WebQuest begins with directions to the teacher to read *I Live in Tokyo* by Mari Takabyashi (2001). The students then choose various activities to complete using web links and finally complete a scrapbook on Japan. As they do this, they can use other books about Japan for more information.

Books

Iijima, G. C. (2002). *The way we do it in Japan.* Morton Grove, IL: Albert Whitman.

Littlefield, H. (1997). *Colors of Japan.* Minneapolis, MN: Carolrhoda Books.

Reynolds, B. (1999). *Tokyo friends.* Tokyo: Tuttle.

Reynolds, J. (2005). *Japan (A to Z).* Grolier, CT: Children's Press.

Takabyashi, M. (2004). *I live in Tokyo.* New York: Sandpiper.

Watanabe, E. (2009). *My Japan.* La Jolla, CA: Kane/Miller.

3RD GRADE–5TH GRADE

The WebQuest "Homelessness" (http://questgarden.com/88/00/7/091112143718/, or go to questgarden.com and search the Curriculum X Grade Level Matrix for Social Studies 3–5) is integrated with literature from the beginning as students are directed to first choose and read one of the books from the list that follows.

After students pick and read a book, they complete a story sheet they print out from the WebQuest. There are links to videos they can watch, and then they can choose between four topics on homelessness—shelter, food, clothing, or medical care—and use a job sheet form on the WebQuest as a research guide to each of these topics, using the links to websites and working in groups. Based on their research, they create a poster and prepare a skit on homelessness.

Books

Bunting, E. (1991). *Fly away home.* New York: Clarion.

Carter, R. (1991). *Mr. Bow Tie.* New York: Houghton Mifflin Harcourt.

DiCamillo, K. (2007). *Great joy.* Cambridge, MA: Candlewick Press.

Evans, D. (1993). *So what do you do?* New York: Hand Print.

Fox, P. (1991). *Monkey Island.* New York: Random House.

Hammond, A. (1993). *This home we have made.* New York: Knopf.

McGovern, A. (1997). *The lady in the box.* Madison, CT: Turtle Books.

Testa, M. (1996). *Someplace to go.* Morton Grove, IL: Albert Whitman.

6TH GRADE–8TH GRADE

An excellent example of a WebQuest for middle school is "Medieval Times Reality Adventure," which can be accessed at http://www.ndariess.k12.in.us/elemshare/Teachers/jweathers/Medieval.htm or from http://bestwebquests.com. With this highly engaging WebQuest, students research the Middle Ages by roles: serf, monk or nun, merchant, princess, knight, lady, king, or queen. Introduce the topic by reading aloud *Crispin: Cross of Lead,* by Avi (2002), a Newbery Award-winning book set in the Middle Ages, or the students could read and discuss the book in literature circles with a class set of the books.

As students begin the WebQuest, the author refers them to specific chapters in Avi's (2002) book that correspond to the different roles and aspects of Medieval life that they are researching. There is also a list of other books, media, and online resources students can use to aid in completing the WebQuest, providing an integration of literature and technology in social studies education through the WebQuest strategy.

Books

Avi. (2002). *Crispin: Cross of lead.* New York: Hyperion.

Cushman, K. (1994). *Catherine, called Birdy.* New York: HarperCollins.

Cushman, K. (1995). *The midwife's apprentice.* New York: Clarion.

Gravett, C. (2000). *Castle.* New York: New York: DK Publishing.

Gray, E. J. (1942). *Adam of the road.* New York: Viking.

Macdonald, F. (1995). *How would you survive in the Middle Ages?* New York: Franklin Watts.

Pofahl, J. (1993). *Knights and castles*. Minneapolis, MN: T.S. Dennison & Company.

Schlitz, L. A. (2008). *Good masters! Sweet ladies! Voices from a medieval village.* Cambridge, MA: Candlewick Press.

ENGLISH LEARNERS

English learners can be supported by the use of visuals on websites with links on WebQuests: icons, photographs, drawings, maps, charts, timelines, and videos. WebQuests allow for the added advantage of increased student to student interaction when students work in small collaborative groups. This also allows for increased scaffolding when circulating among groups, providing focused assessment, feedback, and support for English learners in these groups. There are many WebQuests in languages other than English for bilingual or dual immersion class settings.

STRUGGLING STUDENTS

WebQuests use many features that can help struggling students. WebQuests are always broken down into clear, defined steps. The frequent use of advance organizers, graphic organizers, hypertext study guides, outlines, vocabulary definitions, and annotated lists of websites provide support. There are also frames and templates for students to record information that can be useful for struggling students. Modeling the use of these frames, or taking dictation for students filling in the frames, can provide scaffolding for learning with WebQuests. The additional support of group research online and collaborative learning with other students can be of benefit as well. WebQuests can also be created for a variety of student interests and abilities, and they can be tailored to the needs of a particular class.

ASSESSMENT

Every WebQuest has an assessment component that students can review and use to guide their activities. This assessment, or evaluation, usually takes the form of a rubric. Student artifacts or presentations can also be a part of this assessment.

RESOURCES

Thombs, M. M., Gillis, M. M., & Canestrari, A. S. (2008). *Using WebQuests for social studies: A culturally responsive approach*. Thousand Oaks, CA: Corwin Press.

REFERENCES

Brush, T., & Saye, J. (2000). Implementation and evaluation of a student-centered learning unit: A case study. *Educational Technology, Research and Development, 48*(3), 79–100.

Dodge, B. (1995). WebQuests: A technique for Internet-based learning. *Distance Educator, 1*(2), 10–13.

International Society for Technology in Education (ISTE). (1998). *National Educational Technology Standards.* Eugene, OR: Author.

Lamb, A., & Teclehaimanot, B. (2005). A decade of WebQuests: A retrospective. In M. Orey, J. McClendon, & R. M. Branch (Eds.), *Educational media and technology yearbook* (Vol. 30, pp. 62–81). Englewood, CO: Libraries Unlimited.

March, T. (December 2003/January 2004). The learning power of WebQuests. *Educational Leadership, 6*(14), 42–47.

Milson, A. J. (2002). The Internet and inquiry learning: Integrating medium and method in a sixth grade social studies classroom. *Theory and Research in Social Education, 30*(3), 429–455.

Peterson, C. L., & Koeck, D. C. (2001). When students create their own WebQuests. *Learning and Leading with Technology, 29*(1), 10–15.

Saye, J., & Brush, T. (2006). Comparing teachers' strategies for supporting student inquiry in a problem-based multimedia-enhanced history unit. *Theory and Research in Social Education, 32*(3), 349–378.

Skylar, A. A., Higgins, K., & Boone, R. (2007). Strategies for adapting WebQuests for students with learning disabilities. *Intervention in School and Clinic, 43*(1), 20–28.

Sunal, C. S., & Sunal, D. W. (2003). Teacher candidates' conception of guided inquiry and lesson planning in social studies following web-assisted instruction. *Theory and Research in Social Education, 31*(2), 243–264.

Swan, K. O., & Hofer, M. (2008). Technology and social studies. In L. S. Levstik & C. A. Tyson (Eds.), *Handbook of research in social studies education* (pp. 307–328). New York: Routledge.

Teclehaimanot, B., & Lamb, A. (2004, March/April). Reading, technology, and inquiry-based learning through literature-rich WebQuests. *Reading Online, 7*(4). Retrieved November 15, 2009, from http://www.reading online.org/articles/art_index.asp?HREF=teclehaimanot/in dex.html

VanFossen, P. (2004). Using WebQuest to scaffold higher-order thinking. *Social Studies and the Young Learner, 16*(4), 13–16.

Strategy 16

Service-Learning

A Cub Scout leader talked to her seven 2nd-grade Cub Scouts about doing a service-learning project at their school. They liked the idea and asked the principal what they could do for the school. She said "Flowers! I've always wanted to plant flowers here." The Cub Scouts planted flowers around the kindergarten play yard. The whole 2nd-grade class was interested in their project, so they all made plans to help the kindergarten teacher and her students plant and tend a small vegetable garden. Soon the school had both flowers and vegetables.

RATIONALE

Service-learning is the integration of community-based service experiences and academics combined with structured reflection. The goal of service-learning in social studies education is to create informed and active public citizens (Soslau & Yost, 2007; Wade, 2008). While there is a great variety of learning experiences that fall under the category of service-learning, the Alliance for Service-Learning in Education Reform (ASLER) (1993) offers this definition:

> Service-learning is a method by which young people learn and develop through active participation in thoughtfully-organized service experiences: that meet actual community needs, that are coordinated in collaboration with the school and community, that are integrated into each young person's academic curriculum, that provide structured time for a young person to think, talk, and write about what he/she did and saw during the actual service activity, that provide young people with opportunities to use newly acquired academic skills and knowledge in real life situations in their own communities, that enhance what is taught in the school by extending student learning beyond the classroom, and that help to foster the development of a sense of caring for others.

Service-learning has recently increased in popularity, with 64% of public schools offering service-learning activities (Billig, 2000; Skinner & Chapman, 1999). Research has shown a positive impact on student academic success (e.g. non-disruptive school conduct, subject matter test scores, grade point average, school engagement, and commitment to school; Scales, Blythe, Berkas, & Kielsmeier, 2000), and motivation to learn and student attendance rates (Billig, 2000). The greatest benefits shown by studies, however, is in the area of personal and social development (Billig, 2000; Scales et al., 2000), including increased self-esteem, social responsibility, and identity development (Shumer & Belbas, 1996), more positive results in relating to culturally diverse groups, and a greater concern and sense of responsibility for others (Billig, 2000).

Literature can be used to introduce and provide information for a service-learning project in social studies. When using fiction and nonfiction literature in social studies instruction, research shows that one of the benefits of the narratives in historical fiction or biographies or memoirs was that they could be used to motivate students both collectively and individually to social action, which can be accomplished with service-learning. Service-learning projects should actively engage students in meaningful experiences they see a need for and help choose, plan, and carry out, and which are developmentally appropriate for their grade level (Terry, 2008).

Source: From Expectation of excellence: Curriculum standards for the social studies, by the National Council for the Social Studies, 1994. Washington, DC: Author.

Social Studies Standards

Strand 4: Individual Development and Identity
Strand 5: Individuals, Groups, and Institutions
Strand 10: Civic Ideals and Practices

STRATEGY

Students can be involved in all stages of the development of a service-learning project. Ideally, the project will be carried out in response to a real need identified by or for students in the school, community, or the world. Schools and school districts often identify a school- or districtwide service-learning theme and provide leadership and linkages with community service organizations to support projects in classrooms. Such a theme could also be suggested to engage students in supporting the development of service-learning projects in a school. There are also many sources of ideas for service-learning projects in both books (see Resources) and on websites of organizations focused on service (see Plus Technology).

After a need or objective for service-learning is established, students can be introduced to the project through literature read aloud, books on the subject in the classroom, Internet searches, and by meeting with community representatives of organizations or agencies related to the project. After learning about the need, brainstorm with students about ideas for service activities they can carry out, and they can develop action plans and a timeline. They may need to make contact with individuals and agencies through letters and e-mails, solicit materials or goods and services to meet the need, and plan how to implement the service activities. Develop age-appropriate learning experiences to integrate into the service-learning project (e.g., writing a formal letter or doing an Internet search, developing a budget, learning what materials will be needed, planning transportation if the project requires time away from school, obtaining permissions through forms and district approval, and advertising or communicating the project to the community if needed). Students can continue to read and do research using children's and young adult literature on the project.

If it would serve the need identified, the ongoing or completed service-learning project can be publicized to school families and the community. Often, a final celebration of all participants including students, families, other members of the school and local community, and the population served if appropriate can be a culminating activity.

There are many possible service-learning projects, which require that students participate in the project outside of school hours or away from the school site. The following ideas for service-learning projects integrated with literature and social studies, however, can all be conducted in a classroom or at a school site.

Plus Technology

Several organizations dedicated to the goal of service-learning in schools provide teaching ideas and resources for teachers K through 8 on their websites: National Service-Learning Clearinghouse (www.servicelearning.org), Cesar E. Chavez Foundation (www.chavezfoundation.org), and Martin Luther King, Jr. National Service-Learning Partnership, "Kids Consortium" (www.kidsconsortium.org).

GRADE-LEVEL MODIFICATIONS

K–2ND GRADE

Read Barbara Cooney's (1982) *Miss Rumphius*, about a woman who decided she wanted to make the world a more beautiful place and planted lupines all over the countryside of her native Maine. Lead a discussion of the book using aesthetic reader response questions and prompts: What would you do to make the world more beautiful?

Discuss with students planting flowers to beautify the school or a vegetable garden, and they can make plans for how to do so. Students can write or dictate a letter to the principal requesting permission to plant flowers or vegetables and offering suggestions for where it would be possible. They can also write letters to local nurseries requesting donations of seeds or plants to beautify the school and invite owners to the school to talk to students about plants, gardening, and the environment. They can compose a memo to parents explaining their service-learning project and requesting parent involvement, such as loaning gardening tools or helping with the actual planting. They can also contact the school district and ask for help from staff that maintain the school grounds.

Continue to read books about flowers, vegetables, and gardening, and kindergarten students can keep an interactive writing journal of the project (see Strategy 5: Interactive Writing) or, if they are writing, can keep a journal of the project. Students can also compose and present brief public information announcements to other classes on the purpose and the progress of the project, and they can offer to work as mentors with other classes who would also like to beautify the school.

Books

Bunting, E. (1994). *Flower garden.* New York: Harcourt Brace Jovanovich.

Bunting, E. (1999). *Sunflower house.* New York: Sandpiper.

Cole, H. (1997). *Jack's garden.* New York: Greenwillow.

Cooney, B. (1982). *Miss Rumphius.* New York: Viking.

Ehlert, L. (1987*). Growing vegetable soup.* New York: Harcourt Brace Jovanovich.

Ehlert, L. (1992). *Planting a rainbow.* New York: Sandpiper.

Heller, R. (1999). *The reason for a flower.* New York: Putnam.

Logg, G. (1998). *From seed to sunflower.* Danbury, CT: Children's Press.

3RD GRADE–5TH GRADE

Read aloud *Dear Whiskers* (Nagda, 2000), a story about a 4th-grade girl named Jenny who wishes she had more recognition and praise for what she does in her life. She is paired as a pen pal with a second grader named Sameera in her school. The teachers of both classes wanted the 4th-grade students to experience service learning, and the 2nd-grade students to benefit from an older mentor who can help them write. Jenny is disappointed, however, because Sameera writes very little but still wants Jenny to be her friend. Jenny learns that Sameera has only recently emigrated from Saudi Arabia and has very limited English proficiency. She becomes a strong mentor and friend for Sameera, whose spoken and written English improve because of Jenny, who is praised by her teachers for helping. The self-esteem of both students is improved as well.

Students can discuss the book by responding to reader response questions and prompts: How would you feel if you were Jenny? Sameera? What could you do to help other students? Suggest that students mentor the language and literacy of students and ask for suggestions on how to do so. Some possibilities are becoming pen pals with a younger student or a student who is learning to write in English and needs help; starting a buddy reading project where students would read to a younger buddy on a regularly scheduled basis; or creating an after school read aloud program in the library or classroom where students who are at school after classes would sign up to do read alouds for younger students, or anyone else interested; and a peer-tutor project for help in content areas such as mathematics, or mentoring and tutoring in a computer lab.

Students could plan what they would like to do, write memos or schedule meetings to put their plan into effect, write a letter to parents explaining the project and inviting parent involvement, plan a school or community book drive to make books available for students to take home, and so on. This service-learning project could also be extended to provide support at the school for parents and adult literacy and learning English as a second language for family members.

Books

Mortensen, G. (2009). *Listen to the wind.* New York: Dial.

Nagda, A. W. (2000). *Dear Whiskers.* New York: Holiday House.

Polacco, P. (2001). *Thank you, Mr. Falker.* New York: Philomel.

Winter, J. (2009). *Nasreen's secret school: A true story from Afghanistan.* San Diego, CA: Beach Lane Books.

6TH GRADE–8TH GRADE

Read aloud Ken Robbins' (2009) photo-illustrated book *Food for Thought: The Stories Behind the Things We Eat.* The photographs present an artful display of different types of healthy food, along with extensive information about each food: the nutritional content, history, current method of cultivation, and the food in figures of speech, myth, and folklore.

The students can discuss the book by responding to reader response questions and prompts: Which food interested you the most? What are your thoughts about food and health?

Help students plan an informational healthy food fair for other classes. Students can work in pairs or groups, learning about a food, or a food health issue, using books or doing online research. They can communicate what they learn at a health fair in several ways: through posters and displays, brochures and handouts, or through inviting and scheduling health and medical professionals to speak. Other students, parents, and members of the community can attend the healthy food fair.

Books

Hovious, C. (2005). *The best you can be: A teen's guide to fitness and nutrition.* Broomall, PA: Mason Crest.

Madison, L. (2008). *Food and you: Eating right, being strong, and feeling great.* Middleton, WI: American Girl Publishing.

McTavish, S. (2004). *Life skills: 225 ready to use health activities for success and well being.* San Francisco: Jossey-Bass.

Morris, N. (2007). *Do you know what's in your food? Making healthy food choices.* Chicago: Heinemann-Raintree.

Robbins, K. (2009). *Food for thought: The stories behind the things we eat.* New York: Flash Point.

Schlosser, E., & Wilson, C. (2007). *Chew on this. Everything you don't want to know about fast food.* New York: Sandpiper.

ENGLISH LEARNERS

English learners benefit from the social interaction between and among students in service-learning projects, and they can also bring their special skills into play if they speak a home language that may help other English learners—younger students, peers in class, or parents, family, and community members.

STRUGGLING STUDENTS

Struggling students can play a variety of roles in service learning projects that may not be dependent on their ability to perform traditional school tasks such as reading and writing. They may contribute in other ways, such as by making announcements, illustrating, constructing, or contributing ideas for service-learning projects.

ASSESSMENT

Students can write a *structured reflection,* a reflective essay on their experiences with a service-learning project. Areas they can write about include the following: (1) identification of the problem or need; (2) planning a solution that students themselves carried out; (3) reflecting on their plan and what happened. Take dictation for the reflection from younger students, and older students can write independently or collaborate in groups.

RESOURCES

Kaye, C. B. (2010). *The complete guide to service learning: Proven, practical ways to engage students in civic responsibility, academic curriculum, and social action.* Minneapolis, MN: Free Spirit Publishing.

Lewis, B. A. (2009). *The kid's guide to service projects: Over 500 service ideas for young people who want to make a difference.* Minneapolis, MN: Free Spirit Publishing.

REFERENCES

Alliance for Service Learning in Education Reform (ASLER). (1993). *Standards of quality for school-based service-learning.* Chester, VT: Author.

Billig, S. H. (2000). Research on K-12 school-based service learning: The evidence builds. *Phi Delta Kappan, 81,* 658–664.

Scales, P. E., Blyth, D. A., Berkas, T. H., & Kielsmeier, J. C. (2000). The effects of service-learning on middle school students' social responsibility and academic success. *Journal of Early Adolescence, 20*(3), 332–358.

Shumer, R., & Belbas, B. (1996). What we know about service learning. *Education and Urban Society, 28,* 208–223.

Skinner, R., & Chapman, C. (1999). *Service-learning and community service in K-12 public schools.* Washington, DC: National Center for Education Statistics.

Soslau, E. G., & Yost, D. S. (2007). Urban service-learning: An authentic teaching strategy to deliver a standards-driven curriculum. *Journal of Experiential Education, 30*(1), 36–53.

Terry, A. (2008). Student voices, global echoes: Service-learning and the gifted. *Roeper Review, 39*(1), 45–51.

Wade, R. (2008). Service-learning. In L. S. Levstik & C. A. Tyson (Eds.), *Handbook of research in social studies education* (pp. 109–123). New York: Routledge.

PART III

Mathematics

WHAT RESEARCH HAS TO SAY ABOUT LITERATURE-BASED TEACHING AND MATHEMATICS

The new national standards in mathematics (National Council of Teachers of Mathematics [NCTM], 2000) reflect a shift of focus in mathematics instruction beyond mathematics as computation toward mathematics as "conceptualization, description, and explanation" of the powerful ideas associated with mathematical processes (Lesh & English, 2005). This current view of mathematics education is broad enough to include making connections among language, literacy, and literature in the K through 8 classroom.

The National Council of Teachers of Mathematics (2000) standards include five content standards for numbers and operations, algebra, geometry, measurement, and data analysis and probability, but they also include process standards for problem solving, reasoning and proof, communication, connections, and representation. These process standards reflect a view of mathematics as dynamic rather than static and as constructive rather than prescriptive. This means that in addition to mastering math content, students also learn to communicate their mathematical thinking with other students, use the language of mathematics, apply mathematics in contexts outside of mathematics, and use representation to organize, record, and communicate mathematical ideas. Students are expected to build on their own conceptual thinking rather than rely on standard procedures, and they are expected to make connections among mathematical ideas, but also make connections in other contexts.

Connections between mathematics and other content areas in an integrated curriculum are viewed as essential in classroom instruction (Perry & Dockett, 2008). The National Council of Teachers of Mathematics (2000) maintains that mathematics should be learned in context in order to be meaningful:

> When students can connect mathematical ideas, their understanding is deeper and more lasting. They can see mathematical connections in the rich interplay among mathematical topics, in contexts that relate mathematics to other subjects, and in their own interests and experience. (p. 64)

While commercially published, traditional textbooks have predominated mathematics curriculum materials in American classrooms and have consequently determined teaching practices to a large extent (Goodlad, 1984; Grant, Peterson, & Shojgreen-Downer, 1996). The use of concrete objects, such as manipulatives, real-life phenomenon, and children's literature, should also be used—not only to address the basic content standards, but also to reinforce the notion that mathematics learning can be connected with other contexts.

One of the clearest links between mathematics learning and other contexts is found in children's literature. Ginsburg and Seo (2000) and Cutler, Gilkerson, Parrott, and Bowne (2003) emphasized the instructional value of the many mathematical concepts that can be introduced to students through literature. An investigation of the reading of children's books at home to young children as a context for mathematics learning and the development of strong relationships between the adults and children sharing the reading experience showed many positive affects (Anderson, Anderson, & Shapiro, 2004, 2005).

In a school setting, Hong (1996) found that kindergarten students who were taught mathematics related to stories showed a greater preference and aptitude for mathematics activities than students in a comparison group. In another study of the use of children's literature in the teaching of mathematics, Cotti and Schiro (2004) found that the predominant position taken by teachers was child-centered, meaning that teachers focused on students' engagement with and response to the story. Other researchers have described examples of the range of children's literature related to mathematics and its use in the classroom (Thatcher, 2001; Whitin & Whitin, 2004).

The National Council of Teachers of Mathematics (www.nctm.org) publishes *Teaching Children Mathematics,* a journal for teachers published nine times a year with current research and ideas for best practices, including using children's literature in the teaching of mathematics.

Guidelines For Selecting Books For Teaching Mathematics

In *New Visions for Linking Literature and Mathematics,* a joint publication of the National Council of Teachers of English and the National Council of Teachers of Mathematics, Whitin and Whitin (2004) identified the following criteria for selecting children's and young adult literature for teaching mathematics:

- Mathematical integrity: Fiction, as well as nonfiction, requires that the mathematics components be accurate, mathematic concepts or examples must be used in believable contexts, and the ideas and concepts should be obvious in the text and illustrations.

- Potential for varied response: The tone of the book invites the reader to think and respond in several ways.

- An aesthetic dimension: The book is pleasing to the eye, with informational graphics complementing the text.

National Standards For Mathematics

The National Council of Teachers of Mathematics (2000) standards are divided into five content standards for number and operations, algebra, geometry, measurement, and data analysis and probability and five process standards for problem solving, reasoning and proof, communication, connections, and representation.

Content Standards

1. Numbers and Operations
   - Understand numbers, ways of representing numbers, relationships among numbers, and number systems
   - Understand meanings of operations and how they relate to one another
   - Complete fluently and make reasonable estimates

2. Algebra
   - Understand patterns, relations, and functions
   - Represent and analyze mathematical situations and structures using algebraic symbols
   - Use mathematical models to represent and understand quantitative relationships
   - Analyze change in various contexts

3. Geometry
   - Analyze characteristics and properties of two- and three-dimensional geometric shapes and develop mathematical arguments about geometric relationships
   - Specify locations and describe spatial relationships using coordinate geometry and other representational systems
   - Apply transformations and use symmetry to analyze mathematical situations
   - Use visualization, spatial reasoning, and geometric modeling to solve problems

4. Measurement
   - Understand measurable attributes of objects and the units, systems, and processes of measurement
   - Apply appropriate techniques, tools, and formulas to determine measurements

5. Data Analysis and Probability
   - Formulate questions that can be addressed with data and collect, organize, and display relevant data to answer them
   - Select and use appropriate statistical methods to analyze data
   - Develop and evaluate inferences and predictions that are based on data
   - Understand and apply basic concepts of probability

Process Standards

1. Problem Solving
   - Build new mathematical knowledge through problem solving
   - Solve problems that arise in mathematics and in other contexts
   - Apply and adapt a variety of appropriate strategies to solve problems
   - Monitor and reflect on the process of mathematical problem solving

2. Reasoning and Proof
   - Recognize reasoning and proof as fundamental aspects of mathematics
   - Make and investigate mathematical conjectures
   - Develop and evaluate mathematical arguments and proofs
   - Select and use various types of reasoning and methods of proof

3. Communication
   - Organize and consolidate their mathematical thinking through communication
   - Communicate their mathematical thinking coherently and clearly to peers, teachers, and others

- Analyze and evaluate the mathematical thinking and strategies of others
- Use the language of mathematics to express mathematical ideas precisely

4. Connections
   - Recognize and use connections among mathematical ideas
   - Understand how mathematical ideas interconnect and build on one another to produce a coherent whole
   - Recognize and apply mathematics in contexts outside of mathematics

5. Representation
   - Create and use representations to organize, record, and communicate mathematical ideas
   - Select, apply, and translate among mathematical representations to solve problems
   - Use representation to model and interpret physical, social, and mathematical phenomena

REFERENCES

Anderson, A., Anderson, J., & Shapiro, J. (2004). Mathematical discourse in shared storybook reading. *Journal for Research in Mathematics Education, 35*(1), 5–33.

Anderson, A., Anderson, J., & Shapiro, J. (2005). Supporting multiple literacies: Parents' and children's mathematical talk within storybook reading. *Mathematics Education Research Journal, 16*(3), 5–26.

Cotti, R., & Schiro, M. (2004). Connecting teacher beliefs to the use of children's literature in the teaching of mathematics. *Journal of Mathematics Teacher Education, 3*(2), 155–181.

Cutler, K. M., Gilkerson, D., Parrott, S., & Bowne, M. T. (2003). Developing math games based on children's literature. *Young Children, 58*(1), 22–27.

Ginsburg, H. P., & Seo, K.-H. (2000). Preschoolers' mathematical reading. *Teaching Children Mathematics, 7*(4), 226–229.

Goodlad, J. (1984). *A place called school Prospects for the future.* New York: McGraw-Hill.

Grant, S. G., Peterson, P. L., & Shojgreen-Downer, A. (1996). Learning to teach mathematics in the context of system reform. *American Educational Research Journal, 33*(2), 509–541.

Hong, H. (1996). Effects of mathematics learning through children's literature on math achievement and dispositional outcomes. *Early Childhood Research Quarterly, 11*, 477–494.

Lesh, R., & English, L. D. (2005). Trends in the evolution of models & modeling perspectives on mathematical learning and problem solving. *ZDM International Reviews on Mathematical Education, 37*(6), 487–489.

National Council of Teachers of Mathematics. (2000). *Principles and standards for school mathematics.* Reston, VA: Author.

Perry, B., & Dockett, S. (2008). Young children's access to powerful mathematical ideas. In L. D. English (Ed.), *Handbook of international research in mathematics education* (2nd ed., pp. 75–105). New York: Routledge.

Thatcher, D. H. (2001). Reading in the math class: Selecting and using math books for math investigations. *Young Children, 56*(4), 20–26.

Whitin, D. J., & Whitin, P. (2004). *New visions for linking literature and mathematics.* Urbana, IL: National Council of Teachers of English; Reston, VA: National Council of Teachers of Mathematics.

Finding a Fibonacci

Fourth grade students worked in groups to represent the Fibonacci sequence by mapping it onto graph paper using different colored pencils, shown in Figure 17.1.

Figure 17.1 The Fibonacci sequence on graph paper

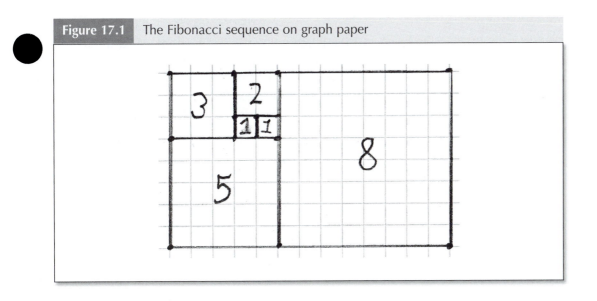

RATIONALE

Use various types of literature to introduce the Fibonacci sequence, which are numbers in the following sequence: 1, 1, 2, 3, 5, 8, 13, 21, 34, 55, 89, 144, and so on. The first two numbers in the sequence are 0 and 1, and each remaining number is the sum of the previous two: $F = F_{n-1} + F_{n-2}$. Fibonacci was the name used by Leonardo of Pisa, a medieval mathematician who described the sequence he had observed in nature.

Research on learning mathematics shows that at a fundamental level, number is conceived of as a composite of units and that children develop a concept of number through counting and the construction of number sequences that lead to the understanding of increasingly more abstract unit types (Steffe, von Glasersfeld, Richards, & Cobb, 1983). Early experiences with patterns and number sequences, and experimenting with various ways of representing them, also opens the possibility of extending students' exposure to generalization tasks over time (Rojano, 2008).

Source: From Principles and standards for school mathematics, by the National Council of Teachers of Mathematics, 2000. Reston, VA: Author.

Mathematics Standards

Content Standards

1. Numbers and Operations: Understand numbers, ways of representing numbers, relationships among numbers, and number systems

2. Algebra: Understand patterns, relations, and functions

Process Standards

5. Representation: Create and use representations to organize, record, and communicate mathematical ideas

---

STRATEGY

Students can discover the pattern of the Fibonacci sequence, where the next number in the sequence is the sum of the preceding two numbers. They can also experience firsthand how Fibonacci numbers exist everywhere in nature.

Read aloud books related to the Fibonacci sequence, such as concept books that use illustrations or photographs that show the pattern in nature, biographies of Fibonacci, and stories and chapter books that use it as a puzzle to be solved in the plot.

Students can look for a Fibonacci sequence in nature by observing natural objects that demonstrate this pattern. Bring these objects to class, or ask students to try to find a Fibonacci pattern outside of the classroom and bring objects to the classroom themselves.

Students can observe and draw the object, simulate the pattern with objects or by standing to form the pattern in the class, represent the pattern with objects such as a unifix cube, or map the pattern with colored pencils on graph paper. Older students can represent the pattern as an operation using numbers.

Because the Fibonacci pattern is often referred to in literature, especially in mysteries, students can read and respond to this literature and try to solve a problem in writing their own mystery.

GRADE-LEVEL MODIFICATIONS

K–2ND GRADE

Read aloud *Growing Patterns: Fibonacci Numbers in Nature* (Campbell, 2010). This concept books uses color photos to show examples of the Fibonacci sequence as it exists in nature. The entire cover is the center of a huge sunflower. Each flower or other plant or object is introduced with a small part of the entire photo, just as the Fibonacci sequence begins small, with one. The photos of the same flower increase in size on subsequent pages, showing the increased size in proportion to the numbers in the sequence. Besides the sunflower, the reader sees other flowers, pine cones, pineapples, and the cutaway chamber of a nautilus shell. Lead a discussion using reader response questions and prompts: Have you seen any of the things pictured in the book? What did you wonder about the Fibonacci numbers?

Students can examine a sunflower, pine cone, pineapple, or other plants or objects that demonstrate the pattern. Students can move through centers, with one of these objects on a table with crayons. They can fold a paper in fourths, and move from center to center, drawing what is on each table in one of the four sections, turning the paper over if more sections are needed. Make a list of words that students can use to label their drawings (e.g., the names of the flowers or fruit).

Represent the sequence on large graph paper on a table. Students can put a unifix cube on a square, then two unifix cubes of a different color to show three, then five to show the sum of three and two, then eight to show the sum of five and three. Each new number in the sequence is the sum of the previous two.

Books

Bunting, E. (1999). *Sunflower house.* Clive, IA: Perfection Learning.

Campbell, S. (2010). *Growing patterns: Fibonacci numbers in nature.* Hondesdale, PA: Boyds Mills Press.

Schaefer, L. M. (2000). *This is the sunflower.* New York: Greenwillow.

3RD GRADE–5TH GRADE

Read aloud the picture book biography *Blockhead: The Life of Fibonacci* (D'Agnese, 2010). When in school, Fibonacci did math so fast in his head that the teacher thought he was day dreaming and other students called him blockhead. But he became the "greatest Western mathematician in the Middle Ages." He observed nature, described the Fibonacci pattern, and promoted so-called Arabic numerals, which he vigorously and rightly ascribes to India. Lead a discussion using reader response questions and prompts: How would you have felt if you were Fibonacci? Have you noticed any of the things he described in his number sequence?

With students, collect the types of things that Fibonacci observed in nature so students can observe them in class (e.g., sunflowers, artichoke, pineapple, pine cone, or the seed pockets of an apple or banana cut in half). In groups, the students can map the sequence on a piece of graph paper, with different colored pencils representing each step in the sequence. They can continue to look for examples of the Fibonacci sequence in nature, bring samples into class, and create a Fibonacci Museum on a table, with the samples and a bulletin board behind it with drawings of the sample and their graph paper representations.

Also read aloud from the Horrible Harry series, which has two titles that use the Fibonacci sequence as part of the plot, or do a book talk on them so that students can read them independently.

Books

D'Agnese, J. (2010). *Blockhead: The life of Fibonacci.* New York: Henry Holt.

Hume, J. N. (2005). *Wild Fibonacci: Nature's secret code revealed.* Berkeley, CA: Tricycle Press.

Kline, S (1998). *Horrible Harry and the dungeon.* New York: Puffin.

Kline, S. (2008). *Horrible Harry cracks the code.* New York: Puffin.

McCallum, A. (2007). *Rabbits, rabbits everywhere: A Fibonacci tale.* Watertown, MA: Charlesbridge.

6TH GRADE–8TH GRADE

Introduce the Fibonacci sequence using objects, such as pine cones, pineapples, and flowers. Students can represent the sequence by mapping it on graph paper or producing the linear sequence by showing that to get any number in the sequence you add the two previous numbers in the sequence. Ask students the following questions: What's happening here? How can you represent this as an operation? (As previously mentioned, the Fibonacci sequence can be written as $F_n = F_{n-1} + F_{n-2}$.)

As students continue to look for samples of the sequence in nature and add them to a class collection, read aloud the chapter book series by Blue Balliett, which has been called the Da Vinci code for middle school students. In *The Wright 3* (2006), the three main characters solve a mystery related to Frank Lloyd Wright's Robie House in Chicago. They use the Fibonacci sequence to help solve it, mentioning irises, buttercups, marigolds, black-eyed Susans, and pansies, and the pattern appears many places in Wright's work, sometimes hidden, sometimes not. The book is full of background information on architecture, Frank Lloyd Wright, literature, geometry, codes, talismans, film, and community activism. A theme throughout all the author's books is the interconnectedness of the universe.

As the book is read chapter by chapter, ask students "How many ways are the Fibonacci numbers used in the book?" Students could keep a list and compare with other students. Many of these things don't appear to be related. Also ask students to list three or four things they like to think about, that don't appear to be related, and invent a way to connect them in a mystery story. The students would be looking for patterns in their own thinking to use in writing. Students could work independently or in groups and write a mystery story using the Fibonacci numbers, or a pattern of their own ideas.

Books

Balliett, B. (2004). *Chasing Vermeer.* New York: Scholastic.

Balliett, B. (2006). *The Wright 3.* New York: Scholastic.

Balliett, B. (2010). *The Calder game.* New York: Scholastic.

Hathout, L. (2007). *Crimes and mathdemeanors.* Natwick, MA: A. K. Peters.

Lee, C., & O'Reilly, G. (2007). *The great number rumble: A story of math in surprising places.* Toronto, Ontario, Canada: Annick Press.

Lichtman, W. (2007). *Do the math: Secrets, lies, and algebra.* New York: Greenwillow.

Lichtman, W. (2008). *Do the math #2: The writing on the wall.* New York: Greenwillow.

ENGLISH LEARNERS

English learners will benefit from the use of visuals, from hands-on experiences with flowers and fruit, and by labeling and graphing the sequence before moving to more abstract numerals. Fibonacci also recognized other non-Western cultures in his investigations of mathematics in the Middle Ages. The Fibonacci sequence was known in ancient India, and the Incas used a *yupana* (Quechua for "counting tool"), a kind of calculator based on the Fibonacci sequence.

Books

Books about mathematicians and important mathematics discoveries from cultures other than Western ones, which may represent the heritage and language of English learners, can be used in the classroom:

Calvert, P. (2005). *The ancient Inca*. Danbury, CT: Franklin Watts.

Schomp, V. (2005). *Ancient India*. Danbury, CT: Children's Press.

Such books can also provide primary language support if they are in the students' home language:

Baquedano, E. (2004). *Aztecs, Incas, Y Mayas* (Spanish Edition). New York: DK Children

STRUGGLING STUDENTS

Take struggling students through the sequence of first using concrete objects such as flowers and fruits, making sure they have enough experience with these before moving on to more abstract representations such as graphing, number sequences, and operations. Using objects on graph paper, such as unifix cubes, for drawing on graph paper may scaffold learning for them as well.

ASSESSMENT

K through 2 students can draw an object that is an example of the Fibonacci sequence, such as a sunflower, pineapple, or pine cone, and label it and write the number sequence of 1, 1, 2, 3, 5, and 8 on their drawing. Grade 3 through 5 students can demonstrate their understanding by graphing the sequence based on real objects and writing the sequence up to 144. Middle grade students can demonstrate understanding by representing the objects and graphing as an operation: $F_n = F_{n-1} + F_{n-2}$.

RESOURCES

Garland, T. H. (1997). *Fibonacci fun: Fascinating activities with intriguing numbers.* Palo Alto, CA: Dale Seymour Publications.

REFERENCES

Rojano, T. (2008). Mathematics learning in the middle school/junior secondary school. In L. D. English (Ed.), *Handbook of international research in mathematics education* (pp. 136–153). New York: Routledge.

Steffe, L. P., von Glasersfeld, E., Richards, J., & Cobb, P. (1983). *Children's counting types: Philosophy, theory, and application.* New York: Praeger Scientific.

Strategy 18

Discovering Pi

The 1st-grade students worked in pairs to measure clean empty cans with tape measures. The teacher recorded their measurements on a chart. The students eagerly asked for more circles to measure and add to the chart. The teacher sent a memo home asking parents to send something round or circular to measure. The parents responded enthusiastically and the class measured many more things and added them to the chart: a Frisbee, a hula hoop, a hoop earring, a plastic bangle bracelet, more clean empty cans, and different sized circles cut out of newspaper.

RATIONALE

Pi is the ratio (3.14) of the circumference of a circle to its diameter. Younger students can learn how to measure and record the measurements of a circle and learn the terms *circumference* and *diameter*. Older students can measure, learn the term *radius*, and use an equation to calculate the ratio of diameter to circumference, as well as do research to discover more about pi. Pi is a value that has puzzled mathematicians for thousands of years, even though with a tin can and a tape measure, students can find a circle's circumference is just over three times its diameter.

Research in the development of students' mathematical understanding identified a learning trajectory with levels of competence that include combining shapes to make pictures and designs and creating and operating on a shape as a unit with measurable attributes (Clements, Wilson, & Sarama, 2004), which can be supported by experiences with measurement of a circle and calculating the meaning of pi.

Source: From *Principles and standards for school mathematics*, by the National Council of Teachers of Mathematics, 2000. Reston, VA: Author.

Mathematics Standards

Content Standards

3. Geometry: Analyze characteristics and properties of two- and three-dimensional geometric shapes and develop mathematical arguments about geometric relationship
4. Measurement: Understand measurable attributes of objects and the units, systems, and processes of measurement; Apply appropriate techniques, tools, and formulas to determine measurements

Process Standards

1. Problem solving: Build new mathematical knowledge through problem solving

STRATEGY

Use literature to introduce measuring the circumference and diameter of a circle for younger students and the equation for calculating the ratio of circumference and diameter to discover the value of pi for older students. Lead a discussion of the books using reader response questions and prompts.

Provide empty, clean cans of all shapes and sizes or ask students to bring them to class, along with measuring tapes, chart paper, and calculators for older students. Students can measure and record the circumference around each can, measure and record the diameter across each can, learn the mathematical terms appropriate for various grade levels, keep a record of the measurements, and older students can use the equation to calculate the ratio of circumference to diameter, and discover the meaning of pi.

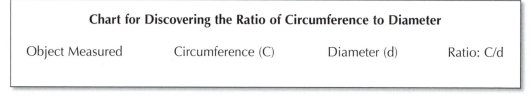

Chart for Discovering the Ratio of Circumference to Diameter			
Object Measured	Circumference (C)	Diameter (d)	Ratio: C/d

Put together a class set of books on the measurement of circles, terms and definitions, and the history, meaning, relevance, and real world applications of pi; older students can read independently or in groups to do research on pi.

GRADE-LEVEL MODIFICATIONS

K–2ND GRADE

Read aloud *Inch by Inch* by Leo Lionni (2010)), a story about an inchworm who is about an inch long and good at measuring. Lead a class discussion asking reader response questions and prompts: What did you wonder about the story? What are some things you have measured?

Model how to measure circles by measuring around the outside and across the top of an empty, clean can with a measuring tape. Then write the terms *around* and *across* at the top of a piece of chart paper for students to copy onto a piece of paper where they will record these measurements. Students can work in pairs measuring a can with the tape measure and recording the measurements on the piece of paper where they have written *around* and *across*.

On the top of the chart, add around = circumference and across = diameter to introduce the terms to the students and then add sentence frames the students can use to report their measurements.

Measuring Cans

Around = Circumference   Across = Diameter

"The circumference of our can is ___."   "The diameter of our can is ____."

Each pair of students can record their measurements on the chart, completing the sentence frame aloud for the rest of the class. Students can also use the sentence frame to record their measurements in a math journal and record measurements of other objects in the room.

Books

Faulkner, K. (2000). *So big! My first measuring book*. New York: Simon & Schuster.

Hightower, S. (1997). *Twelve snails to one lizard: A tale of mischief and measurement*. New York: Simon & Schuster.

Lionni, L. (2010). *Inch by inch*. New York: Knopf.

Loughran, L. (2004). *How long is it?* Danbury, CT: Children's Press.

Pallotta, J. (2002). *Hershey's milk chocolate weights and measures*. New York: Scholastic.

Schwartz, D. M. (2006). *Millions to measure*. New York: HarperCollins.

3RD GRADE–5TH GRADE

Use literature to introduce circumference and area of a circle and the equations to find circumference and area by reading aloud *Sir Cumference and the First Round Table* (Neuschwander, 1997), one of several stories this author has written about mathematics. In this humorous tale, Sir Cumference, his wife Lady Di Ameter, and their son Radius, discover the perfect shape for a table for King Arthur and his knights. Lead a discussion of the book by asking reader response questions and prompts: What questions do you have about the story? What do you know about measuring circumference?

Write the words *circumference* and *diameter* on chart paper and ask students if they know what they mean when measuring a circle—*around* and *across*—and write these in parentheses. Students can then practice measuring circumference and diameter by measuring around (circumference) and across (diameter) an empty, clean can with a measuring tape. Provide the cans and measuring tapes or ask students to bring them to class. The students can do the measurements independently, in pairs, or in small groups, and they can draw a picture of the can, adding the measurements and labeling the measurement for the circumference and diameter.

Ask students if they now know the meaning of each of the words (i.e., *circumference* is the distance around a circle, *diameter* is the distance across a circle, *radius* is the distance from the center to any point in the circle) and have them write the terms on the paper with their drawing and measurements. Students can share the definitions they have written in a discussion, and the class can agree upon one, and they can be recorded on the chart paper.

Next, read *Sir Cumference and the Dragon of Pi* (Neuschwander, 1999), another story with the same characters as *Sir Cumference and the First Round Table,* in which Radius must find the magic number (pi) to save his father who has been turned into a dragon. After a discussion of how he found pi, and how it is used, add the following concepts to the chart: (1) If you know the diameter of a circle, multiply it by pi (3.14) to find the circumference; (2) If you know the circumference, you can find the diameter and radius (circumference divided by pi (3.14) = diameter; diameter divided by 2 = radius).

Using the can measurements of the can they have recorded, each student or group can use calculators to find the circumference, diameter, and radius of the can. They can also find the area of the circle of the can: Multiply pi (3.14) by the square of the radius. The square is found my multiplying the number by itself.

Books

Long, L. (2003). *Groovy geometry: Games and activities that make math easy and fun*. Hoboken, NJ: Wiley.

Neuschwander, C. (1997). *Sir Cumference and the first round table: A math adventure*. Watertown, MA: Charlesbridge.

Neuschwander, C. (1999). *Sir Cumference and the dragon of pi: A math adventure*. Watertown, MA: Charlesbridge.

Ross, C. S. (1993). *Circles: Fun ideas for getting a-round in math*. Old Tappan, NJ: Addison-Wesley.

6th Grade–8th Grade

Students are often given the number for pi, one of the most important numbers that exists, to calculate circumference, diameter, radius, and the area of a circle. Use literature to guide students to explore the origins and meaning of pi in other contexts, since this infinite number was studied thousands of years ago when people realized there was a consistent relationship between the diameter and circumference of a circle. Pi shows up in many fascinating places, from astronomy and probability, random numbers, geometry, square root and calculus to the physics of sound and light.

Providing practice in measuring the circumference and diameter of cans and practicing how to write equations and calculate the circumference, diameter, radius, and area of a circle can lead students from a concrete experience to a more abstract representation and understanding of a mathematical process. Also provide books and online resources for students to research different aspects of pi, a number that has intrigued mathematicians for centuries. Students can form groups, and each group can learn and present information about pi to the other groups in a collaborative jigsaw activity:

1. Learn different ways pi has been calculated

2. Perform a variety of experiments to estimate the value of pi

3. Find the relationship of pi to the alphabet

4. Do a timeline of the history of pi

5. Describe one of the many mathematicians in different eras and areas of the world who studied pi

Students can present their research in a variety of ways:

1. Dramatize scenes from the history of pi

2. Write pi poetry

3. Compile a list of fascinating pi facts

4. Display posters or models showing where and how pi is used

5. Organize a quiz show on pi

Since March 14th is Pi Day each year, it would be a perfect day to do presentations—and eat pie.

Plus Technology

Students can do research online starting at www.joyofpi.com, as well as use books for their research.

Books

Ball, J. (2005). *Go figure! A totally cool book about numbers*. New York: DK Children.

Ball, J. (2009*). Why Pi?* New York: DK Children.

Blatner, D. (1999). *The joy of pi*. New York: Walker & Company.

Pappas, T. (1993). *The joy of mathematics: Discovering mathematics all around you*. San Carlos, CA: Wide World Publishing.

Pappas, T. (1997). *Fractals, googles, and other mathematical tales*. San Carlos, CA: Wide World Publishing.

Pappas, T. (1998). *More joy of mathematics: Exploring mathematics all around you*. San Carlos, CA: Wide World Publishing.

Vorderman, C. (1996). *How math works*. New York: Readers Digest.

ENGLISH LEARNERS

In addition to using concrete objects and having a hands-on measuring experience, English learners benefit from using nonlinguistic ways of representing what they are experiencing, such as a drawing of the can, lines and arrows indicating circumference and diameter, and numerals. They can also use student-student interaction to collaborate with a more English proficient peer.

For students whose home language is Spanish, teach the vocabulary of pi using English-Spanish cognates, which students can use to label their drawings and measurements.

English	Spanish
circumference	circunferencia
diameter	diametro
radius	radio

pi = pi in both languages

Bilingual books can also be used for primary language support.

Books

Ayers, A. (2007). *Midiendo en la exposicion de perros/Measuring at the dog show* (Spanish Edition). Pleasantville, NY: Weekly Reader.

Catala, E. (2005). *Por que medimos?/Why we measure* (Spanish Edition). Chicago: Red Brick.

Martin, E. (2006). *Hay muchos circulos/So many circles* (Bilingual Edition). Mankato, MN: Capstone Press.

STRUGGLING STUDENTS

After modeling measuring, give each student a paper with a word bank and definitions for circumference, diameter, radius, and pi and space to label and record their measurements; for older students, also supply the equations they will need to calculate these.

ASSESSMENT

Assess students' understanding of measurement in Grades K through 2 by reviewing the drawings they made of the can, with measurements and labels added. Older students can trade the papers on which they recorded the measurements of cans or other objects and calculated circumference, diameter, radius, and area of the circle of the can with another student, pair, or group. They can check each other's calculations. In Grades 6 through 8, cocreate a rubric for assessing the presentations of their research on pi.

RESOURCES

Bokhari, N. (2005). *Piece of pi: Wit-sharpening, brain-bruising, number-crunching activities with pi*. Woodway, TX: Prufrock Press.

REFERENCES

Clements, D. H., Wilson, D. C., & Sarama, J. (2004). Young children's composition of geometric figures: A learning trajectory. *Mathematical Thinking and Learning, 6,* 163–184.

Marvelous Mathematicians

The kindergarten teacher asked her students what they would like to name the almanac they would write after the students learned about Benjamin Banneker, a free African American mathematician and scientist who published an almanac from 1792 through 1797. They decided the best name would be "Our Classy Class Almanac."

RATIONALE

The lives of mathematicians reveal information about the way they think, the impact mathematical thinking and discoveries have had on people's lives, and the history of the development of mathematical thinking. By reading biographies and engaging in classroom experiences about important mathematicians, students can deepen their understanding of the nature and role of mathematics in the world. Male students have typically outperformed females in mathematics, and issues of race, power, economic and social disadvantage, and the ways that students participate in mathematics have long been discussed in the research on mathematics education (Gutstein, 2003; Moses & Cobb, 2001). Silver, Smith, and Nelson (1995) maintained that low levels of participation and performance in mathematics by females, ethnic minorities, and the poor were not primarily due to lack of ability or potential but rather to educational practices. Through biographies, students can meet some of the marvelous mathematicians who are not male or white, as well as mathematicians from different times and places in the world who can serve as models for all students.

Source: From Principles and standards for school mathematics, by the National Council of Teachers of Mathematics, 2000. Reston, VA: Author.

Mathematics Standards

Process Standards

1. Problem Solving: Solve problems that arise in mathematics and in other contexts

3. Communication: Analyze and evaluate the mathematical thinking and strategies of others

5. Representation: Create and use representations to organize, record, and communicate mathematical ideas

STRATEGY

Use literature to introduce a mathematician to students by reading an illustrated picture book biography aloud, reading aloud chapters of a biography for older students, and providing a text set of biographies of mathematicians in the classroom.

The students can choose one mathematician as a focus of study, or students can choose among several to read about, research, discuss, and write about. They can then integrate what they have learned into their own study of mathematics and plan ways to present what they have learned about the life and work of one or more mathematicians to the rest of the class, to other classes, or to parents and members of the community.

For example, after reading and researching, students can integrate the ideas of the mathematician into their own math journal, including problems and puzzles posed by the mathematician. They can write poetry, narrative, dialogue, and scripts about them as well, which could be incorporated into a journal or put on a poster for display in the class. Students can use drama such as role play, reader's theatre, writing scripts, and acting out scenes depicting an event in the life of a mathematician, or they can simulate interviews with the mathematician using questions based on research on the person's life, have debates between the mathematician and others who disagreed with their work, or create a video documentary on the mathematician.

GRADE-LEVEL MODIFICATIONS

K–2ND GRADE

First, read aloud the picture book biography, *Molly Bannaky* (McGill, 1999). Molly was born in England and immigrated to the American colonies as an indentured servant. She became the grandmother of Benjamin Banneker. Then, read the picture book biography *Dear Benjamin Banneker*, written by Andrea Pinkney (1998) and illustrated by Brian Pinkney. Benjamin Banneker was a free, self-taught African American mathematician, astronomer, inventor, surveyor, almanac author, and anti-slavery activist who exchanged letters with Thomas Jefferson on the subject in the 18th century. Lead a discussion of the books using reader response questions and prompts: What questions did you have about the life of Benjamin Banneker? Benjamin Banneker loved math. How do you feel about math?

The students will learn that Benjamin Banneker was the author of *Benjamin Banneker's Almanac*, which was published from 1792 to 1797. Banneker based his almanac on his journal—a book of blank pages in which he wrote daily observations of the skies, weather, nature, and events. His friends wrote in his book, and he traded math puzzles with other math lovers as well. Model keeping an *almanac journal* with students, making a list of the things to write and draw about on a piece of chart paper; students can keep the journal by writing or drawing about one or more of the things on the list each day. They can share their observations and notes with the class as well.

After a period of keeping the almanac journal, begin to write an almanac page with students on chart paper each day with the following categories, which were actually in Banneker's almanac. Entries will be based on student observations (such as the weather), information in the daily newspaper (such as rise and set of moon), or on a chosen subject (such as a mathematical calculation or puzzle for the day). Categories in quotations use the same words as were used in Banneker's almanac.

"Our Class Almanac"

- Day and Date
- Weather (student observations and the weather section of the newspaper)
- "Rise and Set of Sun and Moon" (see the daily newspaper or online)
- "Festivals and Other Remarkable Days"
- "Essays in Prose and Verse" (students' writing in their journals)
- "Mathematical Calculations and Puzzles" (teacher-planned or student contributed each day and worked on the chart paper with the whole class)

Students can rotate and take the pen to write interactively (see Strategy 5: Interactive Writing) as scribes on the chart, or dictation can be taken for younger students. Other students can find information in the newspaper or contribute entries from their journals.

Model a mathematical calculation or problem from any math text used in the class, go over an area of mathematics students are struggling with, or find interesting puzzles in books that students can also read, like *Math Curse* (Scieszka, 1995), *Grapes of Math* (Tang, 2004), and *Math for all Seasons* (Tang, 2005).

Plus Technology

With K through 2 students, word process what the students have said and what has been recorded on the chart for the almanac entry each day and publish it as a book. For summaries and links to the actual letters between Benjamin Banneker and Thomas Jefferson on the subject of slavery and abolition, go to www.pbs.org/wgbh/aia/part2/2h71.html and www.pbs.org/wgbh/aia/part2/2h72.html

Books

Blue, R. (2001). *Benjamin Banneker: Mathematicia.* Brookfield, CT: Millbrook Press.

Braun, E. (2005). *Benjamin Banneker.* Mankato, MN: Capstone Press.

Ferris, G. (1990). *What are you figuring now? A story about Benjamin Banneker.* Minneapolis, MN: Carolrhoda Books.

Lassieur, A. (2006). *Benjamin Banneker: Astronomer and mathematician.* Mankato, MN: Capstone Press.

Litwin, L. B. (1999). *Benjamin Banneker: Astronomer and mathematician.* Berkeley Heights, NJ: Enslow Pubishers.

Maupin, M. (2009). *Benjamin Banneker.* Mankato, MN: Child's World.

McGill, A. (1999). *Molly Bannaky.* Boston: Houghton Mifflin.

Pinkney, A. D. (1998). *Dear Benjamin Banneker.* St. Louis, MO: Turtleback.

Scieszka, J. (1995). *Math curse.* New York: Viking Juvenile.

Tang, G. (2004). *Grapes of math.* New York: Scholastic.

Tang, G. (2005). *Math for all seasons.* New York: Scholastic.

Wadsworth, G. (2003). *Benjamin Banneker: Pioneering scientist.* Minneapolis, MN: Carolrhoda.

Weatherly, M. (2006). *Benjamin Banneker: American science pioneer.* Mankato, MN: Compass Point Books.

Welsh, C. A. (2008). *Benjamin Banneker.* Minneapolis, MN: Lerner Publications.

3rd Grade–5th Grade

Use literature to introduce the first notable women in mathematics by reading aloud *Of Numbers and Stars: The Story of Hypatia* (Love, 2006). Hypatia was a Greek scholar in the 4th century who lived in the city of Alexandria in Roman Egypt, home of the great library at Alexandria where her father Theon was a professor. Even though she was a girl, Theon educated Hypatia, which was very unusual for the time, and she became a mathematician, astronomer, and teacher. Her work on a book on cones, and making them understandable, was so well done it survived and was used through many centuries. Lead a discussion of the book using reader response questions and prompts: What do you think of the story of Hypatia? Hypatia loved math. How do you feel about math?

Students can read more books and do online research on Hypatia, and they can also read about cones and write a reader's theatre script to present what they learned about her and cones. A group of five could work together on the script, taking the following parts: Narrator, Theon (her father), Hypatia, and Hypatia Students 1 and 2 (who can demonstrate what they learned about cones from Hypatia using models and charts). (See Strategy 40: Reader's Theatre for more information.)

Other students can read more about Hypatia, the library at Alexandria, cones, and other mathematicians of the ancient world.

Books

Benedick, J. (1995). *Archimedes and the door of science.* Bathgate, ND: Bethlehem Books.

Bradley, M. J. (2006). *Birth of mathematics: Ancient times to 1300.* New York: Facts on File.

Donovan, S. (2008). *Hypatia: Mathematician, inventor, and philosopher.* Mankato, MN: Compass Point Books.

Ellis, J. (2004). *What's your angle, Pythagoras? A math adventure.* Watertown, MA: Charlesbridge.

Hanson, A. (2007). *What in the world is a cone?* Edina, MN: SandCastle.

Hayhurst, C. (2006). *Euclid: The great geometer.* New York: Rosen Central.

Hightower, P. (2009). *The greatest mathematician: Archimedes and his eureka! moment.* Berkeley Heights, NJ: Enslow.

Hoban, T. (2000). *Cubes, cones, cylinders, and spheres.* New York: Greenwillow.

Keating, S. (2002). *Archimedes: Ancient Greek mathematician.* Broomall, PA: Mason Crest.

Lasky, K. (1994). *The librarian who measured the earth.* Boston: Little Brown.

Love, D. A. (2006). *Of numbers and stars: The story of Hypatia.* New York: Holiday House.

Murphy, S. J. (2001). *Captain Invincible and the space shapes.* New York: Harper Collins.

Neuschwander, C. (2003). *Sir Cumference and the sword in the cone: A math adventure.* Watertown, MA: Charlesbridge.

Staeger, R. (2008). *Ancient mathematicians.* Greensboro, NC: Morgan Reynolds.

Trumble, K. (2003). *The library of Alexandria.* New York: Clarion.

6TH GRADE–8TH GRADE

Use literature to introduce Emmy Noether, a famous German mathematician, by reading aloud *Emmy Noether: The Mother of Modern Algebra* (Tent, 2008). Lead a discussion using reader response questions and prompts: What did you think of the story of Emmy Noether? She loved math. How do you feel about math? What parts of her life and her contributions to mathematics interested you most?

Create a class set of books on the lives of mathematicians. Students can read and do online research on other famous mathematicians, including women, and work in pairs to present what they have learned in a *Meet the Press* format. The students can write questions and answers based on the life and work of the mathematician and research the area of mathematics for which they were famous. To present what they have learned, one student will take the part of an interviewer, and the other will take the part of the interviewee—the famous mathematician. After presenting information about their lives and ideas, they can do a demonstration of a concept or problem that the mathematician made famous. They can video record the interview. The interviews for each pair can be video recorded and become a segment of a Meet the Mathematician video documentary by the class.

Books

Bruno, L. C., & Baker, L. W. (1999). *Math and mathematicians: The history of math discoveries around the world.* Farmington Hills, MI: U.X.L.

Henderson, H. (1995). *Modern mathematicians.* New York: Facts on File.

Karamanides, D. (2006). *Pythagoras: Pioneering mathematician and musical theorist of Greece.* New York: Rosen Central.

McElroy, T. (2004). *A to Z of mathematicians*. New York: Facts on File.

Reimer, L., & Reimer, W. (1990). *Mathematicians are people too: Stories from the lives of great mathematicians*: Vol. I. Palo Alto, CA: Dale Seymour.

Reimer, L., & Reimer, W. (1993). *Mathematicians are people too: Stories from the lives of great mathematicians*: Vol. II. Palo Alto, CA: Dale Seymour.

Rosinsky, N. M. (2008). *Sir Isaac Newton: Brilliant mathematician and scientist*. Mankato, MN: Compass Point.

Sherman, J. (2005). *Charles Babbage and the story of the first computer*. Hockessin, DE: Mitchell Lane.

Tent, M. B. W. (2008). *Emmy Noether: The mother of modern algebra*. Natwick, MA: A. K. Peters.

Tent, M. B. W. (2009). *Leonard Euler and the Bernoullis: Mathematicians from Basel*. Natwick, MA: A. K. Peters.

Venkatraman, P. (2008). *Women mathematicians*. Greensboro, NC: Morgan Reynolds Press.

Weir, J. (2009). *Isaac Newton: Groundbreaking physicist and mathematician*. Mankato, MN: Compass Point.

English Learners

English learners from a variety of cultures and language groups can benefit from knowledge about famous mathematicians around the world and through history who share their culture and language. An excellent resource for this for older students is the book *Agnesi to Zeno: Over 100 Vignettes From the History of Math* (Sanderson, 1996). This collection includes vignettes about mathematicians from some of the many cultures represented and second languages spoken by students in American schools, including the following: from China, ideograms, Liu Hui, Shiing-Shen, Mei Wending, Yang Hui, and Zhu Shijie; from India, Brahmagupta's concept of zero; from Latin America, the Mayan step pyramids and concept of zero, the Inca and Aztec calendars, the use of the quipu by the Incas to keep records, and noted educator Jaime Escalante; from Khmer (the language spoken in Cambodia), the temple calendar. There is also a section on ethnomathematics to contextualize mathematics as a human endeavor practiced all over the world throughout history. Each vignette also includes student activities and mathematical problems for use in the classroom.

Books

Sanderson, S. (1996). *Agnesi to Zeno: Over 100 vignettes from the history of math*. Emeryville, CA: Key Curriculum.

STRUGGLING STUDENTS

Struggling students can participate in many of the experiences in reading and learning about mathematicians, but they may also benefit from the use of a frame that was prepared for researching and writing a biography. This frame could be on two pages. One page would pose questions for the students with space to write the information they find. The other would change the sentences into statements that the student can use to write a biography.

Q&A Frame for Writing a Mathematician Biography

Questions

1. What mathematician are you writing about?
2. What city or country did she or he live in?
3. What years did she or he live?
4. What was his or her contribution to mathematics?
5. What are the three most interesting things you learned about the mathematician?

Answers

The mathematician I am writing about is _____. She/he lived in the city/country of _____ during the years _____. Her/his contribution to mathematics was _____

_____.

The three most interesting things I learned about the mathematician were

1. _____.

2. _____.

3. _____.

ASSESSMENT

For students in Grades K through 2, review the almanac journal they kept using a rubric. For older students, use a rubric for the presentation of reader's theatre or another dramatic simulation of the research students conducted on a mathematician. (See Strategy 40: Reader's Theatre for an assessment rubric.)

RESOURCES

Berlinghoff, W. P., & Gouvea, F. O. (2003). *Math through the ages: A gentle history for teachers and others.* Farmington, ME: The Mathematical Association of America: Oxton House Publishing.

References

Gutstein, E. (2003). Teaching and learning mathematics for social justice in an urban Latino school. *Journal for Research in Mathematics Education, 34,* 37–73.

Moses, R. P., & Cobb, C. E. (2001). *Radical equations: Civil rights from Mississippi to the algebra project.* Boston: Beacon Press.

Silver, E. A., Smith, M. S., & Nelson, B. S. (1995). The QUASAR Project: Equity concerns meets mathematics education reform in the middle school. In W. G. Secada, E. Fennema, & L. B. Adajian (Eds.), *New directions for equity in mathematics education* (pp. 9–56). Cambridge, MA: Cambridge University Press.

Math Poetry

First-grade students in Louisiana used the rhyming pattern of the traditional counting song "Over in the Meadow" after the teacher read a picture book of the song illustrated by Ezra Jack Keats. They wrote this class song about where they lived in Cajun country, near the Atchafalaya basin, with its rich array of animal and marine life that the students knew about from their own experience:

"Over on the Bayou"

Over on the bayou in the sand and the sun,

Lived an old mother gator and her little gator one.

"Chomp" said the mother; "I chomp" said the one,

And they chomped and were glad in the sand and the sun.

RATIONALE

Poetry and math have a natural connection in the classroom. Young students can learn counting through repeated rhymes and songs. Older students see that riddles ask the kinds of questions that are used in math problems and puzzles and that words can be arranged and spoken in ways that demonstrate and communicate mathematical understanding.

Young children experience and use numbers in many contexts, one of which is encounters with rhymes and poetry from children's literature (Copley, 2000).

Source: From *Principles and standards for school mathematics,* by the National Council of Teachers of Mathematics, 2000. Reston, VA: Author.

Mathematics Standards

Process Standards

3. Communication: Use the language of mathematics to express mathematical ideas precisely
4. Connections: Recognize and apply mathematics in contexts outside of mathematics
5. Representation: Use representations to model and interpret physical, social, and mathematical phenomena

---

STRATEGY

Use poetry that is about math, such as counting rhymes for younger students, or use different forms of poetry, such as riddles, as a model for students to think about math and write poetry about the math content they are learning.

For all students, read poems that ask the following question: What is math? After listening to or reading these poems, lead a discussion using reader response questions and prompts: Was there anything in the poem that reminded you of what you think or how you feel about math? What would you say in answer to this question: What is math?

Students can respond to these questions, and their responses can be recorded in a list on chart paper, a whiteboard, or an overhead transparency. Students can then write a class list poem titled "Math is. . . ." using the words and phrases recorded on their list of ideas. Take dictation for younger students and write the poem on chart paper. For older students, model writing the poem using the responses from the discussion; students can write a list of their ideas about what math is independently, or in small groups, before they write their own "Math is. . . ." poems. At the beginning of the school year, these poems can become part of an assessment of students' knowledge, beliefs, and feelings about math, and they can provide direction for planning further math instruction.

Also read other rhymes, riddles, and poems about math and use these or other types of poetry as a frame for students to write poetry about math.

GRADE-LEVEL MODIFICATIONS

K–2ND GRADE

Ask students, What do you think math is? Student responses can be recorded on a cluster at the top of a piece of chart paper. Write the title "Math is . . . ." under the cluster and ask students to choose words and phrases to write under the title for a class poem with each line beginning with "Math is. . . ." Words and phrases can be added to the poem throughout the year, and it can be posted in the room. Students who are writing can use this experience as a model to write their own "Math is. . ." poems, which can then be used to conference with the student and assess their knowledge and understanding of math to plan further instruction.

Rhyming counting books, which use repeated rhymes or songs as a framework for teaching the names, words, numerals, and sequence of counting, are an excellent example of math poetry to read aloud with young children. Read aloud one of the many illustrated counting books based on the traditional song "Over in the Meadow," such as *Over in the Meadow*, illustrated by Ezra Jack Keats (1999). This counting rhyme uses a repeated pattern:

"Over in the meadow, in the sand and the sun,
Sat an old mother turtle and her little turtle one.
Swim said the mother, I swim said the one,
And they swam and were glad in the sand and the sun"

The next verse follows the same pattern, but now there are two baby animals. Do repeated readings of the book with students joining in the song, also using gestures like holding up the number of fingers to represent the number in that verse. Also make a chart with the numeral and word for 1 to 10 and point to, or have a student point to, each number as the song is sung.

Use this rhyming song as a model for students to write a class poem using the numbers from 1 to 10, writing either about any content they choose or about a topic they are exploring in class. First, the class can brainstorm the types of words needed in the song.

Place	Describe place	Animal	Number

Students can use the words and the following frame to write their own counting song. Words at the end of each line can rhyme, but they don't have to.

"Over in the . . ."

Over in the _____(place), in the _____ and the _____ (describe place),
Lived an old mother _____ (animal) and her little _____ (animal) ____ (number)
_____ (action) said the mother, I/We _____ (action) said the _____ (number)
And they ____ (action) and were glad in the _____ and the
_____ (describe place).

Verses can be added to the song. The charts with the verses can be illustrated by students, students can copy the verses and illustrate them, and they can be put together in their own book of "Over in the. . . ." There are many children's books based on "Over in the Meadow" and other books using counting rhymes, many of which can be used to make connections with other content areas.

Books

Berkes, M. (2004). *Over in the ocean: In a coral reef*. Nevada City, CA: Dawn.

Berkes, M. (2007). *Over in the jungle: A rainforest rhyme*. Nevada City, CA: Dawn.

Berkes, M. (2008). *Over in the arctic: Where the cold winds blow*. Nevada City, CA: Dawn.

Cabrera, J. (2000). *Over in the meadow*. New York: Holiday House.

Hutchings, A., & Hutchings, R. (1997). *The gummy candy counting book*. New York: Scholastic.

Keats, E. J. (1999). *Over in the meadow.* New York: Viking.

Langstaff, J. (1957). *Over in the meadow.* New York: Harcourt.

March, T. J., & Ward, J. (1999). *Way out in the desert.* Lanham, MD: Rising Moon.

Newcome, Z. (2009). *Ten in the bed and other counting rhymes.* New York: Walker Books.

Pinczes, E. J. (1993). *One hundred angry ants.* Boston: Houghton Mifflin.

Rose, D. L. (2003). *The twelve days of kindergarten: A counting book.* New York: Harry N. Abrams.

Slate, J. (1998). *Miss Bindergarten celebrates the 100th day of kindergarten.* New York: Dutton Juvenile.

Wadsworth, O. A. (2002). *Over in the meadow.* New York: North-South Books.

Ward, J. (2000). *Somewhere in the ocean.* Landham, MD: Rising Moon.

Ward, J. (2002). *Over in the garden.* Landham, MD: Rising Moon.

Ward, J. (2007). *Way up in the arctic.* Landham, MD: Rising Moon.

Yolen, J. (2006). *Count me a rhyme: Animal poems by the number.* Honesdale, PA: Wordsong.

3RD GRADE–5TH GRADE

Read aloud a poem about math from the collection edited by Lee Bennett Hopkins (2001), *Marvelous Math: A Book of Poems*; for example, the title poem "Marvelous Math," by Rebecca Kai Dotlich, and other poems by Karla Kuskin, Janet S. Wong, Lillian M. Fisher, and David McCord, among others. Lead a discussion using reader response questions and prompts such as the following: The poet Rebecca Kai Dotlich thinks math is marvelous. What do you think? Record their responses on a list to create a list poem titled "Math is . . . ."

Another way to link poetry and math is to read and write poems that combine language and math, like math riddle rhymes or the poems written by Betty Franco (2006) in *Mathematickles!*—which use a math equation as the structure of the poem. Write one of these poetic equations on chart paper and create a frame for student writing, using words in place of numbers in the equation.

Addition

(word) + (word) = (word) Example: Peanut butter + jelly + bread = sandwich.

Or Example:

(words)	warm days
(words)	camp
+ (words)	+family reunion
_____	_____
(words) =	summer vacation

Subtraction

(word) − (word) = (word) Example: Days − friends = lonely.

Or Example:

(word)	days
− (word)	− friends
_____	_____
(word) =	lonely

The students can use any equation that will allow them to express what they want to say in the poem, and the poems can be on any topic, including math. As students learn new operations in math, they can use them to write these poetic equations. Many children's books combine language and math in math poetry.

Books

Cleary, B. P. (2008). *On the scale, a weighty tale.* Brookfield, CT: Millbrook.

Franco, B. (2006). *Mathematickles!* New York: Aladdin.

Holub, J. (2003). *Riddle-iculous math riddles and rhymes.* Morton Grove, IL: Albert Whitman.

Hopkins, L. B. (Ed.). (2001). *Marvelous math: A book of poems.* New York: Simon & Schuster.

Lewis, J. P. (2002). *Arithme-Tickle: An even number of odd riddle-rhymes.* San Diego, CA: Harcourt.

Martin, J. (2003). *ABC math riddles.* Columbus, NC: Peel Productions.

Tang, G. (2005). *Math potatoes: Mind-stretching brain food.* New York: Scholastic.

6TH GRADE–8TH GRADE

Read aloud Carl Sandburg's poem "Arithmetic," from the single-edition picture book illustrated by Ted Rand (Sandburg, 1993), or put the poem on an overhead transparency or make an individual copy for each student and have one student at a time read a line. Lead a discussion using reader response questions and prompts: What did you think of the way Carl Sandburg described math? How would you describe what math is? Students can each make a list of what they think math is to write a "Math is. . ." list poem.

Read aloud poems for two voices from Paul Fleischman's (2004) *Joyful Noise: Poems for 2 Voices* and put an example on an overhead projector to model the structure of the poem for students, who will work in pairs and combine their "Math is. . . ." poems and then read them aloud in a poem for two voices. Use a frame to show the structure of the poem.

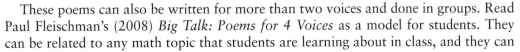

Poem for Two Voices

1st Voice (Student 1)   *2nd Voice (Student 2)*

Together

_____   _____

_____

Student 1 arranges his or her list in a left-hand column, and Student 2 arranges hers or his in a right-hand column. Their ideas are their own. They do not have to concur. If there is an idea they share, they can place it in a middle column. The poem is read by both, left to right and up and down. Student 1 is the 1st voice, Student 2 the 2nd voice, and the lines in the middle are read by both simultaneously.

These poems can also be written for more than two voices and done in groups. Read Paul Fleischman's (2008) *Big Talk: Poems for 4 Voices* as a model for students. They can be related to any math topic that students are learning about in class, and they can work in pairs and groups of four to discuss their understandings, any problems they are having, solutions, and other thoughts.

Books of poetry on math for two or more voices:

Fleischman, P. (1989). *I am Phoenix: Poems for 2 voices.* New York: HarperCollins.

Fleischman, P. (2004). *Joyful noise: Poems for 2 voices.* New York: HarperCollins.

Fleischman, P. (2008). *Big talk: Poems for 4 voices.* Cambridge, MA: Candlewick Press.

Franco, B. (2009). *Messing around on the monkey bars: And other poems for two voices.* Cambridge, MA: Candlewick Press.

Pappas, T. (1993). *Math talk: Mathematical ideas in poems for two voices.* San Carlos, CA: Wide World Publishing.

Sandburg, C. (1993). *Arithmetic.* San Diego, CA: Harcourt Brace Jovanovich.

ENGLISH LEARNERS

Young English learners benefit from the use of repeated rhyme, rhythm, and song, just as children who are learning a home language do when learning cultural sequences like counting. They can also use gestures and Total Physical Response (TPR) by showing a number using their fingers. Many languages use the same numerals as are used in English, so English learners will have familiarity with them. Add the words in English and in the home language to show the connection. Tap into students' prior knowledge because everybody counts in any language. There are also counting books that may match students' home language: for example, *Ten Elephants and a Spider's Web: A Traditional Latin American Counting Rhyme* (Ortiz, 2009) is in Spanish and English.

Books

Ortiz, E. (2009). *Ten elephants and a spider's web: A traditional Latin American counting rhyme.* Orlando, FL: Ortiz Publishing.

STRUGGLING STUDENTS

Use frames for writing math poems, with the addition of word banks—or lists of vocabulary words written on the same paper as the frame so that students can read, recognize, and use the words as they need in the frame. Repeated readings of student-written poetry can also benefit students.

Assessment

Successful completion of math poetry writing can be determined by the student's ability to produce a poem, through participation in a class or group poetry writing experience, or independently. A rubric cocreated with students can address both poetry writing and mathematical understanding for assessment: for example, both the math and language were used appropriately in a counting or equation poem.

Resources

Franco, B. (1999). *Counting caterpillars and other math poems.* New York: Scholastic.

Franco, B. (2006). *Math poetry: Linking language and math in a fresh way.* Tucson, AZ: Good Year Books.

Harrison, D. L., & Holderith, K. (2003). *Using the power of poetry to teach language arts, social studies, math, and more.* New York: Scholastic.

Lewis, J. P., & Robb, L. (2007). *Poems for teaching in the content areas: 75 powerful poems to enhance your history, geography, science, and math lessons.* New York: Scholastic.

Liatsos, S. (1999). *Poems to count on.* New York: Scholastic.

Simpson, J. (2005). *Circle-time poetry math: Delightful poems with activities that help young children build phonemic awareness, oral language, and early math skills.* New York: Scholastic.

References

Copley, J. V. (2000). *The young child and mathematics.* Washington, DC: National Association for the Education of Young Children.

Cubing Math Vocabulary

Figure 21.1   Cubing fraction vocabulary, 3rd grade

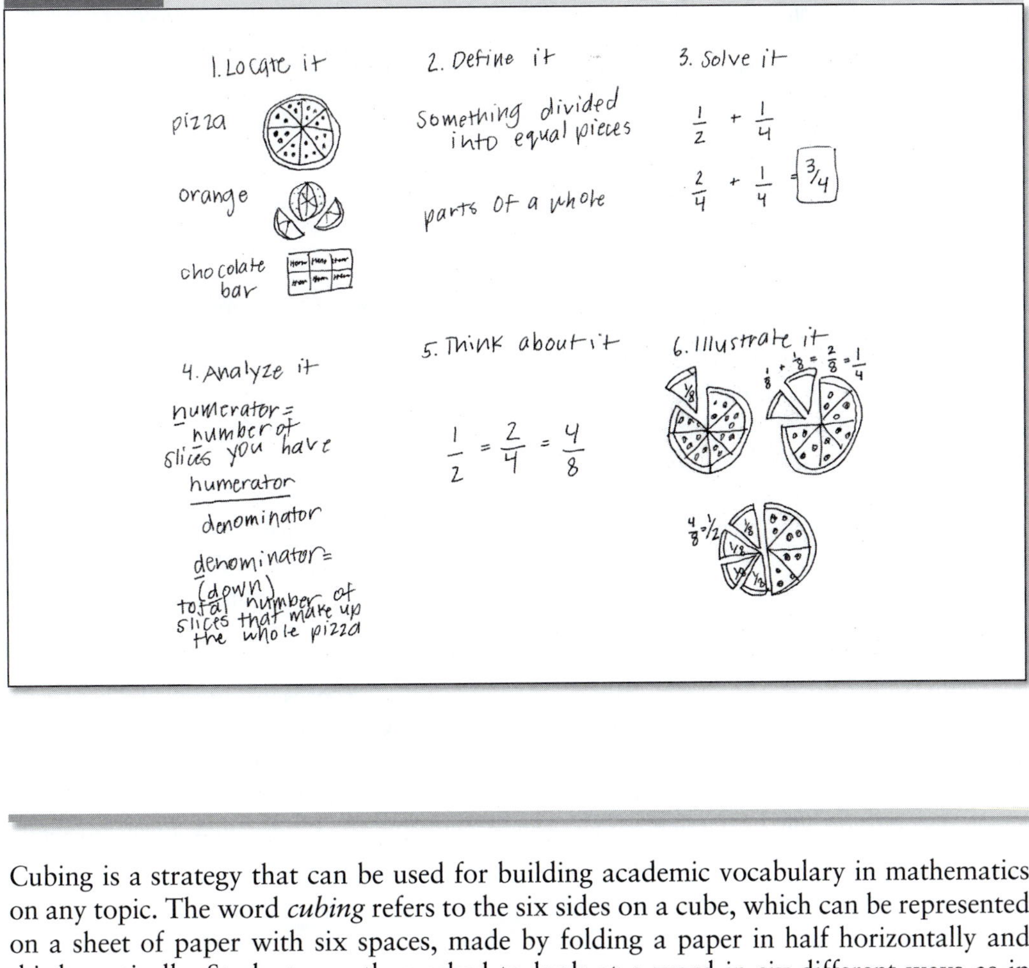

1. Locate it

pizza

orange

chocolate bar

2. Define it

Something divided into equal pieces

parts of a whole

3. Solve it

$\frac{1}{2} + \frac{1}{4}$

$\frac{2}{4} + \frac{1}{4} = \boxed{\frac{3}{4}}$

4. Analyze it

numerator = number of slices you have

$\frac{numerator}{denominator}$

denominator = (down) total number of slices that make up the whole pizza

5. Think about it

$\frac{1}{2} = \frac{2}{4} = \frac{4}{8}$

6. Illustrate it

$\frac{1}{8} + \frac{1}{8} = \frac{2}{8} = \frac{1}{4}$

$\frac{4}{8} = \frac{1}{2}$

RATIONALE

Cubing is a strategy that can be used for building academic vocabulary in mathematics on any topic. The word *cubing* refers to the six sides on a cube, which can be represented on a sheet of paper with six spaces, made by folding a paper in half horizontally and thirds vertically. Students are then asked to look at a word in six different ways as in Figure 21.1. Provide experiences in math, moving from concrete to more abstract and using literature with related concepts and vocabulary. Students respond to probes about the word, such as locate it, define it, solve it, analyze it, think about it, and illustrate it.

The cubing strategy can be adapted to differentiate instruction across grade levels, for English learners and struggling students, and can be based in students' individual needs.

Language is an essential aspect of the development of mathematical ideas in students (Ellerton, Clarkson, & Clements, 2000). Without sufficient language to communicate the ideas they are developing, children will be limited in their ability to interact with the others, and they will lose opportunities to further develop mathematical thinking (Cobb, Yackel, & McClain, 2000). Students need the necessary vocabulary to understand the lessons and other students as explanations of mathematical concepts and processes are given and to allow them to give their own explanations. Typically, specialized vocabulary in a content area such as mathematics is challenging (Pearson, Hiebert, & Kamil, 2007), and math also makes use of common words that have specialized meanings. This is especially important for students for whom English is not their first language.

Source: From *Principles and standards for school mathematics,* by the National Council of Teachers of Mathematics, 2000. Reston, VA: Author.

Mathematics Standards

Process Standards

1. Problem solving: Apply and adapt a variety of appropriate strategies to solve problems

3. Communication: Organize and consolidate their mathematical thinking through communication

4. Connections: Recognize and use connections among mathematical ideas; recognize and apply mathematics in contexts outside of mathematics

---

STRATEGY

Teach a concept in math, beginning with concrete objects and moving to more abstract representation with numbers, operations, and problem solving. These math experiences can be expanded with literature that uses the relevant vocabulary; the words can be read about, discussed, and identified together.

To further explore and understand these words and how they can be used, brainstorm with students a list of the words used in a book on the topic. Model the cubing strategy with one of the words on chart paper or an overhead transparency. As an introduction to the strategy, ask students to look at an object, for example, from six different perspectives by moving it to different positions on a table.

To cube a math vocabulary word, the students can fold a piece of paper in half horizontally, and then in thirds vertically, to make six spaces representing the six sides of a cube. In each of the six spaces on the paper, they can respond to a question and prompts and write about a vocabulary word from a different perspective. The six questions and prompts can be adapted by to differentiate for grade levels and other student differences. Do cubing with younger students as a class by recording their ideas on chart paper, or have students do it independently or in small groups.

GRADE-LEVEL MODIFICATIONS

K–2ND GRADE

Use concrete objects to introduce money: "play money" for students or real money used by the teacher. While teaching the value of coins and bills, basic operations like adding and subtracting money, and counting by ones, fives, and tens, literature can be used to both assess for understanding and to teach students the academic vocabulary of math for money.

Read *The Coin Counting Book* (Williams, 2001), which uses rhymes and large, clear color photographs of coin denominations and of grouping and counting coins arranged in sets with visual equations illustrating their mathematical equivalents. The book ends with a problem for students to solve: What are all the ways a dollar is made? Lead a discussion using reader response questions and prompts: What questions do you have about counting coins? What do you know about money? Read other books on money (see *Books,* which follows).

Ask students for the words about money they heard in the books and make a list on one side of a piece of chart paper (e.g., the names for coins, bills, and, when appropriate, words like *face value, currency,* and *denomination*). Draw a rectangle in the remaining space, divided in half horizontally and in thirds vertically to create six spaces, with a different question and prompt at the top of each space. These can be adapted for each class. Record students' ideas in each space, and have students take the pen and add words and drawings themselves.

Six Questions and Prompts for Cubing Math Vocabulary for Money, K–2

1. Name it: What do we call it?

2. Describe it: What does it look like?

3. Find it: What is an example of it?

4. Compare it: What other thing is it like?

5. Use it: Show a problem with it.

6. Draw it: Make a picture of it.

Books

Axelrod, A. (1997). *Pigs will be pigs: Fun with math and money.* New York: Simon & Schuster.

Dalton, J. (2006). *Counting money.* Danbury, CT: Children's Press.

Dalton, J. (2006). *Making change at the fair.* Danbury, CT: Children's Press.

Doudna, K. (2002). *Let's subtract bills.* Edina, MN: ABDO.

Doudna, K. (2002). *Let's subtract coins.* Edina, MN: ABDO.

Doudna, K. (2003). *Let's subtract money.* Edina, MN: ABDO.

Hill, M. (2005). *Dollars.* Danbury, CT: Children's Press.

Hill, M. (2005). *Quarters.* Danbury, CT: Children's Press.

Rosinsky, N. M. (2003). *All about money.* Mankato, MN: Compass Point.

Wells, R. (1997). *Bunny money.* New York: Dial.

Williams, R. L. (2001). *The coin counting book.* Watertown, MA: Charlesbridge.

3RD GRADE–5TH GRADE

Concurrent with teaching fractions, use literature and the cubing strategy to assess and teach academic math vocabulary related to fractions. Read aloud books by Jerry

Pallotta: *Apple Fractions* (2002) and *The Hershey's Milk Chocolate Fractions Book* (1999). The former uses large color photographs of apples cut in various fractions, and in the latter, the 12 little rectangles of a Hershey's chocolate bar are used to show concepts and introduce vocabulary. Portions of apples or a Hershey's milk chocolate bar can be used to move from the concrete to the abstract in learning about fractions. Make a copy of the Hershey bar from the book for each child, which they can cut into the 12 segments and use as a manipulative.

Lead a class discussion using reader response questions and prompts: What questions do you have about fractions? What do you know about fractions? With students, make a list of the academic math vocabulary related to fractions (e.g., names of fractions, fraction parts, numerator, denominator, etc.).

Students can work in pairs using the cubing strategy for fraction vocabulary. They can fold a piece of paper in half horizontally and in thirds vertically to make six spaces. Each pair can choose or be assigned a vocabulary word and can complete the cube using the following questions and prompts, with a copy given to each pair.

Six Questions and Prompts for Cubing Math Vocabulary for Fractions, 3–5

1. Locate it: Make a list of all the places in which we find fractions in everyday life.

2. Define it: What is a fraction?

3. Solve it: Create and find the answer to a problem with fractions.

4. Analyze it: What are the parts of a fraction? Define the parts and show the relationship among them.

5. Think about it: How many different ways can you represent the same fraction?

6. Illustrate it: Draw a picture of a page in a children's book on fractions you might write.

The pairs can share their completed cube with another pair or with the whole class.

Books

Gifford, S. G. (2008). *Piece = part = portion*. Berkeley, CA: Tricycle Press.

Leedy, L. (1996). *Fraction action*. New York: Holiday House.

Naga, A. W. (2004). *Polar bear math*. New York: Henry Holt.

Pallotta, J. (1999). *The Hershey's milk chocolate fractions book*. New York: Scholastic.

Pallotta, J. (2001). *Twizzlers percentages book*. New York: Scholastic.

Pallotta, J. (2002). *Apple fractions*. New York: Scholastic.

6TH GRADE–8TH GRADE

While teaching data analysis and probability, use literature and the cubing strategy to assess and teach academic math vocabulary. Read aloud *Do You Wanna Bet? Your*

Chances to Find out About Probability (Cushman, 1991) or *A Very Improbable Story: A Math Adventure* (Einhorn, 2008) and lead a discussion using reader response questions and prompts: Can you give an example of data analysis and probability from your own life? During the discussion of the book, make a list of the academic vocabulary associated with data analysis and probability and introduce the cubing activity to assess students' understanding of these words.

Give each student a list of possible ways they can use the vocabulary words while approaching a concept from a variety of perspectives: describe it, compare it, associate it, analyze it, apply it, connect it, illustrate it, change it, solve it, question it, use it, rearrange it, satirize it, evaluate it, relate it to something else, contrast it, investigate it, explain the significance of it, put it in historical perspective, list the cause/effects of it, cartoon it, tell the parts of it, argue for/against it, personify it, and so on. These can be adapted to differentiate by class, student ability, and interests.

Assign, or let students choose, six of these to respond on a cubing sheet—a 12 × 18 or larger piece of paper folded in half horizontally and then in thirds vertically. For example, some perspectives to probe on data analysis and probability could be as follows.

Six Questions and Prompts for Cubing Math Vocabulary for Data Analysis and Probability, 6–8

1. Define it: What is a random stratified sample? When would you use one?

2. Call it into question: Is there such a thing as a truly random sample?

3. Conduct it: Choose a random sample of n = 15 students from class and conduct a survey of their favorite sports team/food/band, and so on. You choose. Describe how you arrived at your sample and create a data display of your results.

4. Argue it: Make an argument for which graphing method is the easiest to read: pie charts, stem-and-leaf plots, bar graphs, or line graphs. Construct a visual model to show why.

5. Evaluate it: Find an opinion poll online or in the newspaper. What type of graph is used to display the results? Do you feel the data display is accurate or misleading?

6. Cartoon it: Create a political cartoon using a graph or commenting on the use of graphs in politics.

Students can complete the cubing activity independently, in pairs, or groups of six, where one student would take primary responsibility for one of the six perspectives and collaborate with other students to complete the activity.

Books

Adelson, B. (1998). *Slam dunk trivia: Secrets, statistics, and little-known facts about basketball.* Minneapolis, MN: Lerner Publications.

Catel, P. (2010). *Graphing money.* London: Heinemann Educational Books.

Cushman, J. (1991). *Do you wanna bet? Your chance to find out about probability.* New York: Clarion.

Einhorn, E. (2008). *A very improbable story: A math adventure.* Watertown, MA: Charlesbridge.

Rand, C. (2010). *Graphing sports.* London: Heinemann Educational Books.

Solway, A. (2010). *Graphing immigration.* London: Heinemann Educational Books.

Solway, A. (2010). *Graphing war and conflict.* London: Heinemann Educational Books.

Somervil, B. A. (2010). *Graphing natural disasters.* London: Heinemann Educational Books.

Tabak, J. (2004). *Probability and statistics: The science of uncertainty.* New York: Facts on File.

Thomas, I. (2008). *Graphing food and nutrition.* London: Heinemann Educational Books.

Thomas, I. (2008). *Graphing population.* London: Heinemann Educational Books.

ENGLISH LEARNERS

Tap into students' prior knowledge and relate the words to their own experiences and life. Visuals, real objects, and hands-on experiences can clarify concepts and words as well. When possible, use cognates in the students' home languages for primary language support. Students who are less proficient in English than others can also draw and illustrate responses and label their drawings with the vocabulary being learned to demonstrate their understanding.

STRUGGLING STUDENTS

Create the six space cubing display for students and print specific questions and prompts on it, along with a word bank of the vocabulary. Students can work in pairs.

ASSESSMENT

Use a student's cubing sheet to assess their understanding of math concepts and their ability to use the academic vocabulary associated with it. In addition, a rubric can be created or cocreated with students or the cubing sheet can be used to conference with students. After reviewing the cubing sheets, give students word problems to solve that require using the vocabulary.

RESOURCES

Fogelberg, E., Skalinder, C., Satz, P., Hiller, B., Berstein, L., & Vitantonio, S. (2008). *Integrating literacy and math: Strategies for K-6 teachers*. New York: The Guilford Press.

REFERENCES

Cobb, P., Yackel, E., & McClain, K. (Eds.). (2000). *Symbolizing and communicating in mathematics classrooms*. Mahwah, NJ: Erlbaum.

Ellerton, N., Clarkson, P., & Clements, M. A. (2000). Language factors in mathematics education. In K. Owens & J. Mousley (Eds.), *Research in mathematics education in Australasia 1996–1999* (pp. 29–95). Sydney: MERGA.

Pearson, P. D., Hiebert, E. H., & Kamil, M. (2007). Vocabulary assessment: What we know and what we need to learn. *Reading Research Quarterly, 42*(2), 282–296.

Strategy 22

Math Stories

The kindergarten teacher had read the counting book *Ten Black Dots*, by Donald Crews, to her class of all English learners, Khmer speaking Cambodian American students. After re-reading and counting together, she gave them blue dot stickers to put on paper to draw a picture, Figure 22.1. Then they wrote a class story together, and the teacher modeled English using the students' ideas for "What Can You Do With Blue Dots?"

"Once upon a time a mother and her little girl went for a walk. There was 1 blue sun in the sky. The little girl had 3 blue ice creams. The sun melted the ice creams and the little girl cried. Her mother gave her 1 blue balloon and she was happy. How many things can you do with blue dots? 5 things."

| Figure 22.1 | "What Can You Do With Blue Dots?" |

RATIONALE

Students can learn math concepts, skills, and vocabulary by writing and illustrating math stories with the math content as an integral part of the story narrative. The structure of a story provides a scaffold for students to use problem solving as they make decisions about the story theme, characters, setting, and plot. Many children's books integrate math content into a story and can be used to model writing math stories with students.

Stories in children's books can provide many meaningful experiences with mathematics for students (Whitin & Whitin, 2004). Using natural language in conversation and interaction leading to communicating ideas in writing has been shown to be associated with success in mathematical problem solving (Ferrari, 1996). Vygotsky (1992) maintained that the transition from oral to written text is considered a prototype for the transition from common knowledge to scientific knowledge in terms of consciousness, intentionality, and systematic organization.

Reading and discussing stories with math content and moving from an oral to a written text through planning and revision can provide this transition in a meaningful context.

Source: From Principles and standards for school mathematics, by the National Council of Teachers of Mathematics, 2000. Reston, VA: Author.

Mathematics Standards

Process Standards

1. Problem Solving: Build new mathematical knowledge through problem solving; Solve problems that arise in mathematics and other contexts
2. Reasoning and Proof: Make and investigate mathematical conjectures; Select and use various types of reasoning and methods of proof
4. Connections: Recognize and apply mathematics in contexts outside of mathematics

---

STRATEGY

Use literature that blends math concepts, skills, and vocabulary into the narrative of a story as a model for students to write their own stories related to any math content they are learning.

Read and discuss a story with students and then model or review the elements of a story (i.e., setting, characters, plot, mood, and theme) as well as the structure of a story (i.e., with a beginning or opening hook or a problem to be solved, a middle and development of events, a climax, and a solution). Also describe what math content, skills, and vocabulary should be included in the story.

The students can generate ideas as a class, or students can work in pairs, groups, or independently to write math stories. Stories can be shared by reading them aloud or by illustrating them and posting them on a bulletin board, or they can be word processed and made into a book of class math stories, dramatized using reader's theatre (using story dramatization and script writing), or videotaped.

GRADE-LEVEL MODIFICATIONS

K–2ND GRADE

Read aloud *Pigs Will Be Pigs: Fun With Math and Money* (Axelrod, 1997), which is about a family of personified pigs who want to go to a Mexican restaurant but realize on their way out that they don't have enough money. They return to the house and search everywhere—for example, under couch cushions—for enough coins and bills to pay for the meal. As the story unfolds, they add up each amount of money they find until they have enough. Lead a discussion using reader response questions and prompts: Has anything like this ever happened to you? Tell about it.

Review the elements and structure of a story with students using this book and add ideas the students have for writing their own story on chart paper.

	Parts of a Story	
Setting (Where)	Characters (Who)	Plot/Order (What/When)
Our Story		

Write the concepts and math vocabulary students need to use in the story. For example, the author of the story about pigs used the concept and skill of adding money, and the vocabulary included the names of the denominations of coins and bills, in both words and numerals, with the cent and dollar sign, decimal point, and equation for an addition problem.

The students can compose the class story, which can be recorded on chart paper. The story writing may take place over several days, adding a new part to the story each day. Students can also take the pen and write on the chart paper, and after each writing session, students can illustrate a part of the story. The students can also monitor to see if they have used all the math concepts, skills, and vocabulary and used them correctly. When the story is complete, it can be published on a bulletin board, or students can make a copy on smaller paper or word process it and illustrate each page to publish as a book.

Many other children's books blend math concepts, skills, and vocabulary with a narrative story line.

Books

Axelrod, A. (1997). *Pigs will be pigs: Fun with math and money.* New York: Simon & Schuster.

Axelrod, A. (1999). *Pigs go to market: Fun with math and shopping.* New York: Aladdin.

Axelrod, A. (1999). *Pigs in the pantry: Fun with math and cooking.* New York: Aladdin.

Axelrod, A. (2000). *Pigs on the ball: Fun with math and games.* New York: Aladdin.

Axelrod, A. (2002). *Pigs on the move: Fun with math and travel.* New York: Aladdin.

Axelrod, A. (2005). *Pigs in the corner: Fun with math and dance.* New York: Aladdin.

Burns, M. (2008). *The greedy triangle.* New York: Scholastic.

Crews, D. (1995). *Ten black dots.* New York: Greenwillow.

Dodds, D. A. (2009). *Full house: An invitation to fractions.* Cambridge, MA: Candlewick Press.

Hightower, S. (1997). *Twelve snails to one lizard: A tale of mischief and measurement.* New York: Simon & Schuster.

Kroll, V. L. (2005). *Equal shmequal.* Watertown, MA: Charlesbridge Publishing.

Moore, I. (1993). *Six-dinner Sid.* New York: Aladdin.

Murphy, S. (1997). *Just enough carrots.* New York: HarperCollins.

Napoli, D. J. (2007). *The wishing club: A story about fractions.* New York: Henry Holt.

Pinczes, E. J. (1995). *A remainder of one.* Boston: Houghton Mifflin.

Schnitzlein, D. (2007). *The monster who did my math.* Atlanta, GA: Peachtree Press.

Wright, A (1997). *Alice in Pastaland.* Watertown, MA: Charlesbridge.

3rd Grade–5th Grade

Read aloud *The King's Chessboard* (Birch, 1993) or *One Grain of Rice: A Mathematical Folktale* (Demi, 1997). Both books use the math concepts of estimation and patterns, wrapped in the narrative of a traditional tale. Lead a discussion using reader response questions and prompts: What was your favorite part of the story? What story would you tell?

Tell the class they will write their own math stories and review literary elements (setting, characters, plot, mood, theme) and structure of a story (beginning, including statement of a problem; middle, including how the problem is being solved; ending, with a final solution). The class can brainstorm ideas for a math problem that could be solved in a story related to what they are learning in math and for types of traditional tales they could use to tell how it was solved. Record their ideas on a T-chart titled "Math Problems and Traditional Tales."

Students can work in groups to write a story, choosing from the ideas on the T-chart or generating their own ideas. The students could present their stories using drama: through reader's theatre or through writing the story as a script and presenting it as a play.

Other children's books combine math content and a story narrative, including many traditional stories.

Books

Birch, P. (1993). *The king's chessboard.* New York: Puffin.

Burns, M. (1997). *Spaghetti and meatballs for all! A mathematical story.* New York: Scholastic.

Calvert, P. (2006). *Multiplying menace: The revenge of Rumpelstiltskin.* Watertown, MA: Charlesbridge.

Demi. (1997). *One grain of rice. A mathematical folktale.* New York: Scholastic.

McCallum, A. (2006). *Beanstalk: The measure of a giant.* Watertown, MA: Charlesbridge.

McCallum, A. (2007). *Rabbits, rabbits everywhere: A Fibonacci tale.* Watertown, MA: Charlesbridge.

Neuschwander, C. (2001). *Sir Cumference and the great knight of angleland: A math adventure.* Watertown, MA: Charlesbridge.

Neuschwander, C. (2006). *Sir Cumference and the Isle of Immeter. A math adventure.* Watertown, MA: Charlesbridge.

Neuschwander, C. (2009). *Mummy math: An adventure in geometry.* Watertown, MA: Charlesbridge.

Neuschwander, C. (2009). *Sir Cumference and all the King's tens: A math adventure.* Watertown, MA: Charlesbridge.

Tompert, A. (1998). *Grandfather Tang's story.* New York: Random House.

6th Grade–8th Grade

Read aloud *Zachary Zormer: Shape Transformer* (Reisberg, 2006). Zachary is a class cut-up who forgets his math homework, which was to bring something to measure to class. Luckily, he has a scrap of paper in his pocket and a vivid imagination. Can you double the length of a strip of paper without cutting it? Zachary Zormer, Shape Transformer can! Math content introduced in the story via Zachary includes area, perimeter, length, width, and a Moebius strip.

Two other collections could also be read. The first collection is titled *The Man who Counted: A Collection of Mathematical Adventures* (Tahan, 2008). Malba Tahan is the creation of a Brazilian mathematician who wrote Arabian night stories about the character Beremiz Samir, who goes on a journey and settles disputes, gives wise advice, overcomes dangerous enemies, and wins fame and fortune. Each story draws on the history of a famous mathematician, and each is built around a classical mathematical puzzle. In the second collection, titled *The Number Devil* (Enzensberger, 2000), the main character is Robert, a boy who hates math. In 12 dreams, he meets a sly number devil who introduces him to the wonder of numbers (e.g., infinite, prime, Fibonacci, etc.). Discuss the stories using reader response questions and prompts: What did you think of the story? What kind of a story would you write?

Review literary elements and story structure on a chart or overhead transparency with students, using the book or one of the stories that were read aloud. Prepare a handout for each student with (1) the literary elements and story structure, and (2) a math concept, skills, and vocabulary. Students can work in groups, writing a story using the math content. The stories could be word processed and compiled in a book or read over time like a series of stories from the Arabian Nights.

Books

Enzensberger, H. M. (2000). *The number devil.* New York: Henry Holt.

Reisberg, J. A. (2006). *Zachary Zormer: Shape transformer.* Watertown, MA: Charlesbridge.

Tahan, M. (2008). *The man who counted: A collection of mathematical adventures.* New York: W. W. Norton.

ENGLISH LEARNERS

Tap into prior knowledge so that students can use their own life experiences in a story. Also of benefit are visuals, writing frames, and any cognates related to the parts of a story. For example, here are some English/Spanish cognates:

Story = historia

Character = character

Sequence = secuencia

Middle = medio

English learners can work in collaborative pairs or groups with more English-proficient peers, contributing ideas which can be clarified and written down by other students. They can also add illustrations to a story to demonstrate their understanding of story structure and the math content.

STRUGGLING STUDENTS

Provide a frame for the structure of a story for each student to use, while the teacher models for the whole class or group.

Parts of a Story

Setting (where the story takes place) _____

Characters (who is in the story)

1.

2.

3.

Plot (what happens in the story) and Sequence (when things happen)

Beginning

Middle

End

Each student could also be given a copy of the math concepts, skills, and vocabulary in a word bank to use as they write the story. Students could also dictate ideas for the parts of a story, which could be recorded on the Parts of a Story Frame. Students could then copy the ideas on a student copy of the frame and transition these ideas into sentences and paragraphs to write the story.

ASSESSMENT

Cocreate a rubric with students for story parts and structure and for the specific math concepts, skills, and vocabulary to be used in the story. The students can use the rubric to both guide their writing and use of math content and to provide a means to evaluate it. Individual students or students writing in groups can also switch stories and provide peer-assessment for the other student or groups.

RESOURCES

Greenberg, D. (2005). *Fractured math fairy tales.* New York: Scholastic.

REFERENCES

Ferrari, P. L. (1996). *On some factors affecting advanced algebraic problem solving.* Proceedings of PME-XX (Vol. 2, pp. 345–352). Valencia, Spain.

Vygotsky, L. S. (1992). *Pensiero e linguaggio. Edizione critica di L. Meccacci.* Bari: Laterza.

Whitin, D. J., & Whitin, P. (2004). *New visions for linking literature and mathematics.* Reston, VA: NCTM.

Strategy
23

Math in the World

A 5th-grade teacher with a class of predominantly English learners asked her father to come to school to show her class how numbers are written in Arabic, explain how to say them, give an example of how to use them in a math problem, and to talk to her students about how he used math in his business. The students were very excited to meet their teacher's father, and they wrote letters to their own parents inviting them to school to teach the class numbers in one of the home languages of the students—Spanish, Khmer, and Korean—and how they used math in the jobs.

RATIONALE

The teacher can contextualize math in the real world for students by introducing counting systems from other languages, countries, and cultures and explaining the many ways math is used in the world, including real world examples in the United States. The teacher can use literature and can also tap into students' prior knowledge and experience if they speak a home language other than English by inviting their family members to school to share their math knowledge with the class.

Darling-Hammond and Ancess (1996) stated the following: "Education for democracy requires more than equal access to technical knowledge. It requires access to social knowledge and understanding forged by participation in a democratic community." (p. 166). Students should see themselves in the curriculum and link mathematics to their everyday lives, and they should see that mathematics is connected to the social needs of the community (Malloy & Malloy, 1998; Tate & Rousseau, 2002; Woodrow, 1997).

Contextual learning, when students are confronted by problems and challenges in their daily lives, as well as integrated learning with literature and the content areas can make meaningful connections with concepts and skills in mathematics and the real world (Perry & Dockett, 2008). Culture is another important aspect of learning mathematics (Barta & Schaelling, 1998). Teachers can relate instruction to the cultures and languages students bring to class, which Bezuska and Kenney called "honest numbers" (1997). Guha (2006) reported on a study based on an Indian method of finger counting as an example of culturally responsive teaching in the early childhood years and concluded the following:

Using culture as a bait to "hook" students who tend to shy away from mathematics education, or students who are considered less interested or even weak in mathematics skills, the teacher can potentially engage all students regardless of race, ethnicity, caste, or socioeconomic status to learn mathematics in a playful way. Although culturally unfamiliar manipulatives or tools may be more interesting for one group of children as compared to others, they can also generate curiosity among the entire group that can assist in their learning endeavor. (p. 32)

Maree and Erasmus (2006) maintained that "mathematics teaching cannot be divorced from the socio-economic context in which it is taught" (p. 16). The international examination PISA (Programme for International Student Assessment), at the middle school level, places a great deal of emphasis on mathematics within context for social usage in the daily lives of students, measuring such capabilities as recognizing and interpreting mathematical problems in everyday life and translating those problems into a mathematical context (http://www.pisa.oecd.org).

Source: From Principles and standards for school mathematics, by the National Council of Teachers of Mathematics, 2000. Reston, VA: Author.

Mathematics Standards

Process Standards

1. Problem Solving: Apply and adapt a variety of appropriate strategies to solve problems
4. Connections: Recognize and apply mathematics in contexts outside of mathematics
5. Representation: Use representations to model and interpret physical, social, and mathematical phenomena

---

STRATEGY

Use literature to introduce counting systems in the home languages of the English learners in his or her classes, as well as counting systems and how math is used in the real world, both here and in other countries. Students can learn to count in other languages by responding to counting books, making posters with different counting systems to post in the class, and reciting a chosen counting system as "Numbers of the Week or Month" in class.

Invite parents and other family members who speak a language other than English to come to class and teach the counting system and show examples of how math is used in other countries and cultures. Students could also interview parents and other family members about a counting system and how they might work a problem in math. The student could then share this information with the rest of the class by teaching them the numbers and how to work a problem.

Students could also interview or survey family and community members on how they use math in the real world. Students could work independently or in groups to plan a math lesson and teach it to the rest of the class, explaining these real world applications. They can model a real problem, and other students can solve the problem. They could also invite guest speakers to share with the class how math is used in their occupations or vocations. Students could research the use of math in an occupation or vocation that interests them.

GRADE-LEVEL MODIFICATIONS

K–2ND GRADE

An excellent book to read aloud is *Can You Count Ten Toes? Count to 10 in 10 Different Languages* (Evans, 2004). The 10 languages are Japanese, Chinese (Mandarin), Hindi, Hebrew, Tagalog (from the Philippines), Russian, Zulu, Korean, Spanish, and French. The book shows numerals, the word for the number transliterated into English, and how to say the word phonetically. There are also maps showing where each of the languages is spoken. Lead a class discussion using reader response questions and prompts: What questions do you have about the book? Can any of you count in another language?

If any student can count in another language, she or he could teach the numbers to the class. Family members could also be invited to come to school to teach the numbers in their home language to the class. With the help of students or family members, the make a chart showing the numeral, the word in the home language, and the word in English to post in class.

How do you count in (home language)?			
Language	Numerals	Word	How you say it

Record each counting system on a poster for a bulletin board with a map showing where in the world the counting systems used in the home languages of the English learners in the class are located, or use another counting system from a children's book, for example.

The class could designate "Numbers of the Week or Month," and the numbers from one language could be recited daily, during the class opening for example. All students can learn the numbers in all the languages spoken in class, or in other languages they choose. Students could also work in writing groups, each group showing the counting system from another language, a description and interesting facts, and names of any students in the class who can count in the language. Students can illustrate the writing and it can be published in a class book: "Our Class Counts Around the World." There are several children's counting books in other languages.

Books

Boueri, M. (2005). *Lebanon 1–2–3: A counting book in three languages*. Exeter, NH: Publishing Works. (English, French, Arabic)

Cheng, A. (2003). *Grandfather counts*. New York: Lee & Low Books. (Chinese)

Evans, L. (2004). *Can you count ten toes? Count to 10 in 10 different languages*. Boston: Houghton Mifflin. (Japanese, Chinese—Mandarin, Hindi, Hebrew, Tagalog—Phillipines, Russian, Zulu, Korean, Spanish, and French)

Feelings, M., & Feelings, T. (1992). *Moja means one: A Swahili counting book*. New York: Dial Press.

Law, D. (2006). *Come out and play: Count around the world in 5 languages.* New York: North-South Books. (English, Spanish, German, French, and Chinese)

Macdonald, M. R., & Taibah, N. J. (2009). *How many donkeys? An Arabic counting tale.* Morton Grove, IL: Albert Whitman.

Morales, Y. (2003). *Just a minute: A trickster tale and counting book.* San Francisco: Chronicle Books. (Spanish)

Shea, P. D., & Weil, C. (2003). *Ten mice for tet!* San Francisco: Chronicle Books. (Vietnamese)

3rd Grade–5th Grade

Read aloud *One Hen! How One Small Loan Made a Big Difference* (Milway, 2008). This book is based on a true story. The main character, Kojo, must quit school after his father dies because the family has no income. The Ashanti village where he lives is trying *microlending,* a system where the village loans money to one family to buy something to improve their lives. Once the loan is paid back, another family borrows money. Kojo borrows a few coins and buys a hen. He starts a business that grows into the largest poultry farm in West Africa, which employs many people and pays taxes that help build roads and medical facilities. Lead a discussion of the book using reader response questions and prompts: What questions did you have about the story? Kojo borrowed money he needed to start a business. How do you receive money? What would you do with a small loan to start a business?

Introduce the economic concepts of microlending, microfinance, and microcredit organizations. Students can read or do online research to learn more. Help students compose a letter to parents and other family members who are in business, inviting them to come to class to tell about how they are able to finance it. Students can then work in groups planning a business they would start with a small loan, or planning how they might help one of the organizations that promotes microcredit in other countries.

There are several children's story books related to microlending, microfinance, microcredit organizations, and fund-raising, and there are nonfiction books on countries where it has been successfully used as well as on investing and starting a business.

Books

Bair, S. (2008). *Isabel's carwash.* Morton Grove, IL: Albert Whitman.

Bateman, K. R. (2001). *The young investor: Projects and activities for making your money grow.* Chicago: Chicago Review Press.

Bochner, A., & Bochner, R. (2007). *The new totally awesome business book for kids.* New York: Newmarket Press.

Bochner, A., & Bochner, R. (2007). *The new totally awesome money book for kids.* New York: Newmarket Press.

Fridell, R. (2003). *The war on hunger.* Brookfield, CT: Twenty First-Century Books.

McBrier, P. (2004). *Beatrice's goat.* New York: Aladdin.

Milway, K. S. (2008). *One hen! How one small loan made a big difference.* Toronto, Ontario, Canada: Kids Can Press.

Mortenson, G. (2009). *Listen to the wind.* New York: Dial Press.

Schwartz, D. M. (1994). *If you made a million.* New York: HarperCollins.

Streissquth, T. (2008). *Bangladesh in pictures.* Brookfield, CT: Twenty First-Century Books.

Streissquth, T. (2009). *Senegal in pictures.* Brookfield, CT: Twenty First-Century Books.

6TH GRADE–8TH GRADE

Read aloud stories from *Real Life Math Mysteries* (Washington, 1995), a book about math problems in the real world, collected from community members, business professionals, and city officials in a variety of roles (e.g., zookeeper, horse stable owner, archeologist, lawyer, pilot, fireman, newspaper editor, Pizza Hut manager, etc.). Lead a discussion asking reader response questions and prompts: Which of the stories interested you the most? What other real-life math stories do you wonder about?

The students can compile their own collection of real-life math mysteries by interviewing family or community members on a topic that interests them. They can develop a list of appropriate questions to ask or create a survey with a cover letter that could be sent home or e-mailed to potential respondents. The cover letter could include an invitation to come to the class as a guest speaker on how the individual uses math in the real world. Students can work independently or in groups to write a story about each person they interviewed or that responded to a survey.

Books

Anoyo, S. L. (2009). *How chefs use math*. New York: Chelsea House.

Anoyo, S. L. (2009). *How crime fighters use math*. New York: Chelsea House.

Bertoletti, J. C. (2009). *How baseball managers use math*. New York: Chelsea House.

Bertoletti, J. C. (2009). *How fashion designers use math*. New York: Chelsea House.

Egan, J. (2009). *How video game designers use math*. New York: Chelsea House.

Glassock, S. (2009). *How nurses use math*. New York: Chelsea House.

Hense, M. (2009). *How astronauts use math*. New York: Chelsea House.

Hense, M. (2009). *How fighter pilots use math*. New York: Chelsea House.

Washington, M. F. (1995). *Real life math mysteries*. Austin, TX: Prufrock Press.

ENGLISH LEARNERS

Determine the home language of ELs in class and send a letter home to parents in both English and the home language inviting family members to come to school to share information about mathematics appropriate to the grade level of the class (e.g., counting in the home language for K–2 or practical applications of math in the real world for 3–5 and 6–8). School staff or community workers should be able to translate a letter in English.

Visuals such as charts of counting systems in other languages with numerals, words in the other language, transliterations in English, and a pronunciation guide for English can benefit English learners. There will also be cognates and similarities in many languages, for example *one* in English, *uno* in Spanish, *un/e* in French, and *ein* in German.

Tapping into students' prior knowledge and past experience, using primary language support with names for numbers in a student's home language, and making home-school connections also benefit English learners.

STRUGGLING STUDENTS

Students can copy a chart with a counting system in a different language—numerals, word in the other language, and transliterated word in English—into a math journal, which, in addition to the chart, they can use to recite the numbers aloud with the class.

ASSESSMENT

Students can volunteer to count in another language the class has learned when they are ready. Students can also write the words for numbers in both English and another language and show the numerals when they are different than those used by English speakers. Students can also assess each other in pairs on successful completion of this task and report the results.

A rubric can be used for students writing reports on real world math problems, for both the elements of nonfiction writing and the math content.

RESOURCES

Aten, J. (1998). *Math for the real world.* Grand Rapids, MI: Instructional Fair.

Krause, M. C. (2000). *Multicultural mathematics materials* (2nd ed.). Reston, VA: National Council of Teachers of Mathematics.

Muschla, J. A., & Muschla, G. R. (2009). *Hands-on math projects with real-life applications.* San Francisco: Jossey-Bass.

Zaslavsky, C. (1995). *The multicultural math classroom: Bringing in the world.* Portsmouth, NH: Heinemann.

REFERENCES

Barta, J., & Schaelling, D. (1998). Games we play: Connecting mathematics and culture in the classroom. *Teaching Children Mathematics, 4,* 388–393.

Bezuska, S. J., & Kenney, M. J. (1997). Honest numbers: A mathematics and language connection. *Mathematics Teaching in the Middle School, 3*(2), 142–147.

Darling-Hammond, L., & Ancess, J. (1996). Democracy and access to education. In R. Soder (Ed.), *Democracy, education, and the schools* (pp. 151–181). San Francisco: Jossey-Bass.

Guha, S. (2006). Using mathematics strategies in early childhood education as a basis for culturally responsive teaching in India. *International Journal of Early Years Education, 14*(1), 15–34.

Malloy, C., & Malloy, W. (1998). Issues of culture in mathematics teaching and learning. *The Urban Review, 30*(3), 245–257.

Maree, J. G., & Erasmus, C. P. (2006). Mathematics skills of Tswana-speaking learners in the North West province of South Africa. *Early Child Development and Care, 176*(1), 1–18.

Perry, B., & Dockett, S. (2008). Young children's access to powerful mathematical ideas. In L. D. English (Ed.), *Handbook of international research in mathematics education* (pp. 75–108). New York: Routledge.

Tate, W., & Rousseau, C. (2002). Access and opportunity: The political and social context of mathematics education. In L. D. English (Ed.), *Handbook of international research in mathematics education* (pp. 271–300). Mahwah, NJ: Erlbaum.

Woodrow, D. (1997). Democratic education: Does it exist—especially for mathematics education? *For the Learning of Mathematics, 17*(3), 11–17.

Strategy
24

Math Puzzle Journals

Two 2nd-grade students were looking at a math puzzle book that included challenges to make animal shapes out of tangrams. They made a cat and traced the outline in their math puzzle journals. Then one said to the other: "Hey, let's make transformers! They can change from one shape to another."

RATIONALE

Puzzles are a way to engage students with problem solving in math. Children's books with math puzzles are often humorous, use rhyme and verse and riddles, and are highly illustrated to help students visualize the puzzle and find a solution. They are typically not sequential, as in a math textbook series, so they can be dipped into, as with a book of stories or poetry, to read, think, and engage with a challenging puzzle in math. Journals are a way for students to work through a puzzle by drawing and labeling the parts, making calculations, and writing a description and explanation.

Such journals reflect the shift of attention beyond mathematics as computation toward mathematics as "conceptualization, description, and explanation" (Lesh & English, 2005).

Mathematics Standards

Content Standards

2. Algebra: Understand patterns, relations, and functions; Use mathematical models to represent and understand quantitative relationships

3. Geometry: Use visualization, spatial reasoning, and geometric modeling to solve problems

5. Data Analysis and Probability: Develop and evaluate inferences and predictions that are based on data

Process Standards

1. Problem Solving: Monitor and reflect on the process of mathematical problem solving

2. Reasoning and Proof: Select and use various types of reasoning and methods of proof

Source: From Principles and standards for school mathematics, by the National Council of Teachers of Mathematics, 2000. Reston, VA: Author.

185

STRATEGY

Use books with collections of math puzzles, riddles, and challenges to engage students in problem solving using math journals. For younger students, read a picture book with a story centered around a math puzzle or choose from a book with a collection of math puzzles. Work the puzzle with students, recording ideas on chart paper. For older students, model solving a puzzle from a story or collection with the whole class.

Students can begin math puzzle journals. Students in Grades K through 2 can make entries by drawing and labeling the parts of a puzzle, using the class chart as a guide. In Grades 3 through 5 they can use a double-entry journal, with drawing and labeling in one column and calculations in the other. Students in Grades 6 through 8 can use a triple-entry journal, with drawing and labeling, calculations, and a third column for a written description of the problem and an explanation of how they solved it.

Math Journals: Single- (K–2), Double- (3–5), and Triple-Entry (6–8)		
Draw/Label	Calculations	Description/Explanation
K–2 _____		
3–5 _____		
6–8 _____		

Students can work in their math journals independently, in pairs, or in groups. They can work puzzles posed in class or choose a puzzle from a class set of math puzzle books on their own.

GRADE-LEVEL MODIFICATIONS

K–2ND GRADE

Read selections from *Math for all Seasons,* one of several books of math riddles in verse by Greg Tang (2005). This title is for younger students, and it encourages problem solving through the use of illustrations as students find ways to group and look for patterns and then add numbers. Lead a discussion using reader response questions and prompts: Which riddle did you like the best? What are your ideas for solving it?

Start a daily class journal modeling problem solving math puzzles and riddles on chart paper as students take the pen to draw and label and try to find a solution for one of the riddles in the book. Students can also start a math journal of their own and either copy the class chart, work through the problem independently, or both. They can also find riddles and puzzles in other books to work on independently.

Do this on a regular basis, first inviting students to share their solutions for any riddles or puzzles the class wasn't able to solve or to demonstrate a problem they solved independently on chart paper for the rest of the class. Encourage students to find puzzles in books or create new puzzles and riddles to share with the class for solving.

Books

Anno, M. (1997). *Anno's math games*. New York: Putnam.

Anno, M. (1997). *Anno's math games 2*. New York: Putnam.

Anno, M. (1997). *Anno's math games 3*. New York: Putnam.

Anno, M. (1999). *Anno's magic seeds*. New York: Putnam.

McGrath, B. B. (2001). *Skittles riddles math*. Watertown, MA: Charlesbridge.

Tang, G. (2003). *Math appeal*. New York: Scholastic.

Tang, G. (2004). *Math fables: Lessons that count*. New York: Scholastic.

Tang, G. (2005). *Math for all seasons*. New York: Scholastic.

Tang, G. (2007). *Math fables too: Making science count*. New York: Scholastic.

3rd Grade–5th Grade

Read aloud Jon Scieszka's (1995) humorous book *Math Curse*. In the book, the teacher, Mrs. Fibonacci, tells her class, "You know, you can think of almost everything as a math problem." The curse is that her students do just that. As the problems are described in a thoroughly engaging way in everyday circumstances, Scieszka covers a great deal of math content: base numbers, Fibonacci series, logic, and combinations. Lead a discussion asking students reader response questions and prompts: Which puzzle puzzled you? Tell about it.

Model solving one of the problems with students on chart paper, whiteboard, or overhead transparency. Choose, or let students choose, the next problem to solve, and students can work in groups, recording the process of their solutions in a double-entry math journal with drawings, labels, and calculations. The class can come together as a whole so students can share the results of their problem solving process.

Provide a text set of books with math puzzles for students to use independently or collaboratively, recording their results in the double-entry journal.

Books

Anno, M., & Anno, M. (1999). *Anno's mysterious multiplying jar*. New York: Putnam.

Burns, M. N. (1991). *The $1.00 word riddle book*. Sausalito, CA: Math Solutions.

Sachar, L. (1994). *Sideways arithmetic from Wayside School*. New York: Scholastic.

Sachar, L. (2004). *More sideways arithmetic from Wayside School*. New York: Scholastic.

Scieszka, J. (1995). *Math curse*. New York: Viking.

Tang, G. (2002). *The best of times: Math strategies that multiply*. New York: Scholastic.

Tang, G. (2003). *Math-terpieces: The art of problem-solving*. New York: Scholastic.

Tang, G. (2004). *Grapes of math*. New York: Scholastic.

Tang, G. (2005). *Math potatoes: Mind-stretching brain food*. New York: Scholastic.

Zaslavsky, C. (1998). *Math games and activities from around the world*. Chicago: Chicago Review Press.

6TH GRADE–8TH GRADE

Read aloud *Zachary Zormer: Shape Transformer* (Reisberg, 2006), a story about a boy who forgets his homework, which was to bring something interesting to measure to class. When it's his turn to share what he brought, he remembers a scrap of paper in his pocket and uses his imagination to pose this math puzzle to the class: "Can you double the length of a strip of paper without cutting it?" Zachary Zormer, Shape Transformer can, and he shows the class how. He demonstrates solving other problems this way as he continues to forget things he's supposed to bring to class for show and tell. Lead a discussion of the book using reader response questions and prompts: What did you think of Zachary's solutions?

Model the problems Zachary posed related to area, perimeter, length, and width, and share his solutions using a Moebius strip, an expanding frame, and a flashlight with the class. The students can work through the solutions in groups and discuss what happened.

Then pose a new puzzle to the class and let students work in groups to solve it, recording their ideas in a triple-entry math journal with space for (1) drawing and labeling the parts of the problem, (2) calculations, and (3) a description and explanation of the solution. Students can share their solutions, they can be assigned puzzles on a regular basis, or students can find problems in books to work independently or in groups in the journals and demonstrate the solutions to the rest of the class.

Books

Miller, M. (2001). *40 fabulous math mysteries kids can't resist.* New York: Scholastic.

Pappas, J. (1993). *Fractals, googols and other mathematical tales.* San Carlos, CA: Wide World Publishing.

Pappas, J. (1997). *The adventures of Penrose the mathematical cat.* San Carlos, CA: Wide World Publishing.

Pappas, J. (2004). *Further adventures of Penrose the mathematical cat.* San Carlos, CA: Wide World Publishing.

Reisberg, J. A. (2006). *Zachary Zormer: Shape transformer.* Watertown, MA: Charlesbridge Publishing.

Wise, B. (2002). *Whodunit math puzzles.* Falls Church, VA: Sterling.

ENGLISH LEARNERS

English learners benefit from the use of visuals usually associated with math puzzles in children's books. Provide concrete objects, such as beans, to provide hands-on experiences as well. Students can use drawings to demonstrate understanding of a problem, and a more proficient English speaking peer can provide labels. Collaboration through student to student interaction in groups also provides support. Primary language support can be provided through books if students can read in their home language.

Driscoll, L. (2009). *El chico del despegue/The Blast-Off Kid* (Spanish Edition). Minneapolis, MN: Kane Press.

STRUGGLING STUDENTS

Struggling students can use dialogue journals with the teacher, teacher's aide, or more capable peers. The students can copy the puzzle into a journal from a chart that was used for modeling. When they have made an entry in the journal, an adult or another student can dialogue with them about it, also providing labels, making written comments they can explain to the student in a conference, and posing questions. Problems from books can be chosen that both interest students and match their ability levels.

ASSESSMENT

Periodically conference with students on a rotating basis, asking them to tell about the math puzzles or riddles they worked on, what they discovered, and what other questions they have. Keep a record of the dates and results of these conferences with anecdotal notes. Assess students' problem solving development and make both further plans for instruction and recommendations to the student for other problems to solve—and books to use as sources of these.

RESOURCES

Ball, J. (2005). *Go figure: A totally cool book about numbers*. New York: DK.

Cipriano, J. S. (2006). *Arithmetricks*. Tucson, AZ: Good Year Books.

Stickels, T. (2009). *Math puzzles and brainteasers*. San Francisco: Jossey-Bass.

REFERENCES

Lesh, R., & English, L. D. (2005). Trends in evolution of models and modeling perspectives on mathematical learning and problem solving. *International Reviews on Mathematical Education, 37*(6), 487–489.

PART IV

Science

WHAT RESEARCH HAS TO SAY ABOUT LITERATURE-BASED TEACHING AND SCIENCE

Inquiry-based, discovery-focused science instruction is widely viewed as best practice today (National Science Teachers Association [NSTA], 2002). What is *inquiry* in science instruction? Here is how the National Science Teachers Association (NSTA) defines inquiry:

> Scientific inquiry refers to the diverse ways in which scientists study the natural world and propose explanations based on the evidence derived from their work. Inquiry also refers to the activities of students in which they develop knowledge and understanding of scientific ideas, as well as an understanding of how scientists study the natural world. (p. 23)

Here are examples of activities that students or scientists would do if they were engaged in inquiry:

1. Make observations

2. Ask questions

3. Read books and look for other sources of information to find out what is already known

4. Plan an investigation

5. Use tools to gather, organize, analyze, and interpret data and information

6. Make predictions and suggest answers and explanations

7. Communicate findings and results to others

While there tends to be less emphasis today on teaching science in elementary and middle schools than on literacy and mathematics, teachers are not opposed to teaching science (Cobern & Loving, 2002). They may feel, however, that there are limited resources and time to teach science or have personal and system perceptions of a lack of importance for science teaching in the classroom. They have also expressed a lack of confidence in their ability to teach science (Lee & Houseal, 2003).

Many science educators believe constructivist principles, such as eliciting children's ideas and encouraging discussion and exploration, are a sound basis for effective science teaching (Akerson, Flick, & Lederman, 2000; Flick, 1995; Kelly, Brown, & Crawford, 2000; Nuthall, 2001). Research (Vosniadou, Ioannides, Dimitrakopoulou, & Papademetriou, 2001) has shown that this kind of scaffolding during inquiry instruction may include the following experiences for students: expressing and supporting their ideas, making and testing hypotheses and predictions, investigating in small groups, comparing ideas, giving scientific explanations and suggesting models, and presenting and debating ideas and conclusions in the whole class.

While the NSTA (2002) recommends a focus on inquiry-based, discovery-focused instructional approaches to science, this is not the only recommended approach. Teachers can use a range of materials and strategies to teach the skills, knowledge, and abilities addressed in the science standards. Furthermore, using hands-on learning in science is not a guarantee of inquiry and discovery outcomes, nor is reading and using literature such as nonfiction and narrative books with science information incompatible with inquiry and discovery learning.

Ideally, a teacher would use both approaches, combining observations of the real world, record-keeping, experiments, and other hands-on science activities with literature, to introduce a science topic and for continued research on the topic in the classroom. Both are necessary to build the foundation of a good science program. In a study of students participating in an experimental group using both science observations and engaging books, Anderson (1998) found that the students in this group acquired more conceptual knowledge than other groups not using the combined approach. The NSTA (2002) also suggested that students learn science best when it is integrated with other areas of the curriculum such as reading, language arts, and mathematics. This would include reading textbooks, newspapers, magazines, online information, and children's and young adult literature, both fiction and nonfiction (Newton, Newton, Blake, & Brown, 2002; Vaughn, Sumrall, & Rose, 1998).

Teachers can build a class collection of books to motivate students to engage in thinking and researching topics in inquiry-based, discovery-focused science (Morrison & Young, 2008). Excellent science trade books are widely available for students K through 8. These are not textbooks, but individual or series books about scientific adventures, biographies of the lives of scientists, and careers in science; they blend factual information about the solar system, living organisms, and the earth with scientific inquiry for students across a range of ages, reading abilities, and interests. Trade books can be used in science education in several ways: to read aloud to a class to introduce a science topic and related facts; to answer student questions and generate further student questions about a topic through discussion of the book; and to further explore a topic combined with hand-on experiences in science. One of the recommendations of The American Association for the Advancement of Science's *Project 2061* (1989) was to integrate literature into the science curriculum. While students can become engaged with scientific phenomenon through observation, recording data, and designing and carrying out experiments, literature can build their understanding of scientific concepts (Bruning & Schweiger, 1997).

Nonfiction trade books can help children acquire science-related information through a presentation of facts, using a well-organized format and graphics such as photographs, charts, maps, tables, and so on. For younger students, scientific concepts and information are often presented following a story line, blending fact and fiction and using narrative to pull the facts through a story. Notable examples of this type of book include many by Eric Carle for young children, such as *The Very Hungry Caterpillar*, and the *Magic School Bus* series, by Joanna Cole, for older students.

Using a collection of trade books on a science-related topic allows a teacher to integrate a theme-based and a project approach to teaching science. The teacher can introduce a topic of choice that addresses the standards and is appropriate for the grade level they are teaching and then build a class collection of books around the topic. Themes such as Change or the Environment cut across curricular areas, including science. Topics may also emerge during the school year that will be of interest to students. For example, during hurricane season in Louisiana with a hurricane forming in the Gulf of Mexico, teachers can plan activities using literature as the source of reading and research on extreme weather.

GUIDELINES FOR SELECTING BOOKS FOR TEACHING SCIENCE

The NSTA publishes a list of "Outstanding Science Trade Books" each year; the books are chosen by a team of science educators who base their decisions on both the content and presentation of each book. Recently, they have grouped their selections according to the eight categories of the science standards. Their selection is based on the following criteria:

- The book has substantial science content.

- Information is clear, accurate, and up-to-date.

- Theories and facts are clearly distinguished.

- Facts are not oversimplified to the point that the information is misleading.

- Generalizations are supported by facts, and significant facts are not omitted.

- Books are free of gender, ethnic, and socioeconomic bias.

For lists of recommended science trade books each year, see the following resources:

- An annual article in *Science and Children* titled "Outstanding Science Trade Books for Students K–12"

- A list on the NSTA website (www.nsta.org), posted under "NSTA Recommends"

Important considerations in choosing books for science instruction are the nature and depth of the science content and the quality of representations of science concepts, although research has indicated that such factors do not always play an important role in newly qualified teachers' selections of science trade books (Peacock & Gates, 2000). Teachers tend to choose trade books to supplement other activities, for alternative and additional instructional ideas, and if they believe the science topics of the books are of interest to their students and will help students achieve goals in science that address expectations of the curriculum and standards (Butts, Koballa, Anderson, & Butts, 1993). While teachers look for books related to the science content they are teaching, they report that, when given a choice, they also tend to choose fiction over nonfiction because they want students to be engaged by a book and enjoy it (Donovan & Smolkin, 2001). It's possible, however, that students may acquire misinformation as well as information, especially with regard to books of fiction (Mayer, 1995). If teachers choose fictional stories related to science content, they should carefully evaluate these books for accuracy and presentation of the content. Introducing a science topic with a book of fiction that has accurate information presented in a narrative form can be highly motivational and engaging to children, and it can then be followed up with nonfiction books that focus on the scientific information.

The *Magic School Bus* series, published by Scholastic, is an example of an artful combination of narrative, characterization, humor, graphic presentation of information, and science content. Written by Joanna Cole and illustrated by Bruce Degen, each book follows the adventures of Ms. Frizzle as she takes her class on scientific adventures in a magic school bus. Magic indeed, the bus can take students on a journey through a city waterworks, to the center of the earth or the ocean floor, into outer space, inside the human body, and back to the time of the dinosaurs. The books also model student questions in speech bubbles; how to present science information in charts, graphs, and models; and examples of student report writing. A teacher can introduce a science topic with one of the books in the series and then introduce a variety of books of nonfiction on the topic to support student learning.

National Standards For Science

The eight categories of the national science content standards are as follows (NSTA, 1996):

1. Unifying concepts and processes in science (measurement, measurement tools)

2. Science as inquiry (asking questions, planning and conducting investigations, using appropriate tools and techniques to gather data)

3. Physical science (properties of objects and materials; position and motion of objects; light, heat, electricity, energy, and magnetism)

4. Life science (organisms, life cycles of organisms, organisms and environments, structure and function in living systems, reproduction and heredity, regulations and behavior, populations and ecosystems; diversity and adaptations of organisms)

5. Earth and space science (properties of Earth materials, objects in the sky, changes in Earth and sky, structure of the Earth system, Earth's history, Earth in the solar system)

6. Science and technology (distinguish between natural objects and objects made by humans, abilities of technological design, understanding about science and technology)

7. Science in personal and social perspectives (personal health, characteristics and changes in populations, types of resources, changes in environments, science and technology in local challenges)

8. History and nature of science (science as human endeavor, nature and history of science)

REFERENCES

Akerson, V. L., Flick, L. B., & Lederman, N. G. (2000). The influence of primary children's ideas in science on teaching practice. *Journal of Research in Science Teaching, 37*(4), 363–385.

American Association for the Advancement of Science. (1989). *Science for all Americans: A Project 2061 report on literacy goals in science, mathematics, and technology.* Washington, DC: Author.

Anderson, E. (1998). Motivational and cognitive influences on conceptual knowledge: The combination of science observation and interesting texts (Doctoral dissertation, University of Maryland, College Park). *Dissertation Abstracts International, 59*(06), 1913A.

Bruning, R., & Schweiger, B. M. (1997). Integrating science and literacy experiences to motivate student learning. In J. T. Guthrie & A. Wigfield (Eds.), *Reading engagement: Motivating readers through integrated instruction* (pp. 149–167). Newark, DE: International Reading Association.

Butts, D. P., Koballa, T., Anderson, M., & Butts, D. P. (1993). Relationship between teacher intentions and their classroom use of Superscience. *Journal of Science Education and Technology, 2*(1), 349–357.

Cobern, W. W., & Loving, C. C. (2002). Investigation of preservice elementary teachers' thinking about science. *Journal of Research in Science Teaching, 39*(10), 1016–1031.

Donovan, C. A., & Smolkin, L. B. (2001). Genre and other factors influencing teachers' book selections for science instruction. *Reading Research Quarterly, 36,* 412–440.

Flick, L. B. (1995). Navigating a sea of ideas: Teacher and students negotiate a course toward mutual relevance. *Journal of Research in Science Teaching, 32*(10), 1065–1082.

Kelly, G. J., Brown, C., & Crawford, T. (2000). Experiments, contingencies, and curriculum: Providing opportunities for learning through improvisation in science teaching. *Science Education, 84,* 624–657.

Lee, C. A., & Houseal, A. (2003). Self-efficacy, standards, and benchmarks as factors in teaching elementary school science. *Journal of Elementary Science Education, 15*(1), 37–55.

Mayer, D. A. (1995). How can we best use literature in teaching science concepts? *Science and Children, 32,* 16–19, 43.

Morrison, J. A., & Young, T. A. (2008). Using science trade books to support inquiry in the elementary classroom. *Childhood Education, 84*(4), 204–208.

National Science Teachers Association. (1996). *National science education standards* (Position statement). Retrieved January 20, 2010, from http://www.nsta.org/about/positions/standards.aspx

National Science Teachers Association. (2002). *Elementary school science* (Position statement). Retrieved January 20, 2010, from http://www.nsta.org/positionstatement&psid=8

Newton, L. D., Newton, D. P., Blake, A., & Brown, K. (2002). Do primary school science books for children show a concern for explanatory understanding? *Research in Science & Technological Education, 20*(2), 227–240.

Nuthall, G. (2001). Understanding how classroom experience shapes students' minds. *Unterrichtswissenschaft, 29*(3), 224–267.

Peacock, A., & Gates, S. (2000). Newly qualified primary teachers' perceptions of the role of text material in teaching science. *Research in Science & Technological Education, 18*(2), 155–171.

Vaughn, M. N., Sumrall, J., & Rose, L. H. (1998). Preservice teachers use the newspaper to teach science and social studies literacy. *Journal of Elementary Science Education, 10*(2), 1–9.

Vosniadou, S., Ioannides, C., Dimitrakopoulou, A., & Papademetriou, E. (2001). Designing learning environments to promote conceptual change in science. *Learning and Instruction, 11,* 381–419.

Graphic Organizers

Strategy 25

A kindergarten teacher plans to teach science as inquiry and life science, specifically as it relates to butterflies. To engage her young students, she first reads *The Very Hungry Caterpillar,* by Eric Carle, aloud, and after a discussion, she asks them to complete a sentence frame from the book about the hungry little caterpillar: "On Monday he ate through one apple...." She records what each student says on a language experience chart. Kate says: "On Monday, Kate ate one apple." Kate draws a picture of this (Figure 25.1) and her teacher writes what she recorded on the chart on the picture. The students' responses and pictures are made into a book called *The Very Hungry Kindergarten Class.* With many books on butterflies in the classroom, the students cocreate a descriptive model chart of a butterfly with their teacher.

Figure 25.1   "On Monday, Kate ate one apple"

RATIONALE

A graphic organizer is a strategy for science instruction that teachers can use to help students record information from direct observation as well as from reading in order to create a descriptive model of an organism or a phenomenon. Graphic organizers are visual illustrations of concepts, information, and verbal statements. They can take many forms useful in teaching inquiry process skills in science: descriptive feature charts, T-charts, flow charts, Venn diagrams, tree diagrams, and semantic maps, among others. Graphic organizers provide a picture of key ideas and information on a topic and the relationship of the parts to the whole. Furthermore, research showed that when students constructed their own graphic representation of material in an explanatory text, they showed better understanding than those who copied an illustration or wrote a summary (Edens & Potter, 2003; Gobert & Clement, 1999; Tomkins & Tunnicliffe, 2001).

When fiction and nonfiction books are integrated into the teaching of a content area such as science, graphic organizers are useful for organizing information and enabling students to classify observations and facts, comprehend the relationships among phenomenon, draw conclusions, develop explanations, and generalize scientific concepts. For example, an important inquiry process skill is comparing. It is a way of creating order from gathering observations from the natural world and making sense of scientific information that has been read. A teacher can use a T-chart to teach this skill. A T-chart is in the shape of the letter *T,* with a horizontal line at the top to signify a broad category and a vertical line that allows students to compare attributes of a concept, organism, or phenomenon. With a topic as the title on the horizontal line, students compare two aspects of the topic on each side of the vertical line. These can be mutually exclusive, such as comparing mammals and nonmammals or insects and spiders, or they can compare two types of spiders with different characteristics.

Charts and other graphic organizers have been found to be effective with students who are struggling with learning content at their grade level or who have difficulty learning (Guastello, Beasley, & Sinatra, 2000). To use charts effectively, Baxendell (2003) offered the following research-based recommendations: (1) Use charts consistently. For example, each time that a process with steps is taught, use a flow chart. (2) Make sure charts clearly show the relationship among key concepts, words, and ideas on a topic. Use clear labels. (3) Be creative when using charts across a lesson or unit in science and across content areas. For example, a chart can be used to introduce a topic after reading a book to activate students' prior knowledge and background experiences, to later clarify problem areas and analyze and synthesize concepts, and, finally, to help students communicate and review what they have learned.

Source: From National science education standards, by the National Science Teachers Association, 1996. Washington, DC: National Academy Press.

Science Standards

2. Science as inquiry (*Abilities necessary to do science inquiry; Understandings about science inquiry*)

4. Life Science (*The characteristics of organisms; Diversity and adaptations of organisms; Life cycles of organisms*)

STRATEGY

Introduce and model the use of graphic organizers as a strategy for inquiry-based, discovery-focused science. Students can learn to organize and analyze observations from the natural world, such as of organisms or objects, but they can also use information from books to begin using charts and to complement and supplement first-hand observations.

Choose, read aloud, and lead discussions on one or more books about living organisms or other topics using reader response questions and prompts to engage students and connect to their experience of the book and prior knowledge. Ask students to describe what they learned from the reading, discussion, and observation of illustrations, photographs, diagrams, charts, maps, and other graphic representations in a book. Then, model how to organize and record the information on various types of charts to classify, clarify, compare, analyze, and interpret it.

The features of an organism can be displayed on a descriptive feature chart with a horizontal and vertical axis to develop a descriptive model of the organism, such as a butterfly. A T-chart can be used to identify differences among organisms, such as insects and spiders or mammals and nonmammals, by placing one on the left side of the vertical line on and the other on the right side. Flow charts can be used to build a descriptive model of the life cycle of an organism.

After modeling the use of a graphic organizer with a class and engaging them in its development, students can practice using it in pairs, groups, or individually. They can come together again as a class to discuss what they have discovered. Students can also use graphic organizers to communicate to others what they have learned, especially if a class is divided into groups with each group studying a different aspect of a science topic or problem using the jigsaw approach. Finally, graphic organizers are also useful tools for students to review a topic, and they can be used for assessment purposes. This same strategy can be used with observations of real world phenomena after modeling with literature.

Graphic organizers produced by students can be displayed as posters in the classroom, as a page in a student-written book, on an overhead projector transparency or in a PowerPoint presentation, or in an online blog on a topic to communicate and clarify for others what the students have discovered.

Plus Technology

Many online sources provide information about charts and other graphic organizers, including how to use them across the K through 8 curriculum, and also offer free, printable versions that students can use on their own after a topic in science has been introduced through literature, class discussions, and modeling using student ideas and responses:

- www.teachervision.com
- www.freeology.com
- www.eduplace.com

GRADE-LEVEL MODIFICATIONS

K–2ND GRADE

Eric Carle's (1986) classic picture book *The Very Hungry Caterpillar* is often read aloud by teachers in the primary grades because of its engaging narrative and captivating illustrations. It's an ideal book for students to read along with the teacher using the illustrations as clues to making predictions for reading comprehension. Teachers also use it for several other instructional purposes: learning the names of the days of the week in sequence, reviewing the names of various foods, counting, and learning about the life cycle of a caterpillar as it turns into a butterfly.

After reading aloud, ask reader response questions tapping into students' own experiences: What food do you like to eat? What is a day that you ate it? How many did you eat? Record student responses in a sentence frame on a language experience chart: "On (day of the week) (name of child) ate (number) (food)." See an example from a kindergarten class at the beginning of this strategy. Students can then draw a picture of themselves eating the food and copy their sentence from the language experience chart onto the picture as a caption. These can be bound into a class book titled *The Very Hungry Kindergarten* (or other grade) *Class*.

Collect a text set of other books on caterpillars and butterflies to read aloud or for students to look at or read on their own, with an adult, in pairs, or in groups. Students can also observe a butterfly specimen, watch butterflies hatch from eggs that can be ordered from a biological supply company, and view images and videos of butterflies online. The website www.butterflywebsite.com is a good source of information, with many links to photographs and video clips of butterflies for students to observe.

Then, use a chart that organizes the characteristics of a butterfly to build a descriptive model of an organism.

Descriptive feature chart for a butterfly				
Body parts	*Number*	*Color & Shape*	*Position*	*Appearance*
Antennae	2	Black, straight line	On head	Thin
Head	1	Black, round	Front of thorax	Tiny, big eyes
Thorax	1	Red & black, oval	Behind head	Bigger than head
Abdomen	1	Yellow, long oval	Behind thorax	Black dots, 8 parts
Legs	6	Black, straight line	Attached to thorax	4 long, 2 short
Wings	2	Yellow & black, curve	Attached to thorax	Large, colorful

As a whole class, in pairs, small groups, or on their own, students can use the descriptive feature chart to write a description of a butterfly, summarizing, analyzing, and interpreting what they observed, organized, and classified on the chart.

Books

Allen, J. (2000). *Are you a butterfly?* New York: Kingfisher.

Bishop, N. (2009). *Butterflies and moths.* New York: Scholastic

Bunting, E. (1999) *Butterfly house.* New York: Scholastic.

Carle, E. (1986). *The very hungry caterpillar.* New York: Philomel.

Gibbons, G. (1989). *Monarch butterfly.* New York: Holiday House.

Lerner, C. (2002). *Butterflies in the garden.* New York: HarperCollins.

Swinbourne, S. (2006). *Wings of light: Butterfly migration.* Honesdale, PA: Boyds Mills Press.

Swinbourne, S. (2009). *A butterfly grows.* Boston: Houghton Mifflin Harcourt.

Wallace, K. (2000). *Born to be a butterfly.* London: Dorling Kindersley.

Zemlicka, S. (2003). *From egg to butterfly.* Minneapolis, MN: Lerner.

3RD GRADE–5TH GRADE

Introduce students to the classification of animals and the diversity that exists among different types of animals. A good fiction book to read aloud is *Animalia,* by Graeme Base (1986), a beautifully illustrated animal alphabet that uses alliteration, such as "Lazy lions lounging in the local library." Students are invited to identify all the things that start with the letter *L* on that page. Follow the reading with a discussion and reader response questions: What do you know about any of the animals in the book? What experiences have you had with any animal?

Then read the nonfiction book *What Is the Animal Kingdom?* by Barbara Kalman (1998), leading into students reading from a text set of books on different animals and discussing the books in small groups or book clubs. Students can take notes in a science journal or take notes for them during a discussion with each of the book clubs.

To model the use of the T-chart, read two other books by Barbara Kalman, *What Is a Vertebrate?* (2007) and *Animals Without Backbones* (2008), and have students list the types of each on the chart. Characteristics of these two types of animals can also be added to the list, including examples of each that they read about in book clubs.

T-chart: Animals	
Vertebrates (5 main groups)	*Invertebrates (6 main groups)*
Mammals	Mollusks (0 legs)
Birds	Annelids (0 legs)
Reptiles	Insects (6 legs)
Amphibians	Arachnids (8 legs)
Fish	Myriapods (20+ legs)
	Crustaceans (10–14 legs)
Examples	*Examples*

As students continue to read, characteristics, descriptions, and examples are added to the T-chart; it can reveal the differences, connections, and relationships among these types of living organisms. In small groups, book clubs, or individually, students can do their own T-charts comparing any two vertebrates or invertebrates, or two examples of any type of animal.

Plus Technology

Use an interactive learning site, which includes games and activities based on a PBS television series using *Animalia* (see www.pbskids.org/animalia). The CGI-animated television show and the website feature two 11-year-old children who have adventures with the animal characters from the book. There is also a PBS DVD based on this series: *Animalia: Welcome to the Kingdom.*

Websites to visit for more information include www.animaldiversity.ummz.umich.edu and www.biokids.umich.edu.

Books

Arnosky, J. (2009). *Crocodile safari.* New York: Scholastic.

Base, G. (1986). *Animalia.* New York: Henry N. Abrams.

Kalman, B. (1997). *What is a mammal?* New York: Crabtree.

Kalman, B. (1998). *What is a bird?* New York: Crabtree.

Kalman, B. (1998). *What is a fish?* New York: Crabtree.

Kalman, B. (1998). *What is a reptile?* New York: Crabtree.

Kalman, B. (1998). *What is the animal kingdom?* New York: Crabtree.

Kalman, B. (2000). *What is an amphibian?* New York: Crabtree.

Kalman, B. (2002). *What is an arthropod?* New York: Crabtree.

Kalman, B. (2007). *What is a vertebrate?* New York: Crabtree.

Kalman, B. (2008). *Animals without backbones.* New York: Crabtree.

Kelly, I. (2009). *Even an ostrich needs a nest: Where birds begin.* New York: Holiday House.

Momatiuk, Y., & Eastcott, J. (2009). *Face to face with penguins.* Washington, DC: National Geographic Children's Books.

Nichols, M. (2009). *Face to face with gorillas.* National Geographic Children's Books.

Parker, S. (2004). *Insect.* New York: DK.

Siwanowicz, I. (2009). *Animals up close.* New York: DK.

Stewart, M. (2009). *A place for birds.* Atlanta, GA: Peachtree.

6TH GRADE–8TH GRADE

Model the use of a flow chart on the life cycle of an organism. A flow chart can show a series or chain of events or the stages in the growth and development of an organism. Flow charts lend themselves to science inquiry, from the steps in the scientific process to how an egg becomes a chicken.

Introduce the concept of the life cycle by reading aloud *This Is Your Life Cycle,* by H. L. Miller (2008). This humorous book is a slapstick spoof on the vintage television show *This is Your Life,* and it takes readers to a swamp where they see the life history of Dahlia, a dragonfly. Ask students reader response questions as they discuss the book: What are the important events in your life? What are some things you remember from when you were younger? How have you changed?

With modeling of the use of a flow chart, students can list the important events in Dahlia the dragonfly's life; they can then read about and research the human life cycle and create a flow chart of their own lives, documenting the important milestones in their own growth and development as humans.

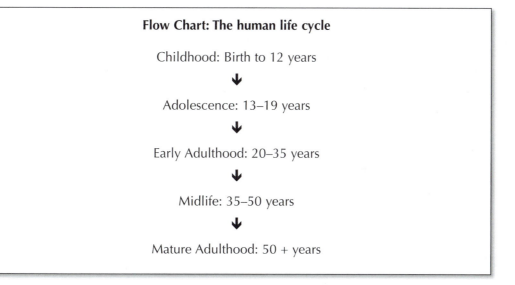

Flow Chart: The human life cycle

Childhood: Birth to 12 years

Adolescence: 13–19 years

Early Adulthood: 20–35 years

Midlife: 35–50 years

Mature Adulthood: 50 + years

Students can be placed in groups, and using a jigsaw strategy, each group can research and create a more detailed flow chart of one specific stage in human growth and development. When completed, the groups can share what they have found with the rest of the class to present a more complete picture of the human life cycle.

Books

Bledsoe, K. (2007). *Human reproduction, growth, and development.* Clive, IA: Perfection Learning.

Glover, D. (2005). *Growing (Humans and animals).* Mankato, MN: Smart Apple Media.

Harris, R. (1994). *It's perfectly normal: Changing bodies, growing up, sex, and sexual health.* Cambridge, MA: Candlewick Press.

Macnair, P. (2004). *Life story: Birth, growth, and development.* New York: Kingfisher.

Miller, H. L. (2008). *This is your life cycle.* New York: Simon & Schuster.

Miller, M. (2005). *Exploring the human body—reproduction and growth.* San Diego, CA: KidHaven Press.

Walker, R. (2009). *Human body.* New York: DK Children.

English Learners

Use the visual information in illustrations, photographs, diagrams, charts, and models in books to make content about a living organism comprehensible to English learners. Tapping into their prior knowledge of any of the organisms supports their learning by relating instruction to their past experiences. The use of real living organisms, specimens, or models is important to provide direct experiences to enhance academic instruction in science as well as in English learning.

Students creating their own charts—either as a whole class, in a pair with a more capable English speaking peer, or in small groups—is especially helpful when teaching content to English learners. Bilingual books, such as the title that follows, on living organisms can provide primary language support as well.

Kalman, B. (2005). *Que es el reino animal? What is the animal kingdom?* (Spanish Edition). New York: Crabtree.

Plus Technology

See the website www.proteacher.com for *ayudas graficas*, graphic organizers written in Spanish.

Struggling Students

Make a copy of a chart for each student that matches the chart he or she will use to model with the whole group or class. While writing down what students say on the group or class chart, also take dictation for individual students who can use the group or class chart for ideas. The chart can also include a word bank of the key vocabulary for the content of each chart, which students can use to help them remember the appropriate words when recording their ideas. The word bank of key vocabulary can also be written on index cards, with a set of cards made for each student or small group. Students can place the key words on the chart and move them to identify relationships before they write them down. Sticky notes can also be used for this purpose.

Assessment

Successful completion of a chart that displays what students have observed through direct experiences with an organism or information they have discovered in books is one way to assess the use of charts in science instruction. A rubric could be cocreated with students to assess each element of the chart, such as appropriate placement of information, accuracy of information, and amount of detail provided.

Students could also write a summary and conclusion of what they learned from the chart as a means of assessment. Since charts can be used to communicate information to others, students could be assessed on a presentation to the class or a group using the chart.

RESOURCES

Bellanca, J. (2007). *A guide to graphic organizers* (2nd ed.). Thousand Oaks, CA: Corwin Press.

Burke, J. (2002). *Tools for thought: Graphic organizers for your classroom.* Portsmouth, NH: Heinemann.

Chang, M. L. (2006). *Science graphic organizers and mini-lessons.* New York: Scholastic.

Tate, M. L. (2007). *Engage the brain: Graphic organizers and other visual strategies, science.* Thousand Oaks, CA: Corwin Press.

REFERENCES

Baxendell, B. W. (2003). Consistent, coherent, creative: The 3 C's of graphic organizers. *Teaching Exceptional Children, 35,* 46–53.

Edens, K. M., & Potter, E. (2003). Using descriptive drawings as a conceptual change strategy in elementary science. *School Science and Mathematics, 103*(3), 135–144.

Gobert, J. D., & Clement, J. J. (1999). Effects of student-generated diagrams versus student-generated summaries on conceptual understanding of causal and dynamic knowledge in plate tectonics. *Journal of Research in Science Teaching, 36*(1), 39–53.

Guastello, E. F., Beasley, T. M., & Sinatra, R. C. (2000). Concept mapping effects on science content comprehension of low-achieving inner-city seventh graders. *Remedial and Special Education, 21,* 356–365.

Tomkins, S. P., & Tunnicliffe, S. D. (2001). Looking for ideas: Observation, interpretation and hypothesis-making by 12-year-old pupils undertaking science investigations. *International Journal of Science Education, 23*(8), 791–813.

Strategy 26

What's in the Sky?

Stan and David were fascinated with the science unit in their 5th-grade class, which the teacher called "Where is the Moon tonight?" They had read books about earth and space, the sun and planets, and the moon. Now they were going to observe the moon for themselves and record what they saw each night. In their excitement to do so, one went to the other's house. As the sun went down and the moon came up, they climbed into a tree house to get a better view, made their observational drawings and notes, and fell asleep. While their parents had a few nervous moments before the two were located, they were pleased with their students' enthusiasm for observing the sky. So was their teacher.

RATIONALE

The National Science Education Standards (NSTA, 1996) identified "making observations" (p. 23) as a key component of inquiry-based, discovery-focused learning in science instruction. This means that students engage with an inquiry question, topic, concept, or problem in science through direct observation of the natural world and develop the skills to record the data from their observations, analyze and interpret it, and infer explanations and draw conclusions from what they have observed (Hanuscin, 2008).

When students practice observing in science, they use their senses to collect information about objects and events related to a question, topic, or problem to solve in science. This information is the data they will organize and analyze to answer questions and learn through discovery. It's important to support students by providing ways to organize their data collection.

Equally important is providing time for students to share and discuss their ideas about their observations as a part of conceptual development and change in science instruction, an approach that reflects a social constructivist theoretical perspective. For example, a study that described how a teacher scaffolded 5th-grade students learning about the earth and moon, beginning with observations of the natural world and models and including opportunities for students to present their ideas to peers and reflect on their own understanding (Barnett & Morran, 2002).

Teachers can effectively scaffold student understanding through careful questioning as students share their observations of the natural world. In a study on the use of teacher questions about students' observations and readings about the moon, Van Zee, Iwasyk, Kurose, Simpson, and Wild (2001) made three assertions about eliciting student thinking: (1) Ask questions that develop conceptual understanding in order to elicit students' experiences (e.g., What can you tell me about the moon?), and then diagnose and further refine students' ideas (e.g., What is your evidence for that idea?); (2) ask students to make their meanings clear and to explore various points of view in a respectful and neutral way, and monitor the discussion and their thinking; and (3) practice quietness as well as reflective questioning by using wait time, listening to students, adding information only as it is needed, and encouraging students to think things through for themselves.

Source: From National science education standards, by the National Science Teachers Association, 1996. Washington, DC: National Academy Press.

Science Standards

2. Science as Inquiry (Abilities necessary to do scientific inquiry)
5. Earth and Space (Objects in the sky; Changes in earth and sky; Earth in the solar system)

STRATEGY

Introduce a topic related to objects in the sky, changes in the sky, and earth in the solar system by reading aloud both fiction and nonfiction children's books; then discuss them with students, using reader response questions to engage students, tap into their prior knowledge, and generate questions for inquiry in space science. The sky and the objects in it is a topic that lends itself to book pairings: a book of fiction, poetry, myth, or traditional tales along with a book of nonfiction at the appropriate level for each grade.

Next, provide a grade-appropriate method for students to directly observe and record information on phenomena in the sky over time, such as taking observational notes, keeping journals, and establishing a place and time to do observations to compare them over time. These data can be kept by the whole class on a chart or students can collect them individually, in pairs, or in small groups. After a period of data collection and discussion of observations, model a means for students to collapse their data using charts—comparing their data with those of other students and compiling a class set of all the data.

During the period of observation and data collection, provide other resources for students to learn more about the phenomena or events they are observing in the sky: text sets of books, DVDs and other visual media, and online resources.

Finally, students can begin to summarize the findings of their data collection and prepare to communicate what they have found through a variety of means: displays of data collected with written summaries, posters and bulletin boards, and video or PowerPoint presentations.

Plus Technology

The website for NASA, www.nasa.gov, has extensive multimedia to add virtual observations to the actual observations made by students (e.g., photographs, on demand videos, NASA TV, interactive features, podcasts and vodcasts, and NASA Kid's Club).

GRADE-LEVEL MODIFICATIONS

K–2ND GRADE

Introduce the topic of the sun in the sky by reading aloud a pair of books, an African folktale and a nonfiction book about the sun. Begin with the classic Caldecott Honor Book *Why the Sun and the Moon Live in the Sky*. It is a retelling by E. Dayrell (1990), of an African *pourquoi*, or *why* folktale, beautifully illustrated by Blair Lent. It demonstrates that long before people had telescopes or means of space travel, they wondered about what they saw in the sky. Lead a discussion, asking reader response questions: What have you wondered about what is in the sky? Write students' comments under the *W* heading in the middle column of a KWL. (What we Know, What we Want to Know, What we Learned.) Follow this reading and discussion with a nonfiction book by Frank Asch (2008), *The Sun Is my Favorite Star*. The main character is a child like the students, and the narrative follows that child's experiences with the sun through a day. Lead a discussion and ask reader response questions: Has anything like this ever happened to you? What do you know about the sun? Add students comments to the KWL chart under the heading *K*. As students carry out their observations of the sun, what they learn can be added to the *L* column.

Lead students in observations of the sun each day. The beginning of the month would be a good time to start. Prepare a large calendar chart with a space for each day and regular times each day when the class will go or look outside to observe the sun. For example, this could be done each hour in a half-day kindergarten class, or every few hours in a full-day kindergarten or 1st- or 2nd-grade class. Also, find a fixed point in the yard such as a tree or utility pole so students can note the position of the sun throughout the day. Other things to note are the sky and weather conditions, such as clouds or rain, and the appearance of the sun as a result. Students can draw and take notes on individual chalk- or whiteboards or on paper on a clipboard, or they can dictate their observations if necessary.

The result would be a month long observation of the sun's movement throughout the day and of its changes in appearance due to changes in the sky. This could be recorded on the large classroom calendar, displayed on a bulletin board with one child's drawing for that day, or made into a book of the day's drawings by each child. Send a letter home to parents explaining the activity and asking them to observe with their student what time the sun goes down each day; the students can bring a drawn or written observation of this to class at the end of a specified time period. Students can use their observations to complete the KWL chart, make additional observations—such as what happens when a magnifying glass is held over a leaf with the sun shining on it or how the sun casts shadows—and record these observations to extend information acquired through reading other books about the sun in the sky.

Books

Asch, F. (2008). *The sun is my favorite star*. San Diego, CA: Harcourt.

Bailey, J. (206). *Sun up, sun down: The story of day and night*. Mankato, MN: Capstone Press.

Branley, F. M. (1986). *What makes day and night?* New York: HarperCollins.

Branley, F. M. (2002). *The sun: Our nearest star*. New York: HarperCollins.

Dayrell, E. (1990). *Why the sun and moon live in the sky*. Boston: Sandpiper.

Fowler, A. (1992). *The sun is always shining somewhere.* Danbury, CT: Children's Press.

Gibbons, G. (1987). *Sun up, sun down.* San Diego, CA: Harcourt Brace Jovanovich.

Simon, S. (1989). *The sun.* New York: HarperCollins.

3RD GRADE–5TH GRADE

Students can launch a month-long period of observations to answer the following question: Where is the moon tonight? Begin by reading two books in the *Magic School Bus* series written by Joanna Cole and illustrated by Bruce Degen. The narrative in each book in this series focuses on an unusual but effective teacher, Ms. Frizzle, who takes her students on amazing field trips in a magic school bus so they can learn about a subject first-hand. Read *The Magic School Bus Lost in the Solar System* (1992) to provide a big picture on everything in the sky, followed by *The Magic School Bus Takes a Moon Walk* (2007). Students can respond to reader response questions and prompts: What have you observed about the moon? What have you wondered about the moon?

Send a letter home to parents requesting permission for their student to participate in observations of the moon each night at home and also requesting their assistance with their student. Each student can make a small booklet by cutting eight pieces of 8 ½ x 11 inch black construction paper into fourths and then stacking and stapling 30 or 31 (depending on the number of days in that month) of these small sheets together in one corner. These can be kept in a plastic sandwich bag with either a white or yellow crayon or piece of chalk. The students can plan to observe the moon from the same position each night (e.g., from a porch or window, at the same time each night). They can note the date and time of each observation, draw a picture of the moon, and make notes on the back of the paper. They can share their observations in small groups the next day and discover that the moon goes through phases and changes shapes.

Books

Branley, F. M. (1987). *The moon seems to change.* New York: HarperCollins.

Branley, F. M. (2000). *What the moon is like.* New York: HarperCollins.

Burleigh, R. (2009). *One giant leap.* New York: Philomel Books.

Chaikin, A. (2009). *Mission Control, this is Apollo: The story of the first voyages to the moon.* New York: Viking.

Cole, J. (1992). *The magic school bus lost in the solar system.* New York: Scholastic.

Cole, J. (2007). *The magic school bus takes a moon walk.* New York: Scholastic.

Floca, B. (2009). *Moonshot: The flight of Apollo.* New York: Atheneum.

Fowler, A. (1991). *So that's how the moon changes shape.* Danbury, CT: Children's Press.

Fowler, A. (1994). *When you look up at the moon.* Danbury, CT: Children's Press.

Gibbons, G. (1998). *The moon book.* New York: Holiday House.

Olson, G. M. (2008). *Phases of the moon.* Mankato, MN: Capstone Press.

Simon, S. (2003). *The moon.* Simon & Schuster.

Stone, J. (2009). *One small step: Celebrating the first men on the moon.* Brookfield, CT: Roaring Brook Press.

6TH GRADE–8TH GRADE

Introduce a unit on observing the stars and their positions and movement in the sky—Star Track—with fiction and poetry that encourages students to reflect on these phenomenon in different ways. The teacher can read the classic book *The Little Prince*, by Antoine de Saint-Exupery. It is a philosophical fable of love, loneliness, and an individual's place in the universe that was first published in French in 1943. A new English translation was published in 2000, and the book has been published in many languages: Latin, German, Spanish, and Italian. Jack Prelutsky (2009), named the nation's first children's poet laureate in 2006, has recently published a collection of 19 poems that are for older students and emerged from his love of the popular television and movie series *Star Trek—The Swamps of Sleethe: Poems From Beyond the Solar System*. Reminiscent of a Tim Burton movie, they verge on the macabre and should appeal to middle school students. More important, both books should engage students in thinking about the universe and the stars by responding to reader response questions: Have you ever felt like the Little Prince? Tell about it. What do you think about the imaginary creatures Jack Prelutsky imagines live beyond the solar system? What do you imagine might be beyond the solar system?

Send a letter home requesting parental permission and support for their student observing stars and other objects in the night sky. Help students plan types of observations, depending on the time of the year and what is visible in the night sky. These observational data can be recorded, classified, analyzed, and interpreted by students, leading to generalizations and conclusions about space science.

Plus Technology

The NASA website, www.nasa.gov, has teacher and student guidelines for constructing a simple telescope.

Books

De Saint-Exupery, A. (2000). *The Little Prince* (R. Howard, Trans.). San Diego, CA: Harcourt.

Lippincott, K. (2008). *Astronomy*. New York: DK Eyewitness.

Prelutsky, J. (2009). *The swamps of sleethe: Poems from beyond the solar system*. New York: Alfred Knopf.

Simon, S. (1991). *Galaxies*. New York: HarperCollins.

Simon, S. (1995). *Star Walk*. New York: HarperCollins.

Simon, S. (2006). *Destination: Space*. New York: HarperCollins.

Simon, S. (2006). *Stars*. New York: HarperCollins.

Simon, S. (2006). *The universe*. New York: HarperCollins.

Simon, S. (2007). *Stars and constellations*. New York: Scholastic.

Simon, S. (2007). *Our solar system*. New York: HarperCollins.

Siy, A. (2009). *Cars on Mars: Roving the red planet*. Watertown, MA: Charlesbridge.

English Learners

English learners benefit from several of the essential strategies used when observing the sky. They rely on their senses to collect information, rather than listening or reading in English. They also use drawing as a means of recording what they observe; an adult or more capable peer can assist in adding written notes to the drawings. They use concrete materials such as drawing paper and journals, and props and realia such as models of the earth or solar system and DVDs or video clips of the sky, which can be accessed online, can be used.

Struggling Students

Provide already formatted journals for observing the sky, with a defined entry space for each observation. The student can add their name. Write the date on a whiteboard, which students can copy onto their observations. Students can also work with you, an aide, or in pairs or small groups to add written notes to their drawn observations. Take dictation for students as they describe their observation, adding written clarification to their drawings. A word bank of needed vocabulary can be posted in the room, and a copy can be provided for each student so they can copy the words they might need.

Assessment

The best assessment for this strategy is a direct demonstration by the student of the data they collected and an explanation to others of their questions, problems to be solved, the resulting data and how they analyzed it, summarization, inferences, interpretations, and conclusions about what they learned. A special day could be set aside for individuals and groups to find ways to do this demonstration and communicate their findings to others. Other students can do a peer-assessment of the students' demonstrations and what they learned from the student. A class could also invite other classes in the school to this event.

Resources

The NASA website, www.nasa.gov, is a rich source of resources for space science. Under the feature for educators, select a grade such as K–4 or 5–8, and also select the type of instructional material desired (e.g., classroom activities, educator guidelines, lesson plans, videos, and websites).

References

Barnett, M., & Morran, J. (2002). Addressing children's alternative frameworks of the Moon's phases and eclipses. *International Journal of Science Education, 24*(8), 859–879.

Hanuscin, D. L., & Park Rogers, M. A. (2008). Learning to observe and infer. *Science and Children, 45*(6), 56–57.

National Science Teachers Association. (1996). *National Science Education Standards.* Washington, DC: National Academy Press.

Van Zee, E. H., Iwasyk, M., Kurose, A., Simpson, D., & Wild, J. (2001). Student and teacher questioning during conversations about science. *Journal of Research in Science Teaching, 38*(2), 159–190.

Strategy 27

Meet the Scientist

Figure 27.1 Einstein explains E=MC² to his 4th-grade teacher

RATIONALE

Teachers can engage students in this research and role play strategy to help them discover that science is a human endeavor. Research has shown the effectiveness of drama and simulations (Bailey & Watson, 1998) and video recordings and puppets (Rollnick, Jones, Perold, & Bahr, 1998) in science instruction. By reading and writing about the lives of real scientists, students can learn more about the nature and history of science and how important scientific discoveries were made; the historical view of science, which stretches back thousands of years; how scientists dealt with other people when their discoveries were not aligned with the prevailing view of the world at the time; and how women and members of other underrepresented groups in the sciences were able to persevere. Students may also begin to see themselves as scientists by trying on scientists' lives for size.

As students learn about science history and the history of scientists, they can discover that there is not only one type of scientist that has made a contribution to the field. Studies have shown that students often perceive scientists to be males who live in a lab, wear a lab coat, and are removed from normal life (Bodzin & Gehringer, 2001; Finson, 2002; McDuffie, 2001). Gender equity in science education is an issue. Beginning in the elementary school years, girls have less favorable attitudes toward science than boys (Andre, Whigham, Hendickson, & Chambers, 1999; Jones, Howe, & Rua, 2000). Students can read about and role play the lives of women scientists, scientists with disabilities, and scientists from different cultural and language heritages than their own and, in the process, not only break down stereotypes they may hold about who a scientist can be, but also open themselves to the idea that any of them can be a scientist—regardless of gender, heritage, language, background, or handicapping conditions (Lee, 2003; Lightbody, 2002). For a look at how 7th-grade students perceived scientists before and after they visited a science laboratory, go to www.science.eastern blot.net/?p=52. There are some very interesting contrasts between the stereotypical before view and the view after the students met and talked with real scientists.

Source: From *National science education standards,* by the National Science Teachers Association, 1996. Washington, DC: National Academy Press.

Science Standard

8. History and nature of science (science as human endeavor, nature and history of science)

STRATEGY

Put together a text set of grade-appropriate books on types of scientists, individual scientists, science and scientists in a specific time period in history, or on a topic that relates in some other ways to the science curriculum in her or his class.

After a period of reading literature or reading online and discussing scientists or the history of science, and further researching in small groups or individually, plan to Meet the Scientist with students. They can use notes to summarize important events and dates in the life of a scientist, what the world around them was like, and the impact their scientific work had on others. This can be done by taking dictation on chart paper for younger students; older students can keep notes on their own.

Next, model one of several ways for the class to prepare to Meet the Scientist, depending on the ages, interests, and abilities of the students. For example, use interactive writing to create a description of scientists with young students. Using this as a script, students can dress as one of these scientists, use appropriate props or do demonstrations, and do a choral reading of the description they have written. Or help students create and perform a reader's theatre script, write a script for a scene or scenes from the life of the scientist, or prepare a script for an interview with the scientist who would answer the questions. To contextualize the scientist's life, especially if they lived in an adversarial world that was not open to their ideas, discoveries, inventions, or innovations, students can research the controversy, choose the pro- or anti-scientist side, and stage a debate.

These dramatic representations of scientists and the history and nature of science can be performed for other members of the class, other classes, or they can be video recorded to communicate what students have learned to others.

Plus Technology

As students pursue a line of inquiry in science in the classroom, they may call on experts in the field through the website www.askascientist.com. To do this, they must have a problem they are trying to solve, be able to identify the problem they are having with solving it, and articulate specific questions they need answered that go beyond the investigation and reading they have already done.

GRADE-LEVEL MODIFICATIONS

K–2ND GRADE

Young students can be introduced to the field of science by learning about different types of scientists. Pose this question: What do scientists do? Books about scientists in different fields can be read and discussed, student ideas can be written on a chart, and interactive writing can be used so that students can take the pen and add to the information on the chart themselves.

The class can work in small groups, each group learning about a different type of scientist (e.g., biologist, naturalist, physicist, or rocket scientist). Write a summary with students in the form of an interactive script with one sentence on each line. Students can be assigned to read each line. They can wear costume pieces that would have been worn by that type of scientist and use props, do demonstrations, or copy gestures used by the scientist. Each line can be color coded and students can read directly off the chart paper.

Students can be put into small groups, with each group writing about a different type of scientist, and they can present their Meet the Scientist activity to the rest of the class.

Here are books about different types of scientists.

Books

Naturalists

Lyon, G. E. (2003). *Mother to tigers*. New York: Atheneum.

Malnor, B., & Malnor, C. L. (2009). *Earth heroes: Champions of the wilderness*. Nevada City, CA: Dawn Publications.

Sheldon, D. (2009). *Into the deep: The life of naturalist and explorer William Beebe*. Watertown, MA: Charlesbridge.

Astronauts

Aldrin, B. (2009). *Look to the stars*. New York: G. P. Putnam's Sons.

Hilliard, R. (2005). *Neil, Buzz, and Mike go to the moon*. Honesdale, PA: Boyds Mills Press.

Inventors

Schanzer, R. (2003). *How Ben Franklin stole the lightning.* New York: HarperCollins.

Physicists

MacDonald, W. (2009). *Galileo's leaning tower experiment.* Charlesbridge Press.

3RD GRADE–5TH GRADE

Read aloud the biography of one scientist and discuss it with the class using reader response questions and prompts: Was there anything you wondered about this scientist? Has anything like this ever happened in your life? How would you feel if you were this scientist?

Do a book talk on several books to introduce different scientists to students, and pre-pare a list of scientists and books to begin reading about them (see *Books* for an example). Students can form groups and choose a scientist from a suggested list. After reading the recommended books, and reading other books and doing online research, the students can write a reader's theatre script. In order for each student in a group of four or five to have a role, the script can be written for parts as follows:

Narrator (to introduce the reader's theatre and provide narration throughout)

Scientist narrator (to tell what is happening to the scientist each time the scientist speaks)

Scientist (only speaking the words of the scientist)

Other character narrators (to introduce other characters in the scientist's life—can be multiple)

Other characters (can be multiple)

Here is a list of books about scientists for students to begin reading and researching:

Books

Adler, D. A. (1999). *A picture book of George Washington Carver.* New York: Holiday House.

Davies, J. (2004). *The boy who drew birds: A story of John James Audubon.* Boston: Houghton Mifflin.

Dend, L., & Boring, M. (2005). *Guinea pig scientists: Bold self-experimenters in science and medicine.* New York: Holt.

Ehrlich, A. (2003). *Rachel: The story of Rachel Carson.* San Diego, CA: Harcourt.

Krull, K. (2009). *Albert Einstein.* New York: Viking Children's Books.

Krull, K. (2009). *The boy who invented TV: The story of Philo Farnsworth.* New York: Alfred A. Knopf.

Mathews, T. (1999). *Always inventing: A photo biography of Alexander Graham Bell.* Washington, DC: National Geographic Society.

McCutcheon, M. (2004). *The kid who named Pluto: And the stories of other extraordinary young people in science.* San Francisco: Chronicle.

Murphy, G. (2009). *Inventions.* New York: Simon & Schuster Books for Young Readers.

Sandler, M. W. (2009). *Secret subway: The fascinating tale of an amazing feat of engineering.* Washington, DC: National Geographic Children's Books.

Thimmesh, C. (2002). *The sky's the limit: Stories of discovery by women and girls.* Boston: Houghton Mifflin.

Wadsworth, G. (2003). *Benjamin Banneker: Pioneering scientist.* Minneapolis, MN: Lerner.

Yaccarino, D. (2009). *The fantastic undersea life of Jacques Cousteau.* New York: Alfred A. Knopf.

6TH GRADE–8TH GRADE

Introduce and read a book about a controversy related to a scientist and lead a discussion using reader response questions and prompts: How do you think the scientist felt? How would you feel if this happened to you? Why do you think this scientist was controversial?

See the following *Books* section for a list of books about controversial scientists. Students can form groups, and each group can pick a scientist and a controversy, do further reading and research (in books and online), and write a script to dramatize each side of the controversy. One member of the group will play the scientist, one half of the rest of the group will play allies who defend him or her, and the other half the group will play opponents. Students can sit at a table with the scientist in the middle and present the dramatization as a debate, each side taking turns defending or attacking the scientist and asking the scientist to present a defense when needed.

The rest of the class can watch, and time can be provided for a Q&A session directed at either the scientist, the allies, or the opponents. Students can wear costume pieces representative of the period and use props and demonstrations to make points if needed.

Darwin and Galileo are two examples of scientists who created controversy, and there are several books about them for students to begin reading and researching—shown here, along with other books about controversies over scientists.

Books

Fortey, J. (2007). *Great scientists.* New York: DK.

Stone, T. L. (2009). *Almost astronauts: 13 women who dared to dream.* Cambridge, MA: Candlewick Press.

Darwin

Ashby, R. (2009). *Young Charles Darwin and the voyage of the beagle.* Atlanta, GA: Peachtree Publishers.

Heiligman, D. (2009). *Charles and Emma: The Darwin's leap of faith.* New York: Henry Holt.

Hopkinson, D. (2005). *Who was Charles Darwin?* New York: Grosset & Dunlop.

McGinty, A. B. (2009). *Darwin*. Boston: Houghton Mifflin.

Schnazer, D. (2009). *What Darwin saw: The journey that changed the world*. Washington, DC: National Geographic Children's Books.

Galileo

Bendick, J. (1999). *Along came Galileo*. San Luis Obispo, CA: Beautiful Feet Books.

Fisher, L. E. (1992). *Galileo*. New York: Atheneum.

MacLachlan, J. (1997). *Galileo Galilei: First physicist*. New York: Oxford University Press.

Nardo, D. (2004). *The trial of Galileo: Science versus the inquisition*. San Diego, CA: Lucent Books.

Sis, P. (2000). *Starry messenger: Galileo Galilei*. New York: Farrar, Straus, & Giroux.

Steele, P. (2008). *Galileo: The genius who faced the inquisition*. Washington, DC: National Geographic Children's Books.

ENGLISH LEARNERS

English learners benefit from engaging activities like dramatization, and they can participate in many different levels of speaking parts. They can also participate through gestures, by doing demonstrations or showing props and models, and because scripts are written, they can learn their lines ahead of time and use the script for support.

Also use online resources to find scientists in the community who are members of the same language groups as students and invite them to speak to the class and answer questions in both English and their first language, thereby providing primary language support for students.

Seek out books on scientists from the same language groups of students (e.g., Carolus Linnaeus, who created the taxonomy of animals).

STRUGGLING STUDENTS

Provide a writing frame to scaffold learning about different types of scientists or about one particular scientist. After reading about a scientist, use guided questioning to enable students to answer the questions, and take dictation and write the students' responses on chart paper with the frame. Students can also use individual copies of the same frame to copy their responses and then add notes after further reading with the help of an adult or peers.

Type or Name of Scientist

What does this scientist do?

What do they use?

When did they live?

What did they discover?

How did their discovery change what we know?

Give an example.

ASSESSMENT

Students can write a summary of what they learned about the scientist they presented to others or write about the scientist presented by another group. A peer-assessment form can be used for students to assess, write comments, and tell what they learned about another groups' Meet the Scientist presentation. Use a rubric to assess the reading, research, and presentation of an individual or group Meet the Scientist.

RESOURCES

Lawson, K. (2003). *Darwin and evolution for kids: His life and ideas with 21 activities.* Chicago: Chicago Review Press.

Panchky, R. (2005). *Galileo for kids: His life and ideas, 25 activities.* Chicago: Chicago Review Press.

REFERENCES

Andre, T., Whigham, M., Hendrickson, A., & Chambers, S. (1999). Competency beliefs, positive affect, gender stereotyping of elementary students and their parents about science versus other school subjects. *Journal of Research in Science Teaching, 36,* 719–747.

Bailey, S., & Watson, R. (1998). Establishing basic ecological understanding in younger pupils: A pilot evaluation of a strategy based on drama/role play. *International Journal of Science Education, 20*(2), 139–152.

Bodzin, A., & Gehringer, M. (2001). Breaking science stereotypes. *Science and Children, 25*(5), 36–41.

Finson, K. D. (2002). Drawing a scientist: What do we know and do not know after fifty years of drawings. *School Science and Mathematics, 102,* 335–345.

Jones, M. G., Howe, A., & Rua, M. J. (2000). Gender differences in students' experiences, interests, and attitudes toward science and scientists. *Science Education, 84,* 180–192.

Lee, S. (2003). Achieving gender equity in middle school science classrooms. *Science Scope, 26*(5), 42–43.

Lightbody, M. (2002). Countering gender bias in the media. *Science Scope, 25*(6), 40–42.

McDuffie, T. E. (2001). Scientists—geeks and nerds. *Science and Children, 38*(8), 16–19.

Rollnick, M., Jones, B., Perold, H., & Bahr, M. A. (1998). Puppets and comics in primary science: The development and evaluation of a pilot multimedia package. *International Journal of Science Education, 20*(5), 533–550.

Strategy 28

Science Notebooks

Figure 28.1 Science notebook, behavior of mealworms, 3/4 grade

Figure 28.1 Science notebook, behavior of mealworms, 3/4 grade

Diagrams

Diagram of Mealworm

Diagram of Pupa

Dorsal   Ventral

Diagram of Beetle

Dorsal   Ventral

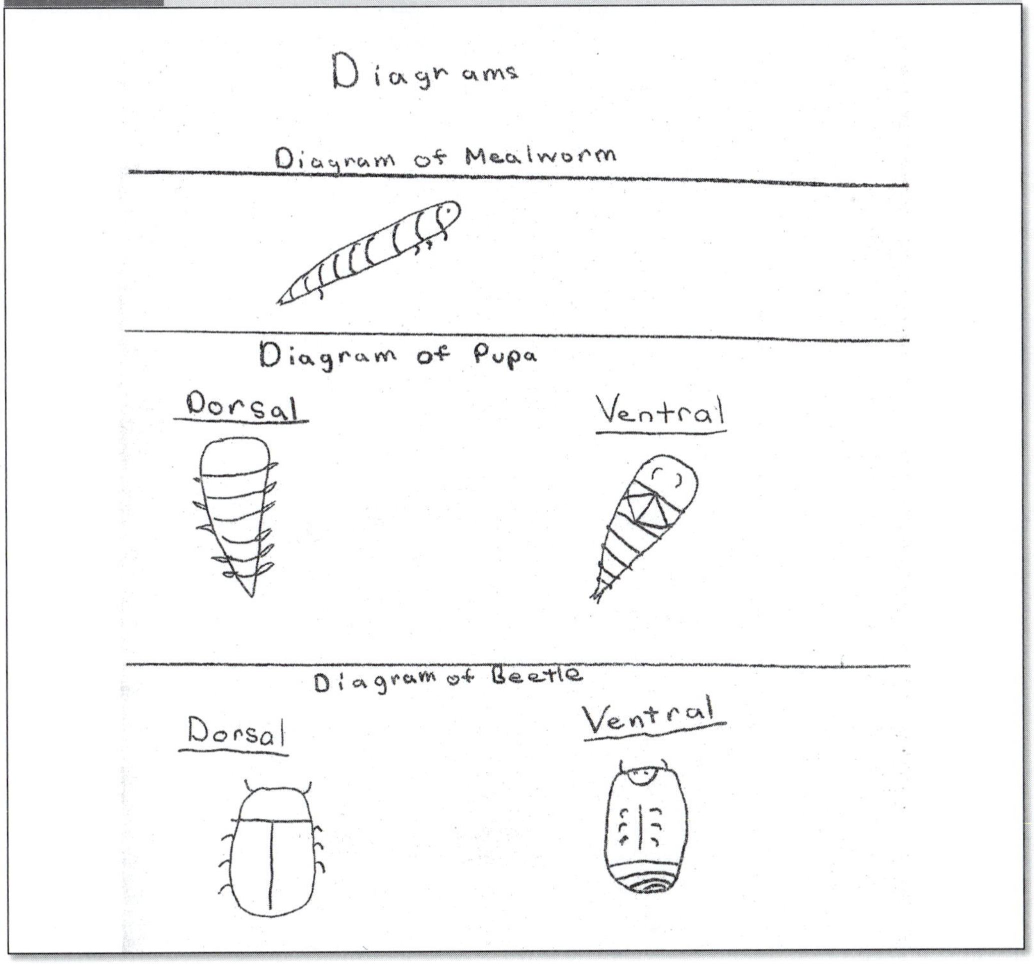

| Figure 28.2 | Science notebook, plant specimen, 6th grade |

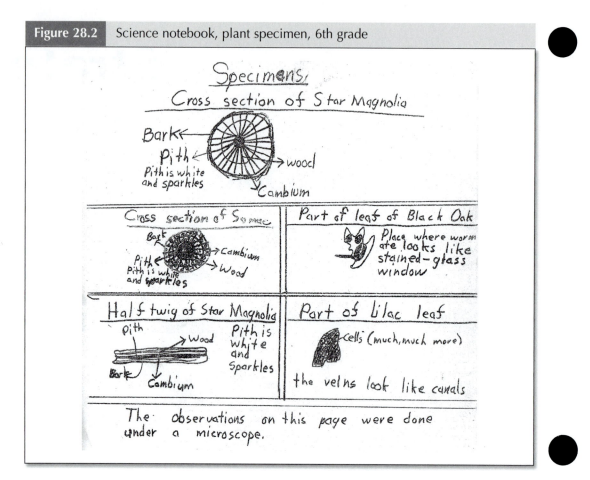

RATIONALE

A science notebook, such as the ones shown in Figures 28.1 and 28.2, is a strategy for students to record and reflect on inquiry-based observations, activities, investigations, and experiments in order to increase their understanding of science instruction. Science notebooks are also an excellent tool for students to communicate their understanding of science concepts, for teachers to provide students with feedback, and, finally, to assess students (Shepardson & Britsch, 2000, 2001). Science notebooks are also a way for teachers to integrate science experiences with literacy and mathematics because they combine science inquiry, written communication, and data using measurement (Gilbert & Kotelman, 2005; Klentschy, 2005; Yore, Bisanz, & Hand, 2003).

Science notebooks are modeled after the way scientists really work, and each scientist's notebook is unique to that person, area of inquiry, type of experiment, and investigation. Student scientists record their observations, ideas, drawings, and other illustrations such as charts, tables, models, and graphs, along with their questions, ideas, and reflections in a running record of their thinking. A notebook may follow a general organization, but the contents can vary from student to student. Writing frames have also proven useful as prompts for students' entries in their notebooks (Warwick, Stephenson, Webster, & Bourne, 2003).

Research has shown that science notebooks support differentiated instruction for English learners through the use of this open format and other useful strategies for teaching English learners such as tapping prior knowledge, the five senses, interaction in groups, and primary language support. (Amaral, Garrison, & Klentschy, 2002). Teachers can use science notebooks to conference with students for purposes of assessment and guidance (Aschbacher & Alonzo, 2006; Ruiz-Primo & Li, 2004).

Source: From *National science education standards,* by the National Science Teachers Association, 1996. Washington, DC: National Academy Press.

Science Standard

1. Unifying concepts and processes in science

STRATEGY

Introduce the use of science notebooks with children's books that are based on the notebooks, journals, diaries, and records of scientists appropriate for each grade level. Discuss the books with students using reader response questions and prompts to engage them. Then model how to use a science notebook before, during, and after classroom science experiences, observations, and investigations.

A template can be used with students on a classroom chart, poster, or overhead transparency, with an individual copy for each student that includes the parts of a notebook—including places where students can formulate and develop their questions, make predictions, record observational data, describe procedures and results, write thoughtful reflections, and keep a record of the new concepts they are learning.

While each teacher will differentiate science notebook organization according to the grade level, interests, abilities, and individual needs of their students, here are the parts of science notebooks frequently used by teachers:

Title Page or Notebook Cover

- Student name
- Teacher name, class, and school
- Decorative cover related to the topic(s) of the notebook

Table of Contents

- Date
- Time: of observation or length of time for activity
- Title of observation, activity, experiment, and so on
- Page number
- Headings: focus questions, hypotheses, observations, experiments, results, conclusions, reflections
- Appendix: tables, measurements, conversions, equations, formulas, facts

Glossary

- Alphabetical list of new vocabulary
- Teacher creates a word wall with words learned to add to glossary
- Students use a one or two page frame with 26 boxes, one for each letter of the alphabet, and add words as they are used to create the glossary
- Students indicate understanding of the word by writing definitions and creating drawings, diagrams, models, charts, graphs, and so on

---

There are several ways to make science notebooks: in a composition book, a spiral notebook, a three ring binder with loose leaf paper and section dividers, or in a three-prong paper folder.

Writing frames can be provided for students to begin their entries, and they can be varied by grade level. For example,

"We are trying to find out. . . ." (Grade 4)

"We made the test fair by. . . ." (Grade 4)

"By carrying out these measurements we are able to find the connection between. . . and . . . ." (Grade 6)

"My results are accurate and reliable because . . . ." (Grade 7)

Plus Technology

Students can also word process notes and use drawing functions and other types of graphics on programs like Word, such as charts, graphs, tables, and so on. Older and more advanced students could keep an online science notebook and create a blog so other students in the class could comment on and compare their findings. In addition to using nonfiction literature to supplement observations and inquiries in a science notebook, students can do online research.

Teachers can find out more about science notebooks at www.sciencenotebooks.org.

GRADE-LEVEL MODIFICATIONS

K–2ND GRADE

Introduce science notebooks on the weather by reading the fictional story *Cloudy With a Chance of Meatballs* (Barrett, 1978). This is a humorous story of a town where the weather comes at breakfast, lunch, and dinner in the form of food. It was recently made into a major motion picture. Discuss the book with reader response questions and prompts: What did you think of the weather in the book? What kind of weather can you imagine?

Other good read aloud books for pre-K or K are *Like a Windy Day* (Asch & Asch, 2008), *When the Wind Stops* (Zolotow, 1997), and *The Storm Book* (Zolotow, 1989); for K through 2 in general is *Oh Say Can You Say What's the Weather Today? All About the Weather* (Cat in the Hat) (Rabe, 2004).

After modeling the use of science notebooks with students, plan daily observations of the weather. Students can note the date, time, and weather conditions, including measurements of the temperature using a thermometer, rainfall using a rain gauge, and wind using an anemometer. For younger students, record students' spoken observations on a large wall chart or calendar. Students can also make their own observations, records, and reflections in an individual notebook. Students can add drawings, charts, graphs, comments, predictions, and questions in these science notebooks.

Bring students together to discuss what they observed and recorded in their notebooks, ask questions, pose problems, and continue with further inquiry about weather. With each change in the weather, read a nonfiction book about it, discuss it with students, do activities, and students can add to their notebooks. Make a list of weather words on a poster in the room and also give each student a list of the words to keep in their notebook. Students can add drawings and definitions and create a glossary for the notebook. A good introduction to weather words is the book *Weather Words and What They Mean* (Gibbons, 1992).

Books

Asch, F., & Asch, D. (2008). *Like a windy day.* New York: Voyager.

Barrett, J. (1978). *Cloudy with a chance of meatballs.* New York: Atheneum.

Branley, F. M. (1997). *Down comes the rain.* New York: Collins.

Branley, F. M. (1999). *Flash, crash, rumble and roll.* New York: Collins.

DeWitt, L. (1993). *What will the weather be?* New York: Collins.

Dorros, A. (1990). *Feel the wind.* New York: Collins.

Flanagan, A. K. (2003). *Sunshine.* Mankato, MN: Child's World.

Flanagan, A. K. (2003). *Wind.* Mankato, MN: Child's World.

Flanagan, A. K. (2010). *Clouds.* Mankato, MN: Child's World.

Flanagan, A. K. (2010). *Rain.* Mankato, MN: Child's World.

Flanagan, A. K. (2010). *Snow.* Mankato, MN: Child's World.

Flanagan, A. K. (2010). *Thunder and lightning.* Mankato, MN: Child's World.

Gibbons, G. (1992). *Weather words and what they mean.* New York: Holiday House.

Moore, J. E. (2000). *Learning about weather.* Monterey, CA: Evan-Moor Educational Publishers.

Paulauski, P. (2005). *W is for wind.* Chelsea, MI: Sleeping Bear Press.

Pratt-Serafini, K. J. (2001). *Salamander rain: A lake and pond journal.* Nevada City, CA: Dawn.

Rabe, T. (2004). *Oh say can you say what's the weather today? All about the weather (Cat in the Hat).* New York: Random House.

Rockwell, A. (2008). *Clouds.* New York: Collins.

Zolotow, C. (1989). *The storm book.* New York: HarperCollins.

Zolotow, C. (1997). *When the wind stops.* New York: HarperCollins.

3RD GRADE–5TH GRADE

Introduce keeping a science notebook by reading aloud the journals of famous scientists, such as *Galileo's Journal, 1609–1610* (Pettenati, 2006) and *My Season With Penguins: An Antarctic Journal* (Webb, 2000). Next, introduce keeping a science notebook on the behavior of mealworms by reading aloud the novel *The Mealworm Diaries* (Kerz, 2009), which is about two students working on a science project together and the personal problems they encounter while doing so. Lead a discussion about these books using reader response questions and prompts: As a scientist, what would you want to write about in your notebook? What are some things you have wondered about worms?

After modeling the use of a science notebook, provide mealworms for students to observe. Mealworms can be obtained from pet stores and biological supply houses. They can be kept in containers with a layer of bran and observed. Students can work in pairs to ask questions about mealworm behavior, pose hypotheses, collect and record data, make predictions, comment, and write reflections. Nonfiction books on mealworms can be used to supplement their observations of a living organism.

Books

Himmelman, J. (2001). *A mealworm's life*. Danbury, CT: Children's Press.

Kerz, A. (2009). *The mealworm diaries*. Victoria, British Columbia, Canada: Orca.

Mason, A. (2001). *Mealworms: Raise them, watch them, see them change*. Toronto, Ontario, Canada: Kids Can Press.

Pettenati, J. (2006). *Galileo's journal, 1609–1610*. Watertown, MA: Charlesbridge.

Rustad, M. E. H. (2009). *Mealworms*. Mankato, MN: Pebble Books.

Salas, L. P. (2008). *From mealworm to beetle: Following the life cycle*. Mankato, MN: Picture Window Books.

Schaffer, D. (2000). *Mealworms*. Mankato, MN: Bridgestone Books.

Webb, S. (2000). *My season with penguins: An Antarctic journal*. Boston: Houghton Mifflin.

6TH GRADE–8TH GRADE

To engage students, introduce science notebooks about plant life and growth by reading aloud a book of fiction. For example, one of the many books in the fantasy series about *The Plant That Ate Dirty Socks* (McArthur, 1988), *Native Plant Stories* by Joseph Bruchac (1995), or traditional stories by Native Americans about the relationships among people, animals, and plants. Lead a discussion using reader response questions and prompts: What did you wonder about the plant(s) in the stories?

The students can begin science notebooks observing plants and plant growth. One way would be to collect samples of tree branches with buds in the spring and keep them in water for observation in the classroom. They can also observe budding branches on trees. Another way is to plant bulbs in pots in the fall for winter plants such as amaryllis or paper white narcissus, or in the spring for many other flowering plants. Students can work in pairs observing what happens to the buds or bulbs over time, and they can record the data in a science notebook. They can record any of the following:

- Hypotheses about factors that affect plant growth, changing factors, and observations of outcomes

- A chart of growth with measurements, times, and drawings; comparisons of two different types of branches or bulbs; and notes

- A labeled diagram of a plant; a cross-section, using a microscope

- Drawings of the parts of a plant (e.g., stamen, pistil)

They can use nonfiction books as resources to identify needed vocabulary and to learn more about the processes they are observing.

Books

Bruchac, J. (1995). *Native plant stories.* New York: Fulcrum Press.

Claybourne, A. (2008). *Growing plants: Plant life processes.* London: Heinemann Educational Books.

Edom, H. (2007). *Science with plants.* London: Usborne Books.

Hoffman, M. A. (2009). *Plant experiments: What affects plant growth?* New York: PowerKids Press.

Hopkins, W. G. (2006). *Plant development.* New York: Chelsea House.

Kravetz, J. (2006). *Learning about plant growth with graphic organizers.* New York: PowerKids Press.

McArthur, N. (1988). *The plant that ate dirty socks.* New York: HarperCollins.

Nadeau, I. (2006). *Plant development and growth.* New York: PowerKids Press.

Spilsbury, R., & Spilsbury, L. (2008). *Plant classification.* London: Heinemann Educational Books.

Spilsbury, R., & Spilsbury, L. (2008). *Plant growth.* London: Heinemann Educational Books.

Spilsbury, R., & Spilsbury, L. (2008). *Plant parts.* London: Heinemann Educational Books.

Spilsbury, R., & Spilsbury, L. (2008). *Plant reproduction.* London: Heinemann Educational Books.

ENGLISH LEARNERS

English learners can use visuals such as drawings, tables, graphs, charts, or models instead of language to make their ideas concrete and to demonstrate their understandings in a nonlinguistic way. Science notebooks also rely on the use of the five senses, tapping into prior knowledge—also excellent strategies for English learners. Group discussions of science notebooks also provide teacher to student or student to student interaction, including the use of primary language support.

Books in students' primary language related to the topic of the science notebook can also be used.

Books

White, A. (2009). *No necesito paraguas/I don't need an umbrella.* Miami, FL: Santillana USA.

STRUGGLING STUDENTS

Writing frames for science notebook entries modeled by the teacher and cocreated with students provide excellent scaffolding for struggling students or students with disabilities. The use of visual entries such as drawings, charts, graphs, diagrams, models, and so on also allow students to make entries even if they are struggling with writing. Take dictation related to these drawings, and so forth, for students to model the writing down of their observations and ideas. A list of the science vocabulary needed for the notebooks can be posted in the room and each student provided with a copy, and materials used for the science notebooks can be labeled so that students can copy the words into their notebooks when needed.

Writing frames for science notebook entries can be posted in the room or on a copy for each student:

"I observed . . . ."

"I (saw, smelled, felt, heard) . . . ."

"My (experiment, investigation) was . . . ."

" I found that . . . ."

"I think this because . . . ."

ASSESSMENT

Student science notebooks can be assessed, at a minimum, for organization and completeness according to the following rubric, Table 28.1:

Table 28.1	Rubric for Science Notebook		
	Science Notebook Rubric		
	4 Excellent 3 Good 2 Fair 1 Poor	Score	Comments/ Suggestions
Table of contents	All parts included Page numbers indicated		
Organization	Titles of activity or section All dates and times All pages numbered		
Written entries and reflections	Appropriately titled Includes main ideas Provides necessary details Shows understanding		
Illustrations: drawings, graphs, charts, tables, diagrams, etc.	Titled and labeled Supports ideas		

With younger students, science notebooks can be an excellent tool to assess student performance, understanding, and needs in a conference. Peer-conferences and peer-assessment using the rubric can be used in Grades 3 through 8, along with periodic conferences where questions can be asked and answered and a dialogue can be shared about the contents of the science notebook.

RESOURCES

Campbell, B., & Fulton, L. (2003). *Science notebooks: Writing about inquiry.* Portsmouth, NH: Heinemann.

REFERENCES

Amaral, O., Garrison, L., & Klentschy, M. (2002). Helping English learners increase achievement through inquiry-based science instruction. *Bilingual Research Journal, 26*(2), 213–239.

Aschbacher, P. R., & Alonzo, A. C. (2006). Examining the utility of elementary science notebooks for formative assessment purposes. *Educational Assessment, 11*(3), 179–203.

Gilbert, J., & Kotelman, M. (2005). Five good reasons to use science notebooks. *Science and Children, 43*(3), 28–32.

Klentschy, M. (2005). Science notebook essentials. *Science and Children, 43*(3), 24–27.

Ruiz-Primo, M. A., & Li, M. (2004). On the use of students' science notebooks as an assessment tool. *Studies in Educational Evaluation, 30,* 61–85.

Shepardson, D. P., & Britsch, S. J. (2000). Analyzing children's science journals. *Science and Children, 38*(3), 29–33.

Shepardson, D., & Britsch, S. (2001). The role of children's journals in elementary school science activities. *Journal of Research in Science Teaching, 38*(1), 43–69.

Warwick, P., Stephenson, P., Webster, J., & Bourne, J. (2003). Developing pupils' written expression of procedural understanding through the use of writing frames in science: Findings from a case study approach. *International Journal of Science Education, 25*(2), 173–192.

Yore, L. S., Bisanz, G. L., & Hand, B. M. (2003). Examining the literacy component of science literacy: 25 years of language arts and science research. *International Journal of Science Education, 25,* 689–725.

Strategy
29

Q&A Reports

After telling her 2nd-grade class that they would be going on a field trip to the local aquarium, the teacher asked them if they had any questions. One boy shot his hand in the air and asked: Do sharks eat people? The rest of the class was stone silent, waiting tensely for the teacher to reply. She in turn asked two questions. First, Who would like to find out if sharks eat people? Every student in the room shot their hand in the air. Second, How do you think we can find the answer to that question?

RATIONALE

Using students' questions as a basis for investigations in science education has been called the *interactive approach* or *question raising approach*. Not only do students pose questions they would like answered, but they are asked to find ways to answer them (Chin & Kayalvizhi, 2002; Gibson, 1998; Watts, Barber, & Alsop, 1997). Teachers have effectively relied on language and literacy teaching approaches by encouraging students to ask questions, engaging in class and small group discussions, and finding other ways to explore ideas through speaking and writing when teaching science (Flick, 1995).

Scientific thinking, exemplified by scientists like Da Vinci, Galileo, and Einstein, is a process of asking questions and seeking explanations. Teachers can begin this process by encouraging and listening to the questions students ask and guiding them through the steps to discovering the answers. In a study of kindergarten and 1st-grade students, Iwasyk (1997) described how a teacher encouraged students to not only ask but answer questions as they investigated them and the conditions that encouraged students to raise questions. Studies have also shown that while direct, hands-on experiences are a necessary element of effective science instruction, they are not sufficient to develop understandings in young children (Butts, Hofman, & Anderson, 1993, 1994). Teachers also need to engage children in exploration of ideas through discussion and instructional conversations. Research has also shown that older elementary and middle school students benefitted from discussing inquiry-based questions, ideas, and explanations in small groups and shared and justified their socially constructed explanations with other groups (Meyer & Woodruff, 1997; Woodruff & Meyer, 1997).

Inquiry process skills in science can begin with students describing phenomena through a process of questioning, observing, enumerating, classifying, measuring, comparing, and communicating. As they explain phenomena, they again begin with questioning, leading to hypothesizing, inferring, interpreting data, and communicating. When they move to experiments, again the first step is questioning, leading to predicting, identifying and controlling variables and experiments, and communicating findings. Questioning is a key first step in using constructivist principles by eliciting students' ideas as a basis for further discussion and reflection in science teaching (Akerson, Flick, & Lederman, 2000; Vosniadou, Ioannides, Dimitrakopoulou, & Papademetriou, 2001).

Source: From National science education standards, by the National Science Teachers Association, 1996. Washington, DC: National Academy Press.

> ## Science Standard
>
> 2. Science as inquiry

STRATEGY

Read aloud a fiction or nonfiction science-related book and lead a discussion asking reader response questions to engage students and to encourage them to ask questions for which they would like to find answers: What did you wonder about while I was reading? List, or have students list, the question on chart paper, on a KWL chart, or on an overhead transparency; these questions can guide further inquiry. The following conditions have been shown to encourage students to raise questions:

- Set up discourse structures such as brainstorming and KWL charts that elicit student questions.

- Engage students in conversations about familiar contexts in which they have made many observations over a long period of time.

- Create comfortable discussion periods where students can try to understand each other's thinking.

- Establish small, collaborative groups.

Students can work in groups to answer different questions using the jigsaw cooperative learning technique. Collect a text set of books on the topic; students can form book clubs to read and research answers to the question they have chosen. They can also do library and online research, investigations, and experiments.

A series of nonfiction children's books that focuses on a science question to be answered in each book can also be used. One of these books could be used to initiate an inquiry for the whole class, a book talk could be done on several of the books, and students could form small groups and each pick a book and a question to research and answer.

GRADE-LEVEL MODIFICATIONS

K–2ND GRADE

Many nonfiction science books use a question and answer format; one of these could be read aloud to model asking and answering questions as a way to learn about a topic in science. For example, the book *Sharks,* by Ann McGovern (1976), uses this format. Each double-page spread of this picture book is a chapter that shows a question in boldface type, followed by an answer, beautifully illustrated by simple but elegant graphite pencil sketches. The table of contents lists each question followed by a page number.

Guided by the list of questions, the class can create their own Q&A book. First, write each question at the top of a piece of chart paper and read aloud other books on the topic, lead class discussions, and then record student ideas about answers to each question on the chart. Interactive writing, where young students take the pen to write on the chart paper, can be used as well. When the questions have been answered on each chart, students in groups can choose and illustrate a chart. To communicate what they have learned, the charts can be placed on a bulletin board.

Here are more books on sharks and a series of books that uses the question and answer format on science content for younger students.

Books

Sharks

Berger, M. (1999). *Chomp! A book about sharks.* New York: Scholastic.

Cerullo, M. (2000). *The truth about great white sharks.* New York: Holiday House.

Dubowski, C. E. (1998). *Shark attack!* New York: DK.

McGovern, A. (1976). *Sharks.* New York: Four Winds Press.

Simon, S. (1995). *Sharks.* New York: HarperCollins.

Q&A series on science: Ask Dr. K. Fisher

Llewellyn, C. (2007). *Ask Dr. K. Fisher about animals.* New York: Kingfisher.

Llewellyn, C. (2007). *Ask Dr. K. Fisher about dinosaurs.* New York: Kingfisher.

Llewellyn, C. (2008). *Ask Dr. K. Fisher about creepy-crawlies.* New York: Kingfisher.

Llewellyn, C. (2008). *Ask Dr. K. Fisher about reptiles.* New York: Kingfisher.

Llewellyn, C. (2009). *Ask Dr. K. Fisher about planet earth.* New York: Kingfisher.

Llewellyn, C. (2009). *Ask Dr. K. Fisher about weather.* New York: Kingfisher.

The format of these books is that questions are mailed to a Dr. K. Fisher, an anthropomorphized kingfisher bird, by other anthropomorphized animal characters who ask questions about themselves that Dr. K. Fisher answers. The books are highly illustrated and humorous but contain factual information in all the answers.

3RD GRADE–5TH GRADE

Introduce a topic in science with a book that uses the Q&A format, and generate a list of questions on a KWL chart. Do a book talk of several of these books in a series, and have students form groups, choose a book and a topic, generate a list of questions, and work in their groups to answer a question through further reading, online research, field trips, interviews, and first-hand experiences.

They can compile their collective Q&A results and communicate them in a variety of ways. For example, they could make a class book, modeled after one of the Q&A series books they have read—with a table of contents listing each question and a page number where question, answer, and illustrations can be found. Other ways they can communicate what they have learned include creating a PowerPoint presentation with a question and answer on each slide, a reader's theatre presentation with the questions and answers in dialogue, and a curriculum-simulated interview with an expert who answers questions posed by interviewers.

Here are two series of nonfiction science books that use a question and answer format that can be used to find information and also model how to communicate the information the students have learned.

Books

Hillman, B. (2007). *How big is it?* New York: Scholastic.

Hillman, B. (2008). *How fast is it?* New York: Scholastic.

Hillman, B. (2008). *How strong is it?* New York: Scholastic.

Hillman, B. (2009). *How weird is it?* New York: Scholastic.

Scholastic Question and Answer Series

Life Science

Berger, M., & Berger, G. (1999). *Did dinosaurs live in your backyard?* New York: Scholastic.

Berger, M., & Berger, G. (1999). *Do whales have belly buttons?* New York: Scholastic.

Berger, M., & Berger, G. (1999). *How do flies walk upside down?* New York: Scholastic.

Berger, M., & Berger, G. (1999). *Why don't haircuts hurt?* New York: Scholastic.

Berger, M., & Berger, G. (2000). *Do all spiders spin webs?* New York: Scholastic.

Berger, M., & Berger, G. (2000). *Do tarantulas have teeth?* New York: Scholastic.

Berger, M., & Berger, G. (2001). *Do penguins get frostbite?* New York: Scholastic.

Berger, M., & Berger, G. (2001). *How do bats see in the dark?* New York: Scholastic.

Berger, M., & Berger, G. (2001). *What do sharks eat for dinner?* New York: Scholastic.

Berger, M., & Berger, G. (2002). *Can snakes crawl backwards?* New York: Scholastic.

Berger, M., & Berger, G. (2002). *Do bears sleep all winter?* New York: Scholastic.

Berger, M., & Berger, G. (2002). *Is a dolphin a fish?* New York: Scholastic.

Berger, M., & Berger, G. (2002). *Where have all the pandas gone?* New York: Scholastic.

Berger, M., & Berger, G. (2002). *Why do wolves howl?* New York: Scholastic.

Berger, M., & Berger, G. (2003). *How do frogs swallow with their eyes?* New York: Scholastic.

Berger, M., & Berger, G. (2003). *Where did the butterfly get its name?* New York: Scholastic.

Earth and Space

Berger, M., & Berger, G. (1999). *Can it rain cats and dogs?* New York: Scholastic.

Berger, M., & Berger, G. (1999). *Do stars have points?* New York: Scholastic.

Berger, M., & Berger, G. (2000). *Do tornadoes really twist?* New York: Scholastic.

Berger, M., & Berger, G. (2000). *Why do volcanoes blow their tops?* New York: Scholastic.

Berger, M., & Berger, G. (2001). *Can you hear a shout in space?* New York: Scholastic.

Berger, M., & Berger, G. (2001). *What makes an ocean wave?* New York: Scholastic.

Berger, M., & Berger, G. (2002). *Does it always rain in the rainforest?* New York: Scholastic.

6TH GRADE–8TH GRADE

Introduce books by David Macauly to middle school students by doing a book talk on each and reading sections aloud. His first book, *The Way Things Work* (1988), used drawings, cross-sections, and other detailed architectural views of mechanical devices and how they work: simple machines, the elements—wind, water, heat, waves (light and sound)—and electronics, from the space shuttles to automobile thermostats. A wooly mammoth guides the reader through the book. This book was extremely popular with adults as well as children and young adults and was on the New York Times Bestseller list for 50 weeks. In 1998, he updated the original book with *The New Way Things Work*, which included the digital world and the significance of computer technology—from levers to lasers and windmills to websites, it is a visual guide to the world of machines today. Multiple copies of the books can be found in libraries.

Provide these copies for students to read in book clubs; each club can generate a question about something in one of the books and read and do further research in books and online to find the answer. For example, How does a pulley work? The students can explore this question by building a model of a pulley and planning a demonstration to the rest of the class with the answers they find.

Books

Macauly, D. (1988). *The way things work.* Boston: Houghton Mifflin.

Macauly, D. (1998). *The new way things work.* Boston: Houghton Mifflin.

ENGLISH LEARNERS

Provide Q&A frames for students to provide visual structure. Each frame can include the question and can change the question to a statement to begin the answer.

Q&A Frame	
Questions	*Answers*
What do sharks eat? Sharks eat. . . .	
Where do sharks live? Sharks live	
What do sharks look like? Sharks look like. . . .	

Most Q&A format nonfiction science books use visuals to convey information, such as drawings, diagrams, models, maps, charts, and graphs, providing comprehensible input for English learners to acquire content information. These books also provide a model for English learners to communicate their ideas through visuals as well as writing.

STRUGGLING STUDENTS

Model and use a frame and sentence starters for struggling students to record both their questions and answers:

Topic

Our topic is . . . .

Question

Our question is . . . ?

Answer

Our answer to the question is . . . .

ASSESSMENT

Students can self-assess to see if they have answered their questions, and they can describe what they learned about the topic and identify what materials, tools, and skills were most useful:

Student Self-Assessment for Q&A

1. What was your question?

2. Why was that an interesting question to you?

3. How did you find answers to the question?

4. What was most useful to you in answering your question?

5. What else would you like to know about the topic of the question?

6. How could you find out?

For younger students, ask questions of groups or the class as a whole; older students can respond in writing or in a teacher conference, where dictation for English learners or struggling students can occur. This type of assessment provides information for planning further instruction for each student.

RESOURCES

Ansberry, K. R., & Morgan, E. (2005). *Picture perfect science lessons: Using children's books to guide inquiry.* Arlington, VA: NSTA Press.

REFERENCES

Akerson, V. L., Flick, L. B., & Lederman, N. G. (2000). The influence of primary children's ideas in science on teaching practice. *Journal of Research in Science Teaching, 37*(4), 363–385.

Butts, D. P., Hofman, H. M., & Anderson, M. (1993). Is hands-on experience enough? A study of young children's views of sinking and floating objects. *Journal of Elementary Science Education, 5*(1), 50–64.

Butts, D. P., Hofman, H. M., & Anderson, M. (1994). Is direct experience enough? A study of young children's views of sounds. *Journal of Elementary Science Education, 6*(1), 1–16.

Chin, C., & Kayalvizhi, G. (2002). Posing problems for open investigations: What questions do pupils ask? *Research in Science & Technological Education, 20*(2), 269–287.

Flick, L. B. (1995). Navigating a sea of ideas: Teacher and students negotiate a course toward mutual relevance. *Journal of Research in Science Teaching, 32*(10), 1065–1082.

Gibson, J. (1998). Any questions any answers? *Primary Science Review, 51,* 20–21.

Iwasyk, M. (1997). Kids questioning kids: "Experts" sharing. *Science and Children, 35*(1), 42–46, 80.

Meyer, K., & Woodruff, E. (1997). Consensually driven explanation in science teaching. *Science Education, 80,* 173–192.

Vosniadou, S., Ioannides, C., Dimitrakopoulou, A., & Papademetriou, E. (2001). Designing learning environments to promote conceptual change in science. *Learning and Instruction, 11,* 381–419.

Watts, M., Barber, B., & Alsop, S. (1997). Children's questions in the classroom. *Primary Science Review, 49,* 6–8.

Woodruff, E., & Meyer, K. (1997). Explanations from intra- and inter-group discourse: Students building knowledge in the science classroom. *Research in Science Education, 27*(1), 25–39.

Strategy 30

Mystery Matter

On Monday, when the 1st-grade students entered the room after a very hot weekend, there were cries of "Eeewww, what stinks?" They quickly discovered the smell was coming from the plastic cup filled with milk that was sitting on the windowsill in the sun with the other cups for their science project "Mystery Matter." The milk had solidified and soured and was giving off a strong odor. They also noticed that the cup with water had a ring showing some of it had evaporated, the piece of apple and banana had dried and there were fruit flies on them, and the piece of bread had some green mold. As they talked about these changes, their teacher said "Get your science notebooks, describe what you see, and tell what you think has happened. It's a mystery we can solve."

RATIONALE

A key part of science instruction is discovery, when a student solves a mystery so to speak—uncovering and learning something they didn't know before. This is a process that relies heavily on observation and description that can lead to explanations. Students can seek verification of explanations by first identifying questions, carrying out investigations based on hypotheses, making predictions, and then engaging in experimentation, data collection, and analysis. This discovery of explanations lays the foundation for inquiry-based science instruction. Research has shown that students working on a genuine, puzzling problem can be an important first step in science teaching (Meyer & Woodruff, 1997).

An approach to teaching toward this goal and toward science curriculum standards is to use direct experiences with students: objects, materials, processes, experiments, field trips, and other things that require that students are learning hands-on by exploring the natural world. The teacher's role is to not only provide contexts for using these objects, materials, and experiences, but to guide students through the discovery process, which leads to explanations, understanding, and learning. Small group work is often used when students engage with new materials during hands-on experiences, and in a study of this type of work, Rath and Brown (1996) identified six "modes of engagement" students use:

- Exploration. Finding out about the phenomenon and studying its basic properties.

- Engineering. Using properties of the phenomenon to make something happen.

- Pet care. A personal connection to the object of study focused on nurturing.

- Procedural. Using the phenomenon as a support for imitation and step-following.

- Performance. Soliciting attention, using the phenomenon or object of study as a prop.

- Fantasy. An imaginative play activity that builds on some aspect of the phenomenon or object of study.

Research has also shown that sustained periods of undirected observation may later help students when more structured, formal instruction begins (Tomkins & Tunnicliffe, 2001), an approach which is consistent with constructivist views of learning in inquiry-focused, discovery-based science teaching. Teacher questioning also plays an important role in scaffolding students' thinking about their observations of materials and relating them to their background knowledge as well as their developing ideas (Beeth, 1998; Beeth & Hewson, 1999; Harlen, 1998). An example of such a teacher questioning sequence from the study by Beeth (1998), with a metacognitive emphasis, is shown in the Strategy section.

Source: From *National science education standards,* by the National Science Teachers Association, 1996. Washington, DC: National Academy Press.

Science Standards

2. Science as inquiry

3. Physical Science (Properties of objects and materials)

5. Earth and Space Sciences (Properties of earth materials)

STRATEGY

Begin this strategy by assembling a collection of related mystery objects (e.g., samples of various types of matter, such as solids and liquids, or rocks) appropriate for the grade level taught. Students can be asked to bring similar mystery objects to class. Create a display of the collection on a table or counter with a bulletin board behind it with the title "Mystery Matter" or "Mystery Rocks" and a large question mark. Allow time for students to add objects to the collection.

Place a class science notebook on the table where students can write descriptions of the objects, make comments, ask questions, and so on about the objects. Add books on the types of mystery objects that students can use to add to their comments and read about for interest. Use the students' written comments as well during a class discussion or to create a KWL chart on the mystery objects.

Form small groups of students and give part of the collection to each group. If rocks are used, each group can keep their part of the collection in an egg carton. Ask students to observe the mystery objects carefully and differentiate among them: How are these objects different? Describe each one. The students can take notes and draw pictures on a sheet for each object. Groups can share their findings with the whole class and then groups can combine to look for similarities and differences in their part of the collection.

After a period of student observation, recording, reflecting on ideas, and discussion in small groups, use a grade-appropriate selection of the following questions with a metacognitive emphasis to further develop student understanding (Beeth, 1998):

1. Can you state your own ideas?

2. Can you talk about why you are attracted to your ideas?

3. Are your ideas consistent?

4. Do you realize the limitations of your ideas and the possibility they might need to change?

5. Can you try to explain your ideas using physical models?

6. Can you explain the difference between understanding an idea and believing an idea? (p. 1093)

Plan further experiences with the mystery objects, using literature, experiments, and more observations.

GRADE-LEVEL MODIFICATIONS

K–2ND GRADE

Place a variety of types of matter in clear plastic cups on a table to create a center, and students can contribute to the collection as well. Place a class science notebook in the center. Students can work in pairs observing the matter and the changes in matter over time. Be sure to include both solids and liquids in the cups, and matter that will change (e.g., solids—bread, piece of fruit, cheese—and liquids—water, milk, juice, honey).

Read aloud *What's the Matter in Mr. Whisker's Room?* (Ross, 2007). The story is about a teacher who lets students explore and interact with matter in class. His students use their senses, make observations, and do mini-experiments that lead to understanding big ideas through independent, open-ended discovery. Lead a discussion asking reader response questions: What did you wonder about the matter in the story? What do you wonder about the matter in our class?

For kindergarten students, record students' responses and questions on chart paper and record students' observations over time on the chart. Students who are writing can record their own observations in a science notebook (see Strategy 28: Science Notebooks).

The big ideas students should discover through observation as well as reading informational books on matter include the following:

- Everything is made of matter.

- Matter exists in three states: solids, liquids, and gases.

- Adding or taking away energy (heat and cold) makes matter change states.

The students will observe that matter can be different: a solid, liquid, or gas (evaporation of liquids, and also the smell associated with it). Some matter changes with time (e.g., bread will mold; milk will sour and become solid and give off gas), and matter can change phases (e.g., water evaporates into air; juice will solidify into a solid and give off gas). Also demonstrate this with experiments, which students conduct.

1. Freezing and thawing water:

   a. Water + cold (freezer in the cafeteria) = ice cube. (Liquid to solid)
   b. Ice cube + heat (room temperature) = water. (Solid to liquid)

2. Melting butter:

   a. Butter + heat (room temperature or microwave/stove) = melted butter. (Solid to liquid)
   b. Melted butter + cold (refrigeration) = firm butter. (Liquid to solid)

3. Making ice cream:

   a. Liquids + solids + cold = ice cream. (Cold changes some liquids to solids)
   b. Procedure (3–5 servings)

      i.   Place ¼ cup sugar, ½ cup Half and Half, ½ cup whipping cream, and ¼ teaspoon vanilla into a one-quart plastic bag. Seal bag and mix.
      ii. Place 2 cups of ice into a one-gallon plastic bag.
      iii. Add ½ cup to ¾ cup rock salt (sodium chloride) to the gallon bag.
      iv. Place the sealed quart bag into the gallon bag and seal.
      v.   Hold the bag by the seal on top and rock from side to side gently. Do not hold the bag. It will be cold enough to cause tissue damage.
      vi. Continue to rock the bag for 10 to 15 minutes.

Students can also record the results of experiments, using dictation if necessary, and read more children's books on matter to discuss and add information to their notebooks and understanding of mystery matter.

Books

Bayrock, F. (2007). *States of matter: A question and answer book.* Mankato, MN: Capstone Press.

Curry, D. L. (2004). *What is matter?* New York: Scholastic.

Garrett, G. (2005). *Solids, liquids, and gases.* New York: Scholastic.

Mason, A. (2005). *Touch it! Materials, matter, and you.* Toronto: Kids Can Press.

Mason, A. (2006). *Change it! Solids, liquids, gases and you.* Toronto: Kids Can Press.

Ontario Science Centre. (1995). *Solids, liquids, and gases.* Toronto: Kids Can Press.

Ross, M. E. (2007). *What's the matter in Mr. Whisker's room?* Cambridge, MA: Candlewick Press.

Stille, D. R. (2004). *Matter: See it, touch it, taste it, smell it.* Mankato, MN: Picture Window Books.

Tocci, S. (2001). *Experiments with solids, liquids, and gases.* New York: Scholastic.

Zoehfeld, K. W. (1998). *What is the world made of? All about solids, liquids, and gases.* New York: Collins.

3RD GRADE–5TH GRADE

Ask students to bring a rock to class to form a collection that they can study. The rocks can be placed on a table with the label "Mystery Rocks." Read aloud *If You Find a Rock* (Christian, 2008), with black and white tinted photos and a lyrical text that describes how a child creates a way of classifying rocks for personal use (e.g., chalk to write, skipping stones, etc.). Lead a discussion using reader response questions and prompts: What did you think of the way rocks were classified in the book? What are some ways you would classify rocks?

Students can begin to group, or classify, rocks. They can work in groups, describing the characteristics of a group of rocks and writing descriptions and reasons they classified those rocks together. Students can discuss the rock groupings, compare them, look for similarities and differences, change groups, or delete some and form new ones. Rocks can be classified by different characteristics: color, size, shape, texture, material, and so on. When they have settled on groupings, they can write a description and put it with the rocks as a label.

Then, read aloud *Rocks and Minerals: A Gem of a Read* (Basher, 2009). In this book, rocks are anthropomorphized and the text is written in the first person for each rock. Each rock has a personality that also describes the characteristics of that type of rock. For example, quartzite says "Nothing wears me down. I'm the definition of true grit!" There is also a short description of each type of rock and a list of basic facts (hardness, chemical formula, etc.).

Students can use the information in this book, and in others in a class text set, to identify the rocks they have classified, regroup if necessary, and add information to the rock display. They can also read to identify the three types of rocks because of the different ways they were made: sedimentary (small pieces of rocks, stuck together), igneous (cooled lava), and metamorphic (rocks altered by pressure and heat).

Plus Technology

For extensive information on rocks and minerals, such as maps showing the distribution and extent of particular rocks and rock types, go to www.usgs.gov.

Books

Bailey, J. (2006). *The rock factory: The story about the rock cycle.* Mankato, MN: Picture Window Books.

Basher, S. (2009). *Rocks and minerals: A gem of a read.* New York: Kingfisher.

Christian, P. (2008). *If you find a rock.* San Diego, CA: Harcourt.

Dussling, J. (2001). *Looking at rocks.* New York: Grosset & Dunlap.

Hooper, M. (1996). *The pebble in my pocket.* New York: Viking.

Rosinsky, N. M. (2004). *Rocks: Hard, soft, smooth, and rough*. Mankato, MN: Picture Window Books.

Symes, R. F. (2008). *Rocks and minerals*. New York: DK.

6TH GRADE–8TH GRADE

Read aloud Byrd Baylor's (1985) poetic text in the illustrated book *Everybody Needs a Rock* and lead a discussion using reader response questions and prompts: What was your favorite part of the book? What do you know about rocks?

Collect mystery rocks with students and do other activities described for Grades 3 through 5. In addition, use Moh's Hardness Scale to observe, describe, characterize, and classify rocks in another way. The relative hardness of a mineral may be determined by scratching it with an object to see if it leaves a mark. The scale measures the hardness from 1 (softest) to 10 (hardest).

Moh's Hardness Scale

Minerals used to determine the hardness scale:

1. Talc
2. Gypsum
3. Calcite
4. Fluorite
5. Apatite
6. Orthoclase (Feldspar)
7. Quartz
8. Topaz
9. Corundum
10. Diamond

How to determine mineral hardness	Scale Number
Can be rubbed off on the fingers	1
Can be scratched with a fingernail	2
Can be scratched with a penny	3
Can be scratched easily with a knife blade	4
Hard to scratch with a knife blade	5
Can be scratched with a file but will not scratch glass	6
Can easily be used to scratch glass	7
Too hard to be tested on this scale	8–10

Create a text set of books on rocks with other information on collecting, earth history and rock formation, the many ways to describe and classify rocks, and the use of rocks and minerals.

Books

Baylor, B. (1985). *Everybody needs a rock*. New York: Aladdin.

Gans, R. (1997). *Let's go rock collecting*. New York: Collins.

Pellant, C. (2001). *Collecting gems and minerals: Hold the treasures of the earth in the palm of your hand*. Falls Church, VA: Sterling.

Pellant, C. (2002). *Smithsonian handbooks: Rocks and minerals*. New York: DK.

Pough, F. H. (1998). *Peterson first guide to rocks and minerals*. Boston: Houghton Mifflin.

Riccinti, E. (2002). *Rocks and minerals*. New York: Scholastic.

Schumann, W. (1993). *Handbook of rocks, minerals, and gemstones*. Boston: Houghton Mifflin.

Shaffer, P. R. (2001). *Rocks and minerals*. New York: St. Martin's Press.

ENGLISH LEARNERS

English learners benefit from the hand-on experience of using real objects, using the five senses, and using drawings, diagrams, or models in a science notebook to demonstrate understanding. Provide, or have a more proficient English speaking peer provide, labels in English for students. Primary language support can be provided through the use of cognates, for example for "Mystery Matter" and "Mystery Rocks."

English	Spanish
Mystery	Misterio
Matter	Materia
Solid	Solido
Liquid	Liquido
Gas	Gas
Mineral	Mineral

STRUGGLING STUDENTS

Prepare frames to help students describe, compare differences, and classify a mystery object based on their observations of the rock characteristics. For example, for "Mystery Rocks," see the frame "How Are Rocks Different?":

How Are Rocks Different?				
Rock (#)	Shape	Color	Feel/Texture	What's Special About It?

Students can work in pairs and groups to share their descriptions, and they can add information with the help of other students.

ASSESSMENT

Science notebooks kept by students can be used to assess student understanding of the process of observing, describing, identifying, and generalizing from experiences with mystery matter. Students can also trade notebooks and dialogue or write comments, questions, and reflections on another student's journal. Have conferences with pairs or groups of students with the dialogue science notebooks.

RESOURCES

Blobaum, C. (1999). *Geology rocks: 50 hands-on activities to explore the earth.* Charlotte, VT: Williamson Publishing.

Calhoun, Y. (2005). *Earth science fair projects: Using rocks, minerals, magnets, and much more.* Berkeley Heights, NJ: Enslow Publications.

Van Cleave, J. (1995). *Janice Van Cleave's rocks and minerals: Mind-boggling experiments you can turn into science fair projects.* Hoboken, NJ: Wiley.

REFERENCES

Beeth, M. (1998). Teaching science in fifth grade: Instructional goals that support conceptual change. *Journal of Research in Science Teaching, 35*(10), 1091–1101.

Beeth, M., & Hewson, P. W. (1999). Learning goals in an exemplary science teacher's practice: Cognitive and social factors in teaching for conceptual change. *Science Education, 83*, 738–760.

Harlen, W. (1998). Teaching for understanding in presecondary science. In B. J. Fraser & K. G. Tobin (Eds.), *International handbook of science education* (pp. 183–198). Dordecht, the Netherlands: Kluwer.

Meyer, K., & Woodruff, E. (1997). Consensually driven explanation in science teaching. *Science Education, 80,* 173–192.

Rath, A., & Brown, D. E. (1996). Modes of engagement in science inquiry: A microanalysis of elementary students' orientations toward phenomena at a summer science camp. *Journal of Research in Science Teaching, 33*(10), 1083–1097.

Tomkins, S. P., & Tunnicliffe, S. D. (2001). Looking for ideas: Observation, interpretation and hypothesis-making by 12-year-old pupils undertaking science investigations. *International Journal of Science Education, 23*(8), 791–813.

Virtual Field Trips on the World Wide Web

The 3rd-grade students bounced up and down with excitement as they looked over the shoulders of ocean explorers using sonar technology to map the deep sea nearly 20,000 feet below the water's surface near Indonesia. The students were on a virtual field trip called "Voyages of Discovery: NOAA's Okeanos Explorer" on the website of the Exploratorium museum (www.exploratorium.com).

RATIONALE

Technology can play an essential role in science instruction through the use of virtual environments in four areas identified by the National Research Council (2002):

- Learners think critically and logically about scientific ideas and compare them with real-life conditions.

- Learners critically evaluate and communicate scientific ideas.

- Learners formulate scientific explanations from evidence.

- Learners use appropriate tools to gather, analyze, and interpret data. (p. 19)

Technologies associated with these learning dimensions include thinking critically with modeling, visualization, and simulation tools (Gobert & Pallant, 2004; Keating, Barnett, Barab, & Hay, 2002; White & Frederiksen, 1998), online interactive and discussion tools (Guzdial & Turns, 2000; Hsi & Hoadley, 1997; Lee & Songer, 2003; Scardamalia & Bereiter, 1994), online scaffolding tools (Davis, 2003; Quintana et al., 2004), and data collection, analysis, and interpretation (Penuel & Yarnal, 2005; Songer, 2006). Using these technology tools can help students experiment and think critically about phenomena they are experiencing first-hand in the real world by using controlled, hypothetical, or virtual environments (Songer, 2007).

Because they have an educational mission and are expected to provide authoritative information, museums and government agencies have created many excellent web-based virtual environments and science field trips for students K through 8 that are recommended by science educators (Bodzin & Cates, 2002; Smith, 1999; Stevenson, 2001). An advantage of these websites over print media is that they can be updated rapidly and can make new, complex, and controversial information readily available. They can also allow children to travel in virtual space, not just in our world but all over the universe.

Source: From National science education standards, by the National Science Teachers Association, 1996. Washington, DC: National Academy Press.

Science Standards

2. Science as Inquiry
6. Science and Technology

STRATEGY

Identify a website that offers a virtual science field trip for students, which can be used in concert with hands-on experiences in the classroom, lessons, and reading nonfiction science trade books on the chosen topic. The following is a list of recommended websites for science education.

- Exploratorium (www.exploratorium.org). The website of the children's science museum in San Francisco offers an array of virtual exhibits that are interactive and include videos, podcasts, photo essays, articles, digital library resources, activities for students, science teaching information, blogs, and much more. The features range in grade-level appropriateness, from very young through secondary students, and many of the activities can be done by students independently. The site is also available in Spanish.

- NASA (www.nasa.gov). The website of the National Aeronautics and Space Administration focuses on earth and space sciences and offers teachers and students many virtual experiences around the Earth and through the universe, including space exploration. For teachers, there are downloadable teaching guides that a teacher can search by grade, science area, and type of activity. The NASA Kid's Club also allows students to search by subject, leading them to many interactive activities.

- USGS (www.usgs.gov). The website of the United States Geological Survey focuses on biology, geography, geology, geospatial, and water. It is constantly updated with FAQs on topics of current interest, with news releases, the latest publications, podcasts, and a multimedia gallery. The Science in Your Backyard section allows students to choose their state and get news releases and real-time information on current events in science. They offer teacher's guides on many topics, student activities, and numerous maps and mapping activities for student participation.

- Boston Museum of Science (www.mos.org). The website of the museum offers teaching resources and guides, and it takes students on virtual field trips related to the museum collection using video, video casts, and podcasts.

- GLOBE (www.globe.gov). The Global Learning and Observation to Benefit the Environment is a worldwide, hands-on primary through secondary school-based science and education program on earth and space science. Students can participate in various research experiences through the program by doing inquiry-based investigations and data entry. This program has a close partnership with NASA and NSF Earth System Science Projects. The site is available in English and Spanish. It is necessary for teachers to join in order to participate.

Preview the sites and current exhibits or features for a virtual field trip with students that will complement classroom instruction and learning goals. Students can be prepared for the visit with an introduction to the site, guidelines on how the virtual field trip will take place, and the expectations for each student.

Before the virtual field trip, introduce the use of the World Wide Web with literature and assemble a text set of nonfiction science trade books on the topic for the field trip. These books could be read aloud and discussed using reader response questions and prompts for whole class participation, used in book clubs on a topic related to the virtual field trip, or read independently by students.

It is also possible to do a post-visit debriefing for student responses, questions, or ideas they might have for further inquiry and activities related to the virtual field trip.

GRADE-LEVEL MODIFICATIONS

K–2ND GRADE

Introduce the World Wide Web to young students by reading aloud the picture book *Willie and the World Wide Web* (Geissen, 1998). This book is a virtual reality fable and tells the story of Willie, who enters a computer on his birthday through a website titled Wonders of Our World and travels on through different site topics such as Our Solar System and The Age of Dinosaurs. While it is a well-illustrated picture story book for children, it also introduces many facts about the web through the narrative of Willie's adventures.

After reading this book, lead a discussion using reader response questions and prompts: If you were Willie, how would you have felt on a trip on the World Wide Web? Was there anything you wondered about? What would you like to find out on the World Wide Web?

Introduce a specific science topic by reading a related book aloud, discussing it, and making a list of questions students would like to have answered as they go on the virtual field trip on the World Wide Web. The whole class can go on the virtual field trip together through the use of a school computer lab with a computer for each one or two students or in the classroom with a Smart Board. Students can also access the site after the initial introduction to do activities on their own.

Books

Brimmer, L. D. (2000). *The world wide web.* New York: Scholastic.

Geissen, S. (1998). *Willie and the world wide web.* New York: Three Leaves Publishing.

3RD GRADE–5TH GRADE

Introduce and read aloud a book on the World Wide Web and have a class set of books that can be read in book clubs or independently by students, as well as a class set of books on the topic related to the virtual field trip. Students can go on the virtual field trip as a class through the use of a Smart Board in the classroom, during time in the computer lab, or they can be rotated through a computer station during assigned times.

Prepare a set of guidelines for the virtual field trip, have students take notes, discuss the field trip with the class after everyone has participated, and then plan further activities.

Books

Bruno, L. C. (1997). *Science and technology breakthroughs: From the wheel to the world wide web.* Farmington Hills, MI: U.X.L.

Jeffries, D. (1999). *Cyber space: Virtual reality and the world wide web.* New York: Crabtree.

6TH GRADE–8TH GRADE

Introduce the virtual science field trip in the classroom by reading *Tim Berners-Lee: Inventor of the World Wide Web* (McPherson, 2010) to put the use of the World Wide Web in scientific, historical, and social context. Lead a discussion using reader response questions and prompts: What are some things you have wondered about the World Wide Web? How would you have felt if you were Tim Berners-Lee? What would you like to see happen with the web?

The virtual field trip related to a science topic could be taken at school in the classroom with the use of a Smart Board, rotating students at classroom computers, or in the computer lab, but students could also take the trip on their own in a computer lab or on a personal computer after being supplied with a guideline for activities. Students could also form small groups and choose different parts of a virtual field trip site, raise questions of their own, and propose independent projects they would like to do.

Books

Gaines, A. (2001). *Tim Berners-Lee and the development of the world wide web.* Hockessin, DE: Mitchell Lane Publishers.

McPherson, S. S. (2010). *Tim Berners-Lee: Inventor of the world wide web.* Brookfield, CT: Twenty-First Century Books.

Wolinsky, A. (2000). *The history of the internet and the world wide web.* Berkeley Heights, NJ: Enslow Book.

ENGLISH LEARNERS

English learners benefit from the use of visuals and auditory sensory information such as photographs, illustrations, and video and audio recordings to provide comprehensible input for the website content. Interactive activities on such websites can engage them, and they can work in pairs or small groups with more proficient English speaking peers for student to student interaction. Many sites are available in Spanish as well to provide primary language support. Websites can be viewed multiple times so that

English learners have repeated opportunities to view, hear, and interact with the website content and activities.

STRUGGLING STUDENTS

Guide students through a website with the use of a Smart Board in the classroom or at an individual computer station with a few or a small group of students. Relevant vocabulary can be introduced with a word bank list of words, and titles of each section of the virtual field trip to find can be shown in order. Students can be guided to choose appropriate activities at a variety of ability levels.

ASSESSMENT

Some sites have included forms of assessment and evaluation that can be used, assessments can be created based on the class's science topic and learning goals, or students can write in response to questions that ask them to evaluate the website and the virtual field trip:

- What did you think of the website and the virtual field trip?
- Were there any questions you have about it?
- What is the most interesting thing you learned on the virtual field trip?
- What else would you like to know?
- How could you find out?

RESOURCES

November, A. (2008). *Web literacy for educators.* Thousand Oaks, CA: Corwin Press.

Sage, K. (1999). *Science activities using the World Wide Web: Grade 4–6+.* Monterey, CA: Evan-Moor Educational Publishers.

REFERENCES

Bodzin, A. M., & Cates, W. M. (2002). Inquiry dot com. *The Science Teacher, 69*(9), 48–52.

Davis, E. (2003). Prompting middle school science students for productive reflection: Generic and directed prompts. *The Journal of the Learning Sciences, 12*(1), 91–142.

Gobert, J. D., & Pallant, A. (2004). Fostering students' epistemologies of models via authentic model-based tasks. *Journal of Science Education and Technology, 13*(1), 7–22.

Guzdial, M., & Turns, J. (2000). Effective discussion through a computer-mediated anchored forum. *The Journal of the Learning Sciences, 91*(4), 437–469.

Hsi, S., & Hoadley, C. (1997). Productive discussion in science: Gender equity through electronic discourse. *Journal of Science Education and Technology, 6*(1), 23–36.

Keating, T., Barnett, M., Barab, S., & Hay, K. (2002). The virtual solar system project: Developing conceptual understanding of astronomical concepts through building three-dimensional computational models. *The Journal of Science Education and Technology, 11*(2), 261–275.

Lee, H. S., & Songer, N. B. (2003). Making authentic science accessible to students. *International Journal of Science Education, 25*(1), 1–26.

National Research Council. (2000). *Inquiry and the national science education standards: A guide for teaching and learning.* Washington, DC: National Academy Press.

Penuel, W. R., & Yarnal, L. (2005). Designing handheld software to support classroom assessment: An analysis of conditions for teacher adoption. *The Journal of Technology, Learning and Assessment, 3*(5), 3–45.

Quintana, C., Reiser, B., Davis, B., Krajcik, J., Fretz, E., Duncan, R., et al. (2004). A scaffolding design framework for software to support science inquiry. *The Journal of the Learning Sciences, 13*(3), 337–386.

Scardamalia, M., & Bereiter, C. (1994). Computer support for knowledge-building communities. *The Journal of the Learning Sciences, 3*(3), 265–283.

Smith, D. A. (1999). Learning the Web: Science magazine site. *Journal of Computers in Mathematics and Science Teaching, 18,* 89–93.

Songer, N. B. (2006). BioKIDS: An animated conversation on the development of curricular activity structures for inquiry science. In R. Keith Sawyer (Ed.), *Cambridge handbook of the learning sciences* (pp. 355–369). New York: Cambridge University Press.

Songer, N. B. (2007). Digital resources versus cognitive tools: A discussion of learning science with technology. In S. K. Abell & N. G. Lederman (Eds.), *Handbook of research on science education* (pp. 471–491). Mahwah, NJ: Lawrence Erlbaum.

Stevenson, S. (2001). Let's get technical: Online learning opportunities for science education. *Multimedia Schools, 8*(6), 42–46.

White, B. T., & Frederiksen, J. R. (1998). Inquiry, modeling, and metacognition: Making science accessible to all students. *Cognition and Instruction, 16*(1), 3–118.

Food Diaries

The students in the 2nd-grade bilingual Spanish-English class wrote an *ABC of Healthy Food* book. Their teacher had read books about food, and students have had hands-on experiences with food in the classroom. They each wrote a Healthy Food Pattern. Here is one by Guadalupe:

Healthy Food Pattern

G is for green beans.

Green beans are a vegetable.

They are green, long, and yummy.

I like green beans because they are good for me.

RATIONALE

Teachers can use literature and model science as inquiry by teaching students how to use a food diary and, therefore, to understand nutrition and healthy eating in a personal and social perspective since they will be recording, analyzing, and reflecting on their own eating habits. The May 2010 report *White House Task Force on Childhood Obesity: Report to the President* (United States Department of Agriculture [USDA], 2010) addresses the challenge of the childhood obesity epidemic in the United States. The report states that one of every three children (31.7%) between the ages of 2 and 19 is overweight or obese, and each has a greater risk of developing diabetes, heart disease, and cancer over their lifetimes. Obesity causes 112, 000 deaths a year in this country and is a burden for the health care system. It costs 150 billion dollars a year to treat obesity-related medical conditions. One third of all children born in the year 2000 are expected to develop diabetes during their lifetime. The current generation of children may have shorter life spans than their parents. The goal of the White House Task Force on Childhood Obesity action plan established by President Obama is to reduce the rate of childhood obesity to 5%, the rate it was before the current rise started in the 1970s.

The first goal of this plan is to create a healthy start on life for American children. Parents, caregivers, and teachers are critical to achieving this goal. Teachers can educate students by having them examine their own behaviors and ideas about eating through the use of food diaries, supported with literature, online research, analysis, discussion, and reflection. In research using teacher's interviews and observations of students' explorations and ideas about food and health, the teachers saw these as a useful pedagogical tool to find out what the students knew and then use it to shape subsequent pedagogy (Turner, 1997).

Source: From *National science education standards,* by the National Science Teachers Association, 1996. Washington, DC: National Academy Press.

Science Standards

2. Science as inquiry

7. Science in personal and social perspectives

STRATEGY

Introduce healthy foods and eating through literature, reading aloud books with food and health as part of a story narrative and nonfiction informational books. Students can respond to reader response questions and prompts about a book, which can lead to self-reflection about their own eating habits.

Direct students to take an inquiry approach to science by using food diaries to record what they eat, and have students use this personal data to explore science content such as types of healthy food; the nutrient groups of carbohydrates, protein, fat, water, vitamins, and minerals; the 2005 United States Department of Agriculture (USDA) revised food pyramid and how to use it; making judgments about fast food; and reading food labels.

Food diaries can be modeled on chart paper for younger students, and older students can use graphic organizers, frames, and templates to record what they eat. Students can also write anecdotal observations in food diaries, make plans to change what they eat, and learn to use food diaries over time to not only understand the impact of the types of foods they eat but to meet the challenge of improving their health.

Plus Technology

The USDA website (www.usda.gov) has information on nutrition, the 2005 food pyramid, and current recommendations for nutrition. Other USDA websites (www.mypyramid.gov/kids; www.nutritionexplorations.org/kids/nutrition-pyramid.asd) that include teaching ideas, resources, and an interactive computer game on nutrition for students can also be visited.

GRADE-LEVEL MODIFICATIONS

K–2ND GRADE

Introduce food diaries by reading aloud *Eating the Alphabet: Fruits and Vegetables From A to Z* by Lois Ehlert (1994). This is a beautifully illustrated large format picture book with repeated rhyme for each fruit or vegetable used for a letter from A to Z, and it includes information about each one. Students can make predictions about which fruit or vegetable will come next, and they can join in the repeated rhyme as the book is read aloud. Lead a discussion using reader response questions and prompts: Which was your favorite part? What fruit or vegetable did you eat today?

Model writing in a food diary of fruits and vegetables on chart paper, recording the fruits and vegetables that students have eaten. The chart can be added to each day to model keeping a food diary for the students. Each student can copy the food diary from the chart, or a writing frame for each student can be prepared for them to create a food diary for a week, recording the fruits and vegetables that they eat:

Food Diary for Fruits and Vegetables, K–2		
	Fruit	Vegetable
Monday		
Tuesday		
Wednesday		
Thursday		
Friday		

Students can share their food diaries, the USDA recommended five servings of fruits and vegetables a day can be introduced. The class can discuss their food diaries, describe their favorite fruits and vegetables, do research on why fruits and vegetables are important and the special value of each one, and plan how to meet the goal of eating five servings a day and discuss why it is important. Continue to read aloud books on healthy food, and provide a class text set for independent reading.

The students can also write their own class book modeled after Lois Ehlert's (1994) book, with each student writing and illustrating a page about one fruit or vegetable. Students can also use a writing frame (e.g., Healthy Food Pattern, the example at the beginning of this strategy; an example in the English Learners section) or use Lois Ehlert's rhyme pattern or make one of their own.

Books

Concannon, L. (2008). *Super sprouts*. Centennial, CO: Life Vest.

Curtis, L. (2009). *More healthy food please*. Philadelphia: Brilliant Learning.

Ehlert, L. (1994*). Eating the alphabet: Fruits and vegetables from A to Z*. San Diego, CA: Harcourt.

Gibbons, G. (2008). *The vegetables we eat*. New York: Holiday House.

Miller, A. (2008). *The monster health book: A guide to eating healthy, being active and feeling great for monsters and kids!* New York: Holiday House.

Rake, T. (2001). *Oh the things you can do that are good for you! All about staying healthy*. New York: Random House.

Russ-Ayon, A. (2009). *We eat food that's fresh*. New York: Our Rainbow Press.

Tourville, A. (2008). *Fuel the body: Eating well*. Mankato, MN: Picture Window Books.

3RD GRADE–5TH GRADE

Introduce healthy eating, the food pyramid, and food diaries by reading aloud *The Edible Pyramid: Good Eating Every Day* (Leedy, 2007). This fictional story book is set in the "Edible Pyramid" restaurant. The diners are personified animals, with a tuxedo-clad cat as the host. He offers a menu that relates to the vertical stripes on the 2005 USDA food pyramid. The book cleverly combines the story with the content of the food pyramid. Lead a discussion using reader response questions and prompts: What did you think of the story? Have you had any experience with the food pyramid? Tell about it.

Introduce the 2005 food pyramid using resources from the USDA, such as a class poster and blank food pyramids for students, or by reading aloud another book, *Good Enough to Eat: A Kid's Guide to Food and Nutrition* (Rockwell, 2009). This book is full of information on the nutrient groups—carbohydrates, protein, fat, water, vitamins and minerals, nutrients functions, which foods contain which nutrients, the food pyramid and how to use it, and so on.

Help students identify the five food groups, plus oils, using the USDA resources of the book by Rockwell (2009), and give each student a food diary based on these that students will keep for a week. They can classify what they eat in each group each day. The groups are color-coded on the food pyramid, and students can add color to their diaries.

Food Pyramid Food Diary, 3–5

	Grains (Orange)	Vegetables (Green)	Fruits (Red)	Milk (Blue)	Meat & Beans (Purple)	Oils (Yellow)
Monday						
Tuesday						
Wednesday						
Thursday						
Friday						

Students can work in six groups using a cooperative learning jigsaw technique to learn about each of the five groups plus oils, using a class set of books, doing online research, or using the USDA resources. Each student group can describe a nutrient group and the foods in it, tell how many servings are recommended each day by the USDA, and show a serving size using actual food if possible. Each group can prepare a one-page fact sheet on the food group they have researched, and these can be attached to the food diaries for reference.

Students can keep the food pyramid food diary for a week or more, and they can analyze and reflect on their eating habits.

Books

Barron, R. (2004). *Showdown at the food pyramid.* New York: Penguin. (Based on the 1992 food pyramid.)

Dickman, N. (2010). *My food pyramid.* London: Heinemann Educational Books.

DK Publishing. (2007). *My food pyramid.* New York: DK Children.

Green, E. K. (2006). *Healthy eating.* Minneapolis, MN: Bellwether.

Hyde, M. O., & Forsyth, E. H. (2003). *Diabetes.* Danbury, CT: Franklin Watts.

Leedy, L. (2007). *The edible pyramid: Good eating every day.* New York: Holiday House.

Rockwell, L. (2009). *Good enough to eat: A kid's guide to food and nutrition.* New York: HarperCollins.

Taylor-Butler, C. (2008). *The food pyramid.* New York: Scholastic.

6TH GRADE–8TH GRADE

To address the issue of eating a balanced healthy diet compared to a diet of fast foods, read excerpts from *Chew on This: Everything You Don't Want to Know About Fast Food* (Schlosser & Winson, 2007). Lead discussions using reader response questions and prompts: What do you think of what the author is saying? Tell about fast food in your diet.

Students can keep a food diary for several weeks, noting everything they eat. They can each also research the USDA recommended servings for the five food groups plus oils and the calorie intake relative to exercise for their specific age and weight. To do this they can use a text set of books for the class, the free teaching materials from the USDA, and online research.

Using food labels and the nutrition information sheets provided in fast food restaurants, they can record the serving size and calories and calculate the amount of stored food energy in the foods they eat and compare it to the amount of energy they expend through exercise to discover if they are eating a diet that will decrease, maintain, or increase their weight. Provide a frame to do these calculations.

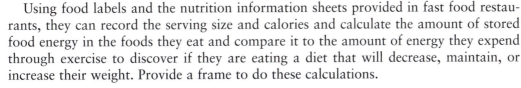

Stored Food Energy				
Food	Grams/Serving	Calories/Serving	Calories/ Gram*	Calories/100 grams**

*Calories divided by grams per serving

**Calories per gram multiplied by 100

Books

Buller, L. (2005). *Food.* New York: DK.

Collins, T. B. (2004). *Fast food.* Farmington Hills, MI: Gale.

Favor, L. J. (2007). *Food as foe: Nutrition and eating disorders.* Tarrytown, NY: Marshall Cavendish.

Jakes, M., & Cheung, L. W. (2003). *Be healthy! It's a girl thing: Food, fitness, and feeling great.* New York: Crown Books.

Knighton, K. (2008). *Why shouldn't I eat junk food?* London: Usborne Books.

Marjolijn, B., & Zoumbaris, S. Z. (2008). *Food and you: A guide to healthy habits for teens.* Santa Barbara, CA: Greenwood.

Ridgwell, J. (1996). *Examining food and nutrition.* London: Heinemann Educational Books.

Schlosser, E., & Wilson, C. (2007). *Chew on this: Everything you don't want to know about fast food.* Boston: Houghton Mifflin.

Tecco, B. D. (2008). *Food for fuel: The connection between food and physical activity.* New York: Rosen Publishing Group.

ENGLISH LEARNERS

English learners can benefit from the opportunity to tap into their prior experience with food and from visuals such as pictures of food, the food pyramid, and charts created by the teacher. If real food is brought to the class, they can also benefit from engaging their five senses.

Provide a writing frame for a Healthy Food Pattern and model writing the frame with the class. This frame provides an either-or choice for students for *is* or *are*, which can be confused by English learners when using the singular or plural forms in English, and many vegetables are written as plurals.

Healthy Food Pattern

(Letter of the alphabet) is for (Name of fruit/vegetable).

(Name of Fruit/vegetable) (Choose is or are) (Choose a fruit or vegetable).

They are (Use three describing words).

I like (Name of fruit/vegetable) because (write a reason).

Also look for cognates: for example, fruit/fruta and pear/pera for Spanish. To provide primary language support, use bilingual books or books in the student's home language.

Plus Technology

The USDA website (www.mypyramid.gov/kids) on nutrition for students, including an interactive computer game, is also in Spanish (click on En Español).

Books

Gaff, J. (2007). *Por que debo comer de forma saludable?/I wonder why I have to eat healthy food?* (Spanish Edition). Corunna, Spain: Everest.

Schaefer, A. (2010). *Alimentos saludables/Healthy food* (Spanish Edition). London: Heinemann Educational Books.

White, A. (2009). *Una fiesta saludable/The healthy food party* (Spanish Edition). Miami, FL: Santillano.

Provide a writing frame for a food diary, as follows:

> Today is (day and date). For breakfast I ate _____. For lunch I ate _____. For dinner I ate _____.

This frame could include a word bank of common food names the students can use to fill in the frame.

ASSESSMENT

Download and print out a blank copy of the 2005 revised food pyramid from the USDA website (www.mypyramid.gov/kids). This can be used as an assessment tool for what students have learned about food, health, and nutrition from literature, the Internet, and from keeping food diaries. The youngest students could color the bars on the food pyramid and label them for each food group. Older students could provide more complex information, such as the description of each nutrient group, nutrient function, recommended daily servings, and calories consumed and used as stored food energy relative to exercise and burning of calories.

RESOURCES

Evers, C. L. (2006). *How to teach nutrition to kids*. Portland, OR: 24 Carrot Press.

REFERENCES

Turner, S. A. (1997). Children's understanding of food and health in primary classrooms. *International Journal of Science Education, 19*(5), 491–508.

United States Department of Agriculture [USDA]. (2010). *White House task force on childhood obesity: Report to the President*. Washington, DC: United States Department of Agriculture.

PART V

The Arts

WHAT RESEARCH HAS TO SAY ABOUT
LITERATURE-BASED TEACHING AND THE ARTS

Educators have advocated over the years for the integration of the arts and other curricular areas such as literature and literacy, using terms such as *interdisciplinary studies, multidisciplinary curriculum,* and *integrated learning* to describe teaching the arts in concert with other content areas. Richard Deasy (2003) referred to arts integration as "the effort to build a set of relationships between learning in the arts and learning in the other skills and subjects of the curriculum" (p. 2).

Acknowledging that learning can be transferred between the arts and other subjects, many in the field advocate for arts integration as learning *through* and *with* the arts (Rabkin & Redmond, 2004, 2006). Arts integration can also be viewed as a curricular connections process by unifying elements of curriculum across several content areas (Krug & Cohen-Evron, 2000; Parsons, 2004). Collaborative engagement among classroom teachers, parents, arts specialists, teaching artists, and members of the community is also seen as important in arts integration (Heath, 2001), and the use of integrated arts theory and a focus on practical applications of concepts, coupled with reflective discussion, can promote conceptual understanding among teachers (Andrews, 2006).

The theory of multiple intelligences put forth by Howard Gardner (1983, 1993, 1999) provides a rationale for integrating the arts with literature in the regular classroom. Gardner describes multiple intelligences students may possess—logical-mathematical, linguistic, musical, spatial, bodily-kinesthetic, interpersonal, and intrapersonal—and suggests that students can be smart and learn in different ways, including through experiences with literature and the visual and performing arts. Elliot Eisner (2002) described curricular structures that can support literature-based teaching and the arts as well as the teaching of the arts across other curricular areas such as social studies, science, and mathematics: (1) focus on a particular historical period or culture, (2) focus on the similarities and differences between and among the art forms themselves, (3) identification of a major theme or idea that can be explored through the arts and other fields as well, and (4) identification of a problem that requires that it be addressed through several disciplines, including the arts.

Studies that provided evidence of enhanced learning and achievement when students engaged in a variety of art experiences were compiled in the report *Champions of Change: The Impact of the Arts on Learning* (Fiske, 1999), developed with the support of the GE Fund, the John D. and Catherine T. MacArthur Foundation, the Arts Education Partnership, and the President's Committee on the Arts and the Humanities. Research from the report showed that students with high involvement in the arts performed better in general in school than students with low involvement (Catterall, Chapleau, & Iwanaga, 1999). Winner and Cooper (2000) investigated the relationship between arts study and academic achievement through a meta-analysis of 31 studies and concluded that "there is indeed a relationship between arts education and composite measures of academic achievement. . ." (p. 24). Research findings from other studies also showed the positive effect of arts integration on student achievement (Burton, Horowitz, & Abeles, 2000; Kinney & Forsythe, 2005; McKean, 2000; Winner & Hetland, 2000).

Consider several questions as you plan to integrate the arts and literature, along with other content areas: What is the content? What is appropriate instruction? Who provides the instruction? What strategies are implemented? How will assessment occur (Brown, 2007)? Smith (2001) described a model of a well-developed, 6th-grade integrated unit on Greek history and art and showed how integration can be successfully applied in the classroom. In the process of studying Greek sculpture, students read an adaptation of Homer's *The Odyssey,* studied Greek history as it was associated with Homer's epic tale, presented a dramatic interpretation of some of the scenes from *The Odyssey,* studied their own bodies in their performance of battle scenes, and finally, they let this inform the design of their sculpture.

Stevenson and Deasy (2005) addressed this primary research question: "How do the arts contribute to the improvement of schools that serve economically disadvantaged communities" (p. 26)? They described 10 case studies across the country where multiple art forms, including poetry, music, theatre, and visual arts, were used to engage students and where there was improved student achievement in reading. For example, in a classroom of students learning English as a second language, students explored the theme of dreams through the poetry of Langston Hughes, the paintings of Marc Chagall, the music of Miles Davis, and the novel *The Long Way to a New Land*, by Joan Sanding. The most common type of integration in all 10 case studies was language arts with drama, which consistently had a positive effect on students' understanding of narrative and characterization in literature.

Illustrated picture books are commonly seen as a way for teachers to integrate visual imagery with written narrative in the classroom (Alejandro, 2005; Chu, 2005; Cornett, 2006; Cowan & Albers, 2006; Greenberg, 2005; Kiefer, 2005; Yolen, 2005). Teachers can draw students' attention to the illustrations, such as black and white or color drawings, mixed media images, photographs, or combinations of these related to the book's fictional story or nonfiction content, and also focus on the illustrator as an artist, with attention paid to the style, media, and choices an artist makes when illustrating a book. They can also plan art experiences based on the art and on artists who illustrate books in any or all of the visual and performing arts: visual, music, dance, and theatre.

The link between the arts, literature, and language arts and reading is especially strong (Mantione & Smead, 2003). Teachers use illustrated picture books and other illustrated books as a basic resource to model and teach reading and writing. In a cross-cultural study exploring the relationship between pictures and words with young children, Soundy and Qui (2006/2007) examined the interplay between the two communication systems of verbal and visual literatures and how they might contribute to the ability of kindergarten students in the United States and China to extract meaning from picture books. The results revealed that children became an engaged audience during picture book reading, experienced the character's thoughts, and learned to visualize through both viewing the art in picture books and creating art themselves. Linking the standards for teaching the language arts and reading with literature and standards for teaching the arts is a natural fit.

An obvious context for this is using drama in the classroom, especially drama based on a book, which can combine the spoken word and text, movement and dance, music, and the visual arts through costuming, backgrounds, and sets. Research has demonstrated the effectiveness of this integration of the arts, literature, and literacy through related speaking, reading, and writing (Podlozny, 2000; Wagner, 1998, 2002).

GUIDELINES FOR SELECTING BOOKS FOR TEACHING THE ARTS

While the content areas of language arts and reading, social studies, mathematics, and science each have a professional organization that offers guidelines for selecting books and publishes the results in their respective journals each year, there is no one central professional organization representing the arts that does this. Furthermore, the many books that teachers can choose to teach the arts in K through 8 classrooms are not limited to books about the arts. Teachers can consider a general guideline for choosing outstanding literature across a wide range of content and topics and for any age.

Temple, Martinez, Yokota, and Naylor (2002) suggested that outstanding children's literature has the following qualities.

QUALITIES OF OUTSTANDING CHILDREN'S LITERATURE

What makes a good book?

- Good books expand awareness. Good books give children names for things in the world and for their own experiences. Good books take children inside other people's perspectives and let children "walk two moons" in their shoes. They broaden children's understanding of the world and capacity for empathy.

- Good books provide an enjoyable read that doesn't overtly teach or moralize. Many children's books turn out to be something—to have themes, in fact—and it is often possible to derive a lesson from them. But if a book seems too obviously contrived to teach a lesson, children (and critics) will not tolerate it.

- Good books tell the truth. Outstanding children's books usually deal with significant truths about the human experience. Moreover, the characters in them are true to life, and the insights the books imply are accurate, perhaps even wise.

- Good books embody quality. The words are precisely chosen and often poetic in their sound and imagery; the plot is convincing, the characters believable, and the description telling.

- Good books have integrity. The genre, plot, language, characters, style, theme, and illustrations, if any, all come together to make a satisfying whole.

- Good books show originality. Excellent children's books introduce readers to unique characters or situations or show them the world from a unique viewpoint; they stretch the minds of readers, giving them new ways to think about the world and new possibilities to think about.

National Standards For Arts Education

The National Standards for Arts Education: What Every Young American Should Know and Be Able to Do in the Arts outlines what every K through 12 student should know and be able to do in the arts. The standards were developed by the Consortium of National Arts Education Associations (1994), which included representatives from the American Alliance for Theatre and Education, the National Art Education Association, Music Educators National Conference, and the National Dance Association. The published standards are specific to dance, drama, music, and the visual arts—though there is one standard that is common to all the arts disciplines: The student understands connections among the various art forms and other disciplines. This standard reflects the approach of integrated arts education, within the arts and across the curriculum.

Dance Content Standards

1. Identifying and demonstrating movement elements and skills in performing dance.
2. Understanding choreographic principles, processes, and structures.
3. Understanding dance as a way to create and communicate meaning.
4. Applying and demonstrating critical and creative thinking skills in dance.
5. Demonstrating and understanding dance in various cultures and historical periods.
6. Making connections between dance and healthful living.
7. Making connections between dance and other disciplines.

Music Content Standards

1. Singing, alone and with others, a varied repertoire of music.
2. Performing on instruments, alone and with others, a varied repertoire of music.
3. Improvising melodies, variations, and accompaniments.
4. Composing and arranging music within specified guidelines.
5. Reading and notating music.
6. Listening to, analyzing, and describing music.
7. Evaluating music and music performances.
8. Understanding relationships between music, the other arts, and disciplines outside the arts.
9. Understanding music in relation to history and culture.

THEATRE CONTENT STANDARDS

1. Script writing by planning and recording improvisations based on personal experience, heritage, imagination, literature, and history (K–4). Script writing by the creation of improvisations and scripted scenes based on personal experience and heritage, imagination, literature, and history (5–8).

2. Acting by assuming roles and interacting in improvisations (K–4). Acting by developing basic acting skills to portray characters who interact in improvised and scripted scenes (5–8).

3. Designing by visualizing and arranging environments for classroom dramatizations (K–4). Designing by developing environments for improvised and scripted scenes (5–8).

4. Directing by planning classroom organizations (K–4). Directing by organizing rehearsals for improvised and scripted scenes (5–8).

5. Researching by finding information to support classroom dramatizations (K–4). Researching by using cultural and historical information to support improvised and scripted scenes (5–8).

6. Comparing and connecting art forms by describing theatre, dramatic media (such as film, television, and electronic media), and other art forms (K–4). Comparing and incorporating art forms by analyzing methods of presentation and audience response for theatre, dramatic media (such as film, television, and electronic media), and other art forms (5–8).

7. Analyzing and explaining personal preferences and constructing meanings from classroom dramatizations and from theatre, film, television, and electronic media productions (K–4). Analyzing, evaluating, and constructing meanings from improvised and scripted scenes and from theatre, film, television, and electronic media productions (5–8).

8. Understanding context by recognizing the role of theatre, film, television, and electronic media in daily life (K–4). Understanding context by analyzing the role of theatre, film, television, and electronic media in the community and in other cultures (5–8).

VISUAL ARTS CONTENT STANDARDS

1. Understanding and applying media, techniques, and processes.
2. Using knowledge of structures and functions.
3. Choosing and evaluating a range of subject matter, symbols, and ideas.
4. Understanding the visual arts in relation to history and cultures.
5. Reflecting upon and assessing the characteristics and merits of their work and the work of others.
6. Making connections between visual arts and other disciplines.

REFERENCES

Alejandro, A. (2005). Like happy dreams: Integrating visual arts, writing, and reading. In J. Flood, S. B. Heath, & D. Lapp (Eds.), *Handbook of research on teaching literacy through the communicative and visual arts* (pp. 794–800). Mahwah, NJ: Lawrence Erlbaum.

Andrews, B. (2006). Re-assessing the effectiveness of an arts partnership in teacher education. *International Review of Education, 52*(5), 443–459.

Brown, S. L. (2007). An arts-integrated approach for elementary level students. *Childhood Education, 83*(3), 172–173.

Burton, J. M., Horowitz, R., & Abeles, H. (2000). Learning in and through the arts: The question of transfer. *Studies in Art Education, 41*(3), 228–257

Catterall, J. S., Chapleau, R., & Iwanaga, J. (1999). Involvement in the arts and human development: General involvement and intensive involvement in music and theater arts. In E. B. Fiske (Ed.), *Champions of change: The impact of the arts on learning* (pp. 1–18). Washington, DC: The Arts Education Partnership.

Chu, J. (2005). Words + pictures = magic: A designer looks at picture books. In J. Flood, S. B. Heath, & D. Lapp (Eds.), *Handbook of research on teaching literacy through the communicative and visual arts* (pp. 862–863). Mahwah, NJ: Lawrence Erlbaum.

Consortium of National Arts Education Associations. (1994). *National standards for arts education: What every young American should know and be able to do in the arts.* Reston, VA: Music Educators National Conference.

Cornett, C. E. (2006). Center stage: Arts-based read alouds. *The Reading Teacher, 60*(3), 234–240.

Cowan, K., & Albers, P. (2006). Semiotic representations: Building complex literacy practices through the arts. *The Reading Teacher, 60*(2), 124–137.

Deasy, R. J. (Ed.). (2003). *Creating quality integrated and interdisciplinary arts programs: A report of the Arts Education National Forum.* Washington, DC: Arts Education Partnership.

Eisner, E. W. (2002). *The arts and the creation of mind.* New Haven, CT: Yale University Press.

Fiske, E. (Ed.). (1999). *Champions of change: The impact of the arts on learning.* Washington, DC: The Arts Education Partnership and the President's Committee on the Arts and the Humanities.

Gardner, H. (1983). *Frames of mind: The theory of multiple intelligences.* New York: Basic Books.

Gardner, H. (1993). *Multiple intelligences: The theory in practice.* New York: Basic Books.

Gardner, H. (1999). *Intelligence reframed: Multiple intelligences for the 21st century.* New York: Basic Books.

Greenberg, J. (2005). Books about art: A joyous vision. In J. Flood, S. B. Heath, & D. Lapp (Eds.), *Handbook of research on teaching literacy through the communicative and visual arts* (pp. 813–815). Mahwah, NJ: Lawrence Erlbaum.

Heath, S. B. (2001). Three's not a crowd: Plans, roles, and focus in the arts. *Educational Researcher, 30*(7), 10–17.

Kiefer, B. (2005). The visual arts made accessible through picture books. In J. Flood, S. B. Heath, & D. Lapp (Eds.), *Handbook of research on teaching literacy through the communicative and visual arts* (pp. 820–821). Mahwah, NJ: Lawrence Erlbaum.

Kinney, C. W., & Forsythe, J. L. (2005, Spring). The effects of the Arts IMPACT curriculum upon student performance on the Ohio fourth-grade proficiency test. *Bulletin of the Council for Research in Music Education, 164,* 35–48.

Krug, D. H., & Cohen-Evron, N. (2000). Curriculum integration positions and practices in art education. *Studies in Art Education, 41*(3), 258–275.

Mantione, R., & Smead, S. (2003). *Weaving through words: Using the arts to teach reading comprehension strategies.* Newark, DE: International Reading Association.

McKean, B. (2000). Arts everyday: Classroom teachers' orientation toward arts education. *Arts and Learning Research, 16*(1), 177–194.

Parsons, M. (2004). Art and integrated curriculum. In E. W. Eisner & M. D. Day (Eds.), *Handbook of research and policy in art education* (pp. 775–794). Mahwah, NJ: Lawrence Erlbaum.

Podlozny, A. (2000). Strengthening verbal skills through the use of classroom drama: A clear link. *Journal of Aesthetic Education, 34*(3/4) 239–275.

Rabkin, N., & Redmond, R. (Eds.). (2004). *Putting the arts in the picture: Reframing education in the 21st century.* Chicago: Columbia College.

Rabkin, N., & Redmond, R. (2006). The arts make a difference. *Educational Leadership, 63*(5), 60–64.

Smith, S. S. (2001). The Ulysses project. *Arts & Activities, 129*(4), 33, 40.

Soundy, C., & Qui, Y. (2006/2007). Portraits of picture power: American and Chinese children explore literacy through the visual arts. *Childhood Education, 83*(2), 68–74.

Stevenson, L. M., & Deasy, R. J. (2005). *Third space: When learning matters.* Washington, DC: Arts Education Partnership.

Temple, C., Martinez, M., Yokota, J., & Naylor, A. (2002). *Children's books in children's hands: An introduction to their literature* (2nd ed.). Boston: Allyn & Bacon.

Wagner, B. J. (1998). *Educational drama and language arts: What research shows.* Portsmouth, NH: Heinemann.

Wagner, B. J. (2002). Understanding drama-based education. In G. Brauer (Ed.), *Body and language: Intercultural learning through drama* (pp. 3–18). Westport, CT: Ablex.

Winner, E., & Cooper, M. (2000). Mute those claims: No evidence (yet) for a causal link between arts study and academic achievement. *Journal of Aesthetic Education, 34*(3/4), 11–75.

Winner, E., & Hetland, L. (2000). The arts and academic achievement: What the evidence shows. *Journal of Aesthetic Education, 34*(3–4).

Yolen, J. (2005). The eye and the ear. In J. Flood, S. B. Heath, & D. Lapp (Eds.), *Handbook of research on teaching literacy through the communicative and visual arts* (pp. 810–812). Mahwah, NJ: Lawrence Erlbaum.

The kindergarten teacher modeled songwriting for her class of all Khmer speaking Cambodian American children who were learning English. She read a picture book of the song "Mary Wore Her Red Dress." The students loved it. During repeated readings, they hummed or sang along when they could say the words in English, and they used a chart with the words written out in very large print so that a student could come up and point to the words each time the class sang the song. The teacher also made a frame with a line for the number of syllables for each line in the song (e.g., six syllables for "Mary wore her red dress"). She asked for a volunteer, and Chinda raised her hand and came to the front of the class. She was wearing a black bow in her hair, so the teacher and the students wrote a new song filling in the lines of the frame: "Chinda wore her black bow, black bow, black bow. Chinda wore her black bow all day long." The class sang the new song every day that week, and Chinda wore her black bow all week long.

RATIONALE

Songwriting integrates several aspects of arts curriculum: oral language, reading, writing, and the structure of language; the literature of rhyme, poetry, and song lyrics; vocal and instrumental music; and thematic and content instruction.

Researchers have explored the connection between music and literacy. Butzlaff (2000) conducted a meta-analysis of 31 research studies that examined the connection between music and writing and found that the 25 correlational studies analyzed showed a strong and statistically reliable link between the study of music and performance on standardized reading and writing tests. For young children, most early music learning in the classroom is focused on the repeated singing of songs where lyrics are learned very well by students.

Numerous studies have also investigated the relationship between music and mathematics achievement. Vaughn (2000) conducted a meta-analysis of 25 studies and found a highly significant positive relationship between music instruction, both vocal and instrumental, and mathematics. This relationship was correlational, and it was not sufficient to suggest a causal relationship.

Source: From *National Standards for arts education: What every young American should know and be able to do in the arts,* by the Consortium of National Arts Education Association, 1994. Reston, VA: Music Educators National Conference.

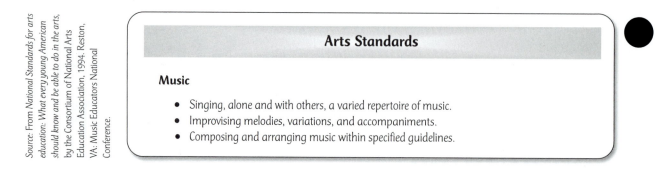

Arts Standards

Music

- Singing, alone and with others, a varied repertoire of music.
- Improvising melodies, variations, and accompaniments.
- Composing and arranging music within specified guidelines.

STRATEGY

You can introduce the strategy of songwriting through literature. For younger students, read aloud a single-edition song picture book—an illustrated book with a text of song lyrics. The students can join in repeated readings by singing the lyrics. Many of these books are based on familiar songs of childhood, and most include the music for the song. For older students, you can introduce song lyrics as a type of poetry and read a variety of poems on a theme aloud, students can read aloud in small groups or for the whole class, and individuals can read on their own from a classroom text set of poems.

Lead the class in writing a song to model the process. Brainstorm ideas with students for a song written by the whole class on a theme, a calendar event, or on a topic in another content area. Record student words and phrases in a cluster on a whiteboard or piece of chart paper.

Since the lines in a song are based on syllables, one syllable per beat, also ask students the number of syllables in each word or phrase recorded on the cluster chart and then write the number next to the word or phrase. Students can also take the pen and do this themselves.

Create a syllable chart as a word bank for songwriting, and either fill it in or have students fill it in according to the number of syllables in words and phrases on the cluster they have brainstormed.

Songwriting Syllable Chart				
Number of Syllables				
One	Two	Three	Four	Five

Prepare a song frame based on a familiar tune, noting the number of syllables per line. Each song frame will vary, depending on the tune upon which it is based. Ask students to suggest words and phrases from the syllable chart to fill in the frame. When the frame is complete, students can sing the song, adding rhythm instruments such as rhythm sticks, rattles, drums, or anything that will create a sound, as well as any musical instruments the students can play. The completed song frame can be posted in the room as a guide for singing the song in the future. Students can also make individual copies of the song, illustrate them, and create their own song lyric picture book that is a collection of class songs.

Plus Technology

Create song frames in a word file that students can download and print out to compose a song in a group or on their own; students could also word process the lyrics to a song they write to print out and share with other students. Students can research the life of a composer on the Internet; they can also do a PowerPoint presentation of a song they write in a group and use it to lead the rest of the class in song.

GRADE-LEVEL MODIFICATIONS

K–2ND GRADE

Read aloud a single edition song lyric picture book of a familiar tune, such as "The Wheels on the Bus" ("go round and round, round and round, round and round. The wheels on the bus go round and round all over town"). An excellent version of this song as a text for a picture book is illustrated by Paul O. Zelinsky (2000), with exciting paper engineering with movable parts such as wheels that spin. Other verses include "The wipers on the bus go swish, swish, swish . . ." and "The babies on the bus go Waah! Waah! Waah!" The book also suggests hand motions to engage students while singing. It comes with music for the lyrics and a song CD. The teacher can lead a class discussion using reader response questions and prompts: What experiences have you had riding a bus?

The frame for "The Wheels on the Bus" looks like this:

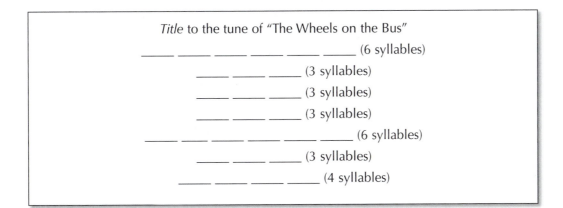

To model the songwriting process for young students in Grades K through 2 from the first day of school, the teacher might suggest starting each verse with the day of school and adding a new verse each day: "The first day of school was fun, fun, fun. . . ."

Plus Technology

A DVD compilation of familiar songs can be found on *The Wheels on the Bus. . . . And More Sing-Along Favorites* (2005, Scholastic Video Collection). The 45 minute color DVD is animated and closed-captioned, and it features the famous Burl Ive's version of "I Know an Old Lady Who Swallowed a Fly."

Books

Kubler, A. (2007). *The wheels on the bus.* Auburn, ME: Child's Play International.

Raffi. (1990). *The wheels on the bus.* St Louis, MO: Turtleback.

Snyder, J. (2009). *The wheels on the bus.* Stow, OH: Twin Sisters Production.

Swan, M. (2006). *The wheels on the bus.* New York: Scholastic.

Zelinsky, P. O. (2000). *The wheels on the bus.* New York: Dutton Juvenile.

DVD

Scholastic Video Collection. (2005). *The wheels on the bus. . . and more sing along favorites.* New York: Scholastic.

Song lyric picture books of other songs include the following:

Hoberman, M. A. (2004). *I know an old lady who swallowed a fly.* Boston: Little Brown.

Hoberman, M. A. (2004). *The eensy weensy spider.* Boston: Little Brown.

Langstaff, J. (1983). *Frog went a-courtin'.* New York: Scholastic.

Langstaff, J. (1989). *Over in the meadow.* St. Louis, MO: Turtleback.

Scholastic. (2007). *Old MacDonald had a farm.* New York: Author.

Spier, P. (1994). *The fox went out on a chilly night.* New York: Dell Picture Yearling.

Trapani, I (1997). *Twinkle, twinkle, little star.* Watertown, MA: Charlesbridge.

Trapani, I. (1998). *I'm a little teapot.* Watertown, MA: Charlesbridge.

Trapani, I. (1998). *Oh where, oh where has my little dog gone?* Watertown, MA: Charlesbridge.

Trapani, I. (2002). *Baa baa black sheep.* Watertown, MA: Charlesbridge.

Trapani, I. (2003). *Mary had a little lamb.* Watertown, MA: Charlesbridge.

Trapani, I. (2004). *How much is that doggie in the window?* Watertown, MA: Charlesbridge.

Trapani, I. (2004). *Row row row your boat.* Watertown, MA: Charlesbridge.

Trapani, I. (2004). *The itsy bitsy spider.* Watertown, MA: Charlesbridge.

Trapani, I. (2006). *Here we go round the mulberry bush.* Watertown, MA: Charlesbridge.

Trapani, I. (2007). *Shoo fly.* Watertown, MA: Charlesbridge.

Trapani, I. (2008). *Jingle bells.* Watertown, MA: Charlesbridge.

Zelinsky, P. O. (2002). *Knick knack paddy whack.* New York: Dutton Juvenile.

3RD GRADE–5TH GRADE

Since song lyrics are poetic verses put to music, you can introduce songwriting by reading aloud from poetry collections and providing a classroom text set of poetry collections that students can read independently, in pairs, or small groups. A collection that clearly makes the connection between poetry and song is *Julie Andrews' Collection of Poems, Songs, and Lullabies,* by Julie Andrews and her daughter Emma W. Hamilton (2009). It includes 150 classic and contemporary poems as well as songs from theatre and movie musicals. The book includes a CD with poems read aloud by Julie Andrews and Emma W. Hamilton and songs by Julie Andrews, such as "My Favorite Things" from the movie *The Sound of Music.* Students can listen for the music inherent in words and poetry through both the book and CD.

Lead a class discussion using reader response questions and prompts: What were you thinking about as you listened to this poem or song? What are some things the poem or song reminded you of in your own life? What are some of the things we could write a song about?

Pick a theme, a calendar event (e.g., season, holiday), or a topic related to another content area with students and brainstorm ideas on a cluster for a class song. Model the songwriting process and record student ideas on the cluster, noting the number of syllables in the words and phrases on the cluster. You or a student recorder can place the words and phrases in a column for the correct number of syllables in the Songwriting Syllable Chart.

Create a song frame using the melody of the familiar French folk song "Frere Jacques," and model songwriting by taking dictation from students using ideas from the cluster of words and phrases they brainstormed. Use the Songwriting Syllable Chart to match the syllables for each line:

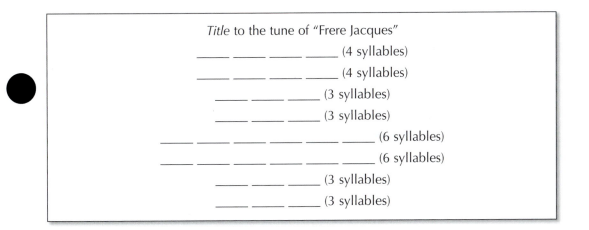

Title to the tune of "Frere Jacques"

_____ _____ _____ _____ (4 syllables)

_____ _____ _____ _____ (4 syllables)

_____ _____ _____ (3 syllables)

_____ _____ _____ (3 syllables)

_____ _____ _____ _____ _____ _____ (6 syllables)

_____ _____ _____ _____ _____ _____ (6 syllables)

_____ _____ _____ (3 syllables)

_____ _____ _____ (3 syllables)

Students can sing the song they have written together. The melody for "Frere Jacques" is often sung as a round. Students can then write songs independently, in pairs, or in groups on other topics. There are many other collections of poetry that can be used to read aloud or can be included in a classroom text set.

Books

Andrews, J. & Hamilton, E. W. (2009). *Julie Andrews' collection of poems, songs, and lullabies.* New York: Little, Brown.

De Regniers, B. S., Moore, E., White, M. M., & Carr, J. (1988). *Sing a song of popcorn: Every child's book of poems.* New York: Scholastic.

Driscoll, M. (2003). *A child's introduction to poetry: Listen while you learn about the magic worlds that have moved mountains, won battles, and made us laugh and cry.* New York: Black Dog & Leventhal.

Hall, P. (2001). *The Oxford illustrated book of American children's poems.* New York: Oxford University Press.

Prelutsky, J. (1983). *The Random House book of poetry for children.* New York: Random House.

Prelutsky, J. (1999). *The 20th century children's poetry treasury.* New York: Alfred A. Knopf.

6TH GRADE–8TH GRADE

Songwriting can be introduced in connection with poetry, showing the relationship between song lyrics and poetic verse, by reading aloud or having students read from books of poetry collections. Read aloud the song lyric picture book *What a Wonderful World* with the words to the song written by David Weiss and Bob Thiele (1995) and made famous by Louis Armstrong. Create a frame for this song and use the process described in the general strategy section to model songwriting and write the first verse of the song with the class.

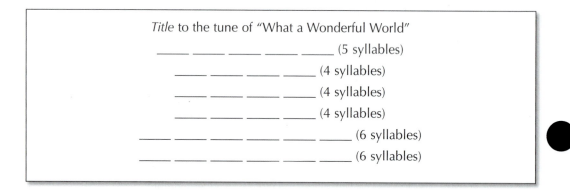

The class can compose one verse together, and then they can form groups to create a different verse to add to the song, record all the verses on chart paper, and sing the song together. Books based on the life of Louis Armstrong and about jazz in America can also be read to or by the class. There are many other collections of poetry that can be read aloud or that students can read independently.

Books

Berry, J., & Mayhew, J. (2003). *Classic poems to read aloud.* New York: Kingfisher.

Mesner, E. S. (2002). *The best poems ever: A collection of poetry's greatest voices.* New York: Scholastic.

Rosen, M. (Ed.). (2009). *Classic poetry: An illustrated collection.* Cambridge, MA: Candlewick Press.

Books on Louis Armstrong and jazz:

Hannah, J. (2005). *Hot jazz special.* Cambridge, MA: Candlewick Press.

McDonough, Y. Z. (2004). *Who was Louis Armstrong?* New York: Penguin Young Readers.

Marsalis, W. (2005). *Jazz ABC: An A to Z collection of jazz portraits.* Cambridge, MA: Candlewick Press.

Myers, W. D. (2008). *Jazz.* New York: Holiday House.

Orgill, R. (1997). *If I only had a horn: Young Louis Armstrong.* Boston: Houghton Mifflin.

Schroeder, A., & Cooper, F. (1999). *Satchmo's blues.* New York: Doubleday.

Weinstein, M. H. (2008). *When Louis Armstrong taught me scat.* San Francisco: Chronicle Books.

Weiss, D., & Thiele, B. (1995). *What a wonderful world.* New York: Atheneum.

ENGLISH LEARNERS

Songwriting includes many elements that provide scaffolding for English learners. The five senses are used, including not only the visuals of picture books and the song chart, but listening to the sound and music, singing the song, the added movement of hand gestures, and the rhythmical counting of syllables to write the song. The songwriting syllable chart and song frame with lines broken down by syllables adds further structure. Student to student interaction is also encouraged as students can write and sing songs in small groups. Students are encouraged to tap into their own life experience as they write songs.

There are also many bilingual books of songs providing primary language support for students. For some examples in Spanish, see the following *Books* section.

Books

Orozco, J. L. (1999). *De colores and other Latin American folksongs for children.* New York: Puffin.

Schiller, P. (2004). *The bilingual book of rhymes, songs, stories, and fingerplays: Over 450 Spanish/English selections.* Silver Spring, MD: Gryphon House.

STRUGGLING STUDENTS

Struggling readers and writers are supported in songwriting efforts through the use of several graphic organizers: cluster charts for brainstorming ideas, songwriting syllable chart, and a song frame. The process can be modeled for the whole class or group on chart paper, or copies of each of these graphic organizers could be provided to students so that they can record the ideas generated by the whole class or group. A book of songs written by the class can be used by students as they learn the words through repeated readings and by engaging in singing.

ASSESSMENT

A blank songwriting syllable frame and song frame can be used to assess a student's understanding of the songwriting process as he or she goes through the steps of songwriting independently: (1) create a cluster of words and phrases for a song on a self-selected theme or topic, (2) place the words and phrases in the appropriate column in the songwriting syllable frame, and (3) write a song using the words and phrases on a song frame. The teacher can provide the frame for the song, or students can choose a tune and create their own frame.

RESOURCES

Andrews, L. J., & Sink, P. E. (2002). *Integrating music and reading instruction: Teaching strategies for upper-elementary grades.* Reston, VA: The National Association for Music Educators.

Garland, T. H., & Kahn, C. V. (1995). *Math and music: Harmonious connections.* Palo Alto, CA: Dale Seymour.

Hansen, D., Bernstorf, E., & Stuber, G. (2004). *The music and literacy connection.* Reston, VA: The National Association for Music Educators.

REFERENCES

Butzlaff, R. (2000). Can music be used to teach reading? *Journal of Aesthetic Education, 34*(3), 167–178.

Vaughn, K. (2000). Music and mathematics: Modest support for the oft-claimed relationship. *Journal of Aesthetic Education, 34*(3/4), 149–166.

Strategy
34

Music Stories

The 1st-grade teacher read a picture book about Saint-Saens music story, "The Carnival of the Animals," played the music for the children, and had them pantomime the movements of the animals to the music. Saint-Saens used the rhythm of the march for the lions, but at recess Alice lined other students up and led them around the playground in a spirited conga line rhythm, encouraging them to roar in time with the step, step, step, kick of the conga. When her teacher asked her about it she said: "I saw the conga on a re-run of *I Love Lucy* on TV. I liked it. If I were the composer, I would have the lions dance the conga."

RATIONALE

Music stories are compositions of a narrative or descriptive sort, and they are intended to depict or suggest nonmusical incidents, ideas, or images, such as those drawn from literature or legend. Students can listen for the story in the music, and this type of music can be integrated with literature, literacy, social studies, science, mathematics, and the other arts. Hope (2003) suggested that music can be integrated into an interdisciplinary curriculum with each area retaining unique integrity (e.g., both literature and the study of narrative or music based on a story).

Burrack and McKenzie (2005) investigated the effect of teaching approaches that associated visual art, the language arts, and music. They found students were better able to develop conceptual connections across these curricular areas: for example, the expressive movements of music to color in art and literature. One student in the study commented as follows: "When the picture mixed with the music, it really brought everything together." Cosenza (2006) made a case for integrating the visual arts and music as well.

Barrett (2001) emphasized the importance of challenging students to relate music to other disciplines and cultures when integrating music into the curriculum, maintaining that "deep understanding often depends upon the intersections and interactions of the disciplines" (p. 27), such as that which can occur when music is related to literature as well as the visual arts. Collett (1991) described a sequential arts education methodology that resulted in students learning more with a curriculum based on integrated thematic units generated by the arts. For example, when two music story pieces were integrated into classroom instruction, Prokofiev's "Peter and the Wolf" and Saint Saens "Carnival of the Animals," achievements in reading, sciences, and attitudes toward school were improved.

Source: From *National Standards for arts education: What every young American should know and be able to do in the arts,* by the Consortium of National Arts Education Association, 1994. Reston, VA: Music Educators National Conference.

Arts Standards

Music

- Listening to, analyzing, and describing music.

- Evaluating music and music performances.

- Understanding relationships between music, the other arts, and disciplines outside the arts.

- Understanding music in relation to history and culture.

STRATEGY

Literature can be used to introduce the story upon which a piece of program music is based. Programmatic music can be selected for grade-level appropriateness, for music related to another content area to practice an interdisciplinary approach to teaching the arts, or for other criteria such as current events or student or teacher interest in a piece of music or a particular composer.

After selecting a piece of programmatic music, introducing it with literature, and playing it for students, use reader response questions and prompts to lead a discussion. What were you thinking about as you listened to the music? Tell about anything the music reminded you of from your own life as you listened. What did you wonder about the music? Tell how you heard the story in the music.

For younger students, create a T-chart to record student ideas in two columns. In the left-hand column, list the Sights/Story, and in the right-hand column, list Sounds/Music. Older students can write responses in a double-entry journal. A double-entry journal uses a page with a vertical line down the middle, similar to a T-chart. In the left-hand column, they can note the sights or part of the story they hear in the music, and in the right-hand column, they can write the sounds of the music that correspond to the sights and the story. Older students can write in their journals while listening and share what they have written in a small group first; then a spokesperson from each group can share what they discussed with the whole class.

You can continue writing in music journals with students and discussing the journal entries, or you can choose from several ways to extend the experience of listening to and writing about programmatic music: You can read literature related to the story or to the author of the story that forms the inspiration for the music; read, write, and learn more about the piece of music, the composer, or the period of history in which it was written; or create interdisciplinary projects related to the music, such as creating a dance choreography, dramatizing the story with the music, or responding to the music with the visual arts.

GRADE-LEVEL MODIFICATIONS

K–2ND GRADE

Read aloud the picture book *Carnival of the Animals* (Lithgow, 2007), which is a narrative of the music composed by Camille Saint-Saens in 1886, reimagined by John Lithgow. In Lithgow's story, a young boy wanders off from a school field trip in a natural history museum and sees his classmates, teachers, and family transformed into a menagerie of the animals that the composer Saint-Saens represented in his musical composition.

Play the music and ask students reader response aesthetic questions and prompts after each animal is introduced in the music: What were you thinking about when you listened to this part of the music? How did the music make you feel? The teacher can take dictation for younger students on chart paper, and older students can write their response in a double-entry journal as described in the general strategy.

The teacher can also read *Carnival of the Animals: Classical Music for Kids* (Saint-Saens & Turner, 1999), which gives an introduction to the music, shows the instruments associated with each animal, and provides commentary. This book comes with a full-length, music only CD. The teacher can use a T-chart with students, asking them to identify the instruments of the orchestra played for each of the animals.

Students can reflect on this piece of programmatic music through the other arts by doing the following: (1) pantomiming the movements of the animals and creating a dance choreography using the movements to the music, (2) drawing or painting illustrations for each of the animals, (3) creating dramatic scenes with the animals with dialogue and conversations among the animals, and (4) writing poems or stories about each of the animals. A good book to read aloud to model drawing and painting is *Can You Hear It?* (Lach & Metropolitan Museum of Art, 2006), which includes a CD and shows 13 examples of pictorial music and visual masterpieces such as a Remington's painting of the Old West and Aaron Copeland's "Billy the Kid: Gun Battle." For poetry writing, the teacher can read *Carnival of the Animals With CD: Poems Inspired by Saint-Saens Music* (Chernaik, 2006), with 13 different poets writing a poem corresponding to each of the animals in the composition.

Books

Chernaik, J. (2006). *Carnival of the animals with CD: Poems inspired by Saint-Saens music*. Cambridge, MA: Candlewick Press.

Hayes, A. (1991). *Meet the orchestra*. San Diego, CA: Harcourt.

Lach, W., & Metropolitan Museum of Art. (2006). *Can you hear it?* New York: Abrams Books for Young Readers.

Lithgow, J. (2007). *Carnival of the animals*. New York: Simon & Schuster.

Moss, L. (2000). *Zin! Zin! Zin! A violin*. New York: Aladdin.

Saint-Saens, C., & Turner, B. C. (1999). *Carnival of the animals: Classical music for kids*. New York: Henry Holt.

3RD GRADE–5TH GRADE

Read aloud Sergei Prokofiev's *Peter and the Wolf* (Schulman & Prokoviev, 2004), which comes with a fully orchestrated and narrated CD. After playing the music, the teacher can lead a class discussion using reader response questions and prompts: What did you picture in your mind as you listened to the story and the music? The students can write in double-entry journals on what they pictured in their mind for each part of the story in the left-hand column, and they can write the sounds and music that corresponded to that part of the story in the right-hand column.

The teacher can make a chart with five columns for (1) characters in the story, (2) description of the characters, (3) the instrument representing each character, (4) the sound of the character in the music, and (5) the mood of the music in that part of the story and how it made them feel. The teacher can read the story and play the music again. Students can take turns at the chart, asking other students to raise their hands when they hear another character in the music.

Students can use the other arts to respond to the book and music by illustrating scenes from the story and music for posting on classroom bulletin boards, for making a class book, or for first pantomiming the characters and then writing scripts for each of the scenes to present as a story dramatization to accompany the music with spoken lines.

Books

Beck, I., & Prokofiev, S. (1995). *Peter and the wolf.* New York: Atheneum.

Prokofiev, S. (1986). *Peter and the wolf.* New York: Penguin Puffin.

Raschka, C., & Prokofiev, S. (2008). *Peter and the wolf.* New York: Atheneum.

Schulman, J., & Prokofiev, S. (2004). *Sergei Prokofiev's Peter and the Wolf with a fully orchestrated and narrated CD.* New York: Alfred A. Knopf.

6TH GRADE–8TH GRADE

The teacher can read Gershwin's *Rhapsody in Blue With CD* (Celenza, 2006) to introduce George Gershwin's musical composition "Rhapsody in Blue." The book describes the creation of Gershwin's 1924 masterpiece after he was surprised by a newspaper announcement that he would write a new jazz concerto. He did not remember agreeing to do so for Paul Whiteman's forthcoming "An Experiment in American Music" concert. Gershwin later said it was the rhythm of a train ride that freed his mental block and led him to the concept of a musical kaleidoscope of America. He wanted to mirror New York of the 1920s, and his musical ideas included the Jewish Klezmer howl of the opening clarinet, the blues, and ragtime as a love song for the city.

Students can write in double-entry journals during and after they listen to a reader response question and prompt: What did they picture in their mind as they listened? (in the left-hand column), and How did they feel as they listened to that part? (in the right-hand column).

Students can form small groups and share from their journals their impressions and feelings about the music. Each student can choose a prompt to write about, based on their journals and discussions: (1) Choose one part of the music and write a description of what they saw as they listened. (2) Compare the way Gershwin pictured New York through music to the way the student would picture their own city (including New York, if that is where they live).

Students can read about Gershwin and do online research on the composer and his times and present what they have learned using the other arts by illustrating their writing or presenting information in a graphic comic or novel form or by writing a reader's theatre script using the words of Gershwin and his brother, lyricist Ira.

Books

Celenza, A. H. (2006). *Gershwin's rhapsody in blue with CD*. Watertown, MA: Charlesbridge.

Ford, C. T. (2008). *George Gershwin: American musical genius*. Berkeley Heights, NJ: Enslow.

Krull, K. (1993). *Lives of the musicians: Good times, bad times, and what the neighbors thought*. San Diego, CA: Harcourt.

Mitchell, B. (1987). *America I hear you: A story about George Gershwin*. Minneapolis, MN: Lerner.

Reef, C. (2000). *George Gershwin: American composer*. Greensboro, NC: Morgan Reynolds.

Venezia, M. (1994). *George Gershwin*. Danbury, CT: Children's.

Vernon, R. (2002). *Introducing Gershwin*. Middlesex, UK: Belitha Press.

Whiting, J. (2005). *The life and times of George Gershwin*. Hockessin, DE: Mitchell Lane.

ENGLISH LEARNERS

Listening to music and focusing on the visual imagery of programmatic music allows English learners to use multiple senses to understand and use English. Create and add to a word bank of musical sounds, terms, and instruments, and use cognates in the students' home language to provide primary language support. The use of charts also scaffolds the learning for English learners. Students can write in double-entry journals with the help of a peer more proficient in English, with the teacher, or they can draw their ideas in journals to later use in discussions. They can also use pantomime and gestures to demonstrate their understanding of the music. Using props and realia like actual musical instruments provides further scaffolding.

STRUGGLING STUDENTS

Create a list of words to describe music and make a copy for each student to use as they discuss music and write in journals. Musical terms, the names of instruments, the words for sounds, and other relevant vocabulary can be on this list that students can access as they respond to music and write in journals. You can also take dictation for student comments on chart paper during whole class or small group discussions, and students can copy these into their journals. Students can also draw and label an image or scene from the music, using the word list.

ASSESSMENT

For younger students, the teacher can direct students to draw a picture of a character or of an image or scene from the story behind the programmatic music. They can then use a frame that the student can complete about their drawing:

> Here is _____. The instrument for _____ is _____.
> It sounds _____. It made me feel _____.

Conference with older students using their double-entry music journals, noting their comments; their understanding of the music, imagery, and stories; and their personal response to the music. During these conferences, you can learn more about the students' interest in types of music and plan further activities with the student related to the programmatic music used in the classroom.

RESOURCES

Barrett, J. R., McCoy, C., & Veblen, K. (1997). *Sound ways of knowing: Music in the interdisciplinary classroom.* Belmont, CA: Wadsworth.

REFERENCES

Barrett, J. R. (2001). Interdisciplinary work and musical integrity. *Music Educators Journal, 87*(5), 27–31.

Burrack, F., & McKenzie, T. (2005). Enhanced student learning through cross-disciplinary projects. *Music Educators Journal, 91*(5), 45–50.

Collett, M. J. (1991). Read between the lines: Music as a basis for learning. *Music Educators Journal, 78,* 42–45.

Cosenza, G. (2006, Winter). Play me a picture, paint me a song: Integrating music learning with visual art. *General Music Today, 19,* 7–11.

Hope, S. (2003). Questions and challenges concerning music's role in education. *Journal for Learning Through Music, 2,* 12–15.

Strategy 35

Collage

Figure 35.1   Julissa's self-portrait collage and face poem

Julissa's
Face Pome

Hair: Black, short, soft.
Smile: Pretty, shiny.
Nose: Looks like
a button, small,
Cute.

RATIONALE

Collage is a mixed media art strategy using paper or other media to compose shapes, colors, and lines, and it is used by many picture book illustrators such as Leo Leonni, Eric Carle, Ezra Jack Keats, Lois Ehlert, and others. Torn paper collage requires only a piece of paper for a background and small pieces of paper attached to it with a glue stick and can be done in classrooms from kindergarten through 8th grade.

Integrating visual arts instruction, such as collage, into literacy instruction has often been suggested as a way to improve student achievement. In a meta-analysis of studies conducted by Burger and Winner (2000), results showed a positive, moderately sized relationship between reading improvement and an integrated arts-reading form of instruction when visual art was integrated as an entry point into reading instruction for students. A study of the benefits of integrating visual art and writing (Andrzejczak, Trainin, & Poldberg, 2005) showed that the creation of visual art also enhanced the writing process. In providing written responses to their visual art in this study, students took more time to elaborate thoughts, produced stronger descriptions, and developed concrete vocabulary.

In a study of reluctant readers, Wilheim (1995) found that during visualization training the students became much more sophisticated readers. They took a more active role in reading, and they began to interpret text rather than just passively read it. Experiences with the visual arts provided a concrete "metacognitive marking point" (p. 489) that allowed these readers to see what they understood. The students also became more motivated to read.

Source: From *National Standards for arts education: What every young American should know and be able to do in the arts,* by the Consortium of National Arts Education Association, 1994. Reston, VA: Music Educators National Conference.

Arts Standards

Visual Arts

- Understanding and applying media, techniques, and processes.
- Using knowledge of structures and functions.
- Reflecting upon and assessing the characteristics and merits of their work and the work of others.

STRATEGY

Literature can be used to introduce collage using books illustrated in this style. Reading aloud and discussing these books, especially the use of the collage technique, contextualizes this strategy. Use reader response questions and responses about collage: What do you think of the illustrations done in collage? Have you had any experience with collage, as a viewer or as an artist? What kind of a collage would you create?

The word *collage* can be analyzed as part of the specific vocabulary of art. With students, the teacher can create a cluster semantic map by drawing a circle with the word collage inside and asking students: What do you know about the word collage? Students can share their ideas and experiences, which can be added around the circle. The root *coll* is found in the word collection, which may help students understand that a collage is a collection of shapes, often made of paper, or objects that are arranged by an artist.

Materials for creating a collage can be simply construction paper and glue sticks. Each student can use a piece of construction paper, or one half of a manila folder, as a background and build a collage with torn pieces of construction or other paper arranged and attached to the background with glue sticks.

The teacher can suggest a focus, such as an animal, self-portrait, still life, a landscape, an event, an idea, or a combination of these, using models from picture book illustrators who use the collage technique, or other fine artists who have used collage.

It is not necessary to use scissors, and the torn paper can create an interesting deckled edge for texture on the paper. Other objects can be added to the collage as well, including some newspaper and magazine images, but a collage made exclusively of these is more on the order of a cut-and-paste activity rather than an art activity where the students create their own images.

GRADE-LEVEL MODIFICATIONS

K–2ND GRADE

Read aloud a picture book by one of several illustrators who use the collage technique: Leo Leonni, Ezra Jack Keats, Eric Carle, or Lois Ehlert. For example, Leo Leonni's (2006) book *A Color of His Own* is about a chameleon who is constantly changing to look like someone else until he learns to love himself. Leonni has created many other books using animals as main characters, which the teacher could also read and discuss with students— not only the story, but the way he uses torn paper to create collage art could be discussed.

With some assistance, the students could make a list of animals they would like to depict in a collage. Each student could pick an animal and suggest ideas for the color, shape, and texture of a collage showing that animal. Each student could create a collage of an animal using construction paper and glue sticks. There are many picture books by illustrators who use collage.

Books

Eric Carle

Carle, E. (1987). *The very hungry caterpillar.* New York: Philomel.

Carle, E. (1990). *The very busy spider.* New York: Scholastic.

Carle, E. (1996). *The grouchy ladybug.* New York: HarperCollins.

Lois Ehlert

Ehlert, L. (1993). *Eating the alphabet: Fruits and vegetables from A to Z.* San Diego, CA: Harcourt.

Ehlert, L. (1999). *Red leaf, yellow leaf.* New York: Scholastic.

Ehlert, L. (2005). *Leaf man.* San Diego, CA: Harcourt Children's Books.

Ezra Jack Keats

Keats, E. J. (2002). *Keats neighborhood: An Ezra Jack Keats Treasury.* New York: Viking Juvenile. (This collection contains 10 of the author's picture books in slightly abridged size: *The snowy day; Goggles!; Whistle for Willie; Peter's chair; Apt. 3; A letter to Amy; Jennie's hat; Hi, cat!; Louie's search;* and *Pet show.*)

Leo Leonni

Leonni, L. (1973). *Frederick.* New York: Dragonfly.

Leonni, L. (1973). *Swimmy.* New York: Dragonfly.

Leonni, L. (1974). *Alexander and the wind-up mouse*. New York: Dragonfly.

Leonni, L. (1974). *Fish is fish*. New York: Dragonfly.

Leonni, L. (2006). *A color of his own*. New York: Knopf Books for Young Readers.

Leonni, L. (2010). *Inch by inch*. New York: Knopf Books for Young Readers.

3RD GRADE–5TH GRADE

Read aloud an illustrated book about Frida Kahlo, a Mexican artist whose work includes many self-portraits, many of which combine a realistic study of her face with imagery of how she imagines she might look: for example, *Frida Kahlo: The Artist who Painted Herself* (Frith, 2003), illustrated by Tomie de Paolo. Use reader response questions and prompts to lead a class discussion: What were you thinking when you looked at Frida Kahlo's self-portraits? What did you wonder about her self-portraits? How would you show yourself in a portrait?

The teacher can use a tree chart to record students' responses to the last question, classifying their ideas by feature, including imaginary images.

Name	Face	Hair	Eyes	Nose	Mouth	Ears	Imaginary Images

The students can use the torn paper collage technique to create a self-portrait. They can also do a Think-Pair-Share activity with a partner: Each student asks the other to tell about and describe the self-portrait. The partners can share this description with the rest of the class in pairs, telling the class how their partner described their self-portrait as the partner holds the self-portrait over their face.

The teacher can also read aloud *Frida: Viva la Vida! Long Live Life!* (Bernier-Grand, 2007), with poems by the author, illustrated with Frida Kahlo's paintings. The students can write a face poem using three describing words for each feature using the following frame:

Face Poem

First Name

Hair _____ _____ _____

Eyes _____ _____ _____

Nose _____ _____ _____

Mouth _____ _____ _____

Ears _____ _____ _____

Imaginary Images _____ _____ _____

Last Name

Books

Bernier-Grand, C. T. (2007). *Frida: Viva la vida! Long live life!* Tarrytown, NY: Marshall Cavendish.

Frith, M. (2003). *Frida Kahlo: The artist who painted herself*. New York: Grosset & Dunlap.

Hillstrom, L. (2008). *Frida Kahlo: The 20th century's most influential Hispanics*. San Diego, CA: Lucent Books.

Holzey, M. (2003). *Frida Kahlo: The artist in the blue house*. New York: Prestel.

Johnston, L. (2006). *Frida Kahlo: Painter of strength*. Mankato, MN: Capstone Press.

Kent, D. (2004). *Frida Kahlo: An artist celebrates life*. Mankato, MN: Child's World.

Klein, A. G. (2006). *Frida Kahlo*. Edina, MN: Checkerboard Books.

Laidlaw, J. (2006). *Frida Kahlo*. Danbury, CT: Franklin Watts.

Novesky, A. (2010). *Me, Frida*. New York: Abrams Books for Young Readers.

Venezia, M. (1999). *Frida Kahlo: Getting to know the world's great artists*. Danbury, CT: Children's Press.

Winter, J. (2002). *Frida*. New York: Arthur A. Levine Books.

Wooten, S. M. (2005). *Frida Kahlo: Her life in paintings*. Berkeley Heights, NJ: Enslow.

6TH GRADE–8TH GRADE

Introduce the collage strategy by reading aloud *Henri Matisse: Drawing With Scissors* (O'Connor, 2002), which describes the Fauve movement in art and Matisse's shift from painting to cut paper collage to represent the essentials of color, shape and form, and lines. Ask students reader response questions and prompts: What did you wonder about the way Matisse showed objects in a still life? As an artist, how would you represent objects in a still life?

The teacher can record students responses to these questions on a tree chart describing how Matisse represented objects and how the students would represent objects in a still life by colors, shape and form, and line.

	Colors	Shape/Form	Line
Matisse			
Students			

With students, choose objects to arrange a still life in class, one for the whole class or one for each table groups of students. Students can create a collage of the still life using the torn paper technique or use painted papers and scissors to use the same techniques that Matisse used in his still lifes.

The young adult themed novel *Matisse on the Loose* (Bragg, 2009) can also be read aloud or read independently by students.

Books

Anholt, L. (2007). *Matisse the king of color*. Hauppauge, NY: Barron's Educational Series.

Baillet, Y., & Goodman, J. (1995). *Matisse: Painter of the essential*. New York: Chelsea House.

Bragg, G. (2009). *Matisse on the loose*. New York: Delacorte.

Flux, P. (2003). *The life and work of Henri Matisse*. Portsmouth, NH: Heinemann Library.

LeTord, B. (1999). *A bird or 2: A story about Henri Matisse*. Grand Rapids, MI: Eerdmans Books for Young Readers.

Mason, A. (2002). *Matisse*. Danbury, CT: Franklin Watts.

Merberg, J., & Bober, S. (2002). *A magical day with Matisse*. San Francisco: Chronicle Books.

Niepold, M., & Verdu, J. (2007). *Oooh! Matisse*. Berkeley, CA: Tricycle Press.

O'Connor, J. (2002). *Henri Matisse: Drawing with scissors*. New York: Grosset & Dunlap.

Stephens, P. G. (2004). *Dropping in on Matisse*. Glenview, IL: Crystal Productions.

Sturm, E. (2003). *Matisse*. Mankato, MN: Bridgestone Books.

Venezia, M. (1997). *Henri Matisse*. Danbury, CT: Children's Press.

Welton, J. (2002). *Henri Matisse*. Danbury, CT: Children's Press.

ENGLISH LEARNERS

Collage is an excellent strategy for English learners because it relies on several techniques for sheltering English and academic language: visuals, the five senses, using real objects such as art materials, and student collaboration when using Think-Pair-Share to tell the class about a partner's collage art.

The word *collage* has a cognate in Spanish in the word *collecion*. Create a Venn diagram, putting the root *coll* in the middle where the two circles of a Venn diagram overlap, and then search for and write other words that share that root in English in one circle and other words that share that root in Spanish in the other circle.

Books in Spanish, Hindi, and bilingual Spanish/English can be brought into the classroom to provide primary language support for English learners.

Books

Carle, E. (2008). *The very hungry caterpillar*. (Hindi Edition). Chennai, India: Karadi Tales Company.

Guzman, L., & Guzman, R. (2007). *Frida Kahlo: Pinto su vida/Painting her life*. Berkeley Heights, NJ: Enslow Elementary.

Leonni, L. (2005). *Frederick*. (Spanish Edition). Lyndhurst, NJ: Lectorum.

Leonni, L. (2005). *Nadarin/Swimmy*. (Spanish Edition). Lyndhurst, NJ: Lectorum.

Winter, J. (2002). *Frida*. (Spanish Edition). New York: Arthur A. Levine.

STRUGGLING STUDENTS

Create a frame for poetry writing integrated with the collage strategy, for example a Face Poem if students make a self-portrait. The students can brainstorm ideas for describing words for each of the features of the face, the teacher can record the responses, and the students can use this list to complete a Face Poem frame:

Face Poem Frame

My name is _____

My hair is _____

My eyes are _____

My nose is _____

My mouth is _____

My ears are _____

My face is _____

ASSESSMENT

Younger students can complete a frame to demonstrate their understanding of the collage technique. For the youngest students, English learners in the early stages of acquiring English, or struggling readers and writers, add a word bank below the frame so that students have access to words needed to complete the frame:

Today I made a _____. It is made of _____.

I made it by _____. It shows _____.

I think collage is _____.

Something special about collage is _____.

Word Bank:

   Collage

   Collection

   Construction paper

   Tearing

   Gluing

   Shape

   Color

   Texture

Older students can use the semantic cluster map for collage and write a paragraph describing the technique, other artists who have used the technique, their own collage, and how they felt about creating it. The completed frame or descriptive paragraphs can be attached to the back of each student's collage and added to a student's art portfolio.

RESOURCES

Hetland, L., Winner, E., Veenema, S., & Sheridan, K. M. (2007). *Studio thinking: The real benefits of visual arts education.* New York: Teachers College Press.

REFERENCES

Andrzejczak, N., Trainin, G., & Poldberg, M. (2005). From image to text: Using images in the writing process. *International Journal of Education and the Arts, 6*(12), 1–17.

Burger, K., & Winner, E. (2000). Instruction in visual art: Can it help children learn to read? *Journal of Aesthetic Education, 34*(3/4), 277–293.

Wilheim, J. D. (1995). Reading is seeing: Using visual response to improve the literary reading of reluctant readers. *Journal of Reading Behavior, 27*(4), 467–503.

I Am the Artist

The 7th-grade class was so excited about their I Am the Renaissance Artist projects that their teacher decided to stage a Renaissance Fair at the school to showcase the students' efforts. The principal helped the teacher set up tables and roll whiteboards to display the art and written work. Other classes, parents, and members of the community were invited. On the day of the big event, students came to school dressed in Renaissance attire and staged several of their I Am the Renaissance Artist projects: a roving reporter doing interviews with Leonardo, Michelangelo, and Raphael; a debate between Michelangelo and the Pope on why he hadn't finished the ceiling of the Sistine Chapel; a demonstration of Leonardo's flying machine; and a video documentary on life and art during the Renaissance, among others. Punch and cookies were served.

RATIONALE

When students step into the life of a famous artist, they learn about the artist and a particular artistic style or school of art in a period of art history and use what they have learned to report or present the information to the rest of the class, or other classes, parents, and members of the community. They can choose from a variety of options to present what they have learned by integrating the visual arts with literature, literacy, and the other arts—drama, music, and dance. The study of an artist or style or period of art can be related to a theme or to topics in the other content areas of social studies, science, and mathematics.

In a study of thematic project-based units that integrated the arts in an urban middle school that examined resulting achievement and collaboration among students, standardized test scores showed improvement, especially for struggling students (Bolak, Bialach, & Dunphy, 2005). These results are substantiated by Winner and Hetland's (2000) observation in the REAP study that test scores do improve when arts learning is in place, although researchers cannot exactly say why this is so.

Source: From National Standards for arts education: What every young American should know and be able to do in the arts, by the Consortium of National Arts Education Association, 1994. Reston, VA: Music Educators National Conference.

Arts Standards

Visual Arts

- Choosing and evaluating a range of subject matter, symbols, and ideas.
- Understanding the visual arts in relation to history and cultures.
- Making connections between visual arts and other disciplines.

STRATEGY

Literature can be used to introduce an artist, style, or period of art by reading books on the subject aloud and gathering a text set of books for the classroom, which students can read and use to do research. The culminating project "I Am the Artist" is where they can step into the role of the artist and communicate what they have learned through assuming the artist's identity.

Students can focus on the same artist, style, or period or choose to do different artists representing a style or period. Provide guidelines and support for student research, and offer and model a set of options for students to use either as individuals, pairs, or groups, depending on the age, interests, and abilities of the students.

Options for reporting or presenting "I Am the Artist" include the following:

- Creating art using the preferred media and style of the artist and explaining the process and the art work in a gallery showing in the classroom. An opening show can be planned with invitations, scheduled talks and other events, and refreshments.

- Dramatizing the life story of an artist through scenes and vignettes with important events and people and samples of their art.

- Interviews and guest speakers could be used to simulate a *This Is Your Life* television show, with a moderator, the artist, and appearances by significant other people in the artist's life, along with samples of their art.

- A debate could be planned between the artist or advocates for their style of art and critics of the style, each taking turns to speak for or against the artist. Samples of the artist's work could be shown during the debate.

- A monologue or an "I Am the Artist" report by the artist explaining their life and work.

- A newspaper or online news report written by a group or class of students on an artist, including articles written by the artist, interviews with the artist, and reports of events in the artist's life.

- A documentary video on the artist using "archival" footage created by students to show events in the artist's life, interviews with the artist, and others commenting on the artist's life.

GRADE-LEVEL MODIFICATIONS

K–2ND GRADE

Introduce the artist Picasso to the class by reading aloud one of the many illustrated picture books about Picasso that has a narrative that tells a story about a period in the artist's life, rather than a nonfiction book that gives biographical information and describes his work. For example, *Paris in the Spring With Picasso* (Yolleck, 2010) tells a story of the young Picasso going to the home of Gertrude Stein and meeting other intellectuals and artists in Paris at that time, such as Max Jacob. Lead a discussion using reader response questions and prompts: What did you wonder about the artist Picasso? If you have seen art by Picasso, tell about it.

Because Picasso's art can be classified in several periods, from his early to later works, a good book to read aloud next describes the beginning of his career as an artist: *Picasso and Minou* (Maltbie, 2008). This is an engaging fictionalized version of a slice of his life when he was so poor he couldn't afford to feed his cat Minou. The paintings he produced at this time are called his Blue Period. The teacher can then read *Pablo Picasso: Breaking all the Rules* (Kelly, 2002), which uses the format of a child writing a report on Picasso, to model the class writing language experience stories about Picasso.

Read, or have students read, other books about Picasso and do a series of language experience stories, recording students' ideas from their reading and discussions on a piece of chart paper or asking students to take the pen and write on the chart paper. Students can also create paintings using the colors, subjects, and style of each of the periods. The result could be a period of reading, discussing, art making, and writing five group stories about Picasso: The Early Years, Blue Period, Rose Period, Cubism, and Later Years.

To model the art making process, read *Oooh! Picasso* (Niepold, 2009), which uses photos of found object sculptures in a slow reveal process where a part of something is seen as something else until the whole thing is shown for what it is.

When the class has written language experience stories about all periods of Picasso's life, they can form groups to dramatize it. In each group, one child can speak for Picasso and other children for other people in his life at the time, telling about his life and art. The classroom could become a gallery for the student work in the style of Picasso, each period in a different section. The students playing a scene from his life could use that section of the gallery as a backdrop for their scene.

Books

Anholt, L. (2007). *Picasso and the girl with the ponytail: A story of Pablo Picasso.* Hauppauge, NY: Barron's Educational Series.

Kelly, T. (2002). *Pablo Picasso: Breaking all the rules.* New York: Grosset & Dunlap.

Kelly, T. (2009). *Who was Pablo Picasso?* New York: Grosset & Dunlap.

Lepscky, I. (1993). *Pablo Picasso.* Hauppauge, NY: Barron's Educational Series.

Mahlberger, R. (1994). *What makes a Picasso a Picasso?* New York: Viking Juvenile.

Maltbie, P. I. (2008). *Picasso and Minou.* Watertown, MA: Charlesbridge.

Niepold, M. (2009). *Oooh! Picasso.* Berkeley, CA: Tricycle Press.

Salvador, A. (2008). *Draw with Pablo Picasso*. London: Frances Lincoln Children's Books.

Scarborough, K. (2002). *Pablo Picasso*. Danbury, CT: Watts.

Spence, D. (2010). *Picasso*. Kent, UK: Tick Tock Books.

Yolleck, J. (2010). *Paris in the spring with Picasso*. New York: Schwartz & Wade.

3RD GRADE–5TH GRADE

Introduce Impressionism as a style of art through literature by reading aloud a picture book that engages students with a story, such as *Katie Meets the Impressionists* (Mayhew, 2007). Katie visits an art museum with her grandmother and views paintings of the Impressionists. When she closes her eyes, she is inside the paintings of Monet, Renoir, and Degas. Two other picture story books can engage children. *Charlotte in Giverny* (Knight, 2000) is about a fictional young American diarist who moves to Giverny to study painting *en plein air* with the Impressionists; she meets their neighbor, the Impressionist painter Claude Monet. In *Charlotte in Paris* (Knight, 2003), the family moves to Paris in 1893 and she meets other Impressionist painters: Cassat, Degas, and Renoir. Lead a class discussion using reader response questions and prompts: What did you think of the Impressionists and their paintings? What did you wonder about this style of art and their lives? What was your favorite thing about the Impressionists?

The teacher can put together a set of classroom books on the Impressionists that students can read in book clubs, each group choosing to focus on an artist. After a period of reading and discussing the books, they can create artworks in the style and with a focus on the subject matter of the painter they have chosen. Each group can create a gallery of their work on a bulletin board.

Each group can then participate in a jigsaw activity, learning more about the artist they have chosen and choosing a way to communicate what they have learned about this Impressionist to the other groups, who will also choose a way to present what each of them has learned. For example, they can stage an interview with the artist or a debate between their artist and critics of the style, or they can use other options as previously described.

Books

Anholt, L. (2007). *Degas and the little dancer*. Hauppauge, NJ: Barron's Educational Series.

Anholt, L. (2007). *The magical garden of Claude Monet*. Hauppauge, NJ: Barron's Educational Series.

Bolton, L. (2000). *Impressionism*. New York: Peter Bedrick.

Boutan, M. (2010). *Renoir and me*. London: A & C Black Books.

Dickens, R. (2009). *The Impressionists*. London: Usborne Books.

Gunderson, J. (2008). *Impressionism*. Mankato, MN: Creative Education.

Harris, L. (2007). *Mary Cassat: Impressionist painter*. Gretna, LA: Pelican.

Kalen, S. A. (2009). *Impressionism*. San Diego, CA: Lucent Books.

Knight, J. (2000). *Charlotte in Giverny*. San Francisco: Chronicle Books.

Knight, J. (2003). *Charlotte in Paris*. San Francisco: Chronicle Books.

Koja, S., & Miksovsky, K. (1997). *Claude Monet: The magician of colour*. New York: Prestel.

Mayhew, J. (2007). *Katie meets the Impressionists*. New York: Scholastic.

Montanari, E. (2009). *Chasing Degas*. New York: Abrams Books for Young Readers.

Muhlberger, R. (1994). *What makes a Cassat a Cassat?* New York: Viking Juvenile.

Muhlberger, R. (2002). *What makes a Monet a Monet?* New York: Viking Juvenile.

Muhlberger, R. (2002). *What makes a Degas a Degas?* New York: Viking Juvenile.

Raimondo, J. (2004). *Picture this! Activities and adventures in Impressionism*. New York: Watson-Guptill.

Rayfield, S. (1998). *First impressions: Pierre Auguste Renoir*. New York: Harry N. Abrams.

Sabbeth, C. (2002). *Monet and Impressionism for kids*. Chicago: Chicago Review Press.

Salvi, F., & Galanate, L. R. (2001). *The Impressionists: The origins of modern painting*. New York: Peter Bedrick.

Spence, D. (1997). *Monet and Impressionism*. Hauppauge, NY: Barron's Educational Series.

Streissquth, T. (1998). *Mary Cassatt: Portrait of an American Impressionist*. Minneapolis, MN: Carolrhoda Books.

Waldron, A. (2007). *Who was Claude Monet?* New York: Grosset & Dunlap.

Welton, J. (1999). *Eyewitness: Monet*. New York: DK Children.

Welton, J. (2000). *Eyewitness: Impressionism*. New York: DK Children.

6TH GRADE–8TH GRADE

Introduce a period in the history of art, such as Classical, Medieval, or the Renaissance, by reading an illustrated picture book aloud. For example, there are several well-illustrated picture books with an interesting narrative based on the life of one of the great Renaissance artists that can be read to and discussed with the whole class in a short period of time. Diane Stanley has written two beautiful biographies: *Leonardo da Vinci* (2000), and *Michelangelo* (2003). Another beautiful picture book biography is *Leonardo: Beautiful Dreamer* (Byrd, 2003). Two picture books with interesting stories are *Leonardo and the Flying Boy* (Anholt, 2007), and *Katie and the Mona Lisa* (Mayhew, 1998). For an overview of the period, do a picture walk through *Painting in the Renaissance* (D'Elia, 2009). Lead a discussion and ask reader response questions and prompts: What part of the lives of these artists interested you most? Tell anything you know about Renaissance art and artists.

Put together a classroom set of books on Renaissance artists, and the class can form groups to read and learn about a different artist or aspect of this period of art history. The students and teacher can plan to do a documentary video in the style of a CNN special, with each group choosing to do a different aspect and presentation style: an introduction to the period and the origins and sources of Renaissance art, simulated first person accounts from or interviews with the artists and other important figures of the time, displays of examples of the art, maps, timelines, debates among "experts" on the pros and cons of the art and artists, "I" reports or first-hand witness accounts, and panels of experts.

Students can also read, or have read to them, the young adult novel *My Astonishing Life as Leonardo da Vinci's Servant* (Grey, 2008).

Books

Anholt, L. (2007). *Leonardo and the flying boy.* Hauppauge, NY: Barron's Educational Series.

Blanch, G., & Stathis, R. (2003). *Renaissance artists who inspired the world.* Brea, CA: Ballard & Tighe.

Byrd, R. (2003). *Leonardo: Beautiful dreamer.* New York: Dutton Children's Books.

Cole, A. (2000). *Eyewitness: Renaissance.* New York: DK Children.

Corrain, L. (2001). *The art of the Renaissance.* Citrus Heights, CA: Brighter Child.

D'Elia, U. (2009). *Painting in the Renaissance.* New York: Crabtree.

Edwards, R. (2005). *Who was Leonardo da Vinci?* New York: Grosset & Dunlap.

Elliott, L. (2009). *The Renaissance in Europe.* New York: Crabtree.

Emert, P. (2008). *Renaissance art.* San Diego, CA: Lucent Books.

Fitzpatrick, A. (2005). *The Renaissance: Movements in art.* Mankato, MN: Creative Education.

Grey, C. (2008). *My astonishing life as Leonardo da Vinci's servant.* New York: Atheneum.

Hebert, J. (1998). *Leonardo da Vinci for kids: His life and ideas.* Chicago: Chicago Review Press.

Kallen, S. (2002). *The working life—A Renaissance painter's studio.* San Diego, CA: Lucent Books.

Klein, A. G. (2006). *Raphael.* Edina, MN: Checkerboard Books.

Mayhew, J. (1998). *Katie and the Mona Lisa.* Danbury, CT: Orchard Books.

Merlo, C. (1999). *Three masters of the Renaissance: Leonardo, Michelangelo, Raphael.* Hauppauge, NY: Barron's Juveniles.

Mofford, J. (2010). *Raphael.* Hockessin, DE: Mitchell Lane.

Murphy, L., & Matthews, R. (2010). *Art and culture of the Renaissance.* New York: Rosen Central.

O'Connor, B. (2002). *Leonardo da Vinci: Renaissance genius.* Minneapolis, MN: Carolrhoda Books.

Phillips, J. (2008). *Leonardo da Vinci: The genius who defined the Renaissance.* Washington, DC: National Geographic Children's Books.

Romei, F. et al. (2001). *Leonardo da Vinci: Artist, inventor, & scientist of the Renaissance*. New York: Peter Bedrick Books.

Somervil, B. A. (2005). *Michelangelo: Sculptor and painter*. Mankato, MN: Compass Point Books.

Stanley, D. (2000). *Leonardo da Vinci*. New York: Harper Collins.

Stanley, D. (2003). *Michelangelo*. New York: Harper Collins.

Venezia, M. (2001). *Raphael*. Danbury, CT: Children's Press.

ENGLISH LEARNERS

Instruction for English learners is supported by the use of many visuals, the five senses when engaged with painting, props and realia and concrete objects such as art media, and tapping into student's prior knowledge of art.

Culturally sensitive instruction can be practiced with English learners by introducing artists from the cultures of the students. For example, for Mexican American students, introduce Frida Kahlo and her husband Diego Rivera. If studying a period of Western art history such as Impressionism or the Renaissance, introduce the study of the art in Asia at the same time, such as Korean, Chinese, Vietnamese, Cambodian, and Japanese art.

STRUGGLING STUDENTS

Do vocabulary instruction with semantic maps on words specific to an artist or period of art history, such as *cubism* and *Impressionism*. After introducing an artist or period of art and engaging students in collaborative group activities, such as dramatizations about the life of an artist, model the use of an "I Am the Artist" frame adapted for a specific group of students:

"I Am" Report

I am _____ (name of artist). I was born in _____ in the
year _____ and I died in _____ in the year _____.

As a child I _____.

I would describe my art as _____.

Problems I had as an artist were _____.

The most important things about my art were _____.

ASSESSMENT

To assess what students have learned as demonstrated by the presentations of their reading and research when different groups have researched different artists or different aspects of an artist's life, students can do Peer-Assessments of each other's groups and write what they learned about the artist:

Peer-Assessment of Group _____

The group I assessed presented on the artist _____.

The best thing about the presentation was _____.

A suggestion I would make would be

_____.

Three things I learned about the artist from the presentation were

1.

2.

3.

RESOURCES

Kohl, M. F., & Solga, K. (1997). *Discovering great artists: Hands-on art for children in the styles of the great masters.* Bellingham, WA: Bright Ring.

Kohl, M. F., & Solga, K. (2008). *Great American artists for kids: Hands-on art experiences in the styles of the great masters.* Bellingham, WA: Bright Ring.

REFERENCES

Bolak, K., Bialach, D., & Dunphy, M. (2005). Standards-based thematic units integrate the arts and energize students and teachers. *Middle School Journal, 36*(5), 9–19.

Winner, E., & Hetland, L. (2000). The arts and academic achievement: What the evidence shows. *Journal of Aesthetic Education, 34*(3–4).

Strategy 37

Dance a Poem

Fourth-grade students had listened to their teacher read Mary O'Neill's collection of poetry about color, *Hailstones and Halibut Bones,* and they had written their own color poems. They also choreographed a dance to go with each color poem, which they performed to a tape of their own voice reading the poem with music in the background. Here is Mariko's poem "Silver," which she danced wearing a silver tutu from her first ballet class dance recital:

WHAT IS SILVER?

Silver feels like a fairy that's gliding through the night.

Silver means peace and quiet.

Silver is a sleeping feeling.

Silver is a merry color like bells ringing.

◆

RATIONALE

Combining the literature of poetry, writing original poems, choreographing movement and dance to express the poem, and dancing it to music allows students to clearly make connections between dance and other disciplines in an active, engaging, and personally meaningful experience.

Blecher and Jaffee (1998) are team teacher researchers in a 1st- and 2nd-grade multi-age classroom where they place a heavy emphasis on creating a community of learners in a "languages-rich environment with music and movement" (p. 16), and they have found positive effects from combining poetry and movement. Middle school educators describe a successful approach to integrating the study of literature with the arts (Wright & Kowalczyk, 2000). The students read and wrote poetry with some natural phenomenon or weather pattern at that time of the year as a theme (e.g., the gold of autumn leaves in September, snow in December, green in March). They incorporated these poems into a dance performance to the music of Vivaldi's "Four Seasons" in an integrated language arts and arts approach.

Benefits have also been found for students with disabilities in a program that combined movement and poetry instruction (Mentzer & Boswell, 1995). The instruction began with an introduction followed by a movement and poetry section that involved the teacher reading the poem aloud twice while the students read along, the students creating individual movement sequences for the lines they selected from the poem, and then sharing their movement sequences. Students also began to write and create movement for original poetry they "spontaneously spoke," which was recorded by the teacher and later compiled into a book. The study suggests that, when combined, poetry and movement may contribute to engagement, development of creativity, and social or motor learning in children with behavioral disorders.

Source: From *National Standards for arts education: What every young American should know and be able to do in the arts,* by the Consortium of National Arts Education Association, 1994. Reston, VA: Music Educators National Conference.

Arts Standards

Dance

- Understanding dance as a way to create and communicate meaning.

- Making connections between dance and other disciplines.

STRATEGY

Read aloud a poem related to a theme (e.g., animals, color imagery, nature) and discuss it with students using reader response questions and prompts: What did you think of the poem? What did you picture in your mind? Tell about anything in your own life that the poem reminded you of. Finally, the teacher can ask students: Which lines in the poem made you picture a dance move? What kind of music would match the poem and the movements?

Record student responses on a chart. Charts can vary depending on the age of students, their abilities, and the type of poem. For younger students, the general concept of movement in the poem can be a focus. For example, after reading animal poems, the teacher can use a cluster chart on how one animal moves or a T-chart listing animals on one side and their movements on the other. The whole class can move and dance with music to the same poem at the same time.

The focus can also be on certain lines in a poem using a tree chart with three branches: lines in the poem, movement, and music. Not all lines in the poem need to have movement and music. The teacher and students can add to the chart a few lines at a time. The students can be divided into groups and each group can choose lines and create the movements for these lines in the poem, adding music. The poem can be read aloud by one or several students, and each group can dance to the lines.

Model this process with older students who can then also choose a poem as individuals or in pairs or groups; create dance movements to music they choose and other nonverbal means of expressing their response to a poem.

GRADE-LEVEL MODIFICATIONS

K–2ND GRADE

Use paired books to lead young students to dance a poem. For example, first read *Move!* by Robin Page and Steve Jenkins (2006). This imaginative book uses a variety of verbs for movement, showing a type of animal that uses the movement and later explaining why animals move in different ways (e.g., gibbons swing). Also, *Animal Action ABC* (Pandell, 2003) combines a letter of the alphabet, an action word, a poem about an animal, a photo of the animal, and another photo of the children imitating the animal's movement.

Pair books of poetry about animals with either or both of these two books, and students can listen for descriptions of animal movement in the poem. Favorite poems can be copied onto chart paper for re-reading as a class.

The teacher can lead a discussion of animal poems using reader response questions and prompts: How did you picture the animals in your mind? How do you think the animals would move? The teacher can record student responses on a T-chart:

Animal	Movement

The students can experiment with moving like each animal as the teacher or another student re-reads a poem about the animal. Students can create movement and dance to several animal poems each time the poems are re-read or recited.

Books

Ackerman, D. (2003). *Animal sense.* New York: Alfred A. Knopf.

Florian, D. (1998). *Beast feast: Poems.* Clive, IA: Perfection Learning.

Florian, D. (2004). *Omnibeasts: Animal poems and paintings.* Harcourt Children's Books.

Florian, D. (2005). *Zoo's who.* San Diego, CA: Harcourt.

Hague, M. (2007). *Animal friends: A collection of poems for children.* New York: Henry Holt.

Heard, G. (1997). *Creatures of earth, sea, and sky: Poems.* Honesdale, PA: Boyds Mills Press.

Hollander, J. (Ed.). (2004). *Animal poems.* Falls Church, VA: Sterling.

Page, R., & Jenkins, S. (2006). *Move!* Boston: Houghton Mifflin.

Pandell, K. (2003). *Animal action ABC.* New York: Handprint.

Prelutsky, J. (2006). *The beauty of the beast: Poems from the animal kingdom.* New York: Alfred A. Knopf.

Worth, V. (2007). *Animal poems.* New York: Farrar, Straus, & Giroux.

Yolen, J. (1995). *Alphabestiary: Animal poems from A to Z.* Honesdale, PA: Boyds Mills Press.

3RD GRADE–5TH GRADE

Introduce poems about color by reading aloud Mary O'Neill's classic poetry collection *Hailstones and Halibut Bones*, first published in 1961 and re-issued in 1989. Each poem begins with the name of the color and the word *is*: for example, "White is hailstones and halibut bones." Lead a discussion of the book asking reader response questions and prompts: What did you picture in your mind for a color? Tell about your favorite color poem by Mary O'Neill.

Model poetry writing for students by doing a cluster map on a color and recording students' ideas and images for the color. The words and phrases can be arranged as a poem following the beginning of the line: (Name of color) is_____. Students can also write poems in pairs, groups, or on their own.

To dance a color poem, students can choose a poem by Mary O'Neill or one they have written. Model planning to dance a poem with the whole class with a tree chart. Students select the lines in the poem, suggest dance movements for the lines, and think of music to match the words and music.

Dance a Poem Plan for the Color _____		
Line in poem	*Dance movement*	*Music*

Students can work in groups, each creating a dance with music for a different color.

Books

Hamanaka, S. (1999). *All the colors of the earth*. New York: HarperCollins.

Hindley, J. (1998). *A song of colors*. Cambridge, MA: Candlewick Press.

Iyengar, M. M. (2009). *Tan to tamarind: Poems about the color brown*. San Francisco: Children's Book Press.

Nordine, K. (2000). *Colors*. San Diego, CA: Harcourt.

O'Neill, M. (1989). *Hailstones and halibut bones*. New York: Doubleday.

Sidman, J. (2009). *Red sings from treetops: A year in colors*. Boston: Houghton Mifflin.

Yolen, J. (2003). *Color me a rhyme: Nature poems for young people*. Honesdale, PA: Boyds Mills Press.

6TH GRADE–8TH GRADE

Read aloud poetry with nature imagery: for example, read poems by American poet Robert Frost. One of his poems serves as the text of an illustrated picture book, beautifully illustrated by Susan Jeffers: *Stopping by Woods on a Snowy Evening* (Frost, 2001). The picture book format lends itself to reading the poem and showing the illustrations to the whole class.

Lead a discussion of the poem using reader response questions and prompts: What did you picture in your mind? How did the poem make you feel? What movements could go with the poem? Record student responses on a cluster chart. Read other poems aloud and create a classroom collection of poetry with nature imagery for students to read independently.

To dance a poem, students can work in pairs, pick a poem, and discuss how the poem makes them feel and how they could express these feelings nonverbally with movement, dance, and music. After creating a dance, one pair can share it with and teach it to another pair, and vice versa. Each student can write about the experience of creating a dance to a poem, teaching it to another pair of students, and learning a dance from them. Finally, they can write about how words, movement, dance, and music can be connected and integrated as an art form.

Books

Demi. (1994). *In the eyes of the cat: Japanese poetry for all seasons.* New York: Henry Holt.

Frank, J., & Locker, T. (1995). *Snow toward evening: A year in a river valley/nature poems.* New York: Puffin.

Frost, R. (2001). *Stopping by woods on a snowy evening.* New York: Dutton Juvenile.

Hoberman, M. A., & Winston, L. (2009). *The tree that time built: A celebration of nature, science, and time.* Naperville, IL: Sourcebooks.

Janeczko, P. (2000). *Stone bench in an empty park.* New York: Scholastic.

Michael, P. (2008). *River of words: Young poets and artists on the nature of things.* Minneapolis, MN: Milkweed Editions.

Schmidt, G. D. (2008). *Poetry for young people: Robert Frost.* Falls Church, VA: Sterling.

Yolen, J. (2009). *A mirror to nature: Poems about reflection.* Honesdale, PA: Wordsong.

ENGLISH LEARNERS

English learners benefit from this nonverbal approach to poetry by using the five senses, gestures, movement, dance, music, student to student interaction, and tapping into their life experiences. Engaging students with words through movement and music provides comprehensible input as they listen to and read and re-read the poems they are dancing.

There are also many books of bilingual poetry, which provide primary language support as well as allow for culturally responsive teaching by using poems that may contain familiar cultural and linguistic content.

Books

Alaracon, F. X. (2008). *Animal poems of the Iguazu/ Animalario del Iguazu.* San Francisco: Children's Book Press.

Lujan, J. (2008). *Colors! Colores!* Toronto, Ontario, Canada: Groundwood Books.

STRUGGLING STUDENTS

Support struggling students by developing a written plan with them for dancing a poem—with lines of the poem, the movement and dance, and music—with the addition of drawings and illustrations to indicate the words of the poem and the movements of the dance. Both teacher and student can add these images to the plan and a copy can be made for each child as a guide during rehearsals.

ASSESSMENT

Students can write a self-assessment of their experience of dancing a poem that addresses the following questions:

How did you feel about dancing a poem?

How is a poem different from a dance? How is it alike?

What did you like best about dancing a poem?

RESOURCES

Blecher, S., & Jaffee, K. (1998). *Weaving in the arts: Widening the learning circle.* Portsmouth, NH: Heinemann.

REFERENCES

Blecher, S., & Jaffee, K. (1998). *Weaving in the arts: Widening the learning circle.* Portsmouth, NH: Heinemann.

Mentzer, M. C., & Boswell, B. B. (1995). Effects of a movement poetry program on creativity of children with behavioral disorders. *Impulse, 3,* 183–199.

Wright, M. F., & Kowalczyk, S. (2000). Peace by piece: The freeing power of language and literacy through the arts. *English Journal, 89*(5), 55–63.

Strategy
38

Dance
Improvisation

The 5th-grade class was reading about immigration to the United States and looking at the heritage of their own families, many of whom came to this country speaking a language other than English. The grandparents and parents and some of the students who had immigrated were not yet fluent English speakers. A native-English speaking student wondered aloud what it must be like to come to this country and not be able to communicate. The teacher suggested they form groups and improvise dances that would show the problems, frustrations, and solutions these immigrant families might have experienced, using music and any dances they knew from the different countries of origin.

RATIONALE

Students can improvise movements and dance to literature, their own writing, or any topic or subject in other content areas. Many students, especially English learners or students who struggle with reading, writing, and other traditional school tasks, can use this nonverbal means of expressing their ideas and feelings before moving to verbal means.

Research has shown the positive effect of dance instruction on reading, and especially on nonverbal reasoning (Keinanen, Hetland, & Winner, 2000). Classes in hip hop and jazz have been shown to have a positive effect on the confidence, tolerance, and persistence related to dance instruction on incarcerated and low-income, non-English proficient middle school students, with the researcher (Ross, 2000) suggesting that "Patience, and sometimes even compassion, can be social by-products of aesthetic engagement, and new regard for the human body (is what) dance can introduce" (p. 4).

Bradley (2002) maintained that research has shown that dance can be an engaging and effective means of developing three aspects of creative thinking: fluency, originality, and abstractness—especially when improvisation is taught. Other benefits include improvements in reading and writing, critical thinking, and interacting with the world of ideas.

Source: From *National Standards for arts education: What every young American should know and be able to do in the arts,* by the Consortium of National Arts Education Association, 1994. Reston, VA: Music Educators National Conference.

Arts Standards

Dance

- Identifying and demonstrating movement elements and skills in performing dance.
- Understanding choreographic principles, processes, and structures.
- Understanding dance as a way to create and communicate meaning.
- Applying and demonstrating critical and creative thinking skills in dance.

STRATEGY

Initiate dance improvisation with literature by reading aloud a book on how machines of different types work and move. The teacher and students can discuss the book using reader response questions and prompts and brainstorm ideas for ways that students can move their bodies in rhythm or to music in a dance improvisation that simulates some type of machine.

The teacher can record their ideas on a tree chart with branches for the type of machine, the parts that move, and how students can move. Students can experience moving like the machine or different machine parts. Different types of machines or parts of a machine can be chosen by different students, and they can begin to build a machine with themselves as moving parts. Students can create sketches of the machine and how it works, assigning each student to a movement.

As a class or in groups, students and teacher can also create a flow chart showing the order of the movement. Music can be added to the different stages of the movement of the machine. Students can assess their movements as a machine, make changes on their sketches or flow chart, and further develop their dance improvisation.

GRADE-LEVEL MODIFICATIONS

K–2ND GRADE

Use literature to introduce dance improvisations of vehicles used for transportation, such as cars, trucks, boats, trains, and planes, by reading aloud Chris Van Dusen's (2007) engaging story *If I Built a Car*. In the story, a young boy plans to design a car and begins to sketch it, with safety features, a pool, a robot driver, a fireplace, and a snack bar. The car can drive underwater as well as fly and is reminiscent of the muscle cars of the 1950s and 1960s; it looks like a combination of a Cadillac, a train, a zeppelin, and a vintage plane.

Lead a discussion of the story using reader response questions and prompts: What was your favorite part of the car? What would a car you built look like? Record the students' responses on a cluster chart. The students can design a car using ideas from the chart on a large piece of poster paper, and different students can take the pen and add a feature to the car.

As a class, the students can improvise movements for the different parts of the car and add music to their movements. Each student can choose a part of the car (e.g., wheels, doors, steering wheel, engine, lights, and other special features they have added, like a robot driver), and they come together and make the car. The car can move as they use their improvised movements for each part and move the car forward together.

Students can also improvise dance movements for multiple vehicles in an environment, such as cars, trucks, and buses on the freeway; planes at the airport and in the air; boats in the harbor and at sea; and different cars on various types of trains (e.g., passenger, freight, or circus trains). Chris Van Dusen and Donald Crews wrote other children's books that feature vehicles.

Books

Crews, D. (1991). *Truck.* New York: Greenwillow.

Crews, D. (1992). *Freight train.* New York: Greenwillow.

Crews, D. (1993). *Flying.* San Diego, CA: Harcourt Brace.

Crews, D. (1993). *School bus.* New York: Greenwillow.

Crews, D. (2000). *Sail away.* New York: Greenwillow.

Crews, D. (2002). *Inside freight train.* New York: Scholastic.

Crews, D. (2004). *Harbor.* St. Louis, MO: Turtleback.

Van Dusen, C. (2003). *A camping spree with Mr. Magee.* San Francisco: Chronicle Books.

Van Dusen, C. (2006). *Down to the sea with Mr. Magee.* San Francisco: Chronicle Books.

Van Dusen, C. (2007). *If I built a car.* New York: Puffin Books.

Van Dusen, C. (2009). *The circus ship.* Cambridge, MA: Candlewick Press.

3RD GRADE–5TH GRADE

Read aloud Tana Hoban's (1997) photo-illustrated book *Construction Zone*, which shows the various types of heavy machinery used in a construction zone—each of which has a different purpose and moves in different ways: forklift cranes, bulldozers, dump trucks, cherry picker crane, back hoes, jack hammers, and so on. Discuss the book using reader response questions and prompts: What did you wonder about the machines? Tell about your favorite machine. What do you know about how any of these machines move?

The students can imagine a construction zone and imagine what would be built there. Make a list of the machines that would be needed and how they move. Students can put themselves in a position to resemble the machine, and they may work together in pairs or groups to create a machine. They can improvise dance movements to music as they become the machine and go to work. The classroom can become the imaginary construction zone as the students do dance improvisations as the heavy machinery.

For more detailed information on how a particular machine works, students can use David Macaulay's (1988) *The Way Things Work.*

Books

Hoban, T. (1992). *Dig, drill, dump, fill*. New York: Mulberry Books.

Hoban, T. (1997). *Construction zone*. New York: Greenwillow.

Jennings, T. (2009). *Construction vehicles: How machines work*. Mankato, MN: Smart Apple Media.

Lewis, K. (2008). *My truck is stuck*. New York: Scholastic.

Macaulay, D. (1988). *The way things work*. Boston: Houghton Mifflin.

Olson, K. C. (2004). *Construction countdown*. New York: Henry Holt.

Pallotta, J. (2006). *The construction alphabet*. Watertown, MA: Charlesbridge.

Sobel, J. (2006). *B is for bulldozer: A construction ABC*. Fairbanks, AK: Gulliver Books.

6TH GRADE–8TH GRADE

Put together a classroom set of books on how new technologies work—computers, digital cameras, CDs, cell phones, and other digital devices, as well as how they can be interconnected. David Macaulay's well-known book *The Way Things Work*, published in 1988, has been updated as *The New Way Things Work* (1998). It includes the digital world and is an excellent and entertaining source of information.

Ask students for ideas for technological and communication devices that they use and ask them how they think they work, recording their ideas on chart paper. Students can form groups, each group choosing a different type of device and using one of the books in the classroom set to find out information on how it works to add to what they already know.

Then ask students to discuss the device they have been reading about and how they would move if they were actually that device. They can create movements to develop a dance improvisation. They can each be the device, or they can join together as different parts of it. They can create a rhythm by clapping, using any rhythm instrument, or adding music.

When each group has developed their device, the class can plan how to connect the devices in a dance improvisation that represents a network of the devices.

Books

Macaulay, D., & Ardley, N. (1998). *The new way things work*. Boston: Houghton Mifflin.

Oxlade, C. (2005). *The way things work: The complete illustrated guide to the amazing world of technology*. London: Lorenz Books.

Woodford, C. (2008). *Cool stuff exploded*. New York: DK.

Woodford, C. (2008). *How cool stuff works*. New York: DK.

Woodford, C. (2009). *Cool stuff and how it works*. New York: DK.

Woodford, C. (2010). *Cool stuff 2.0: And how it works*. New York: DK.

ENGLISH LEARNERS

Gestures, movement, and dance are excellent nonverbal means of expression for English learners. In these dance improvisations of types of machines and devices, they also work in groups and benefit from the support of student to student interaction. Visuals, music, and the senses provide additional scaffolding.

Attach labels with the words in English to students representing a machine and, if possible, in the child's home language for primary language support.

STRUGGLING STUDENTS

Struggling students can be fully integrated into dance improvisation as it does not rely heavily on traditional skills of reading and writing. Students can use gestures, movement, mime, and dance to express themselves nonverbally.

ASSESSMENT

Students could write a response to several open questions about dance improvisation: How did you feel about the dance improvisation? What was your favorite part of doing the improvisation? What would you do differently? What did you learn?

RESOURCES

Dunkin, A. (2006). *Dancing in your school: A guide for preschool and elementary school teachers.* Hightstown, NJ: Princeton Book Company.

REFERENCES

Bradley, K. K. (2002). Informing and reforming dance education research. In R. J. Deasy (Ed.), *Critical links: Learning in the arts and student academic and social development* (pp. 16–18). Washington, DC: Arts Education Partnership.

Keinanen, M., Hetland, L., & Winner, E. (2000, Fall). Teaching cognitive skill through dance: Evidence for near but not far transfer. *Journal of Aesthetic Education, 34*(3–4), 295–306.

Ross, J. (2000, April). *Art and community: Creating knowledge through service in dance.* Paper presented at the meeting of the American Educational Research Association, New Orleans, LA.

Strategy
39

Story Dramatization

A 4th-grade class was learning about Asia as a part of their study of the world. In a story dramatization of the 2500-year-old epic story "The Ramayana," which is still read and performed as a play all over India and Southeast Asia, the Demon King Ravana was trying to kidnap Princess Sita, wife of Prince Rama. But Carolyn, as Sita, had thrown herself into the role and was successfully resisting Ravana. Jeff, as Ravana, was frustrated but stayed in role and finally improvised a line that kept the story moving forward: "I am the Demon King Ravana and I have ten heads. Can my other nine heads get over here and help me kidnap Sita?" Other students playing demons rushed to his aid, Sita was kidnapped, and the story dramatization continued and played to a successful end.

RATIONALE

Learning theory supports the use of drama in the classroom. From his extensive research on child development, Piaget (1962) found that language development goes through three stages: (1) actual experience with an action or object, (2) dramatic reliving of this experience, and (3) words that represent this whole schema verbally. From Vygotsky's (1986) sociohistorical theory of learning, *activity* is the major explanatory concept in the development of human thought and language. The use of drama in the classroom, then, reflects a social constructivist perspective of learning that is active, social, centered in students' experience, and provides an effective way to teach not only the arts, but language, literacy, and other content (Wagner, 2003).

Story dramatizations are based on a story that students are familiar with. While it is planned by students, a script is not necessary. Students know the story and characters well enough to improvise action and dialogue. The dramatization can be recast with different students playing different parts each time it is played so that everyone has an opportunity to step into the roles. Many stories have characters and elements that can be played by several students so that all can participate in a story dramatization.

Research has shown the positive effects of improvised story dramatization on language development and student achievement in oral and written story recall, writing, and reading for both younger students (Pellegrini, 1997) and students through middle school (Deasy, 2002; Fiske, 1999).

Source: From National Standards for arts education: What every young American should know and be able to do in the arts, by the Consortium of National Arts Education Association, 1994. Reston, VA: Music Educators National Conference.

Arts Standards

Drama

- Script writing by planning and recording improvisations based on personal experience and heritage, imagination, literature, and history.
- Designing by visualizing and arranging environments for classroom dramatizations.
- Directing by planning classroom dramatizations.

STRATEGY

Choose a book to dramatize that is grade-level appropriate and that may be related to other content areas of study in the classroom. Picture books with repeated phrases that students can chant are good choices for younger children. Traditional literature, such as folk tales and myths and legends which may be related to the study of American history, the history and traditions of world cultures, or the ancient world, are good choices for older students. Stories with a clear story line, strong characters, repeated dialogue, and especially a character or element that many students can play at the same time, so that all students can be involved in each playing of a story dramatization, are ideal. Since story dramatizations do not require a written script, students should be very familiar with the story and characters so that they can improvise a character's actions and speech and so that different students can play different roles each time the story is played.

Read the book aloud to both older and younger students, and older students may read different stories in groups related to a single genre of story (e.g., Greek myths). Lead discussions using reader response questions and prompts, tapping into students' personal experiences of the story. The teacher and students can then plan and play a story dramatization:

---

1. Re-read and discuss the story: So that students are completely familiar with the story, the teacher can do repeated read alouds of picture books for younger students, and older students can read and discuss a story in groups. Ask students to note the setting, characters, and sequence of events or plot, as well as the most exciting parts, the climax, the way the story ended (i.e., the resolution), mood and theme, and important phrases and characteristic things characters say.

2. Make a story chart: The teacher can record students' ideas about each of these on chart paper for younger students and to model planning a story dramatization, and older students may do this independently in groups:

Plan for Story Dramatization

Setting/s	Character/s	Sequence of Events/Plot
1.		
2.		
3.		

3. Make a story map: Use the whole classroom space, adjusting furniture as necessary. Make a map of the classroom and place the settings needed for the story. Add the numbered sequence of events of the plot, with arrows showing the direction of the flow of the action.

4. Take volunteers for the first cast: Do a walkthrough of the story with the first cast. All students can be engaged in each dramatization by using stories that have a type of character that can be played by many students. Or students not playing in the story can be the audience, and then vice versa.

5. Play the scene: A narrator can be added to read parts of the story. This could be the teacher for younger students, who would also guide students through the actions.

6. Debrief and discuss: Ask questions that emphasize the positive and make plans for the next playing of the story:

   a. What did you see that you liked?
   b. Who did something really interesting (or exciting, realistic, funny, etc.)?
   c. What can we do next time to make the play even better?

7. Play the story again: The teacher can take new volunteers to play characters in the story so that all students have the opportunity to step into one of the roles.

GRADE-LEVEL MODIFICATIONS

K–2ND GRADE

Read aloud the classic children's book by Wanda Gag (2006) *Millions of Cats*. This is a traditional-type folk tale with two main characters: an old man and an old woman who wish they had a little cat because they are so lonely. The old man goes on a journey to find a cat and instead finds millions of cats. There is a repeated phrase used several times throughout the book, and students can join in with the teacher during the read aloud. Lead a discussion using reader response questions and prompts: What was your favorite part of the story? What did you wonder about? What would you put in a play of the story?

Make a chart to plan the story dramatization and re-read the story as students fill in each of the sections of the story structure as it appears in the story.

A Story Dramatization Plan for Millions of Cats		
Setting	Characters	Sequence/Plot
Nice clean house with flowers around	Very old man Very old woman	1. They are lonely. Old woman wants a cat.
Over the hill		2. Old man looks for a cat.
A hill	Millions of cats	3. He chooses them all.
Over the hills		Cats follow him.

A pond	4. Cats drink water.
Hill with grass	5. Cats eat grass.
Home to the house	6. Old woman says too many cats. Old man askswhich is prettiest.
	7. Cats all say I am and fight. Cats ate each other up.
One little cat	8. One little cat is left. They take care of her and are happy.

Figure 39.1   Story Map of Millions of Cats

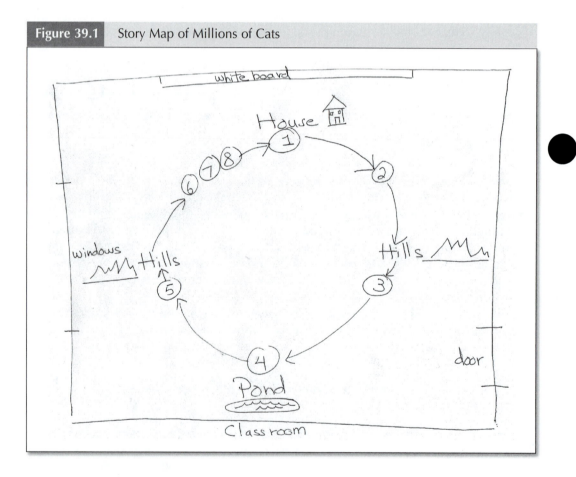

Make a map of the room with students on chart paper and show where each of the setting parts will be in the room by labeling them (Figure 39.1). Students can also draw arrows to show which way the students will move as they play the story and number each of the parts of the steps of the sequence and plot those on the map as well. Simple costume pieces such as a shawl for the old woman, a hat for the old man, headbands with cat ears attached for the cats, or simple paper cat masks can be added.

Ask for volunteers to play the old man, the old woman, and one little cat. The other students can be the millions of cats. The students can take their positions at the beginning of the story. The old man and the old woman are in the house, the cats are on the hills. For younger students, read, or have a student narrator who is already reading, begin to read the book, and pause for the student playing the old man and woman to talk to each other. They can improvise the dialogue. When the old man moves to the hills, the narrator can follow along. All the cats can say the repeated phrase about millions of cats together, follow the old man home, and so on.

After asking students what they liked, adjustments can be made in the story dramatization, new volunteers can be found to play the old man and woman and little cat, and the story can be played again.

There are many excellent picture books with repeated phrases or sounds that all students who are not playing main characters can say so that all students can participate in each story dramatization. The characters or things the students represent, as well as what they can say, are noted in parentheses after the book listing.

Books

Asbjornsen, P. C., & Moe, J. E. (1991). *The three billy goats gruff.* San Diego, CA: Sandpiper. (All Students form bridge, say "trip trap" etc. when goats cross.)

Gag, W. (2006). *Millions of cats.* New York: Puffin. (All Students playing cats say "millions of cats" repeated phrase.)

Sendak, M. (1988). *Where the wild things are.* New York: HarperCollins. (All Students playing Wild Things roar, gnash their teeth, roll their eyes, etc.)

Slobodkina, E. (1987). *Caps for sale: A tale of a peddler, some monkeys, and their monkey business.* New York: HarperCollins. (All Students playing monkeys throw hats and say "tsk, tsk.")

3RD GRADE–5TH GRADE

Because of the clear and often familiar plot lines and archetypal characters, traditional world tales are excellent choices for story dramatization for students in the middle grades. For example, "The Ramayana" is one of the oldest stories in the world, believed to have been written down by the great Sanskrit poet Valmiki 2,500 years ago. It is famous in India, Indonesia, Thailand, and all over Southeast Asia in books, music, dance, plays, and paintings. There are thousands of versions told in hundreds of languages.

The tale of the Ramayana contains many stories, but the basic plot tells the story of Rama, a Prince of Ayodha, who was exiled for 14 years to the forest with his wife, Sita, and brother, Lakshmana, because of a jealous stepmother. They have many adventures and fight demons. Ravana, a King of the Demons with ten heads, kidnaps Sita, and Rama gets help from the superhero monkey King Hanuman and his army. Hanuman can leap over oceans, carry mountains, and is a symbol of loyalty to Rama. In the end, good triumphs over evil. "The Ramayana" is the basis for the celebration of Divaali, when children perform versions of the stories in India.

Read aloud a picture book version *Rama and the Demon King: An Ancient Tale From India* (Souhami, 2005) or read aloud chapters from longer versions of the story, for example *The Story of Divaali* (Verma, 2007) or *Ramayana: Divine Loophole,* adapted and illustrated by S. Patel (2010), a film animator for Pixar studios. Students could also read the stories independently or in book clubs.

Lead discussions using reader response questions and prompts: What was your favorite part of the Ramayana? Which character did you like the most? Which character would you like to play in a story dramatization?

Plan a dramatization by listing the setting, characters, and sequence of events with numbers in one of the stories in the Ramayana students will play. Students can also draw a large map of the room and show the settings of the story on the map and the numbers of the sequence of events with arrows showing the progression of the action. The main characters are listed here. The setting and plot or sequence of events would depend on which part of the Ramayana students would choose to play.

The Ramayana

Setting	Characters	Plot
	Vishnu, a god and Preserver of the Universe	
	King Dashratha, of the great city of Ayodhya	
	Rama's father	
	Bharata, Rama's stepbrother, son of Kaikeyi	
	Rama, Prince of Ayodhya, son of king Dashratha	
	Lakshmana, Rama's younger brother	
	King Janaka, father of Princess Sita	
	Sita, daughter of King Janaka and Rama's wife	
	Hanuman, the Monkey King	
	Kaikeyi, Rama's stepmother	
	Ravana, Demon King of Lanka	

Ask for volunteers for the main characters to dramatize the story. Students can improvise the dialogue to tell the story. All students can participate at the same time. Any students not playing one of the characters can form a group that can all be the Demon King Ravana because he has ten heads. Students playing Ravana can link arms and stand in a semicircle to signify that they are all the same character. Ravana can speak from any one of his many heads. Other students not playing main characters can be monkey soldiers in Hanuman's army.

After playing the story, debrief with students—ask them what they saw that they liked and make adaptations for another playing where students take on parts different from those played the first time. Students can add simple costume pieces such as lengths of cloth over one shoulder, crowns for Rama and Sita, masks for the ten heads of the demon king, or monkey masks for Hanuman and his army.

Students can read the many versions of the Ramayana independently or in book clubs, or the stories can continue to be read aloud.

Books

Acharya, M. (1998). *The Ramayana for young readers*. India: HarperCollins.

Gray, J. E. B. (2001). *Tales from India*. New York: Oxford University Press.

Greene, J. (2009). *Hanuman: The heroic monkey god*. San Rafael, CA: Mandala Publishing.

Patel, S. (2010). *Ramayana: Divine loophole.* San Francisco: Chronicle Books.

Sekar, R. (2007). *Hanuman.* Mumbai, India: Vakils, Feffer, & Simons.

Sharma, B. (2004). *The Ramayana for children.* New York: Penguin.

Souhami, J. (2005). *Rama and the demon king: An ancient tale from India.* London: Frances Lincoln Children's Books.

Sperling, V. (2006). *Hanuman's journey to the medicine mountain.* Rochester, VT: Bear Cub Books.

Sperling, V. (2006). *Ram the demon slayer.* Rochester, VT: Bear Cub Books.

Verma, J. (2007). *The story of Divaali.* New York: Barefoot Books.

Weitzman, D. (2002). *Rama and Sita: A tale from ancient Java.* Boston: David R. Godine.

Woods, C. (2009). *Where's Hanuman?* Badger, CA: Torchlight Publishing.

6TH GRADE–8TH GRADE

Greek myths and stories of the ancient gods, goddesses, monsters, heroes, and mortals, as well as the stories from the classic *Iliad, Odyssey,* and *Aeneid,* are excellent for story dramatization and can align with learning about the ancient world for middle school students. Read aloud from one of the many collections of these stories, and model planning and mapping a story dramatization. The students can play this story several times, rotating students into the main character parts each time. Many students can participate in a story dramatization of a classic Greek story by adding a Greek chorus. Students can plan what the chorus will say (i.e., phrases to comment on the characters' actions).

Students can then form groups and read from collections of classic Greek stories, and each group can choose a different story to dramatize using the steps described in the Strategy section. See also the K–2 and 3–5 sections for ideas. Strips of white cloth can be added for costume pieces over one shoulder and belted or used as headbands and sandals.

Books

Colum, P. (2004). *The children's Homer: The adventures of Odysseus and the tale of Troy.* New York: Aladdin.

Colum, P. (2004). *The golden fleece: And the heroes who lived before Achilles.* New York: Aladdin.

D'Aulaire, I., & D'Aulaire, E. (1992). *D'Aulaire's book of Greek myths.* New York: Delacorte.

Green, R. L. (1995). *The tale of Troy: Retold from the ancient author.* New York: Puffin.

Green, R. L. (2009). *Tales of the Greek heroes.* New York: Puffin.

Kimmel, E. A. (2008). *The McElderry book of Greek myths.* New York: Margaret K. McElderry.

Lively, P. (2006). *In search of a homeland: The story of the Aeneid.* London: Frances Lincoln Children's Books.

McCaugherean, G. (1992). *The orchard book of Greek myths*. Danbury, CT: Orchard Books.

McCaugherean, G. (1997). *The Odyssey*. New York: Puffin.

Sutcliff, R. (2005). *Black ships before Troy: The story of the Iliad*. New York: Laurel Leaf.

Sutcliff, R. (2005). *The wanderings of Odysseus*. New York: Laurel Leaf.

Vinge, J. D. (1999). *The Random House book of Greek myths*. New York: Random House.

English Learners

Several English language development strategies are used in story dramatization. Visuals such as book illustrations and charts for planning and mapping a story dramatization are used. English learners can participate in a drama using nonverbal means such as facial expression, gestures, and movement to communicate meaning and demonstrate understanding. The collaborative nature of drama provides student to student interaction in a meaningful context. Stories from the cultural heritage of the English learners in the class can also be chosen. For example, the example in the 3–5 section uses the Ramayana, an epic tale known, read, and performed in India and all over Southeast Asia. English learners of Indian or Southeast Asian heritage, such as Thai, Vietnamese, or Indonesian students, can benefit from prior knowledge they may have of this story and the characters. The students' heritages are also being acknowledged in class.

Books

Amery, H. (2002). *Stories from around the world*. London: Usborne.

Struggling Students

Struggling students can fully participate in story dramatizations. Listening to the stories read aloud and viewing charts and maps for planning a dramatization can scaffold learning. Students can also pair up with a drama buddy in parts that can be played by more than one student for peer support.

ASSESSMENT

A self-assessment that requires students to reflect on the story and their role in dramatizing it can be used with questions and prompts such as the following:

1. Tell about the story.
2. Tell about the character or characters you played in the story.
3. What was the most important thing about the story?
4. What was the most important thing about your character or characters?
5. What did you like best about dramatizing the story?

RESOURCES

Heinig, R. B. (1992). *Improvisation with favorite tales: Integrating drama into the reading/writing classroom.* Portsmouth, NH: Heinemann.

REFERENCES

Deasy, R. (Ed.). (2002). *Critical links: Learning in the arts and student academic and social development.* Washington, DC: Arts Education Partnership.

Fiske, E. (Ed.). (1999). *Champions of change: The impact of the arts on learning.* Washington, DC: The Arts Education Partnership and The President's Committee on the Arts.

Pellegrini, A. D. (1997). Dramatic play, context, and children's communicative behavior. In J. Flood, S. B. Heath, & D. Lapp (Eds.), *Handbook of research on teaching literacy through the communicative and visual arts* (pp. 486–491). New York: Macmillan.

Piaget, J. (1962). *Play, dreams, and imitation in childhood.* New York: Norton.

Vygotsky, L. (1986). *Thought and language.* Cambridge, MA: MIT.

Wagner, B. J. (2003). Imaginative expression. In J. Flood, D. Lapp, M. R. Squire, & J. M. Jensen (Eds.), *Handbook of research on teaching the English language arts* (2nd ed., pp. 1008–1025). Sponsored by the International Reading Association/National Council of Teachers of English. Mahwah, NJ: Erlbaum.

Strategy 40

Reader's Theatre

A 2nd-grade Spanish-English bilingual class was learning about people who make a difference. Their teacher read picture book biographies, discussed each book with students, and recorded their ideas about what each person said and why they made a difference on a graphic organizer. They used these ideas to create a reader's theatre script, which they performed:

People Who Make a Difference

Narrator: Many people in American have made a difference. Here is what they said.

Cesar Chavez Narrator: Cesar Chavez was the leader of the United Farm Workers union because he wanted everyone to be treated fairly and with respect. He said:

Cesar Chavez: Si, se puede!

Martin Luther King, Jr. Narrator: Martin Luther King, Jr. was the leader of the Civil Rights movement because he dreamed that African Americans would have equal rights. He said:

Martin Luther King, Jr.: I have a dream.

Rosa Parks Narrator: Rosa Parks was an African American who refused to give up her seat at the front of the bus during the Civil Rights Movement. She said:

Rosa Parks: No!

Barack Obama Narrator: Barack Obama is the first African American president of the United States and wants to change things. He said:

Barack Obama: Yes, we can!

RATIONALE

Recent research recommended the arts strategy of reader's theatre as a means to increase reading fluency (NICHD, 2000). Research-based practices to promote reading fluency include modeling reading aloud for students, repeated reading, performance reading, and reader's theatre (NICHD, 2000; Rasinski & Hoffman, 2003). Research on the reading behaviors of English learners has also identified fluency as important (August & Shanahan, 2006). The same has been found true in research on struggling students (Therrien, 2004).

Reader's theatre can be on literature that uses the words spoken by important individuals that students are learning about (Flynn, 2005). Speeches and original documents can easily be adapted for reader's theatre scripts.

Source: From National Standards for arts education: What every young American should know and be able to do in the arts, by the Consortium of National Arts Education Association, 1994. Reston, VA: Music Educators National Conference.

Arts Standards

Theatre

- Script writing by planning and recording improvisations based on personal experience, heritage, imagination, literature, and history.

- Acting by assuming roles and interacting in improvisations.

- Designing by visualizing and arranging environments for classroom dramatizations.

STRATEGY

Reader's theatre is a strategy that uses scripts adapted from literature or other print sources that are read aloud and interpreted by students. Scripts can be adapted and read aloud from nonfiction literature such as biographies, informational books, or contemporary news media texts such as newspapers, news magazines, or online news reports. The words of the speaker can be divided into parts so that several students can read them, and each part can have a narrator part to provide an introduction. Reader's theatre can use any type of book or text, and students can write their own texts as well.

Steps for adapting a book or speech text for reader's theatre:

1. Choose the spoken words of the person or persons that will be used in the script.

2. Divide the words into parts for the number of students who will speak them.

3. Add narrator parts for things like the period of time, place, and scene. Each character speaking can also have a narrator to introduce them.

4. Put the words of the speakers and narrators in a script format:
    - Narrator (Introduction)
    - Narrator for Speaker 1
    - Speaker 1
    - Narrator for Speaker 2
    - Speaker 2, and so on

Steps for putting reader's theatre into practice:

1. Introduce the book or text. Read aloud a picture book for young children, or older students can take turns reading a book aloud. Lead a discussion using reader response questions and prompts:

- What did you think of the book and the words of this person?
- Which part of what they said most attracted your attention?
- What would you have thought or how would you have felt if you were saying those words?

2. Explain reader's theatre. If this is the first time students have done reader's theatre, explain how it works: the physical arrangement and movements (students can stand in a semicircle and turn in and out of the scene when not speaking), the roles of narrators and characters, the uses of facial expressions and gestures, and how to prepare and use a script.

3. Cast the script. Read through the script letting different students read the parts of each character. Students should become familiar with all the parts and comfortable with the script. Take volunteers for each of the parts for the performance. Adjustments can be made as students practice. Students can also play different parts for different performances.

4. Block, stage, and practice playing the script. The students can practice the physical arrangement of characters before and during practices, and they can make adjustments as needed. Some general guidelines for reader's theatre:

   - Students often stand or sit in a semicircle.
   - Narrators for characters can stand next to or behind the character.
   - Students may hold the script or use a music stand or lectern.
   - Students may take a step forward when they speak and step back when they are finished. Students not speaking can also have their backs to the audience and turn to face it when it is their turn to speak. There is a minimum of floor movement in reader's theatre.
   - Students can wear a nametag for their character or use simple costume pieces to go with their character, such as an appropriate hat.

5. Sharing reader's theatre: Students can perform a reader's theatre script in an open space in the classroom. If several groups are performing different scripts on the same person or topic, they can stand in different parts of the room to perform or take turns coming to the same place in the room. They can also perform for other classes in the school.

GRADE-LEVEL MODIFICATIONS

K–2ND GRADE

Read aloud a picture book biography or informational book that uses the real words of a person students are learning about. After reading, lead a discussion using reader response questions and prompts: What did you think of the person? Has anything like this ever happened to you? How would you feel or what would you do if you were that person?

Write a reader's theatre script with students on chart paper. The teacher can model the structure of a script:

Script Title: _____

Character or Narrator: Words They Speak

_____   _____

Re-read each page of the book that is the source of words for the reader's theatre script, discuss with students which words to choose, and record them on the script on the chart paper. When the script is completed, students can read the script together aloud, guided by the teacher, and take turns reading parts of the script individually. When students are familiar with the words, they can practice reading with expression.

For the performance, young children stand facing the script on chart paper and read it with the guidance of the teacher, pointing to the words rather than each child holding a smaller printed script. Children who are reading can each hold a copy of the script.

Books about people who have made a difference are a common theme in K through 2, and there are several books that use the actual words spoken by these people:

Books

Parks, R., with J. Haskings. (1994). *Rosa Parks: My story.* New York: Dial.

Rappaport, T. D. (2007). *Martin's big words.* New York: Hyperion.

Rappaport, T. D. (2008). *Abe's honest words.* New York: Hyperion.

3RD GRADE–5TH GRADE

Put together a classroom text set of books about people using their own words. After introducing the strategy of reader's theatre, students can write a script with the teacher or form groups and work cooperatively to write scripts.

Students can use books that present one person's viewpoint, conflicting or opposing points of view, or multiple perspectives from different people on the same issue in their own words.

Books

Allen, T. B. (2001). *Remember Pearl Harbor: Japanese and American survivors tell their stories.* Washington, DC: National Geographic Society.

Fradin, F. M. (2001). *Duel! Burr and Hamilton's deadly war of words.* New York: Bloomsbury.

Levine, F. (1993). *Freedom's children: Young civil rights activists tell their own stories.* New York: Putnam.

Rappaport, T. D. (2002). *No more! Stories and songs of slave resistance.* Cambridge, MA: Candlewick Press.

Winters, J. (2008). *Colonial voices: Hear them speak.* New York: Penguin, Dutton.

6TH GRADE–8TH GRADE

Students can work in groups and research different people with different perspectives on world events. Using the library and Internet, they can find comments, addresses, and speeches by these people. Introduce the steps used in reader's theatre and provide a printed guideline for students to follow. Different groups could read scripts using the words of different individuals in a single presentation, but rotating—perhaps chronologically. The individuals could have exchanges and agree or disagree on an issue.

Plus Technology

Sources of original statements, speeches, addresses, and other oral texts in the words of people since the advent of motion picture and video cameras can be found on the Internet. Go to Google (www.google.com) and click on Video or go to YouTube (www.youtube.com) and search for specific people, events, or speeches.

ENGLISH LEARNERS

Beginning English learners can participate nonverbally by using facial expressions and gestures while another student speaks. More proficient speakers can take a smaller speaking part as a narrator introducing a character. They can also share a role with another more English-proficient student.

STRUGGLING STUDENTS

Scaffold learning for struggling students through the use of frames and templates for writing a reader's theatre script.

Reader's Theatre Script
Narrator: _____
Narrator for Speaker 1: _____
Speaker 1: _____

Pairing students with different abilities can also provide support. Students can also echo, or repeat, the lines another student has just read.

ASSESSMENT

Authentic assessment in the form of post-rehearsal and post-performance discussions, peer-evaluations, journals, notes kept by students, and written responses to the experience can be used.

RESOURCES

Polette, N. (2008). Whose tale is true? *Reader's theatre to introduce and research 49 amazing women.* Denver, CO: Libraries Unlimited.

Sanders, N. I. (2008). *Readers theatre for African American history.* Denver, CO: Libraries Unlimited.

Sloyer, S. (2003). *From the page to the stage: The educator's complete guide to reader's theatre.* Westport, CT: Teacher Ideas Press.

REFERENCES

August, E., & Shanahan, T. (2006). *Developing literacy in second-language learners: Report of the National Literacy Panel on Language-Minority Children and Youth.* Mahwah, NJ: Erlbaum.

Flynn, R. (2005). Curriculum-based Reader's Theatre: Setting the stage for reading and retention. *The Reading Teacher, 58*(4), 360–365.

National Institute of Child Health and Human Development (NICHD). (2000). *Report of the National Reading Panel: Teaching children to read: An evidence-based assessment of the scientific research literature on reading and its implications for reading instruction* (NIH Publication 00–4769). Washington, DC: U.S. Government Printing Office.

Rasinski, T. V., & Hoffman, J. V. (2003). Theory and research into practice: Oral reading in the school literacy curriculum. *Reading Research Quarterly, 38*(4), 510–522.

Therrien, B. (2004). Fluency and comprehension gains as a result of repeated reading: A meta-analysis. *Remedial and Special Education, 25*(4), 252–261.

Index

M

Map making strategy
assessments, 85
description of, 81–82
English learner modifications, 85
grade-level modifications, 82–84
K–2nd grade modifications, 82–83
rationale for, 80–82
6th grade–8th grade modifications, 84
struggling student considerations, 85
3rd grade–5th grade modifications, 83–84

Marvelous mathematicians strategy
assessments, 153
description of, 148
English learner modifications, 152
grade-level modifications, 148–152
K–2nd grade modifications, 148–150
rationale for, 147
6th grade–8th grade modifications, 151–152
struggling student considerations, 153
3rd grade–5th grade modifications, 150–151

Math in the world strategy
assessments, 184
description of, 180
English learner modifications, 183
grade-level modifications, 181–183
K–2nd grade modifications, 181–182
rationale for, 179–180
6th grade–8th grade modifications, 183
struggling student considerations, 184
3rd grade–5th grade modifications, 182

Math poetry strategy
assessments, 161
description of, 156
English learner modifications, 160
grade-level modifications, 156–160
K–2nd grade modifications, 156–158
rationale for, 155
6th grade–8th grade modifications, 159–160
struggling student considerations, 160
3rd grade–5th grade modifications, 158–159

Math puzzle journals strategy
assessments, 189
description of, 186
English learner modifications, 188
grade-level modifications, 186–188
K–2nd grade modifications, 186–187
rationale for, 185
6th grade–8th grade modifications, 188
struggling student considerations, 189
3rd grade–5th grade modifications, 187

Math stories strategy
assessments, 177
description of, 172
English learner modifications, 176
grade-level modifications, 173–175
K–2nd grade modifications, 173–174
rationale for, 172
6th grade–8th grade modifications, 175

struggling student considerations, 176
3rd grade–5th grade modifications, 174–175

Mathematics
cubing math vocabulary strategy for, 163–169
discovering Pi strategy for, 141–146
finding a Fibonacci strategy for, 135–140
literature-based teaching of, 131–132
marvelous mathematicians strategy for, 147–154
math in the world strategy for, 179–184
math puzzle journals strategy for, 185–189
math stories strategy for, 171–177
music and, 267
national standards in, 131–134
what's in the sky? strategy for, 207–212

Meet the scientist strategy
assessments, 219
description of, 214–215
English learner modifications, 218
grade-level modifications, 215–218
K–2nd grade modifications, 215–216
rationale for, 213–214
6th grade–8th grade modifications, 217–218
struggling student considerations, 218–219
3rd grade–5th grade modifications, 216–217

Modes of engagement, 239–240

Multiple intelligences, 261

Multiple perspectives jigsaw strategy
assessments, 118
description of, 112
English learner modifications, 117
grade-level modifications, 112–117
K–2nd grade modifications, 112–114
rationale for, 111–112
6th grade–8th grade modifications, 115–117
struggling student considerations, 117–118
3rd grade–5th grade modifications, 114–115

Music content standards, 264

Music journals, 276

Music stories strategy
assessments, 280
description of, 276
English learner modifications, 279
grade-level modifications, 277–279
K–2nd grade modifications, 277
rationale for, 275–276
6th grade–8th grade modifications, 278–279
struggling student considerations, 279–280
3rd grade–5th grade modifications, 278

Mystery matter strategy
assessments, 246
description of, 240–241
English learner modifications, 245
grade-level modifications, 241–245
K–2nd grade modifications, 241–243
rationale for, 239–240
6th grade–8th grade modifications, 244–245
struggling student considerations, 245–246
3rd grade–5th grade modifications, 243–244

About the Author

Carole Cox taught elementary school in Los Angeles, California and Madison, Wisconsin, and received a PhD from the University of Minnesota. As a professor at Louisiana State University, Baton Rouge, and now at California State University, Long Beach, she has taught courses in language arts, reading, and children's literature. Carole's research focuses on children's responses to literature from a reader response perspective, specifically Louise Rosenblatt's transactional model of the reading process. She is the author of many articles and books in education, most recently *Teaching Language Arts: A Student-Centered Classroom* (Pearson/Allyn & Bacon, 2008), *Engaging English Learners: Exploring Literature, Developing Literacy, and Differentiating Instruction* co-authored with Paul Boyd-Batstone (Pearson/Allyn & Bacon, 2009), and *Shakespeare Kids: Speaking his Words, Performing his Plays* (Libraries Unlimited, 2010). In 2001, she was named the Outstanding Professor at California State University, Long Beach. The greatest honor she has ever received, however, occurred when students she had taught in 3rd through 5th grade in the 1960s and 1970s organized a reunion of her classes in Madison, Wisconsin, and the mayor declared July 2, 2005, as Carole Cox Day. She and her former elementary students are currently writing an historical ethnography of their classroom experiences together. They will hold another reunion in the summer of 2011.

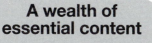